The Expositor's Bible
The Prophecies Of Jeremiah With A Sketch Of His Life And Times

by

C. J. Ball

Double 9 BOOKS

The Expositor's Bible
The Prophecies Of Jeremiah With A Sketch Of His Life And Times
by C. J. Ball

ISBN: 978-93-61158-22-3

Published by

DOUBLE 9 BOOKS
2/13-B, Ansari Road
Daryaganj, New Delhi – 110002
info@double9books.com
www.double9books.com
Tel. 011-40042856

ABOUT THE AUTHOR

C. J. Ball's "The Expositor's Bible" stands as one in every of his masterpieces, showcasing his brilliance as a creator. With a profound dedication to bridging the nation-states of non-secular literature, Ball's paintings serves as a conduit for fostering connections and mutual information amongst readers. His writing is a testament to creativity and ardour, skillfully navigating various geographical regions of human experience. Through eloquent prose, Ball introduces readers to a rich tapestry of emotions and varied landscapes. His writings, characterised through each beauty and accessibility, invite everybody to partake within the entertainment of his excellent stories. C. J. Ball's literary contributions go beyond mere narratives, serving as a way to light up the shared human revel in and forge connections thru the universal language of storytelling.

CONTENTS

PRELIMINARY SKETCH OF THE LIFE AND TIMES OF JEREMIAH

A priest by birth, Jeremiah became a prophet by the special call of God. His priestly origin implies a good literary training, in times when literature was largely in the hands of the priests. The priesthood, indeed, constituted a principal section of the Israelitish nobility, as appears both from the history of those times, and from the references in our prophet's writings, where kings and princes and priests are often named together as the aristocracy of the land (i. 18, ii. 26, iv. 9); and this fact would ensure for the young prophet a share in all the best learning of his age. The name of Jeremiah, like other prophetic proper names, seems to have special significance in connexion with the most illustrious of the persons recorded to have borne it. It means *Iahvah foundeth*, and, as a proper name, The Man that Iahvah foundeth; a designation which finds vivid illustration in the words of Jeremiah's call: "Before I moulded thee in the belly, I knew thee; and before thou camest forth from the womb, I consecrated thee: a spokesman to the nations did I make thee" (i. 5). The not uncommon name of Jeremiah—six other persons of the name are numbered in the Old Testament—must have appeared to the prophet as invested with new force and meaning, in the light of this revelation. Even before his birth he had been "founded"[1] and predestined by God for the work of his life.

The Hilkiah named as his father was not the high priest of that name,[2] so famous in connexion with the reformation of king Josiah. Interesting as such a relationship would be if established, the following facts seem decisive against it. The prophet himself has omitted to mention it, and no hint of it is to be found elsewhere. The priestly family to which Jeremiah belonged was settled at Anathoth (i. 1, xi. 21, xxix. 27). But Anathoth in Benjamin (xxxvii. 12), the present `Anâtâ, between two and three miles NNE. of Jerusalem, belonged to the deposed line of Ithamar (1 Chron. xxiv. 3; comp. with 1 Kings ii. 26, 35). After this it is needless to insist that the prophet, and presumably his father, resided at Anathoth, whereas Jerusalem was the usual residence of the high priest. Nor is the identification of Jeremiah's family with that of the ruling high priest helped by the observation that the father of the high priest was named Shallum (1 Chron. v. 39), and that the prophet had an uncle of this name (Jer. xxxii. 7). The names Hilkiah[3] and Shallum are too common to justify any conclusions from such data. If the prophet's father was head of one of the twenty-four classes or guilds of the priests, that might explain the influence which Jeremiah could exercise with some of the grandees of the court. But we are not told more than that Jeremiah ben Hilkiah was a member of the priestly community settled at Anathoth. It is, however, a gratuitous disparagement of one of the greatest names in Israel's history, to suggest that, had Jeremiah belonged to the highest ranks of his caste, he would not have been equal to the self-renunciation involved in the assumption of the unhonoured and thankless office of a prophet.[4] Such a suggestion is certainly not warranted by the portraiture of the man as delineated by himself, with all the distinctive marks of truth and nature. From the moment that he became decisively convinced of his mission, Jeremiah's career is marked by struggles and vicissitudes of the most painful and perilous kind; his perseverance in his allotted path was met by an ever increasing hardness on the part of the people; opposition and ridicule became persecution, and the messenger of Divine truth persisted in proclaiming his message at the risk of his own life. That life may, in fact, be called a prolonged martyrdom; and, if we may judge of the unknown by the known, the tradition that the prophet was stoned to death by the Jewish refugees in Egypt is only too probable an account of its final scene. If "the natural shrinking of a somewhat feminine character" is traceable in his own report of his conduct at particular junctures, does not the fact shed an intenser glory upon the man, who overcame this instinctive timidity, and persisted, in face of the most appalling dangers, in the path of duty? Is not the victory of a constitutionally timid and shrinking character a nobler moral triumph than that of the man who never knew fear—who marches to the conflict with others, with a light heart, simply because it is his nature to do so—because he has had no experience of the agony of a previous conflict with self? It is easy to sit in one's library and criticize the heroes of old; but the modern censures of Jeremiah betray at once a want of historic imagination, and a defect of sympathy with the sublime fortitude of one who struggled on in a battle which he knew to be lost. In a protracted contest such as that which Jeremiah was called upon to maintain, what wonder if courage sometimes flags, and hopelessness utters its forsaken cry? The moods of the saints are not always the same; they vary, like those of common men, with the stress of the hour. Even our Saviour could cry from the cross, "My God, My God, why hast Thou forsaken Me?" It is not by passing expressions, wrung from their torn hearts by the agony of the hour, that men are to be judged. It is the issue of the crisis that is all-important; not the cries of pain, which indicate its overwhelming pressure.

"It is sad," says a well known writer, with reference to the noble passage, xxxi. 31-34, which he justly characterizes as "one of those which best deserve to be called the Gospel before Christ," "It is sad that Jeremiah could not always keep his spirit under the calming influence of these high thoughts. No book of the Old Testament, except the book of Job and the Psalms, contains so much which is difficult to reconcile with the character of a self-denying servant of Jehovah. Such expressions as those in xi. 20, xv. 15, and especially xviii. 21-23, contrast powerfully with Luke xxiii. 34, and show that the typical character of Jeremiah is not absolutely complete." Probably not. The writer in question is honourably distinguished from a crowd of French and German critics, whose attainments are not superior to his own, by his deep sense of the inestimable value to mankind of those beliefs which animated the prophet, and by the sincerity of his manifest endeavours to judge fairly between Jeremiah and his detractors. He has already remarked truly enough that "the baptism of complicated suffering," which the prophet was called upon to pass through in the reign of Jehoiakim, "has made him, in a very high and true sense, a type of One greater than he." It is impossible to avoid such an impression, if we study the records of his life with any insight or sympathy. And the impression thus created is deepened, when we turn to that prophetic page which may be called the most *appealing* in the entire range of the Old Testament. In the 53rd of Isaiah the martyrdom of Jeremiah becomes the living image of that other martyrdom, which in the fulness of time was to redeem the world. After this, to say that "the typical character of Jeremiah is not absolutely complete," is no more than the assertion of a truism; for what Old Testament character, what character in the annals of collective humanity, can be brought forward as a perfect type of the Christ, the Man whom, in His sinlessness and His power, unbiassed human reason and conscience instinctively suspect to have been also God? To deplore the fact that this illustrious prophet "could not always keep his spirit under the calming influence of his highest thoughts," is simply to deplore the infirmity that besets all human nature, to regret that natural imperfection which clings to a finite and fallen creature, even when endowed with the most splendid gifts of the spirit. For the rest, a certain degree of exaggeration is noticeable in founding upon three brief passages of so large a work as the collected prophecies of Jeremiah the serious charge that "no book of the Old Testament, except the book of Job and the Psalms, contains so much which is difficult to reconcile with the character of a self-denying servant of Jehovah." The charge appears to me both ill-grounded and misleading. But I reserve the further consideration of these obnoxious passages for the time when I come to discuss their context, as I wish now to complete my sketch of the prophet's life. He has himself recorded the date of his call to the prophetic office. It was in the thirteenth year of the good king Josiah, that the young[5] priest was summoned to a higher vocation by an inward Voice whose urgency he could not resist.[6] The year has been variously identified with 629, 627, and 626 b.c. The place has been supposed to have been Jerusalem, the capital, which was so near the prophet's home, and which, as Hitzig observes, offered the amplest scope and numberless occasions for the exercise of prophetic activity. But there appears no good reason why Jeremiah should not have become known locally as one whom God had specially chosen, before he abandoned his native place for the wider sphere of the capital. This, in truth, seems to be the likelier supposition, considering that his reluctance to take the first decisive step in his career excused itself on the ground of youthful inexperience: "Alas, my Lord Iahvah! behold, I know not (how) to speak; for I am but a youth."[7] The Hebrew term may imply that he was about eighteen or twenty: an age when it is hardly probable that he would permanently leave his father's house. Moreover, he has mentioned a conspiracy of his fellow-townsmen against himself, in terms which have been taken to imply that he had exercised his ministry among them, before his removal to Jerusalem. In chap. xi. 21, we read: "Therefore thus said Iahvah Sabaoth upon the men of `Anathoth that were seeking thy life, saying, Prophesy not in the name of Iahvah, that thou die not by our hand! Therefore thus said Iahvah Sabaoth: Behold I am about to visit it upon them: the young men shall die by the sword; their sons and their daughters shall die by the famine. And a remnant they shall have none; for I will bring evil unto the men of `Anathoth, (in) the year of their visitation." It is natural to see in this wicked plot against his life the reason for the prophet's departure from his native place (but cf. p. 265). We are reminded of the violence done to our Lord by the men of "His own country" (ἡ πάτρις αὐτοῦ), and of His final and, as it would seem, compulsory departure from Nazareth to Capernaum (St. Luke iv. 16-29; St. Matt. iv. 13). In this, as in other respects, Jeremiah was a true type of the Messias.

The prophetic discourses, with which the book of Jeremiah opens (ii. 1-iv. 2), have a general application to all Israel, as is evident not only from the ideas expressed in them, but also from the explicit address, ii. 4: "Hear ye the word of Iahvah, O house of Jacob, and all the clans of the house of Israel!" It is clear enough, that although Jeremiah belongs to the southern kingdom, his reflexions here concern the northern tribes as well, who must be included in the comprehensive phrases "house of Jacob," and "all the clans of the house of Israel." The fact is accounted for by the circumstance that these two discourses are summaries of the prophet's teaching on many distinct occasions, and as such might have been composed anywhere. There can be no doubt, however, that the principal contents of his book have their scene in Jerusalem. In chap. ii. 1, 2, indeed, we have what looks like the prophet's introduction to the scene of his future activity. "And there fell a word of Iahvah unto me, saying, Go and cry in the ears of Jerusalem." But the words are not found in the LXX., which begins chap. ii. thus: "And he said, These things saith the Lord, I remembered the lovingkindness (ἔλεος) of thy youth, and the love of thine espousals (τελείωσις)." But whether these words of the received Hebrew text be genuine or not, it is plain that if, as the terms of the prophet's commission affirm, he was to be "an embattled city, and a pillar of iron, and walls of bronze ... to the kings of Judah, to her princes, to her priests," as well as "to the country folk" (i. 18), Jerusalem, the residence of kings and princes and chief priests, and the centre of the land, would be the natural sphere of his operations. The same thing is implied in the Divine statement: "A *nabî'* to *the nations* have I made thee" (i. 5). The prophet of Judea could only reach the *gôyîm*—the surrounding foreign peoples—through the government of his own country, and through his influence upon Judean policy. The leaving of his native place, sooner or later, seems to be involved in the words (i. 7, 8): "And Iahvah said unto me, Say not, I am a youth: for upon whatsoever (journey) I send thee, thou shalt go (Gen. xxiv. 42); and with whomsoever I charge thee, thou shalt speak (Gen. xxiii. 8). Be not afraid of them!" The Hebrew is to some extent ambiguous. We might also render: "Unto whomsoever I send thee, thou shalt go; and whatsoever I charge thee, thou shalt speak." But the difference will not affect my point, which is that the words seem to imply the contingency of Jeremiah's leaving Anathoth. And this implication is certainly strengthened by the twice-given warning: "Be not afraid of them!" (i. 8), "Be not dismayed at them, lest I dismay thee (indeed) before them!" (17). The young prophet might dread the effect of an unpopular message upon his brethren and his father's house. But his fear would reach a far higher pitch of intensity, if he were called upon to confront with the same message of unwelcome truth the king in his palace, or the high priest in the courts of the sanctuary, or the fanatical and easily excited populace of the capital. Accordingly, when after his general prologue or exordium, the prophet plunges at once "into the agitated life of the present,"[8] it is to "the men of Judah and Jerusalem" (iv. 3), to "the great men" (v. 5), and to the throng of worshippers in the temple (vii. 2), that he addresses his burning words. When, however (v. 4), he exclaims: "And for me, I said, They are but poor folk; they *do* foolishly (Num. xii. 11), for they know not the way of Iahvah, the rule (*i.e.*, *religion*) of their God (Isa. xlii. 1): I will get me unto the great men, and will speak with them; for *they* know the way of Iahvah, the rule of their God:" he again seems to suggest a prior ministry, of however brief duration, upon the smaller stage of Anathoth. At all events, there is nothing against the conjecture that the prophet may have passed to and fro between his birthplace and Jerusalem, making occasional sojourn in the capital, until at last the machinations of his neighbours (xi. 19 *sqq.*), and as appears from xii. 6, his own kinsmen, drove him to quit Anathoth for ever. If Hitzig be right in referring Psalms xxiii., xxvi.-xxviii. to the prophet's pen, we may find in them evidence of the fact that the temple became his favourite haunt, and indeed his usual abode. As a priest by birth, he would have a claim to live in some one of the cells that surrounded the temple on three sides of it. The 23rd Psalm, though written at a later period in the prophet's career—I shall refer to it again by-and-by—closes with the words, "And I will return unto (Ps. vii. 17; Hos. xii. 7) the house of Iahvah as long as I live," or perhaps, "And I will return (and dwell) in" etc., as though the temple were at once his sanctuary and his home. In like manner, Ps. xxvi. speaks of one who "washed his hands, in innocency" (*i.e.* in a state of innocency; the symbolical action corresponding to the real state of his heart and conscience), and so "compassed the altar of Iahvah"; "to proclaim with the sound of a psalm of thanksgiving, and to rehearse all His wondrous works." The language here seems even to imply (Ex. xxx. 19-21), that the prophet took part, as a priest, in the ritual of the altar. He continues: "Iahvah, I love the abode of thine house, And the place of the dwelling of Thy glory!" and concludes, "My foot, it standeth on a plain; In the congregations I bless Iahvah," speaking as one continually present at the temple services. His prayers "Judge me," *i.e.*, Do me justice, "Iahvah!" and "Take not away my soul among sinners, Nor my life among men of bloodshed!" may point either to the conspiracies of the Anathothites, or to subsequent persecutions at Jerusalem. The former seem to be intended both here, and in Ps. xxvii., which is certainly most appropriate as an Ode of Thanksgiving for the prophet's escape from the murderous attempts of the men of Anathoth. Nothing could be more apposite than the allusions to "evil-doers drawing near against him to eat up his flesh" (*i.e.*, according to the common Aramaic metaphor, to slander him, and destroy him with false accusations); to the "lying witnesses, and the man (or men) breathing out (or panting after) violence" (ver. 12); and to having been forsaken even by his father and mother (ver. 10). With the former, we may compare the prophet's words, chap. ix. 2 *sqq.*, "O that I were in the wilderness, in a lodge of wayfaring men; that I might forsake my people, and depart from among them! For all of them are adulterous, an assembly of traitors. And they have bent their tongue, (as it were) their bow for lying; and it is not by sincerity that they have grown strong in the land. Beware ye, every one of his friend, and have no confidence in any brother: for every brother will assuredly supplant" (בקעי בוקע a reference to Jacob and Esau), "and every friend will gad about for slander. And each will deceive his friend, and the truth they will not speak: they have taught their tongue to speak lies; with perverseness they have wearied themselves. Thy dwelling is in the midst of deceit.... A murderous arrow is their tongue; deceit hath it spoken; with his mouth one speaketh peace with his neighbour, and inwardly he layeth an ambush for him." Such language, whether in the psalm or in the prophetic oration, could only be the fruit of bitter personal experience. (Cf. also xi. 19 *sqq.*, xx. 2 *sqq.*, xxvi. 8, xxxvi. 26, xxxvii. 15, xxxviii. 6). The allusion of the psalmist to being forsaken by father and mother (Ps. xxvii. 10) may be illustrated by the prophet's words, chap. xii. 6.

Jeremiah came prominently forward at a serious crisis in the history of his people. The Scythian invasion of Asia, described by Herodotus (i. 103-106), but not mentioned in the biblical histories of the time, was threatening Palestine and Judea. According to the old Greek writer, Cyaxares the Mede, while engaged in besieging Nineveh, was attacked by a great horde of Scythians, under their king Madyes, who had entered Asia in pushing their pursuit of the Cimmerians, whom they had expelled from Europe.[9] The Medes lost the battle, and the barbarous victors found themselves masters of Asia. Thereupon they marched for Egypt, and had made their way past Ascalon, when they were met by the envoys of Psammitichus I. the king of Egypt, whose "gifts and prayers," induced them to return. On the way back, some few of them lagged behind the main body, and plundered the famous temple of Atergatis-Derceto, or as Herodotus calls the great Syrian goddess, Ourania Afrodite, at Ascalon (the goddess avenged herself by smiting them and their descendants with impotence—θήλειαν νοῦσον, cf. 1 Sam. v. 6 *sqq.*). For eight and twenty years the Scythians remained the tyrants of Asia, and by their exactions and plundering raids brought ruin everywhere, until at last Cyaxares and his Medes, by help of treachery, recovered their former sway. After this, the Medes took Nineveh, and reduced the Assyrians to complete subjection; but Babylonia remained independent. Such is the story as related by Herodotus, our sole authority in the matter. It has been supposed[10] that the 59th Psalm was written by king Josiah, while the Scythians were threatening Jerusalem. Their wild hordes, ravenous for plunder, like the Gauls who at a later time struck Rome with panic, are at any rate well described in the verse

"They return at eventide,
They howl like the dogs,

the famished pariah dogs of an eastern town—

And surround the city."

But the Old Testament furnishes other indications of the terror which preceded the Scythian invasion, and of the merciless havoc which accompanied it. The short prophecy of Zephaniah, who prophesied "in the days of Josiah ben Amon king of Judah," and was therefore a contemporary of Jeremiah, is best explained by reference to this crisis in the affairs of Western Asia. Zephaniah's very first word is a startling menace. "I will utterly away with everything from off the face of the ground, saith Iahvah." "I will away with man and beast, I will away with the birds of the air, and the fishes of the sea, and the stumblingblocks along with the wicked (*i.e.* the idols with their worshippers); and I will exterminate man from off the face of the ground, saith Iahvah." The imminence of a sweeping destruction is announced. Ruin is to overtake every existing thing; not only the besotted people and their dumb idols, but beasts and birds and even the fish of the sea are to perish in the universal catastrophe. It is exactly what might be expected from the sudden appearance of a horde of barbarians of unknown numbers, sweeping over a civilised country from north to south, like some devastating flood; slaying whatever crossed their path, burning towns and temples, and devouring the flocks and herds. The reference to the fishes of the sea is explained by the fact that the Scythians marched southward by the road which ran along the coast through Philistia. "Gaza," cries the prophet, "shall be forsaken," —there is an inimitable paronomasia in his words[11]—"And Ascalon a desolation: as for Ashdod, at noonday they shall drive her into exile; and Ekron shall be rooted up. Alas for the dwellers by the shore line, the race of the Cherethites! The word of Iahvah is against you, O Canaan, land of the Philistines! And I will destroy thee, that there shall be no inhabitant." It is true that Herodotus relates that the Scythians, in their retreat, for the most part marched past Ascalon without doing any harm, and that the plunder of the temple was the work of a few stragglers. But neither is this very probable in itself, nor does it harmonize with what he tells us afterwards about the plunder and rapine that marked the period of Scythian domination. We need not suppose that the information of the old historian as to the doings of these barbarians was as exact as that of a modern state paper. Nor, on the other hand, would it be very judicious to press every detail in a highly wrought prophetic discourse, which vividly sets forth the fears of the time, and gives imaginative form to the feelings and anticipations of the hour; as if it were intended by the writer, not for the moral and spiritual good of his contemporaries, but to furnish posterity with a minutely accurate record of the actual course of events in the distant past.

The public danger, which stimulated the reflexion and lent force to the invective of the lesser prophet, intensified the impression produced by the earlier preaching of Jeremiah. The tide of invasion, indeed, rolled past Judea, without working much permanent harm to the little kingdom, with whose destinies were involved the highest interests of mankind at large. But this respite from destruction would be understood by the prophet's hearers as proof of the relentings of Iahvah towards His penitent people; and may, for the time at least, have confirmed the impression wrought upon the popular mind by Jeremiah's passionate censures and entreaties. The time was otherwise favourable; for the year of his call was the year immediately subsequent to that in which the young king Josiah "began to purify Judah and Jerusalem from the high places and the Asherim, and the carven images and the molten images," which he did in the twelfth year of his reign, *i.e.* in the twentieth year of his age, according to the testimony of the Chronicler (2 Chron. xxxiv. 3), which there is no good reason for disallowing. Jeremiah was probably about the same age as the king, as he calls himself a mere youth (na`ar). After the Scythians had retired—if we are right in fixing their invasion so early in the reign—the official reformation of public worship was taken up again, and completed by the eighteenth year of Josiah, when the prophet might be about twenty-five. The finding of what is called "the book of the Law," and "the book of the Covenant,"[12] by Hilkiah the high priest, while the temple was being restored by the king's order, is represented by the histories as having determined the further course of the royal reforms. What this book of the Law was, it is not necessary now to discuss. It is clear from the language of the book of Kings, and from the references of Jeremiah, that the substance of it, at any rate, closely corresponded with portions of Deuteronomy. It appears from his own words (chap. xi. 1-8) that at first, at all events, Jeremiah was an earnest preacher of the positive precepts of this book of the Covenant. It is true that his name does not occur in the narrative of Josiah's reformation, as related in Kings. There the king and his counsellors inquire of Iahvah through the prophetess Huldah (2 Kings xxii. 14). Supposing the account to be both complete and correct, this only shows that five years after his call, Jeremiah was still unknown or little considered at court. But he was doubtless included among the "prophets," who, with "the king and all the men of Judah and all the inhabitants of Jerusalem," "and the priests ... and all the people, both small and great," after the words of the newfound book of the Covenant had been read in their ears, bound themselves by a solemn league and covenant, "to walk after Iahweh, and to keep His commandments, and His laws, and His statutes, with all the heart, and with all the soul" (2 Kings xxiii. 3). It is evident that at first the young prophet hoped great things of this national league and the associated reforms in the public worship. In his eleventh chapter, he writes thus: "The word that fell to Jeremiah from Iahvah, saying: Hear ye the words of this covenant"—presumably the words of the newfound book of the Torah—"And speak ye to the men of Judah, and to the inhabitants of Jerusalem. And thou shalt say unto them"—the change from the second plural "hear ye," "speak ye," is noticeable. In the first instance, no doubt, the message contemplates the leaders of the reforming movement generally; the prophet is specially addressed in the words, "And *thou* shalt say unto them, Thus said Iahvah, the God of Israel, Cursed is the man that will not hear the words of this covenant, which I commanded your fathers, in the day when I brought them forth from the land of Egypt, from the iron furnace, saying, Hearken to My voice, and do them, according to all that I command you; and ye shall become to Me a people, and I—I will become to you Elohim: in order to make good the oath that I sware to your fathers, to give them a land flowing with milk and honey, as at this day.

"And I answered and said, So be it, Iahvah!

"And Iahvah said unto me, Proclaim all these words in the cities of Judah and in the streets of Jerusalem, saying, Hear ye the words of this covenant, and do them. For I solemnly adjured your fathers, at the time when I brought them up out of the land of Egypt, (and) unto this day, with all earnestness [earnestly and incessantly], saying, Hearken ye to My voice. And they hearkened not, nor inclined their ear, and they walked individually in the stubbornness of their evil heart. So I brought upon them all the words of this covenant"—*i.e.*, the curses, which constituted the sanction of it: see Deut. iv. 25 *sqq.*, xxviii. 15 *sqq.*—"(this covenant) which I commanded them to do, and they did it not." [Or perhaps, "Because I bade them *do*, and they *did* not;" implying a general prescription of conduct, which was not observed. Or, "I who had bidden them do, and they did not"—justifying, as it were, God's assumption of the function of punishment. *His* law had been set at nought; the national reverses, therefore, were *His* infliction, and not another's.] This, then, was the first preaching of Jeremiah. "Hear ye the words of this covenant!"—the covenant drawn out with such precision and legal formality in the newfound book of the Torah. Up and down the country, "in the cities of Judah" and "in the streets of Jerusalem," everywhere within the bounds of the little kingdom that acknowledged the house of David, he published this panacea for the actual and imminent evils of the time, insisting, we may be sure, with all the eloquence of a youthful patriot, upon the impressive warnings embodied in the past history of Israel, as set forth in the book of the Law. But his best efforts were fruitless. Eloquence and patriotism and enlightened spiritual beliefs and lofty purity of purpose were wasted upon a generation blinded by its own vices and reserved for a swiftly approaching retribution. Perhaps the plots which drove the prophet finally from his native place were due to the hostility evoked against him by his preaching of the Law. At all events, the account of them immediately follows, in this eleventh chapter (vers. 18 *sqq.*). But it must be borne in mind that the Law-book was not found until *five* years after his call to the office of prophet. In any case, it is not difficult to understand the popular irritation at what must have seemed the unreasonable attitude of a prophet, who, in spite of the wholesale destruction of the outward symbols of idolatry effected by the king's orders, still declared that the claims of Iahweh were unsatisfied, and that something more was needed than the purging of Judah and Jerusalem from the high places and the Asherim, if the Divine favour were to be conciliated, and the country restored to permanent prosperity. The people probably supposed that they had sufficiently fulfilled the law of their God, when they had not only demolished all sanctuaries but His, but had done away with all those local holy places where Iahvah was indeed worshipped, but with a deplorable admixture of heathenish rites. The law of the one legal sanctuary, so much insisted upon in Deuteronomy, was formally established by Josiah, and the national worship was henceforth centralized in Jerusalem, which from this time onward remained in the eyes of all faithful Israelites "the place where men ought to worship." It is entirely in accordance with what we know of human nature in general, and not merely of Jewish nature, that the popular mind failed to rise to the level of the prophetic teaching, and that the reforming zeal of the time should have exhausted itself in efforts which effected no more than these external changes. The truth is that the reforming movement began from above, not from below; and however earnest the young king may have been, it is probable that the mass of his subjects viewed the abolition of the high-places, and the other sweeping measures, initiated in obedience to the precepts of the book of the Covenant, either with apathy and indifference, or with feelings of sullen hostility. The priesthood of Jerusalem were, of course, benefited by the abolition of all sanctuaries, except the one wherein they ministered and received their dues. The writings of our prophet amply demonstrate that, whatever zeal for Iahvah, and whatever degree of compunction for the past may have animated the prime movers in the reformation of the eighteenth of Josiah, no radical improvement was effected in the ordinary life of the nation. For some twelve years, indeed, the well-meaning king continued to occupy the throne; years, it may be presumed, of comparative peace and prosperity for Judah, although neither the narrative of Kings and Chronicles nor that of Jeremiah gives us any information about them. Doubtless it was generally supposed that the nation was reaping the reward of its obedience to the law of Iahvah. But at the end of that period, circ. b.c. 608, an event occurred which must have shaken this faith to its foundations. In the thirty-first year of his reign, Josiah fell in the battle of Megiddo, while vainly opposing the small forces at his command to the hosts of Egypt. Great indeed must have been the "searchings of heart" occasioned by this unlooked-for and overwhelming stroke. Strange that it should have fallen at a time when, as the people deemed, the God of Israel was receiving His due at their hands; when the injunctions of the book of the Covenant had been minutely carried out, the false and irregular worships abolished, and

Jerusalem made the centre of the cultus; a time when it seemed as if the Lord had become reconciled to His people Israel, when years of peace and plenty seemed to give demonstration of the fact; and when, as may perhaps be inferred from Josiah's expedition against Necho, the extension of the border, contemplated in the book of the Law, was considered as likely to be realised in the near future. The height to which the national aspirations had soared only made the fall more disastrous, complete, ruinous.

The hopes of Judah rested upon a worldly foundation; and it was necessary that a people whose blindness was only intensified by prosperity, should be undeceived by the discipline of overthrow. No hint is given in the meagre narrative of the reign as to whether the prophets had lent their countenance or not to the fatal expedition. Probably they did; probably they too had to learn by bitter experience, that no man, not even a zealous and godfearing monarch, is *necessary* to the fulfilment of the Divine counsels. And the agony of this irretrievable disaster, this sudden and complete extinction of his country's fairest hopes, may have been the means by which the Holy Spirit led Jeremiah to an intenser conviction that illicit modes of worship and coarse idolatries were not the only things in Judah offensive to Iahvah; that something more was needed to win back His favour than formal obedience, however rigid and exacting, to the letter of a written code of sacred law; that the covenant of Iahvah with His people had an inward and eternal, not an outward and transitory significance; and that not the letter but the spirit of the law was the thing of essential moment. Thoughts like these must have been present to the prophet's mind when he wrote (xxxi. 31 *sqq*.): "Behold, a time is coming, saith Iahvah, when I will conclude with the house of Israel and with the house of Judah a fresh treaty, unlike the treaty that I concluded with their forefathers, at the time when I took hold of their hand, to bring them out of the land of Egypt; when they, on their part, disannulled my treaty, and I—I disdained[13] them, saith Iahvah. For this is the treaty that I will conclude with the house of Israel after those days [*i.e.* in due time], saith Iahvah: I will put my Torah within them and upon their heart will I grave it; and I will become to them a God, and they—they shall become to me a people."

It is but a dull eye which cannot see beyond the metaphor of the covenant or treaty between Iahvah and Israel; and it is a strangely dark understanding that fails to perceive here and elsewhere a translucent figure of the eternal relations subsisting between God and man. The error is precisely that against which the prophets, at the high watermark of their inspiration, are always protesting—the universal and inveterate error of narrowing down the requirements of the Infinitely Holy, Just and Good, to the scrupulous observance of some accepted body of canons, enshrined in a book and duly interpreted by the laborious application of recognised legal authorities. It is so comfortable to be sure of possessing an infallible guide in so small a compass; to be spared all further consideration, so long as we have paid the priestly dues, and kept the annual feasts, and carefully observed the laws of ceremonial purity! From the first, the attention of priests and people, including the official prophets, would be attracted by the ritual and ceremonial precepts, rather than by the earnest moral teaching of Deuteronomy. As soon as first impressions had had time to subside, the moral and spiritual element in that noble book would begin to be ignored, or confounded with the purely external and mundane prescriptions affecting public worship and social propriety; and the interests of true religion would hardly be subserved by the formal acceptance of this code as the law of the state. The unregenerate heart of man would fancy that it had at last gotten that for which it is always craving—something final—something to which it could triumphantly point, when urged by the religious enthusiast, as tangible evidence that it was fulfilling the Divine law, that it was at one with Iahvah, and therefore had a right to expect the continuance of His favour and blessing. Spiritual development would be arrested; men would become satisfied with having effected certain definite changes bringing them into external conformity with the written law, and would incline to rest in things as they were. Meanwhile, the truth held good that to make a fetish of a code, a system, a holy book, is not necessarily identical with the service of God. It is, in fact, the surest way to forget God; for it is to invest something that is not He, but, at best, a far-off echo of His voice, with His sole attributes of finality and sufficiency.

The effect of the downfall of the good king was electrical. The nation discovered that the displeasure of Iahvah had not passed away like a morning cloud. Out of the shock and the dismay of that terrible disillusion sprang the conviction that the past was not atoned for, that the evil of it was irreparable. The idea is reflected in the words of Jeremiah (xv. 1): "And Iahvah said unto me, If Moses were to stand before Me (as an intercessor), and Samuel, I should not incline towards this people: dismiss them from My presence, and let them go forth! And when they say unto thee, Whither are we to go forth? thou shalt say unto them, Thus said Iahvah, They that are Death's to death; and they that are the Sword's to the sword; and they that are Famine's to famine; and they that are Captivity's to captivity. And I will set over them four families, saith Iahvah; the sword to slay, and the dogs to draw (2 Sam. xvii. 13), and the birds of the air, and the beasts of the earth, to devour and to destroy. And I will give them for worry (Deut. xxviii. 25) to all the realms of earth; *because of* (Deut. xv. 10, xviii. 12; ללנב) *Manasseh ben Hezekiah king of Judah; for what he did in Jerusalem.*" In the next verses we have what seems to be a reference to the death of Josiah (ver. 7). "I fanned them with a fan"—the fan by which the husbandman separates wheat from chaff in the threshing floor—"I fanned them with a fan, in the gates of the land"—at Megiddo, the point where an enemy marching along the maritime route might enter the land of Israel; "I bereaved, I ruined my people (ver. 9). She that had borne seven, pined away; she breathed out her soul; *her sun went down while it was yet day.*" The national mourning over this dire event became proverbial, as we see from Zech. xii. 11: "In that day, great shall be the mourning in Jerusalem; like the mourning of Hadadrimmon in the valley of Megiddo."

The political relations of the period are certainly obscure, if we confine our attention to the biblical data. Happily, we are now able to supplement these, by comparison with the newly recovered monuments of Assyria. Under Manasseh, the kingdom of Judah became tributary to Esarhaddon; and this relation of dependence, we may be sure, was not interrupted during the vigorous reign of the mighty Ashurbanipal, b.c. 668-626. But the first symptoms of declining power on the side of their oppressors would undoubtedly be the signal for conspiracy and rebellion in the distant parts of the loosely amalgamated empire. Until the death of Ashurbanipal, the last great sovereign who reigned at Nineveh, it may be assumed that Josiah stood true to his fealty. It appears from certain notices in Kings and Chronicles (2 Kings xxiii. 19; 2 Chron. xxxiv. 6) that he was able to exercise authority even in the territories of the ruined kingdom of Israel. This may have been due to the fact that he was allowed to do pretty much as he liked, so long as he proved an obedient vassal; or, as is more likely, the attention of the Assyrians was diverted from the West by troubles nearer home in connection with the Scythians or the Medes and Babylonians. At all events, it is not to be supposed that when Josiah went out to oppose the Pharaoh at Megiddo, he was facing the forces of Egypt alone. The thing is intrinsically improbable. The king of Judah must have headed a coalition of the petty Syrian states against the common enemy. It is not necessary to suppose that the Palestinian principalities resisted Necho's advance, in the interests of their nominal suzerain Assyria. From all we can gather, that empire was now tottering to its irretrievable fall, under the feeble successors of Ashurbanipal. The ambition of Egypt was doubtless a terror to the combined peoples. The further results of Necho's campaign are unknown. For the moment, Judah experienced a change of masters; but the Egyptian tyranny was not destined to last. Some four years after the battle of Megiddo, Pharaoh Necho made a second expedition to the North, this time against the Babylonians, who had succeeded to the empire of Assyria. The Egyptians were utterly defeated in the battle of Carchemish, circ. b.c.

606-5, which left Nebuchadrezzar in virtual possession of the countries west of the Euphrates (Jer. xlvi. 2). It was the fourth year of Jehoiakim, son of Josiah, king of Judah, when this crisis arose in the affairs of the Eastern world. The prophet Jeremiah did not miss the meaning of events. From the first he recognised in Nebuchadrezzar, or Nabucodrossor, an instrument in the Divine hand for the chastisement of the peoples; from the first, he predicted a judgment of God, not only upon the Jews, but upon all nations, far and near. The substance of his oracles is preserved to us in chapters xxv. and xlvi.-xlix. of his book. In the former passage, which is expressly dated from the fourth year of Jehoiakim, and the first of Nebuchadrezzar, the prophet gives a kind of retrospect of his ministry of three-and-twenty years, affirms that it has failed of its end, and that Divine retribution is therefore certain. The "tribes of the north" will come and desolate the whole country (ver. 9), and "these nations"—the peoples of Palestine—"shall serve the king of Babel seventy years" (ver. 11). The judgment on the nations is depicted by an impressive symbolism (ver. 15). "Thus said Iahvah, the God of Israel, unto me, Take this cup of wine, the (Divine) wrath, from My hand, and cause all the nations, unto whom I send thee, to drink it. And let them drink, and reel, and show themselves frenzied, because of the sword that I am sending amongst them!" The strange metaphor recalls our own proverb: *Quem Deus vult perdere, prius dementat.* "So I took the cup from the hand of Iahvah, and made all the nations drink, unto whom Iahvah had sent me." Then, as in some list of the proscribed, the prophet writes down, one after another, the names of the doomed cities and peoples. The judgment was set for that age, and the eternal books were opened, and the names found in them were these (ver. 18): "Jerusalem, and the cities of Judah, and her kings, and her princes. Pharaoh king of Egypt, and his servants, and his princes, and all his people. And all the hired soldiery, and all the kings of the land of Uz, and all the kings of the land of the Philistines, and Ashkelon, and Gaza, and Ekron, and the remnant of Ashdod. Edom, and Moab, and the benê Ammon. And all the kings of Tyre, and all the kings of Sidon, and the kings of the island (*i.e.* Cyprus) that is beyond the sea. Dedan and Tema and Buz and all the tonsured folk. And all the kings of Arabia, and all the kings of the hired soldiery, that dwell in the wilderness. And all the kings of Zimri, and all the kings of Elam, and all the kings of Media. And all the kings of the north, the near and the far, one with another; and all the kingdoms of the earth that are upon the surface of the ground."

When the mourning for Josiah was ended (2 Chron. xxxv. 24 *sqq.*), the people put Jehoahaz on his father's throne. But this arrangement was not suffered to continue, for Necho, having defeated and slain Josiah, naturally asserted his right to dispose of the crown of Judah as he thought fit. Accordingly, he put Jehoahaz in bonds at Riblah in the land of Hamath, whither he had probably summoned him to swear allegiance to Egypt, or whither, perhaps, Jehoahaz had dared to go with an armed force to resist the Egyptian pretensions, which, however, is an unlikely supposition, as the battle in which Josiah had fallen must have been a severe blow to the military resources of Judah. Necho carried the unfortunate but also unworthy king (2 Kings xxiii. 32) a prisoner to Egypt, where he died (*ibid.* 34). These events are thus alluded to by Jeremiah (xxii. 10-12): "Weep ye not for one dead (*i.e.* Josiah), nor make your moan for him: weep ever for him that is going away; for he will not come back again, and see his native land! For thus hath Iahvah said of Shallum (*i.e.* Jehoahaz, 1 Chron. iii. 15) ben Josiah, king of Judah, that reigned in the place of Josiah his father, who is gone forth out of this place (*i.e.* Jerusalem, or the palace, ver. 1), He will not come back thither again. For in the place whither they have led him into exile, there he will die; and this land he will not see again." The pathos of this lament for one whose dream of greatness was broken for ever within three short months, does not conceal the prophet's condemnation of Necho's prisoner. Jeremiah does not condole with the captive king as the victim of mere misfortune. In this, as in all the gathering calamities of his country, he sees a retributive meaning. The nine preceding verses of the chapter demonstrate the fact.

In the place of Jehoahaz, Necho had set up his elder brother Eliakim, with the title of Jehoiakim (2 Kings xxiii. 34). This prince also is condemned in the narrative of Kings (ver. 37), as having done "the evil thing in the eyes of Iahvah, according to all that his forefathers had done;" an estimate which is thoroughly confirmed by what Jeremiah has added to his lament for the deposed king his brother. The pride, the grasping covetousness, the high-handed violence and cruelty of Jehoiakim, and the doom that will overtake him, in the righteousness of God, are thus declared: "Woe to him that buildeth his house by injustice, and his chambers by iniquity! that layeth on his neighbour work without wages, and giveth him not his hire! That saith, I will build me a lofty house, with airy chambers; and he cutteth him out the windows thereof, panelling it with cedar, and painting it with vermilion. Shalt thou *reign*, that thou art hotly intent upon cedar?" (Or, according to the LXX. Vat., thou viest with Ahaz—LXX. Alex., with Ahab; perhaps a reference to "the ivory house" mentioned in 1 Kings xxii. 39). "Thy father, did he not eat and drink and do judgment and justice? Then it was well with him. He judged the cause of the oppressed and the needy: then it was well. Was not this to know Me? saith Iahvah. For thine eyes and thine heart are set upon nought but thine own lucre [thy plunder], and upon the blood of the innocent, to shed it, and upon extortion and oppression to do it. Therefore, thus hath Iahvah said of Jehoiakim ben Josiah, king of Judah: They shall not lament for him with Ah, my brother! or Ah, sister! They shall not lament for him with Ah, lord! or Ah, his majesty! With the burial of an ass shall he be buried; with dragging and casting forth beyond the gates of Jerusalem!"

In the beginning of the reign of this worthless tyrant, the prophet was impelled to address a very definite warning to the throng of worshippers in the court of the temple (xxvi. 4 *sqq.*). It was to the effect that if they did not amend their ways, their temple should become like Shiloh, and their city a curse to all the nations of the earth. There could be no doubt of the meaning of this reference to the ruined sanctuary, long since forsaken of God (Ps. lxxviii. 60). It so wrought upon that fanatical audience, that priests and prophets and people rose as one man against the daring speaker; and Jeremiah was barely rescued from immediate death by the timely intervention of the princes. The account closes with the relation of the cruel murder of another prophet of the school of Jeremiah, by command of Jehoiakim the king; and it is very evident from these narratives that, screened as he was by powerful friends, Jeremiah narrowly escaped a similar fate.

We have reached the point in our prophet's career when, taking a broad survey of the entire world of his time, he forecasts the character of the future that awaits its various political divisions. He has left the substance of his reflexions in the 25th chapter, and in those prophecies concerning the foreign peoples, which the Hebrew text of his works relegates to the very end of the book, as chapters xlvi.-li., but which the Greek recension of the Septuagint inserts immediately after chap. xxv. 13. In the decisive battle at Carchemish, which crippled the power of Egypt, the only other existing state which could make any pretensions to the supremacy of Western Asia, and contend with the trans-Euphratean empires for the possession of Syria-Palestine, Jeremiah had recognised a signal indication of the Divine Will, which he was not slow to proclaim to all within reach of his inspired eloquence. In common with all the great prophets who had preceded him, he entertained a profound conviction that the race was not necessarily to the swift, nor the battle to the strong; that the fortune of war was not determined simply and solely by chariots and horsemen and big battalions; that behind all material forces lay the spiritual, from whose absolute will they derived their being and potency, and upon whose sovereign pleasure depended the issues of victory and defeat, of life and death. As his successor, the second Isaiah, saw in the polytheist Cyrus, king of Anzan, a chosen servant of Iahvah, whose whole triumphant career was foreordained in the counsels of heaven; so Jeremiah saw in the rise of the Babylonian domination, and the rapid development of the new empire upon the ruins of the old, a manifest token of the Divine purpose, a revelation of a Divine secret. His point of view is strikingly illustrated by the warning which he was directed to send a few years later to the kings who were seeking to draw Judah into the common alliance against Babylon (chap. xxvii. 1 *sqq.*). "In the beginning of the reign of Zedekiah[14] ben Josiah, king of Judah, fell this word to Jeremiah from Iahvah. Thus said Iahvah unto me, Make thee thongs and poles, and put them upon thy neck; and send them to the king of Edom, and to the king of Moab, and to the king of the benê Ammon, and to the king of Tyre, and to the king of Zidon, by the hand of the messengers that are come to Jerusalem, unto Zedekiah the king of Judah. And give them a charge unto their masters, saying, Thus said Iahvah Sabaoth, the God of Israel, Thus shall ye say to your masters: I it was that made the earth, mankind, and the cattle that are on the face of the earth, by My great strength, and by Mine outstretched arm; and I give it to whom it seemeth good in My sight. And now, I will verily give all these countries into the hand of Nebuchadrezzar king of Babel, *My servant; and even the wild creatures of the field will I give unto him to serve him.*"

Nebuchadrezzar was invincible, and the Jewish prophet clearly perceived the fact. But it must not be imagined that the Jewish people generally, or the neighbouring peoples, enjoyed a similar degree of insight. Had that been so, the battle of Jeremiah's life would never have been fought out under such cruel, such hopeless conditions. The prophet saw the truth, and proclaimed it without ceasing in reluctant ears, and was met with derision, and incredulity, and intrigue, and slander, and pitiless persecution. By-and-by, when his word had come to pass, and all the principalities of Canaan were crouching abjectly at the feet of the conqueror, and Jerusalem was a heap of ruins, the scattered communities of banished Israelites could remember that Jeremiah had foreseen and foretold it all. In the light of accomplished facts, the significance of his prevision began to be realised; and when the first dreary hours of dumb and desperate suffering were over, the exiles gradually learned to find consolation in the few but precious promises that had accompanied the menaces which were now so visibly fulfilled. While they were yet in their own land, two things had been predicted by this prophet in the name of their God. The first was now accomplished; no cavil could throw doubt upon actual experience. Was there not here some warrant, at least for reasonable men, some sufficient ground for trusting the prophet at last, for believing in his Divine mission, for striving to follow his counsels, and for looking forward with steadfast hope out of present affliction, to the gladness of the future which the same seer had foretold, even with the unwonted precision of naming a limit of time? So the exiles were persuaded, and their belief was fully justified by the event. Never had they realised the absolute sovereignty of their God, the universality of Iahvah Sabaoth, the shadowy nature, the blank nothingness of all supposed rivals of His dominion, as now they did, when at length years of painful experience had brought home to their minds the truth that Nebuchadrezzar had demolished the temple and laid Jerusalem in the dust, not, as he himself believed, by the favour of Bel-Merodach and Nebo, but by the sentence of the God of Israel; and that the catastrophe, which had swept them out of political existence, occurred not because Iahvah was weaker than the gods of Babylon, but because He was irresistibly strong; stronger than all powers of all worlds; stronger therefore than Israel, stronger than Babylon; stronger than the pride and ambition of the earthly conqueror, stronger than the self-will, and the stubbornness, and the wayward rebellion, and the fanatical blindness, and the frivolous unbelief, of his own people. The conception is an easy one for us, who have inherited the treasures both of Jewish and of Gentile thought; but the long struggle of the prophets, and the fierce antagonism of their fellow-countrymen, and the political extinction of the Davidic monarchy, and the agonies of the Babylonian exile, were necessary to the genesis and germination of this master-conception in the heart of Israel, and so of humanity.

To return from this hasty glance at the remoter consequences of the prophet's ministry, it was in the fourth year of Jehoiakim, and the first of Nebuchadrezzar (xxv. 1) that, in obedience to a Divine intimation, he collected the various discourses which he had so far delivered in the name of God. Some doubt has been raised as to the precise meaning of the record of this matter (xxxvi.). On the one hand, it is urged that "An historically accurate reproduction of the prophecies would not have suited Jeremiah's object, which was not historical but practical: he desired to give a salutary shock to the people, by bringing before them the fatal consequences of their evil deeds:" and that "the purport of the roll (ver. 29) which the king burned was [only] that the king of Babylon should 'come and destroy this land,' whereas it is clear that Jeremiah had uttered many other important declarations in the course of his already long ministry." And on the other hand, it is suggested that the roll, of which the prophet speaks in chap. xxxvi., contained no more than the prophecy concerning the Babylonian invasion and its consequences, which is preserved in chap. xxv., and dated from the fourth year of Jehoiakim.

Considering the unsatisfactory state of the text of Jeremiah, it is perhaps admissible to suppose, for the sake of this hypothesis, that the second verse of chap. xxv., which expressly declares that this prophecy was spoken by its author "to all the people of Judah, and to all the inhabitants of Jerusalem," is "a loose inaccurate statement due to a later editor;" although this inconvenient statement is found in the Greek of the LXX. as well as in the Massoretic Hebrew text. But let us examine the alleged objections in the light of the positive statements of chap. xxxvi. It is there written thus: "In the fourth year of Jehoiakim ben Josiah king of Judah, this word fell to Jeremiah from Iahvah. Take thee a book-roll, and write on it all the words that I have spoken unto thee, concerning Israel and Judah and all the nations, from the day when I (first) spake unto thee,—from the days of Josiah,—unto this day." This certainly seems plain enough. The only possible question is whether the command was to collect within the compass of a single volume, a sort of author's edition, an indefinite number of discourses preserved hitherto in separate MSS. and perhaps to a great extent in the prophet's memory; or whether we are to understand by "all the words" the *substance* of the various prophecies to which reference is made. If the object was merely to impress the people on a particular occasion by placing before them a sort of historical review of the prophet's warnings in the past, it is evident that a formal edition of his utterances, so far as he was able to prepare such a work, would not be the most natural or ready method of attaining that purpose. Such a review for practical purposes might well be comprised within the limits of a single continuous composition, such as we find in chap. xxv., which opens with a brief retrospect of the prophet's ministry during twenty-three years (vers. 3-7), and then denounces the neglect with which his warnings have been received, and declares the approaching subjugation of all the states of Phenicia-Palestine by the king of Babylon. But the narrative itself gives not a single hint that such was the sole object in view. Much rather does it appear from the entire context that, the crisis having at length arrived, which Jeremiah had so long foreseen, he was now impelled to gather together, with a view to their preservation, all those discourses by which he had laboured in vain to overcome the indifference, the callousness, and the bitter antagonism of his people. These utterances of the past, collected and revised in the light of successive events, and illustrated by their substantial agreement with what had actually taken place, and especially by the new danger which seemed to threaten the whole West, the rising power of Babylon, might certainly be expected to produce a powerful impression by their coincidence with the national apprehensions; and the prophet might even hope that warnings, hitherto disregarded, but now visibly justified by events in course of development, would at last bring "the house of Judah" to consider seriously the evil that, in God's Providence, was evidently impending, and "return every man from his evil way," that even so late the consequences of their guilt might be turned aside. This doubtless was the immediate aim, but it does not exclude others, such as the vindication of the prophet's own claims, in startling contrast with those of the false prophets, who had opposed him at every step, and misled his countrymen so grievously and fatally. Against these and their delusive promises, the volume of Jeremiah's past discourses would constitute an effective protest, and a complete justification of his own endeavours. We must also remember that, if the repentance and salvation of his own contemporaries was naturally the first object of the prophet in all his undertakings, in the Divine counsels prophecy has more than a temporary value, and that the writings of this very prophet were destined to become instrumental in the conversion of a succeeding generation.

Those twenty-three years of patient thought and earnest labour, of high converse with God, and of agonised pleading with a reprobate people, were not to be without their fruit, though the prophet himself was not to see it. It is matter of history that the words of Jeremiah wrought with such power upon the hearts of the exiles in Babylonia, as to become, in the hands of God, a principal means in the regeneration of Israel, and of that restoration which was its promised and its actual consequence; and from that day to this, not one of all the goodly fellowship of the prophets has enjoyed such credit in the Jewish Church as he who in his lifetime had to encounter neglect and ridicule, hatred and persecution, beyond what is recorded of any other.

"So Jeremiah called Baruch ben Neriah; and Baruch wrote, from the mouth of Jeremiah, all the words of Iahvah, that He had spoken unto him, upon a book-roll" (ver. 4). Nothing is said about time; and there is nothing to indicate that what the scribe wrote at the prophet's dictation was a single brief discourse. The work probably occupied a not inconsiderable time, as may be inferred from the datum of the ninth verse (*vid. infr.*). Jeremiah would know that haste was incompatible with literary finish; he would probably feel that it was equally incompatible with the proper execution of what he had recognised as a Divine command. The prophet hardly had all his past utterances lying before him in the form of finished compositions. "And Jeremiah commanded Baruch, saying: I am detained (or confined); I cannot enter the house of Iahvah; so enter *thou*, and read in the roll, that thou wrotest from my mouth, the words of Iahvah, in the ears of the people, in the house of Iahvah, upon a day of fasting: and also in the ears of all Judah (the Jews), that come in (to the temple) from their (several) cities, thou shalt read them. Perchance their supplication will fall before Iahvah, and they will return, every one from his evil way; for great is the anger and the hot displeasure that Iahvah hath spoken (threatened) unto this people. And Baruch ben Neriah did according to all that Jeremiah the prophet commanded him, reading in the book the words of Iahvah in Iahvah's house." This last sentence might be regarded as a general statement, anticipative of the detailed account that follows, as is often the case in Old Testament narratives. But I doubt the application of this well-known exegetical device in the present instance. The verse is more likely an interpolation; unless we suppose that it refers to divers readings of which no particulars are given, but which preceded the memorable one described in the following verses. The injunction,

"And also in the ears of all Judah that come out of their cities thou shalt read them!" might imply successive readings, as the people flocked into Jerusalem from time to time. But the grand occasion, if not the only one, was without doubt that which stands recorded in the text. "And it came to pass in the *fifth* year of Jehoiakim ben Josiah king of Judah, in the *ninth* month, they proclaimed a fast before Iahvah,—all the people in Jerusalem and all the people that were come out of the cities of Judah into Jerusalem. And Baruch read in the book the words of Jeremiah, in the house of Iahvah, in the cell of Gemariah ben Shaphan the scribe, in the upper (inner) court, at the entry of the new gate of Iahvah's house, in the ears of all the people." The dates have an important bearing upon the points we are considering. It was in the fourth year of Jehoiakim that the prophet was bidden to commit his oracles to writing. If, then, the task was not accomplished before the *ninth* month of the *fifth* year, it is plain that it involved a good deal more than penning such a discourse as the twenty-fifth chapter. This datum, in fact, strongly favours the supposition that it was a record of his principal utterances hitherto, that Jeremiah thus undertook and accomplished. It is not at all necessary to assume that on this or any other occasion Baruch read the entire contents of the roll to his audience in the temple. We are told that he "read *in* the book the words of Jeremiah," that is, no doubt, some portion of the whole. And so, in the famous scene before the king, it is not said that the entire work was read, but the contrary is expressly related (ver. 23): "And when Jehudi had read *three columns or four*, he (the king) began to cut it with the scribe's knife, and to cast it into the fire." Three or four columns of an ordinary roll might have contained the whole of the twenty-fifth chapter; and it must have been an unusually diminutive document, if the first three or four columns of it contained no more than the seven verses of chap. xxv. (3-6), which declare the sin of Judah, and announce the coming of the king of Babylon. And, apart from these objections, there is no ground for the presumption that "the purport of the roll which the king burnt was [only] that the king of Babylon should 'come and destroy this land.'" As the learned critic, from whom I have quoted these words, further remarks, with perfect truth, "Jeremiah had uttered many other important declarations in the course of his already long ministry."

That, I grant, is true; but then there is absolutely nothing to prove that this roll did not contain them all. Chap. xxxvi. 29, cited by the objector, is certainly not such proof. That verse simply gives the angry exclamation with which the king interrupted the reading of the roll, "Why hast thou written upon it, The king of Babylon shall surely come and destroy this land, and cause to cease from it man and beast?"

This may have been no more than Jehoiakim's very natural inference from some one of the many allusions to the enemy "from the north," which occur in the earlier part of the book of Jeremiah. At all events, it is evident that, whether the king of Babylon was directly mentioned or not in the portion of the roll read in his presence, the verse in question assigns, not the sole import of the entire work, but only the particular point in it, which, at the existing crisis, especially roused the indignation of Jehoiakim. The 25th chapter may of course have been contained in the roll read before the king.

And this may suffice to show how precarious are the assertions of the learned critic in the *Encyclop. Brit.* upon the subject of Jeremiah's roll. The plain truth seems to be that, perceiving the imminence of the peril that threatened his country, the prophet was impressed with the conviction that now was the time to commit his past utterances to writing; and that towards the end of the year, after he had formed and carried out this project, he found occasion to have his discourses read in the temple, to the crowds of rural folk who sought refuge in Jerusalem, before the advance of Nebuchadrezzar. So Josephus understood the matter (*Ant.*, x. 6, 2).

On the approach of the Babylonians, Jehoiakim made his submission; but only to rebel again, after three years of tribute and vassalage (2 Kings xxiv. 1). Drought and failure of the crops aggravated the political troubles of the country; evils in which Jeremiah was not slow to discern the hand of an offended and alienated God. "How long," he asks (xii. 4), "shall the country mourn, and the herbage of the whole field wither? From the wickedness of them that dwell therein the beasts and the birds perish." And in chap. xiv. we have a highly poetical description of the sufferings of the time.

"Judah mourneth, and her gates languish;
They sit in black on the ground;
And the outcry of Jerusalem hath gone up.
And their nobles, they sent their menial folk for water;
They came to the pits, they found no water;
They returned with their vessels empty;
They were ashamed and confounded and covered their
head.
On account of ye ground that is chapt,
For rain hath not fallen in the land,
The plowmen are ashamed—they cover their head.
For even the hind in the field—
She calveth and forsaketh her young;
For there is no grass.
And the wild asses, they stand on the scaurs;

They snuff the wind[15] like jackals;
Their eyes fail, for there is no herbage."

And then, after this graphic and almost dramatic portrayal of the sufferings of man and beast, in the blinding glare of the towns, and in the hot waterless plains, and on the bare hills, under that burning sky, whose cloudless splendours seemed to mock their misery, the prophet prays to the God of Israel.

"If our misdeeds answer against us,
O Iahvah, work for Thy name sake!
Verily, our fallings away are many;
Towards thee we are in fault.
Hope of Israel, that savest him in time of trouble!
Why shouldst thou be as a sojourner in the land,
And as a traveller, that turneth aside to pass the night?
Why shouldst thou be as a man stricken dumb,
As a champion that cannot save?
Yet Thou art in our midst, O Iahvah,
And Thy name is called over us:Leave us not!"

And again, at the end of the chapter,

"Hast Thou wholly rejected Judah?
Hath Thy soul loathed Zion?
Why hast Thou smitten us,
That there is no healing for us?
We looked for welfare, but bootlessly,
For a time of healing, and behold terror!
We know, Iahvah, our wickedness, the guilt of our fathers:
Verily, we are in fault toward Thee!
Be not scornful, for Thy name's sake!
Dishonour not Thy glorious throne! [*i.e.* Jerusalem.]
Remember, break not Thy covenant with us!
Among the Vanities of the nations are there indeed
raingivers?
Or the heavens, can they yield showers?
Art not Thou He (that doeth this), Iahvah our God?
And we wait for Thee,
For 'tis Thou that madest all this world."

In these and the like pathetic outpourings, which meet us in the later portions of the Old Testament, we may observe the gradual development of the dialect of stated prayer; the beginnings and the growth of that beautiful and appropriate liturgical language in which both the synagogue and the church afterwards found so perfect an instrument for the expression of all the harmonies of worship. Prayer, both public and private, was destined to assume an increasing importance, and, after the destruction of temple and altar, and the forcible removal of the people to a heathen land, to become the principal means of communion with God.

The evils of drought and dearth appear to have been accompanied by inroads of foreign enemies, who took advantage of the existing distress to rob and plunder at will. This serious aggravation of the national troubles is recorded in chap. xii. 7-17. There it is said, in the name of God, "I have left My house, I have cast off My heritage; I have given the Darling of My soul into the hands of her enemies." The reason is Judah's fierce hostility to her Divine Master: "Like a lion in the forest she hath uttered a cry against Me." The result of this unnatural rebellion is seen in the ravages of lawless invaders, probably nomads of the desert, always watching their opportunity, and greedy of the wealth, while disdainful of the pursuits of their civilised neighbours. It is as if all the wild beasts, that roam at large in the open country, had concerted a united attack upon the devoted land; as if many shepherds with their innumerable flocks had eaten bare and trodden down the vineyard of the Lord. "Over all the bald crags in the wilderness freebooters (Obad. 5) are come; for a sword of Iahweh's is devouring: from land's end to land's end no flesh hath security" (ver. 12). The rapacious and heathenish hordes of the desert, mere human wolves intent on ravage and slaughter, are a sword of the Lord's, for the chastisement of His people; just as the king of Babylon is His "servant" for the same purpose.

Only ten verses of the book of Kings are occupied with the reign of Jehoiakim (2 Kings xxiii. 34-xxiv. 6); and when we compare that flying sketch with the allusions in Jeremiah, we cannot but keenly regret the loss of that "Book of the chronicles of the kings of Judah," to which the compiler of Kings refers as his authority. Had that work survived, many things in the prophets, which are now obscure and baffling, would have been clear and obvious. As it is, we are often obliged to be contented with surmises and probabilities, where certainty would be right welcome. In the present instance, the facts alluded to by the prophet appear to be included in the statement that the Lord sent against Jehoiakim bands of Chaldeans, and bands of Arameans, and bands of Moabites, and bands of benê Ammon. The Hebrew term implies marauding or predatory bands, rather than regular armies, and it need not be supposed that they all fell upon the country at the same time or in accordance with any preconcerted scheme. In the midst of these troubles, Jehoiakim died in the flower of his age, having reigned no more than eleven years, and being only thirty-six years old (2 Kings xxiii.

36). The prophet thus alludes to his untimely end. "Like the partridge that sitteth on eggs that she hath not laid, so is he that maketh riches, and not by right: in the midst of his days they leave him; and in his last end he proveth a fool" (xvii. 11). We have already considered the detailed condemnation of this evil king in the 22nd chapter. The prophet Habakkuk, a contemporary of Jeremiah, seems to have had Jehoiakim in his mind's eye, when denouncing (ii. 9) woe to one that "getteth an evil gain for his house, that he may set his nest on high, that he may escape from the hand of evil!" The allusion is to the forced labour on his new palace, and on the defences of Jerusalem, as well as to the fines and presents of money, which this oppressive ruler shamelessly extorted from his unhappy subjects. "The stone out of the wall," says the prophet, "crieth out; and the beam out of the woodwork answereth it."

The premature death of the tyrant removed a serious obstacle from the path of Jeremiah. No longer forced to exercise a wary vigilance in avoiding the vengeance of a king whose passions determined his conduct, the prophet could now devote himself heart and soul to the work of his office. The public danger, imminent from the north, and the way to avert it, is the subject of the discourses of this period of his ministry. His unquenchable faith appears in the beautiful prayer appended to his reflexions upon the death of Jehoiakim (xvii. 12 *sqq.*). We cannot mistake the tone of quiet exultation, with which he expresses his sense of the absolute righteousness of the catastrophe. "A throne of glory, a height higher than the first (?), (or, higher than any before) is the place of our sanctuary." Never before in the prophet's experience has the God of Israel so clearly vindicated that justice which is the inalienable attribute of His dread tribunal.

For himself, the immediate result of this renewal of an activity that had been more or less suspended, was persecution and even violence. The earnestness with which he besought the people to honestly keep the law of the Sabbath, an obligation which was recognised in theory though disregarded in practice; and his striking illustration of the true relations between Iahvah and Israel as parallel to those that hold between the potter and the clay (chap. xvii. 19 *sqq.*), only brought down upon him the fierce hostility and organised opposition of the false prophets, and the priests, and the credulous and self-willed populace, as we read in chap. xviii. 18 *sqq.* "And they said, Come, and let us contrive plots against Jeremiah.... Come, and let us smite him with the tongue, and let us not listen to any of his words. Should evil be repaid for good, that they have digged a pit for my life?" And after his solemn testimony before the elders in the valley of Ben-Hinnom, and before the people generally, in the court of the Lord's house (chap. xix.), the prophet was seized by order of Pashchûr, the commandant of the temple, who was himself a leading false prophet, and cruelly beaten, and set in the stocks for a day and a night. That the spirit of the prophet was not broken by this shameful treatment, is evident from the courage with which he confronted his oppressor on the morrow, and foretold his certain punishment. But the apparent failure of his mission, the hopelessness of his life's labour, indicated by the deepening hostility of the people, and the readiness to proceed to extremities against him thus evinced by their leaders, wrung from Jeremiah that bitter cry of despair, which has proved such a stumbling-block to some of his modern apologists.

Soon the prophet's fears were realised, and the Divine counsel, of which he alone had been cognisant, was fulfilled. Within three short months of his accession to the throne, the boy-king Jeconiah (or Jehoiachin or Coniah), with the queen-mother, the grandees of the court, and the pick of the population of the capital, was carried captive to Babylon by Nebuchadrezzar (2 Kings xxiv. 8 *sqq.*; Jer. xxiv. 1).

Jeremiah has appended his forecast of the fate of Jeconiah, and a brief notice of its fulfilment, to his denunciations of that king's predecessors (xxii. 24 *sqq.*). "As I live, saith Iahvah, verily, though Coniah ben Jehoiakim king of Judah be a signet ring upon My own right hand, verily thence will I pluck thee away! And I will give thee into the hand of them that seek thy life, and into the hand of those of whom thou art afraid; and into the hand of Nebuchadrezzar king of Babel, and into the hand of the Chaldeans. And I will cast thee forth, and thy mother that bare thee, into the foreign land, wherein ye were not born; and there ye shall die. But unto the land whither they long to return, thither shall they not return. Is this man Coniah a despised broken vase, or a vessel devoid of charm? Why were he and his offspring cast forth, and hurled into the land that they knew not? O land, land, land, hear thou the word of Iahvah. Thus hath Iahvah said, Write ye down this man childless, a person that shall not prosper in his days: for none of his offspring shall prosper, sitting on the throne of David, and ruling again in Judah."

No better success attended the prophet's ministry under the new king Zedekiah, whom Nebuchadrezzar had placed on the throne as his vassal and tributary. So far as we can judge from the accounts left us, Zedekiah was a wellmeaning but unstable character, whose weakness and irresolution were too often played upon by unscrupulous and scheming courtiers, to the fatal miscarriage of right and justice. Soon the old intrigues began again, and in the fourth year of the new reign (xxviii. 1) envoys from the neighbour-states arrived at the Jewish court, with the object of drawing Judah into a coalition against the common suzerain, the king of Babylon. This suicidal policy of combination with heathenish and treacherous allies, most of whom were the heirs of immemorial feuds with Judah, against a sovereign who was at once the most powerful and the most enlightened of his time, called forth the prophet's immediate and strenuous opposition. Boldly affirming that Iahvah had conferred universal dominion upon Nebuchadrezzar, and that consequently all resistance was futile, he warned Zedekiah himself to bow his neck to the yoke, and dismiss all thought of rebellion. It would seem that about this time (circ. 596 b.c.) the empire of Babylon was passing through a serious crisis, which the subject peoples of the West hoped and expected would result in its speedy dissolution. Nebuchadrezzar was, in fact, engaged in a life-and-death struggle with the Medes; and the knowledge that the Great King was thus fully occupied elsewhere, encouraged the petty princes of Phenicia-Palestine in their projects of revolt. If chaps. l., li., are genuine, it was at this juncture that Jeremiah foretold the fall of Babylon; for, at the close of the prophecy in question (li. 59), it is said that he gave a copy of it to one of the princes who accompanied Zedekiah to Babylon *in the fourth year of his reign*, i.e. in 596 b.c. But the style and thought of these two chapters, and the general posture of things which they presuppose, are decisive against the view that they belong to Jeremiah. At all events the prophet gave the clearest evidence that he did not himself share in the general delusion that the fall of Babylon was near at hand. He declared that all the nations must be content to serve Nebuchadrezzar, and his son, and his son's son (xxvii. 7); and as chap. xxix. shows, he did his best to counteract the evil influence of those fanatical visionaries, who were ever promising a speedy restoration to the exiles who had been deported to Babylon with Jeconiah. At last, however, in spite of all Jeremiah's warnings and entreaties, the vacillating king Zedekiah, was persuaded to rebel; and the natural consequence followed—the Chaldeans appeared before Jerusalem. King and people had refused salvation, and were now no more to be saved.

During the siege, the prophet was more than once anxiously consulted by the king as to the issue of the crisis. Although kept in ward by Zedekiah's orders, lest he should weaken the defence by his discouraging addresses, Jeremiah showed that he was far above the feeling of private ill-will, by the answers he returned to his sovereign's inquiries. It is true that he did not at all modify the burden of his message; to the king as to the people he steadily counselled surrender. But strongly as he denounced further resistance, he did not predict the king's death; and the tone of his prophecy concerning Zedekiah is in striking contrast with that concerning his predecessor Jehoiakim. It was in the tenth year of Zedekiah and the eighteenth of Nebuchadrezzar, that is to say, circ. 589 b.c., when Jeremiah was imprisoned in the court of the royal guard, within the precincts of the palace (xxxii. 1 *sqq.*); when the siege of Jerusalem was being pressed on with vigour, and when of all the strong cities of Judah, only two, Lachish and Azekah, were still holding out against the Chaldean blockade; that the prophet thus addressed the king (xxxiv. 2 *sqq.*): "Thus hath Iahvah said, Behold, I am about to give this city into the hand of the king of Babel, and he shall burn it with fire. And thou wilt not escape out of his hand; for thou wilt certainly be taken, and into his hand thou wilt be given. And thine eyes shall see the king of Babel's eyes, and his mouth shall speak with thy mouth, and to Babel wilt thou come. But hear thou Iahvah's word, O Zedekiah king of Judah! Thus hath Iahvah said upon thee, Thou wilt not die by the sword. In peace wilt thou die; and with the burnings of thy fathers, the former kings that were before thee, so will men burn (spicery) for thee, and with Ah, Lord! will they wail for thee; for a promise have *I* given, saith Iahvah." Zedekiah was to be exempted from the violent death, which then seemed so probable; and was to enjoy the funeral honours of a king, unlike his less worthy brother Jehoiakim, whose body was cast out to decay unburied like that of a beast. The failure of Jeremiah's earnest and consistent endeavours to bring about the submission of his people to what he foresaw to be their inevitable destiny, is explained by the popular confidence in the defences of Jerusalem, which were enormously strong for the time, and were considered impregnable (xxi. 13); and by the hopes entertained that Egypt, with whom negotiations had long been in progress, would raise the siege ere it was too late. The low state of public morals is vividly illustrated by an incident which the prophet has recorded (chap. xxxiv. 7 *sqq.*). In the terror inspired by the approach of the Chaldeans, the panic-stricken populace of the capital bethought them of that law of their God, which they had so long set at nought; and the king and his princes and the entire people bound themselves by a solemn covenant in the temple, to release all slaves of Israelitish birth, who had served six years and upwards, according to the law. The enfranchisement was accomplished with all the sanctions of law and of religion; but no sooner had the Chaldeans retired from before Jerusalem in order to meet the advancing army of Egypt, than the solemn covenant was cynically and shamelessly violated, and the unhappy freedmen were recalled to their bondage. After this, further warning was evidently out of place; and nothing was left for Jeremiah but to denounce the outrage upon the majesty of heaven, and to declare the speedy return of the besiegers, and the desolation of Jerusalem. His own liberty had not yet been restricted (xxxvii. 4) when these events happened; but a pretext was soon found for venting upon him the malice of his enemies. After assuring the king that the respite was not to be permanent, but that Pharaoh's army would return to Egypt without accomplishing any deliverance, and that the Chaldeans would "come again, and fight against the city, and take it, and burn it with fire" (xxxvii. 8), Jeremiah availed himself of the temporary absence of the besieging forces, to attempt to leave his City of Destruction; but he was arrested in the gate by which he was going out, and brought before the princes on a charge of attempted desertion to the enemy. Ridiculous as was this accusation, when thus levelled against one whose whole life was conspicuous for sufferings entailed by a lofty and unflinching patriotism and a devotion, at the time almost unique, to the sacred cause of religion and morality; it was at once received and acted upon. Jeremiah was beaten and thrown into a dungeon, where he languished for a long time in subterranean darkness and misery, until the king desired to consult him again. This was the saving of the prophet's life; for after once more declaring his unalterable message, וְתִנַּת לְבַב הֶּלֶמ רִיְב, "Into the king of Babel's hand thou wilt be given!" he made indignant protest against his cruel wrongs, and obtained from Zedekiah some mitigation of his sentence. He was not sent back to the loathsome den under the house of Jonathan the scribe, in whose dark recesses he had well nigh perished (xxxvii. 20), but was detained in the court of the guard, receiving a daily dole of bread for his maintenance. Here he appears to have still used such opportunity as he had, in dissuading the people from continuing the defence. At all events, four of the princes induced the king to deliver him into their power, on the ground that he "weakened the hands of the men of war," and sought not the welfare but the hurt of the nation (xxxviii. 4). Unwilling for some reason or other, probably a superstitious one, to imbrue their hands in the prophet's blood, they let him down with cords into a miry cistern (רֹוּב) in the court of the guard, and left him there to die of cold and hunger. Timely help sanctioned by the king rescued Jeremiah from this horrible fate; but not before he had undergone sufferings of the severest character, as may easily be understood from his own simple narrative, and from the indelible impression wrought upon others by the record of his sufferings, which led the poet of the Lamentations to refer to this time of deadly peril, and torture both mental and physical, in the following terms:

> "They chased me sore like a bird,
> They that were my foes without a cause.
> They silenced my life in the pit,
> And they cast a stone upon me.
> Waters overflowed mine head;
> Methought, I am cut off.
> I called Thy name, Iahvah,
> Out of the deepest pit.
> My voice Thou heardest (saying),

'Hide not Thine ear at my breathing, at my cry.'
Thou drewest near when I called Thee;
Thou saidst, 'Fear not'!
Thou pleadedst, O Lord, my souls pleadings;
Thou ransomedst my life."

After this signal escape, Jeremiah's counsel was once more sought by the king, in a secret interview, which was jealously concealed from the princes. But neither entreaties, nor assurances of safety, could persuade Zedekiah to surrender the city. Nothing was now left for the prophet, but to await, in his milder captivity, the long foreseen catastrophe. The form now taken by his solitary musings was not anxious speculation upon the question whether any possible resources were as yet unexhausted, whether by any yet untried means king and people might be convinced, and the end averted. Taking that end for granted, he looks forth beyond his own captivity, beyond the scenes of famine and pestilence and bloodshed that surround him, beyond the strife of factions within the city, and the lines of the besiegers without it, to a fair prospect of happy restoration and smiling peace, reserved for his ruined country in the far-off yet ever-approaching future (xxxii., xxxiii.).

Strong in this inspired confidence, like the Roman who purchased at its full market value the ground on which the army of Hannibal lay encamped, he did not hesitate to buy, with all due formalities of transfer, a field in his native place, at this supreme moment, when the whole country was wasted with fire and sword, and the artillery of the foe was thundering at the walls of Jerusalem. And the event proved that he was right. He believed in the depth of his heart that God had not finally cast off His people. He believed that nothing, not even human error and revolt, could thwart and turn aside the Eternal purposes. He was sure—it was demonstrated to him by the experience of an eventful life—that, amid all the vicissitudes of men and things, one thing stands immutable, and that is the will of God. He was sure that Abraham's family had not become a nation, merely in order to be blotted out of existence by a conqueror who knew not Iahvah; that the torch of a true religion, a spiritual faith, had not been handed on from prophet to prophet, burning in its onward course with an ever clearer and intenser flame, merely to be swallowed up before its final glory was attained, in utter and eternal darkness. The covenant with Israel would no more be broken than the covenant of day and night (xxxiii. 20). The laws of the natural world are not more stable and secure than those of the spiritual realm; for both have their reason and their ground of prevalence in the Will of the One Unchangeable Lord of all. And as the prophet had been right in his forecast of the destruction of his country, so did he prove to have been right in his joyful anticipation of the future renascence of all the best elements in Israel's life. The coming time fulfilled his word; a fact which must always remain unaccountable to all but those who believe as Jeremiah believed.

After the fall of the city, special care was taken to ensure the safety of Jeremiah, in accordance with the express orders of Nebuchadrezzar, who had become cognisant of the prophet's consistent advocacy of surrender, probably from the exiles previously deported to Babylonia, with whom Jeremiah had maintained communications, advising them to settle down peaceably, accepting Babylon as their country for the time being, and praying for its welfare and that of its rulers. Nebuzaradan, the commander-in-chief, further allowed the prophet his choice between following him to Babylon, or remaining with the wreck of the population in the ruined country. Patriotism, which in his case was identified with a burning zeal for the moral and spiritual welfare of his fellow-countrymen, prevailed over regard for his own worldly interests; and Jeremiah chose to remain with the survivors—disastrously for himself, as the event proved (xxxix. 2, xl. 1).

An old man, worn out with strife and struggle, and weighed down by disappointment and the sense of failure, he might well have decided to avail himself of the favour extended to him by the conqueror, and to secure a peaceful end for a life of storm and conflict. But the calamities of his country had not quenched his prophetic ardour; the sacred fire still burnt within his aged spirit; and once more he sacrificed himself to the work he felt called upon to do, only to experience again the futility of offering wise counsel to headstrong, proud, and fanatical natures. Against his earnest protestations, he was forced to accompany the remnant of his people in their hasty flight into Egypt (xlii.); and, in the last glimpse afforded us, we see him there among his fellow-exiles making a final, and alas! ineffectual protest against their stubborn idolatry (xliv.). A tradition mentioned by Tertullian and St. Jerome which may be of earlier and Jewish origin, states that these apostates in their wicked rage against the prophet stoned him to death (cf. Heb. xi. 37).

The last chapter of his book brings the course of events down to about 561 b.c. The fact has naturally suggested a conjecture that the same year witnessed the close of the prophet's life. In that case, Jeremiah must have attained to an age of somewhere about ninety years; which, taking all the circumstances into consideration, is hardly credible. A celibate life is said to be unfavourable to longevity; but however that may be, the other conditions in this instance make it extremely unlikely. Jeremiah's career was a vexed and stormy one; it was his fate to be divided from his kindred and his fellow-countrymen by the widest and deepest differences of belief; like St.

Athanasius, he was called upon to maintain the cause of truth against an opposing world. "Woe's me, my mother!" he cries, in one of his characteristic fits of despondency, which were the natural fruit of a passionate and almost feminine nature, after a period of noble effort ending in the shame of utter defeat; "Woe's me, that thou gavest me birth, a man of strife, and a man of contention to all the land! Neither lender nor borrower have I been; yet all are cursing me" (xv. 10). The persecutions he endured, the cruelties of his long imprisonment, the horrors of the protracted siege, upon which he has not dwelt at length, but which have stamped themselves indelibly upon his language (xviii. 21, 22, xx. 16), would certainly not tend to prolong his life. In the 71st Psalm, which seems to be from his pen, and which wants the usual heading "A Psalm of David," he speaks of himself as conscious of failing powers, and as having already reached the extreme limit of age. Writing after his narrow escape from death in the miry cistern of his prison, he prays

"Cast me not off in the time of old age;
Forsake me not, when my strength faileth."

And again,

"Yea, even when I am old and grey-headed,
O God forsake me not!"

And, referring to his signal deliverance,

"Thou that shewedst me many and sore troubles,
Thou makest me live again;
And out of the deeps of the earth again Thou bringest me up."

The allusion in the 90th Psalm, as well as the case of Barzillai, who is described as extremely old and decrepit at fourscore (2 Sam. xix. 33), proves that life in ancient Palestine did not ordinarily transcend the limits of seventy to eighty years. Still, after all that may be urged to the contrary, Jeremiah may have been an exception to his contemporaries in this, as in most other respects. Indeed, his protracted labours and sufferings seem almost to imply that he was endowed with constitutional vigour and powers of endurance above the average of men; and if, as some suppose, he wrote the book of Job in Egypt, to embody the fruits of his life's experience and reflexion, as well as arranged and edited his other writings, it is evident that he must have sojourned among the exiles in that country for a considerable time.

The tale is told. In meagre and broken outline I have laid before you the known facts of a life which must always possess permanent interest, not only for the student of religious development, but for all men who are stirred by human passion, and stimulated by human thought. And fully conscious as I am of failure in the attempt to reanimate the dry bones of history, to give form and colour and movement to the shadows of the past; I shall not have spent my pains for nought, if I have awakened in a single heart some spark of living interest in the heroes of old; some enthusiasm for the martyrs of faith; some secret yearning to cast in their own lot with those who have fought the battle of truth and righteousness and to share with the saints departed in the victory that overcometh the world. And even if in this also I have fallen short of the mark, these desultory and imperfect sketches of a good man's life and work will not have been wholly barren of result, if they lead any one of my readers to renewed study of that truly sacred text which preserves to all time the living utterances of this last of the greater prophets.

I
THE CALL AND CONSECRATION

In the foregoing pages we have considered the principal events in the life of the prophet Jeremiah, by way of introduction to the more detailed study of his writings. Preparation of this kind seemed to be necessary, if we were to enter upon that study with something more than the vaguest perception of the real personality of the prophet. On the other hand, I hope we shall not fail to find our mental image of the man, and our conception of the times in which he lived, and of the conditions under which he laboured as a servant of God, corrected and perfected by that closer examination of his works to which I now invite you. And so we shall be better equipped for the attainment of that which must be the ultimate object of all such studies; the deepening and strengthening of the life of faith in ourselves, by which alone we can hope to follow in the steps of the saints of old, and like them to realise the great end of our being, the service of the All-Perfect.

I shall consider the various discourses in what appears to be their natural order, so far as possible, taking those chapters together which appear to be connected in occasion and subject. Chap. i. evidently stands apart, as a self-complete and independent whole. It consists of a chronological superscription (vv. 1-3), assigning the temporal limits of the prophet's activity; and secondly, of an inaugural discourse, which sets before us his first call, and the general scope of the mission which he was chosen to fulfil. This discourse, again, in like manner falls into two sections, of which the former (vv. 4-10) relates how the prophet was appointed and qualified by Iahvah to be a spokesman for Him; while the latter (vv. 11-19), under the form of two visions, expresses the assurance that Iahvah will accomplish His word, and pictures the mode of fulfilment, closing with a renewed summons to enter upon the work, and with a promise of effectual support against all opposition.

It is plain that we have before us the author's introduction to the whole book; and if we would gain an adequate conception of the meaning of the prophet's activity both for his own time and for ours, we must weigh well the force of these prefatory words. The career of a true prophet, or spokesman for God, undoubtedly implies a special call or vocation to the office. In this preface to the summarized account of his life's work, Jeremiah represents that call as a single and definite event in his life's history. Must we take this in its literal sense? We are not astonished by such a statement as "the word of the Lord came unto me;" it may be understood in more senses than one, and perhaps we are unconsciously prone to understand it in what is called a natural sense. Perhaps we think of a result of pious reflexion pondering the moral state of the nation and the needs of the time: perhaps of that inward voice which is nothing strange to any soul that has attained to the rudiments of spiritual development. But when we read such an assertion as that of ver. 9, "Then the Lord put forth His hand, and touched my mouth," we cannot but pause and ask what it was that the writer meant to convey by words so strange and startling. Thoughtful readers cannot avoid the question whether such statements are consonant with what we otherwise know of the dealings of God with man; whether an outward and visible act of the kind spoken of conforms with that whole conception of the Divine Being, which is, so far as it reflects reality, the outcome of His own contact with our human spirits. The obvious answer is that such corporeal actions are incompatible with all our experience and all our reasoned conceptions of the Divine Essence, which fills all things and controls all things, precisely because it is not limited by a bodily organism, because its actions are not dependent upon such imperfect and restricted media as hands and feet. If, then, we are bound to a literal sense, we can only understand that the prophet saw a vision, in which a Divine hand seemed to touch his lips, and a Divine voice to sound in his ears. But *are* we bound to a literal sense? It is noteworthy that Jeremiah does not say that Iahvah Himself appeared to him. In this respect, he stands in conspicuous contrast with his predecessor Isaiah, who writes (vi. 1), "In the year that king Uzziah died, I saw the Lord sitting upon a throne, high and lifted up;" and with his successor Ezekiel, who affirms in his opening verse (i. 1) that on a certain definite occasion "the heavens opened," and he saw "visions of God." Nor does Jeremiah use that striking phrase of the younger prophet's, "The hand of Iahvah was upon me," or "was strong upon me." But when he says, "Iahvah put forth His hand and touched my mouth," he is evidently thinking of the seraph that touched Isaiah's mouth with the live coal from the heavenly altar (vi. 7). The words are identical (עֲגִיו יפ לֹעַ), and might be regarded as a quotation. It is true that, supposing Jeremiah to be relating the experience of a trance-like condition or ecstasy, we need not assume any conscious imitation of his predecessor. The sights and sounds which affect a man in such a condition may be partly repetitions of former experience, whether one's own or that of others; and in part wholly new and strange. In a dream one might imagine things happening to oneself, which one had heard or read of in connexion with others. And Jeremiah's writings generally prove his intimate acquaintance with those of Isaiah and the older prophets. But as a trance or ecstasy is itself an involuntary state, so the thoughts and feelings of the subject of it must be independent of the individual will, and as it were imposed from without. Is then the prophet describing the experience of such an abnormal state—a state like that of St. Peter in his momentous vision on the housetop at Joppa, or like that of St. Paul when he was "caught up to the third heaven," and saw many wonderful things which he durst not reveal? The question has been answered in the negative on two principal grounds. It is said that the vision of vv. 11, 12, derives its significance not from the visible thing itself, but from the name of it, which is, of course, not an object of sight at all; and consequently, the so-called vision is really "a well-devised and ingenious product of cool reflexion." But is this so? We may translate the original passage thus: *And there fell a word of Iahvah unto me, saying, What seest thou, Jeremiah? And I said, A rod of a wake-tree (i.e.* an almond) *is what I see. And Iahvah said unto me, Thou hast well seen; for wakeful am I over My word, to do it.* Doubtless there is here one of those plays on words which are so well known a feature of the prophetic style; but to admit this is by no means tantamount to an admission that the vision derives its force and meaning from the "invisible name" rather than from the visible thing. Surely it is plain that the significance of the vision depends on the fact which the name implies; a fact which would be at once suggested by the sight of the tree. It is the well known characteristic of the almond tree that it wakes, as it were, from the long sleep of winter before all other trees, and displays its beautiful garland of blossom, while its companions remain leafless and apparently lifeless. This quality of early wakefulness is expressed by the Hebrew name of the almond tree; for *shāqēd* means *waking* or *wakeful*. If this tree, in virtue of its remarkable peculiarity, was a proverb of watching and waking, the sight of it, or of a branch of it, in a prophetic vision would be sufficient to suggest that idea, independently of the name. The allusion to the name, therefore, is only a literary device for expressing with inimitable force and neatness the significance of the visible symbol of the "rod of the almond tree," as it was intuitively apprehended by the prophet in his vision.

Another and more radical ground is discovered in the substance of the Divine communication. It is said that the anticipatory statement of the contents and purpose of the subsequent prophesyings of the seer (ver. 10), the announcement beforehand of his fortunes (vv. 8, 18, 19), and the warning addressed to the prophet personally (ver. 17), are only conceivable as results of a process of abstraction from real experience, as prophecies conformed to the event (*ex eventu*). "The call of the prophet," says the writer whose arguments we are examining, "was the moment when, battling down the doubts and scruples of the natural man (vv. 7, 8), and full of holy courage, he took the resolution (ver. 17) to proclaim God's word. Certainly he was animated by the hope of Divine assistance (ver. 18), the promise of which he heard inwardly in the heart. More than this cannot be affirmed. But in this chapter (vv. 17, 18), the measure and direction of the Divine help are already clear to the writer; he is aware that opposition awaits him (ver. 19); he knows the content of his prophecies (ver. 10). Such knowledge was only possible for him in the middle or at the end of his career; and therefore the composition of this opening chapter must be referred to such a later period. As, however, the final catastrophe, after which his language would have taken a wholly different complexion, is still hidden from him here; and as the only edition of his prophecies prepared by himself, that we know of, belongs to the fourth year of Jehoiakim (xxxvi. 45); the section is best referred to that very time, when the posture of affairs promised well for the fulfilment of the threatenings of many years (cf. xxv. 9 with vv. 15, 10; xxv. 13 with vv. 12-17; xxv. 6 with ver. 16. And ver. 18 is virtually repeated, chap. xv. 20, which belongs to the same period)."

The first part of this is an obvious inference from the narrative itself. The prophet's own statement makes it abundantly clear that his conviction of a call was accompanied by doubts and fears, which were only silenced by that faith which moves mountains. That lofty confidence in the purpose and strength of the Unseen, which has enabled weak and trembling humanity to endure martyrdom, might well be sufficient to nerve a young man to undertake the task of preaching unpopular truths, even at the risk of frequent persecution and occasional peril. But surely we need not suppose that, when Jeremiah started on his prophetic career, he was as one who takes a leap in the dark. Surely it is not necessary to suppose him profoundly ignorant of the subject-matter of prophecy in general, of the kind of success he might look for, of his own shrinking timidity and desponding temperament, of "the measure and direction of the Divine help." Had the son of Hilkiah been the first of the prophets of Israel instead of one of the latest; had there been no prophets before him; we might recognise some force in this criticism. As the facts lie, however, we can hardly avoid an obvious answer. With the experience of many notable predecessors before his eyes; with the message of a Hosea, an Amos, a Micah, an Isaiah, graven upon his heart; with his minute knowledge of their history, their struggles and successes, the fierce antagonisms they roused, the cruel persecutions they were called upon to face in the discharge of their Divine commission; with his profound sense that nothing but the good help of their God had enabled them to endure the strain of a lifelong battle; it is not in the least wonderful that Jeremiah should have foreseen the like experience for himself. The wonder would have been, if, with such speaking examples before him, he had not anticipated "the measure and direction of the Divine help"; if he had been ignorant "that opposition awaited him"; if he had not already possessed a general knowledge of the "contents" of his own as of all prophecies. For there is a substantial unity underlying all the manifold outpourings of the prophetic spirit. Indeed, it would seem that it is to the diversity of personal gifts, to differences of training and temperament, to the rich variety of character and circumstance, rather than to any essential contrasts in the substance and purport of prophecy itself, that the absence of monotony, the impress of individuality and originality is due, which characterises the utterances of the principal prophets.

Apart from the unsatisfactory nature of the reasons alleged, it is very probable that this opening chapter was penned by Jeremiah as an introduction to the first collection of his prophecies, which dates from the fourth year of Jehoiakim, that is, circ. b.c. 606. In that case, it must not be forgotten that the prophet is relating events which, as he tells us himself (chap. xxv. 3), had taken place three and twenty years ago; and as his description is probably drawn from memory, something may be allowed for unconscious transformation of facts in the light of after experience. Still, the peculiar events that attended so marked a crisis in his life as his first consciousness of a Divine call must, in any case, have constituted, cannot but have left a deep and abiding impress upon the prophet's memory; and there really seems to be no good reason for refusing to believe that that initial experience took the form of a twofold vision seen under conditions of trance or ecstasy. At the same time, bearing in mind the Oriental passion for metaphor and imagery, we are not perhaps debarred from seeing in the whole chapter a figurative description, or rather an attempt to describe through the medium of figurative language, that which must always ultimately transcend description—the communion of the Divine with the human spirit. Real, most real of real facts, as that communion was and is, it can never be directly communicated in words; it can only be hinted and suggested through the medium of symbolic and metaphorical phraseology. Language itself, being more than half material, breaks down in the attempt to express things wholly spiritual.

I shall not stop to discuss the importance of the general superscription or heading of the book, which is given in the first three verses. But before passing on, I will ask you to notice that, whereas the Hebrew text opens with the phrase *Dibrê Yirmeyáhu* (וְהִגְּמְרִי יַרְבְּד), "The words of Jeremiah," the oldest translation we have, viz. the Septuagint, reads: "The word of God which came to Jeremiah" (τὸ ῥῆμα τοῦ Θεοῦ ὃ ἐγένετο ἐπὶ Ἰερεμίαν). It is possible, therefore, that the old Greek translator had a Hebrew text different from that which has come down to us, and opening with the same formula which we find at the beginning of the older prophets Hosea, Joel, and Micah. In fact, Amos is the only prophet, besides Jeremiah, whose book begins with the phrase in question (סומ ירבד—Λόγοι Ἀμώς); and although it is more appropriate there than here, owing to the continuation "And he said," it looks suspicious even there, when we compare Isaiah i. 1, and observe how much more suitable the term "vision" (חֲזוֹן) would be. It is likely that the LXX. has preserved the original reading of Jeremiah, and that some editor of the Hebrew text altered it because of the apparent tautology with the opening of ver. 2: "To whom the word of the Lord (LXX. τοῦ Θεοῦ) came in the days of Josiah."

Such changes were freely made by the scribes in the days before the settlement of the O. T. canon; changes which may occasion much perplexity to those, if any there be, who hold by the unintelligent and obsolete theory of verbal and even literal inspiration, but none at all to such as recognise a Divine hand in the facts of history,[16] and are content to believe that in holy books, as in holy men, there is a Divine treasure in earthen vessels. The textual difference in question may serve to call our attention to the peculiar way in which the prophets identified their work with the Divine will, and their words with the Divine thoughts; so that the words of an Amos or a Jeremiah were in all good faith held and believed to be self-attesting utterances of the Unseen God. The conviction which wrought in them was, in fact, identical with that which in after times moved St. Paul to affirm the high calling and inalienable dignity of the Christian ministry in those impressive words, "Let a man so account of us as of the ministers of Christ, and stewards of the mysteries of God."

Vv. 5-10, which relate how the prophet became aware that he was in future to receive revelations from above, constitute in themselves an important revelation. Under Divine influence he becomes aware of a special mission. *Ere I began to form* (mould, fashion, יצר, as the potter moulds the clay) *thee in the belly, I knew thee; and ere thou begannest to come forth from the womb,* [17] *I had dedicated thee,* not "*regarded* thee as holy," Isa. viii. 13; nor perhaps "*declared* thee holy," as Ges.; but "*hallowed* thee," *i.e.* dedicated thee to God, Judg. xvii. 3; 1 Kings ix. 3; especially Lev. xxvii. 14; of money and houses. The pi. of *consecrating* priests, Ex. xxviii. 41; altar, Ex. xxix. 36, temple, mountain, etc.; perhaps also, "*consecrated* thee" for the discharge of a sacred office. Even soldiers are called *consecrated* (מיושֶקַמ Isa. xiii. 3), as ministers of the Lord of Hosts, and probably as having been formally devoted to His service at the outset of a campaign by special solemnities of lustration and sacrifice; while guests bidden to a sacrificial feast had to undergo a preliminary form of *consecration* (1 Sam. xvi. 5; Zeph. i. 7), to fit them for communion with Deity.

With the certainty of his own Divine calling, it became clear to the prophet that the choice was not an arbitrary caprice; it was the execution of a Divine purpose, conceived long, long before its realisation in time and space. The God whose foreknowledge and will directs the whole course of human history—whose control of events and direction of human energies is most signally evident in precisely those instances where men and nations are most regardless of Him, and imagine the vain thought that they are independent of Him (Isa. xxii. 11, xxxvii. 26)—this sovereign Being, in the development of whose eternal purposes he himself, and every son of man was necessarily a factor, had from the first "known him,"—known the individual character and capacities which would constitute his fitness for the special work of his life;—and "sanctified" him; devoted and consecrated him to the doing of it when the time of his earthly manifestation should arrive. Like others who have played a notable part in the affairs of men, Jeremiah saw with clearest vision that he was himself the embodiment in flesh and blood of a Divine idea; he knew himself to be a deliberately planned and chosen instrument of the Divine activity. It was this seeing himself as God saw him, which constituted his difference from his fellows, who only knew their individual appetites, pleasures and interests, and were blinded, by their absorption in these, to the perception of any higher reality. It was the coming to this knowledge of *himself*, of the meaning and purpose of HIS individual unity of powers and aspirations in the great universe of being, of his true relation to God and to man, which constituted the first revelation to Jeremiah, and which was the secret of his personal greatness.

This knowledge, however, might have come to him in vain. Moments of illumination are not always accompanied by noble resolves and corresponding actions. It does not follow that, because a man sees his calling, he will at once renounce *all*, and pursue it. Jeremiah would not have been human, had he not hesitated a while, when, after the inward light, came the voice, *A spokesman*, or Divine interpreter (איבן), *to the nations appoint I thee*. To have passing flashes of spiritual insight and heavenly inspiration is one thing; to undertake *now*, in the actual present, the course of conduct which they unquestionably indicate and involve, is quite another. And so, when the hour of spiritual illumination has passed, the darkness may and often does become deeper than before.

And I said, Alas! O Lord Iahvah, behold I know not how to speak; for I am but a youth. The words express that reluctance to begin which a sense of unpreparedness, and misgivings about the unknown future, naturally inspire. To take the first step demands decision and confidence; but confidence and decision do not come of contemplating oneself and one's own unfitness or unpreparedness, but of steadfastly fixing our regards upon God, who will qualify us for all that He requires us to do. Jeremiah does not refuse to obey His call; the very words "My Lord Iahvah"—'Adonai, Master, or my Master—imply a recognition of the Divine right to his service; he merely alleges a natural objection. The cry, "Who is sufficient for these things?" rises to his lips, when the light and the glory are obscured for a moment, and the reaction and despondency natural to human weakness ensue. *And Iahvah said unto me, Say not, I am but a youth; for unto all that I send thee unto, thou shalt go, and all that I command thee thou shalt speak. Be not afraid of them; for with thee am I to rescue thee, is the utterance of Iahvah.* "Unto all that I send thee unto"; for he was to be no local prophet; his messages were to be addressed to the surrounding peoples as well as to Judah; his outlook as a seer was to comprise the entire political horizon (ver. 10, xxv. 9, 15, xlvi. *sqq.*). Like Moses (Ex. iv. 10), Jeremiah objects that he is no practised speaker; and this on account of youthful inexperience. The answer is that his speaking will depend not so much upon himself as upon God: "All that I command thee, thou shalt speak." The allegation of his youth also covers a feeling of timidity, which would naturally be excited at the thought of encountering kings and princes and priests, as well as the common people, in the discharge of such a commission. This implication is met by the Divine assurance: "Unto all"—of whatever rank—"that I send thee unto, thou shalt go"; and by the encouraging promise of Divine protection against all opposing powers: "Be not afraid of them; for with thee am I to rescue thee."[18]

And Iahvah put forth His hand and touched my mouth: and Iahvah said unto me, Behold I have put My words in thy mouth! This word of the Lord, says Hitzig, is represented as a corporeal substance; in accordance with the Oriental mode of thought and speech, which invests everything with bodily form. He refers to a passage in Samuel (2 Sam. xvii. 5) where Absalom says, "Call now Hushai the Archite, and let us hear *that which is in his mouth* also;" as if what the old counsellor had to say were something *solid* in more senses than one. But we need not press the literal force of the language. A prophet who could write (v. 14): "Behold I am about to make my words in thy mouth fire and this people logs of wood; and it shall devour them;" or again (xv. 16), "Thy words were found, and I did eat them; and Thy word became unto me a joy and my heart's delight," may also have written, "Behold I have put My words in thy mouth!" without thereby becoming amenable to a charge of confusing fact with figure, metaphor with reality. Nor can I think the prophet means to say that, although, as a matter of fact, the Divine word already dwelt in him, it was now "put in his mouth," in the sense that he was henceforth to utter it. Stripped of the symbolism of vision, the verse simply asserts that the spiritual change which came over Jeremiah at the turning point in his career was due to the immediate operation of God; and that the chief external consequence of this inward change was that powerful preaching of Divine truth, by which he was henceforth known. The great Prophet of the Exile twice uses the phrase, "I have set My words in thy mouth" (Isa. li. 16, lix. 21) with much the same meaning as that intended by Jeremiah, but without the preceding metaphor about the Divine hand.

See I have this day set thee over the nations and over the kingdoms, to root out and to pull down, and to destroy and to overturn; to rebuild and to replant. Such, following the Hebrew punctuation, are the terms of the prophet's commission; and they are well worth consideration, as they set forth with all the force of prophetic idiom his own conception of the nature of that commission. First, there is the implied assertion of his own official dignity: the prophet is made a *paqîd* (Gen. xli. 34, "officers" set by Pharaoh over Egypt; 2 Kings xxv. 19 a military prefect) a prefect or superintendent of the nations of the world. It is the Hebrew term corresponding to the ἐπίσκοπος of the New Testament and the Christian Church (Judg. ix. 28; Neh. xi. 9). And secondly, his powers are of the widest scope; he is invested with authority over the destinies of all peoples. If it be asked in what sense it could be truly said that the ruin and renascence of nations was subject to the supervision of the prophets, the answer is obvious. The word they were authorised to declare was the word of God. But God's word is not something whose efficacy is exhausted in the human utterance of it. God's word is an irreversible command, fulfilling itself with all the necessity of a law of nature. The thought is well expressed by a later prophet: "For as the rain cometh down, and the snow from heaven, and returneth not thither, but watereth the earth, and maketh it bring forth and spring; and yieldeth seed to the sower and bread to the eater: so shall My word become, that goeth forth out of My mouth; it shall not return to Me empty (מקיר), but shall surely do that which I have willed, and shall carry through that for which I sent it" (or "shall prosper him whom I have sent," Isa. lv. 10, 11). All that happens is merely the selfaccomplishment of this Divine word, which is only the human aspect of the Divine will. If, therefore, the absolute dependence of the prophets upon God for their knowledge of this word be left out of account, they appear as causes, when they are in truth but instruments, as agents when they are only mouthpieces. And so Ezekiel writes, "when I came to destroy the city" (Ezek. xliii. 3), meaning when I announced the Divine decree of its destruction. The truth upon which this peculiar mode of statement rests—the truth that the will of God must be and always is done in the world that God has made and is making—is a rock upon which the faith of His messengers may always repose. What strength, what staying power may the Christian preacher find in dwelling upon this almost visible fact of the self-fulfilling will and word of God, though all around him he hear that will questioned, and that word disowned and denied! He knows—it is his supreme comfort to know—that, while his own efforts may be thwarted, that will is invincible; that though *he* may fail in the conflict, that word will go on conquering and to conquer, until it shall have subdued all things unto itself.

II
THE TRUST IN THE SHADOW OF EGYPT

Jeremiah ii. 1-iii. 5.

The first of the prophet's public addresses is, in fact, a sermon which proceeds from an exposure of national sin to the menace of coming judgment. It falls naturally into three sections, of which the first (ii. 1-13) sets forth Iahvah's tender love to His young bride Israel in the old times of nomadic life, when faithfulness to Him was rewarded by protection from all external foes; and then passes on to denounce the unprecedented apostasy of a people from their God. The second (14-28) declares that if Israel has fallen a prey to her enemies, it is the result of her own infidelity to her Divine Spouse; of her early notorious and inveterate falling away to the false gods, who are now her only resource, and that a worthless one. The third section (ii. 29-iii. 5) points to the failure of Iahvah's chastisements to reclaim a people hardened in guilt, and in a self-righteousness which refused warning and despised reproof; affirms the futility of all human aid amid the national reverses; and cries woe on a too late repentance. It is not difficult to fix the time of this noble and pathetic address. That which follows it, and is intimately connected with it in substance, was composed "in the days of Josiah the king" (iii. 6), so that the present one must be placed a little earlier in the same reign; and, considering its position in the book, may very probably be assigned to the thirteenth year of Josiah, *i.e.* b.c. 629, in which the prophet received his Divine call. This is the ordinary opinion; but one critic (Knobel) refers the discourse to the beginning of the reign of Jehoiakim, on account of the connexion with Egypt which is mentioned in vv. 18, 36, and the humiliation suffered at the hands of the Egyptians which is mentioned in ver. 16; while another (Graf) maintains that chaps. ii.-vi. were composed in the fourth year of Jehoiakim, as if the prophet had committed nothing to writing before that date—an assumption which seems to run counter to the implication conveyed by his own statement, chap. xxxvi. 2. This latter critic has failed to notice the allusions in chaps. iv. 14, vi. 8, to an approaching calamity which may be averted by national reformation, to which the people are invited;—an invitation wholly incompatible with the prophet's attitude at that hopeless period. The series of prophecies beginning at chap. iv. 3 is certainly later in time than the discourse we are now considering; but as certainly belongs to the immediate subsequent years.

It does not appear that the first two of Jeremiah's addresses were called forth by any striking event of public importance, such as the Scythian invasion. His new-born consciousness of the Divine call would urge the young prophet to action; and in the present discourse we have the firstfruits of the heavenly impulse. It is a retrospect of Israel's entire past and an examination of the state of things growing out of it. The prophet's attention is not yet confined to Judah; he deplores the rupture of the ideal relations between Iahvah and His people as a whole (ii. 4; cf. iii. 6). As Hitzig has remarked, this opening address, in its finished elaboration, leaves the impression of a first outpouring of the heart, which sets forth at once without reserve the long score of the Divine grievances against Israel. At the same time, in its closing judgment (iii. 5), in its irony (ii. 28), in its appeals (ii. 21, 31), and its exclamations (ii. 12), it breathes an indignation stern and deep to a degree hardly characteristic of the prophet in his other discourses, but which was natural enough, as Hitzig observes, in a first essay at moral criticism, a first outburst of inspired zeal.

In the Hebrew text the chapter begins with the same formula as chap. i. (ver. 4): "And there fell a word of Iahvah unto me, saying." But the LXX. reads: "And he said, Thus saith the Lord," (καὶ εἶπε, τάδε λέγει κύριος); a difference which is not immaterial, as it may be a trace of an older Hebrew recension of the prophet's work, in which this second chapter immediately followed the original superscription of the book, as given in chap. i. 1, 2, from which it was afterwards separated by the insertion of the narrative of Jeremiah's call and visions (רְמָאיו: cf. Amos i. 2). Perhaps we may see another trace of the same thing in the fact that whereas chap. i. sends the prophet to the rulers and people of Judah, this chapter is in part addressed to collective Israel (ver. 4); which constitutes a formal disagreement. If the reference to Israel is not merely retrospective and rhetorical,—if it implies, as seems to be assumed, that the prophet really meant his words to affect the remnant of the northern kingdom as well as Judah,—we have here a valuable contemporary corroboration of the much disputed assertion of the author of Chronicles, that king Josiah abolished idolatry "in the cities of Manasseh and Ephraim and Simeon even unto Naphtali, to wit, in their ruins round about" (2 Chron. xxxiv. 6), as well as in Judah and Jerusalem; and that Manasseh and Ephraim and "the remnant of Israel" (2 Chron. xxxiv. 9, cf. 21) contributed to his restoration of the temple. These statements of the Chronicler imply that Josiah exercised authority in the ruined northern kingdom, as well as in the more fortunate south; and so far as this first discourse of Jeremiah was actually addressed to Israel as well as to Judah, those disputed statements find in it an undesigned confirmation. However this may be, as a part of the first collection of the author's prophecies, there is little doubt that the chapter was read by Baruch to the people of Jerusalem in the fourth year of Jehoiakim (chap. xxxvi. 6).

Go thou and cry in the ears of Jerusalem: Thus hath Iahvah said (or *thought*: This is the Divine thought concerning thee!) *I have remembered for thee the kindness of thy youth, the love of thine espousals; thy following Me* (as a bride follows her husband to his tent) *in the wilderness, in a land unsown. A dedicated thing* (שֶׁרֶק: like the high priest, on whose mitre was graven הַוֹהִיַל שֶׁרֶק) *was Israel to Iahvah, His firstfruits of increase; all who did eat him were held guilty, ill would come to them, saith Iahvah* (vers. 2, 3).—"I have remembered for thee," *i.e.* in thy favour, to thy benefit—as when Nehemiah prays, "Remember in my favour, O my God, for good, all that I have done upon this people," (Neh. v. 19)—"the kindness"—חֶסֶד—the warm affection of thy youth, "the love of thine espousals," or the charm of thy bridal state (Hos. ii. 15, xi. 1); the tender attachment of thine early days, of thy new born national consciousness, when Iahvah had chosen thee as His bride, and called thee to follow Him out of Egypt. It is the figure which we find so elaborately developed in the pages of Hosea. The "bridal state" is the time from the Exodus to the taking of the covenant at Sinai (Ezek. xvi. 8), which was, as it were, the formal instrument of the marriage; and Israel's young love is explained as consisting in turning her back upon "the flesh-pots of Egypt" (Ex. xvi. 3), at the call of Iahvah, and following her Divine Lord into the barren steppes. This forsaking of all worldly comfort for the hard life of the desert was proof of the sincerity of Israel's early love. [The evidently original words "in the wilderness, a land unsown," are omitted by the LXX., which renders: "I remembered the mercy of thy youth, and the love of thy nuptials (τελείωσις, consummation), so that thou followedst the Holy One of Israel, saith Iahvah."] Iahvah's "remembrance" of this devotion, that is to say, the return He made for it, is described in the next verse. Israel became not "holiness" but a holy or hallowed thing; a dedicated object, belonging wholly and solely to Iahvah, a thing which it was sacrilege to touch; Iahvah's "firstfruits of increase" (Heb. התאובת תישאר). This last phrase is to be explained by reference to the well-known law of the firstfruits (Ex. xxiii. 19; Deut. xviii. 4, xxvi. 10), according to which the first specimens of all agricultural produce were given to God. Israel, like the firstlings of cattle and the firstfruits of corn and wine and oil, was הוהיל שדק consecrated to Iahweh; and therefore none might eat of him without offending. "To eat" or devour is a term naturally used of vexing and destroying a nation (x. 25, l. 7; Deut. vii. 16, "And thou shalt eat up all the peoples, which Jehovah thy God is about to give thee;" Isa. i. 7; Ps. xiv. 4, "Who eat up My people as they eat bread"). The literal translation is, "All his eaters become guilty (or are treated as guilty, punished); evil cometh to them;" and the verbs, being in the imperfect, denote what happened again and again in Israel's history; Iahvah suffered no man to do His people wrong with impunity. This, then, is the first count in the indictment against Israel, that Iahvah had not been unmindful of her early devotion, but had recognised it by throwing the shield of sanctity around her, and making her inviolable against all external enemies (vv. 1-3). The prophet's complaint, as developed in the following section (vv. 4-8), is that, in spite of the goodness of Iahvah, Israel has forsaken *Him* for idols. *"Hear ye the word of Iahvah, O house of Jacob, and all the clans of the house of Israel!"* All Israel is addressed, and not merely the surviving kingdom of Judah, because the apostasy had been universal. A special reference apparently made in ver. 8 to the prophets of Baal, who flourished only in the northern kingdom. We may compare the word of Amos "against *the whole clan*," which Iahvah "brought up from the land of Egypt" (Amos iii. 1), spoken at a time when Ephraim was yet in the heyday of his power.

Thus hath Iahvah said, What found your fathers in Me, that was unjust, (לְוֶל) a single act of injustice, Ps. vii. 4; not to be found in Iahvah, Deut. xxxii. 4) *that they went far from Me and followed the Folly and were befooled* (or *the Delusion and were deluded*) (ver. 5). The phrase is used 2 Kings xvii. 15 in the same sense; לְבְהָ "the (mere) breath," "the nothingness" or "vanity," being a designation of the idols which Israel went after (cf. also chap. xxiii. 16; Ps. lxii. 11; Job xxvii. 12); much as St. Paul has written that "an idol is nothing in the world" (1 Cor. viii. 4), and that, with all this boasted culture, the nations of classical antiquity "became vain," or were befooled "in their imaginations" (ἐματαιώθησαν = ולבהיו), "and their foolish heart was darkened" (Rom. i. 21). Both the prophet and the apostle refer to that judicial blindness which is a consequence of persistently closing the eyes to truth, and deliberately putting darkness for light and light for darkness, bitter for sweet, and sweet for bitter, in compliance with the urgency of the flesh. For ancient Israel, the result of yielding to the seductions of foreign worship was, that "They were stultified in their best endeavours. They became false in thinking and believing, in doing and forbearing, because the fundamental error pervaded the whole life of the nation and of the individual. They supposed that they knew and honoured God, but they were entirely mistaken; they supposed they were doing His will, and securing their own welfare, while they were doing and securing the exact contrary" (Hitzig). And similar consequences will always flow from attempts to serve two masters; to gratify the lower nature, while not breaking wholly with the higher. Once the soul has accepted a lower standard than the perfect law of truth, it does not stop there. The subtle corruption goes on extending its ravages farther and farther; while the consciousness that anything is wrong becomes fainter and fainter as the deadly mischief increases, until at last the ruined spirit believes itself in perfect health, when it is, in truth, in the last stage of mortal disease. Perversion of the will and the affections leads to the perversion of the intellect. There is a profound meaning in the old saying that, Men make their gods in their own likeness. As a man is, so will God appear to him to be. "With the loving, Thou wilt shew Thyself loving; With the perfect, Thou wilt shew Thyself perfect; With the pure, Thou wilt shew Thyself pure; And with the perverse, Thou wilt shew Thyself froward" (Ps. xviii. 25 *sq.*). Only hearts pure of all worldly taint see God in His purity. The rest worship some more or less imperfect semblance of Him, according to the varying degrees of their selfishness and sin.

And they said not, Where is Iahvah, who brought us up out of the land of Egypt, that guided us in the wilderness, in a land of wastes and hollows (or desert and defile), in a land of drought and darkness (dreariness תוֹמְלֵצ), *in a land that no man passed through, and where no mortal dwelt* (ver. 6). "They said not, Where is Iahvah, who brought us up out of the land of Egypt." It is the old complaint of the prophets against Israel's black ingratitude. So, for instance, Amos (ii. 10) had written: "Whereas I—I brought you up from the land of Egypt, and guided you in the wilderness forty years;" and Micah (vi. 3 *sq.*): "My people, what have I done unto thee, and how have I wearied thee? Answer against Me. For I brought thee up from the land of Egypt, and from a house of bondmen redeemed I thee." In common gratitude, they were bound to be true to this mighty Saviour; to enquire after Iahvah, to call upon Him only, to do His will, and to seek His grace (cf. xxix. 12 *sq.*). Yet, with characteristic fickleness, they soon forgot the fatherly guidance, which had never deserted them in the period of their nomadic wanderings in the wilds of Arabia Petræa; a land which the prophet poetically describes as "a land of wastes and hollows"—alluding probably to the rocky defiles through which they had to pass—and "a land of drought and darkness;"[19] the latter an epithet of the Grave or Hades (Job x. 21), fittingly applied to that great lone wilderness of the south, which Isaiah had called "a fearsome land" (xxi. 1), and "a land of trouble and anguish" (xxx. 6), whither, according to the poet of Job, "The caravans go up and are lost" (vi. 18).

And I brought you into the garden land, to eat its fruits and its choicest things (הַבּוֹט Isa. i. 19; Gen. xlv. 18, 20, 23); *and ye entered and defiled My land, and My domain ye made a loathsome thing!* (ver. 7). With the wilderness of the wanderings is contrasted the "land of the *carmel*," the land of fruitful orchards and gardens, as in chap. iv. 26.; Isa. x. 18, xvi. 10, xxix. 17. This was Canaan, Iahvah's own land, which He had chosen out of all countries to be

His special dwelling-place and earthly sanctuary; but which Israel no sooner possessed, than they began to pollute this holy land by their sins, like the guilty peoples whom they had displaced, making it thereby an abomination to Iahvah (Lev. xviii. 24 *sq.*, cf. chap. iii. 2).

The priests they said not, Where is Iahvah? and they that handle the law, they knew (*i.e.* regarded, heeded) *Me not; and as for the shepherds* (*i.e.* the king and princes, ver. 26), *they rebelled against Me, and the prophets, they prophesied by* (through) *the Baal, and them that help not* (*i.e.* the false gods) *they followed* (ver. 8). In the form of a climax, this verse justifies the accusation contained in the last, by giving particulars. The three ruling classes are successively indicted (cf. ver. 26, ch. xviii. 18). The priests, part of whose duty was to "handle the law," *i.e.* explain the Torah, to instruct the people in the requirements of Iahvah, by oral tradition and out of the sacred law-books, gave no sign of spiritual aspiration (cf. ver. 6); like the reprobate sons of Eli, "they knew not" (1 Sam. ii. 12) "Iahvah," that is to say, paid no heed to Him and His will as revealed in the book of the law; the secular authorities, the king and his counsellors ("wise men," xviii. 18), not only sinned thus negatively, but positively revolted against the King of kings, and resisted His will; while the prophets went further yet in the path of guilt, apostatizing altogether from the God of Israel, and seeking inspiration from the Phenician Baal, and following worthless idols that could give no help. There seems to be a play on the words Baal and Belial, as if Baal meant the same as Belial, "profitless," "worthless" (cf. 1 Sam. ii. 12: "Now Eli's sons were sons of Belial; they knew not Iahvah." The phrase ולעוֹי־אֹל "they that help not," or "cannot help," suggests the term לַעֲיְלֹב Belial; which, however, may be derived from יְלֹב "not," and לֹע "supreme," "God," and so mean "not-God," "idol," rather than "worthlessness," "unprofitableness," as it is usually explained). The reference may be to the Baal-worship of Samaria, the northern capital, which was organised by Ahab, and his Tyrian queen (chap, xxiii. 13).

Therefore—on account of this amazing ingratitude of your forefathers,—*I will again plead* (reason, argue forensically) *with you* (the present generation in whom their guilt repeats itself) *saith Iahvah, and with your sons' sons* (who will inherit your sins) *will I plead*. The nation is conceived as a moral unity, the characteristics of which are exemplified in each successive generation. To all Israel, past, present, and future, Iahvah will vindicate his own righteousness. *For cross* (the sea) *to the coasts of the Citieans* (the people of Citium in Cyprus) *and see; and to Kedar* (the rude tribes of the Syrian desert) *send ye, and mark well, and see whether there hath arisen a case like this. Hath a nation changed gods—albeit they are no-gods? Yet My people hath changed his* (true) *glory for that which helpeth not* (or is worthless). *Upheave, ye heavens* (סימם שמו, a fine paronomasia), *at this, and shudder* (and) *be petrified* (וּבְרָה דֹּאֵם) Ges., "be sore amazed" = שָׁמֵם; but Hitzig "be dry" = stiff and motionless, like syn. שָׁבִי in 1 Kings xiii. 4), *saith Iahvah; for two evil things hath My people done: Me they have forsaken—a Fountain of living water—to hew them out cisterns, broken cisterns, that cannot* (imperf. = potential) *hold water* (Heb. *the* waters: generic article) (vv. 9-13). In these five verses, the apostasy of Israel from his own God is held up as a fact unique in history—unexampled and inexplicable by comparison with the doings of other nations. Whether you look westward or eastward, across the sea to Cyprus, or beyond Gilead to the barbarous tribes of the Cedrei (Ps. cxx. 5), nowhere will you find a heathen people that has changed its native worship for another; and if you did find such, it would be no precedent or palliation of Israel's behaviour. The heathen in adopting a new worship simply exchanges one superstition for another; the objects of his devotion are "non-gods" (ver. 11). The heinousness and the eccentricity of Israel's conduct lies in the fact that he has bartered truth for falsehood; he has exchanged "his Glory"—whom Amos (viii. 7) calls the Pride (A.V. Excellency) of Jacob—for a useless idol; an object which the prophet elsewhere calls "The Shame" (iii. 24, xi. 13), because it can only bring shame and confusion upon those whose hopes depend upon it. The wonder of the thing might well be supposed to strike the pure heavens, the silent witnesses of it, with blank astonishment (cf. a similar appeal in Deut. iv. 26, xxxi. 28, xxxii. 1, where the earth is added). For the evil is not single but twofold. With the rejection of truth goes the adoption of error; and both are evils. Not only has Israel turned his back upon "a fountain of living waters;" he has also "hewn him out cisterns, broken cisterns, that cannot hold water." The "broken cisterns" are, of course, the idols which Israel made to himself. As a cistern full of cracks and fissures disappoints the wayfarer, who has reckoned on finding water in it; so the idols, having only the semblance and not the reality of life, avail their worshippers nothing (vv. 8, 11). In Hebrew the waters of a spring are called "living" (Gen. xxi. 19), because they are more refreshing and, as it were, life-giving, than the stagnant waters of pools and tanks fed by the rains. Hence by a natural metaphor, the mouth of a righteous man, or the teaching of the wise, and the fear of the Lord, are called a fountain of life (Prov. x. 11, xiii. 14, xiv. 27). "The fountain of life" is with Iahvah (Ps. xxxvi. 10); nay, He is Himself the Fountain of living waters (Jer. xvii. 13); because all life, and all that sustains or quickens life, especially spiritual life, proceeds from Him. Now in Ps. xix. 8 it is said that "The law of the Lord—or, the teaching of Iahvah—is perfect, reviving (or restoring) the soul" (cf. Lam. i. 11; Ruth iv. 15); and a comparison of Micah and Isaiah's statement that "Out of Zion will go forth the law, and the word of the Lord from Jerusalem" (Isa. ii. 3; Mic. iv. 2), with the more figurative language of Joel (iii. 18) and Zechariah (xiv. 8), who speak of "a fountain going forth from the house of the Lord," and "living waters going forth from Jerusalem," suggests the inference that "the living waters," of which Iahvah is the perennial fountain, are identical with His law as revealed through priests and prophets. It is easy to confirm this suggestion by reference to the river "whose streams make glad the city of God" (Ps. xlvi. 4); to Isaiah's poetic description of the Divine teaching, of which he was himself the exponent, as "the waters of Shiloah that flow softly" (viii. 6), Shiloah being a spring that issues from the temple rock; and to our Lord's conversation with the woman of Samaria, in which He characterises His own teaching as "living waters" (St. John iv. 10), and as "a well of waters, springing up unto eternal Life" (*ibid.* 14).

Is Israel a bondman, or a homeborn serf? Why hath he become a prey? Over him did young lions roar; they uttered their voice; and they made his land a waste; his cities, they are burnt up (or *thrown down*), *so that they are uninhabited. Yea, the sons of Noph and Tahpan(h)es, they did bruise thee on the crown. Is not this what* (the thing that) *thy forsaking Iahvah thy God brought about for thee, at the time He was guiding thee in the way?* (vv. 14-17). As Iahvah's bride, as a people chosen to be His own, Israel had every reason to expect a bright and glorious career. Why was this expectation falsified by events? But one answer was possible, in view of the immutable righteousness, the eternal faithfulness of God. *The ruin of Israel was Israel's own doing.* It is a truth which applies to all nations, and to all individuals capable of moral agency, in all periods and places of their existence. Let no man lay his failure in this world or in the world to come at the door of the Almighty. Let none venture to repeat the thoughtless blasphemy which charges the All-Merciful with sending frail human beings to expiate their offences in an everlasting hell! Let none dare to say or think, God might have made it otherwise, but He would not! Oh, no; it is all a monstrous misconception of the true relations of things. You and I are free to make our choice now, whatever may be the case hereafter. We may choose to obey God, or to disobey; we may seek His will, or our own. The one is the way of life; the other, of death, and nothing can alter the facts; they are part of the laws of the universe. Our destiny is in our own hands, to make or to mar. If we qualify ourselves for nothing better than a hell—if our daily progress leads us farther and farther from God and nearer and nearer to the devil—then hell will be our eternal home. For God is love, and purity, and truth, and glad obedience to righteous laws; and these things, realized and rejoiced in, are heaven. And the man that lives without these as the sovereign aims of his existence— the man whose heart's worship is centred upon something else than God— stands already on the verge of hell, which is "the place of him that knows not (and cares not for) God." And unless we are prepared to find fault with that natural arrangement whereby like things are aggregated to like, and all physical elements gravitate towards their own kind; I do not see how we can disparage the same law in the spiritual sphere, in virtue of which all spiritual beings are drawn to their own place, the heavenly-minded rising to the heights above, and the contrary sort sinking to the depths beneath.

The precise bearing of the question (ver. 14), "Is Israel a bondman, or a homeborn slave?" is hardly self-evident. One commentator supposes that the implied answer is an affirmative. Israel *is* a "servant," the servant, that is, the worshipper of the true God. Nay, he is more than a mere bondservant; he occupies the favoured position of a slave born in his lord's house (cf. Abram's three hundred and eighteen young men, Gen. xiv. 14), and therefore, according to the custom of antiquity, standing on a different footing from a slave acquired by purchase. The "home" or house is taken to mean the land of Canaan, which the prophet Hosea had designated as Iahvah's "house" (Hosea ix. 15, cf. 3); and the "Israel" intended is supposed to be the existing generation born in the holy land. The double question of the prophet then amounts to this: If Israel be, as is generally admitted, the favourite bondservant of Iahvah, how comes it that his lord has not protected him against the spoiler? But, although this interpretation is not without force, it is rendered doubtful by the order of the words in the Hebrew, where the stress lies on the terms for "bondman" and "homeborn slave"; and by its bold divergence from the sense conveyed by the same form of question in other passages of the prophet, *e.g.* ver. 31 *infr.*, where the answer expected is a negative one (cf. also chap. viii. 4, 5, xiv. 19, xlix. 1. The formula is evidently characteristic). The point of the question seems to lie in the fact of the helplessness of persons of servile condition against occasional acts of fraud and oppression, from which neither the purchased nor the homebred slave could at all times be secure. The rights of such persons, however humane the laws affecting their ordinary status, might at times be cynically disregarded both by their masters and by others (see a notable instance, Jer. xxxiv. 8 *sqq.*). Moreover, there may be a reference to the fact that slaves were always reckoned in those times as a valuable portion of the booty of conquest; and the meaning may be that Israel's lot as a captive is as bad as if he had never known the blessings of freedom, and had simply exchanged one servitude for another by the fortune of war. The allusion is chiefly to the fallen kingdom of Ephraim. We must remember that Jeremiah is reviewing the whole past, from the outset of Iahvah's special dealings with Israel. The national sins of the northern and more powerful branch had issued in utter ruin. The "young lions," the foreign invaders, had "roared against" Israel properly so called, and made havoc of the whole country (cf. iv. 7). The land was dispeopled, and became an actual haunt of lions (2 Kings xvii. 25), until Esarhaddon colonised it with a motley gathering of foreigners (Ezra iv. 2).

Judah too had suffered greatly from the Assyrian invasion in Hezekiah's time, although the last calamity had then been mercifully averted (Sanherib boasts that he stormed and destroyed forty-six strong cities, and carried off 200,000 captives, and an innumerable booty). The implication is that the evil fate of Ephraim threatens to overtake Judah; for the same moral causes are operative, and the same Divine will, which worked in the past, is working in the present, and will continue to work in the future. The lesson of the past was plain for those who had eyes to read and hearts to understand it. Apart from this prophetic doctrine of a Providence which shapes the destinies of nations, in accordance with their moral deserts, history has no value except for the gratification of mere intellectual curiosity.

Aye, and the children of Noph and Tahpanhes they bruise (? *used to bruise; are bruising*: the Heb. וערי may mean either) *thee on the crown* (ver. 16). This obviously refers to injuries inflicted by Egypt, the two royal cities of Noph or Memphis, and Tahpanhes or Daphnæ, being mentioned in place of the country itself. Judah must be the sufferer, as no Egyptian attack on Ephraim is anywhere recorded; while we do read of Shishak's invasion of the southern kingdom in the reign of Rehoboam, both in the Bible (1 Kings xiv. 25), and in Shishak's own inscriptions on the walls of the temple of Amen at Karnak. But the form of the Hebrew verb seems to indicate rather some contemporary trouble; perhaps plundering raids by an Egyptian army, which about this time was besieging the Philistine stronghold of Ashdod (*Herod.*, ii. 157). "The Egyptians are bruising (or crushing) thee" seems to be the sense; and so it is given by the Jewish commentator Rashi (וצרי diffringunt). Our English marginal rendering ("fed on") follows the traditional pronunciation of the Hebrew term (וְעֵרִי), which is also the case with the Targum and the Syriac versions; but this can hardly be right, unless we suppose that the Egyptians infesting the frontier are scornfully compared to vermin (read וְעֹרִי with J. D. Mich.) of a sort which, as Herodotus tells us, the Egyptians particularly disliked (but cf. Mic. v. 5; Ges., depascunt, "eating down.")

The A.V. of ver. 17 presents a curious mistake, which the Revisers have omitted to correct. The words should run, as I have rendered them, "Is not *this*"—thy present ill fortune—"the thing that thy forsaking of Iahvah thy God did for thee—at the time when He was guiding thee in the way?" The Hebrew verb does not admit of the rendering in the perf. tense, for it is an impf., nor is it a 2nd pers. fem. (השעת *not* ישעת) but a 3rd. The LXX. has it rightly (οὐχὶ ταῦτα ἐποίησέ σοι τὸ καταλιπεῖν σε ἐμέ;), but leaves out the next clause which specifies the time. The words, however, are probably original; for they insist, as vv. 5 and 31 insist, on the groundlessness of Israel's apostasy. Iahvah had given no cause for it; He was fulfilling His part of the covenant by "guiding them in the way." Guidance or leading is ascribed to Iahvah as the true "Shepherd of Israel" (chap. xxxi. 9; Ps. lxxx. 1). It denotes not only the spiritual guidance which was given through the priests and prophets; but also that external prosperity, those epochs of established power and peace and plenty, which were precisely the times chosen by infatuated Israel for defection from the Divine Giver of her good things. As the prophet Hosea expresses it, ii. 8 *sq.*, "She knew not that it was I who gave her the corn and the new wine and the oil; and silver I multiplied unto her, and gold, which they made into the Baal. Therefore will I take back My corn in the time of it, and My new wine in its season, and will snatch away My wool and My flax, which were to cover her nakedness." And (chap. xiii. 6) the same prophet gives this plain account of his people's thankless revolt from their God: "When I fed them, they were sated; sated were they, and their heart was lifted up: therefore they forgot Me." It is the thought so forcibly expressed by the minstrel of the Book of the Law (Deut. xxxii. 15), first published in the early days of Jeremiah: "And Jeshurun waxed fat and kicked; Thou waxedst fat, and gross and fleshy! And he forsook the God that made him, And made light of his protecting Rock." And, lastly, the Chronicler has pointed the same moral of human fickleness and frailty in the case of an individual, Uzziah or Azariah, the powerful king of Judah, whose prosperity seduced him into presumption and profanity (2 Chron. xxvi. 16): "When he grew strong, his heart rose high, until he dealt corruptly, and was unfaithful to Iahvah his God." I need not enlarge on the perils of prosperity; they are known by bitter experience to every Christian man. Not without good reason do we pray to be delivered from evil "In all time of our wealth;" nor was that poet least conversant with human nature who wrote that "Sweet are the uses of adversity."

And now—a common formula in drawing an inference and concluding an argument—*what hast thou to do with the way of Egypt, to drink the waters of Shihor* (the Black River, the Nile); *and what hast thou to do with the way to Assyria, to drink the waters of the River?* (*par excellence, i.e.,* the Euphrates). *Thy wickedness correcteth thee, and thy revolts it is that chastise thee. Know then, and see that evil and bitter is thy forsaking Iahvah thy God, and thine having no dread of Me, saith the Lord Iahvah Sabaoth* (vv. 18, 19). And now—as the cause of all thy misfortunes lies in thyself—what is the use of seeking a cure for them abroad? Egypt will prove as powerless to help thee now, as Assyria proved in the days of Ahaz (ver. 36 *sq.*). The Jewish people, anticipating the views of certain modern historians, made a wrong diagnosis of their own evil case. They traced all that they had suffered, and were yet to suffer, to the ill will of the two great Powers of their time; and supposed that their only salvation lay in conciliating the one or the other. And as Isaiah found it necessary to cry woe on the rebellious children, "that walk to go down into Egypt, and have not asked at My mouth; to strengthen themselves in the strength of Pharaoh, and to trust in the shadow of Egypt!" (Isa. xxx. 1 *sq.*), so now, after so much experience of the futility and positive harmfulness of these unequal alliances, Jeremiah has to lift his voice against the same national folly.

The "young lions" of ver. 15 must denote the Assyrians, as Egypt is expressly named in ver. 16. The figure is very appropriate, for not only was the lion a favourite subject of Assyrian sculpture; not only do the Assyrian kings boast of their prowess as lion-hunters, while they even tamed these fierce creatures, and trained them to the chase; but the great strength and predatory habits of the king of beasts made him a fitting symbol of that great empire whose irresistible power was founded upon and sustained by wrong and robbery. This reference makes it clear that the prophet is contemplating the past; for Assyria was at this time already tottering to its fall, and the Israel of his day, *i.e.* the surviving kingdom of Judah, had no longer any temptation to court the countenance of that decaying if not already ruined empire. The sin of Israel is an old one; both it and its consequences belong to the past (ver. 20 compared with ver. 14); and the national attempts to find a remedy must be referred to the same period. Ver. 36 makes it evident that the prophet's contemporaries concerned themselves only about an Egyptian alliance.

It is an interesting detail that for "the waters of Shihor," the LXX. gives "waters of Gihon" (Γηῶν), which it will be remembered is the name of one of the four rivers of Paradise, and which appears to have been the old Hebrew name of the Nile (Ecclus. xxiv. 27; Jos., *Ant.*, i. 1, 3). Shihor may be an explanatory substitute. For the rest, it is plain that the two rivers symbolize the two empires (cf. Isa. viii. 7; chap. xlvi. 7); and the expression "to drink the waters" of them must imply the receiving and, as it were, absorption of whatever advantage might be supposed to accrue from friendly relations with their respective countries. At the same time, a contrast seems to be intended between these earthly waters, which could only disappoint those who sought refreshment in them, and that "fountain of living waters" (ver. 13) which Israel had forsaken. The nation sought in Egypt its deliverance from self-caused evil, much as Saul had sought guidance from witches when he knew himself deserted by the God whom by disobedience he had driven away. In seeking thus to escape the consequences of sin by cementing alliances with heathen powers, Israel added sin to sin. Hence (in ver. 19) the prophet reiterates with increased emphasis what he has already suggested by a question (ver. 17): "Thy wickedness correcteth thee, and thy revolts it is that chastise thee. Know then, and see that evil and bitter is thy forsaking of Iahweh thy God, and thine having no dread of Me!" Learn from these its bitter fruits that the thing itself is bad (Read יְלֹא יִתְחָק as a 2nd pers. instead of יִתְחָם. Job xxi. 33, quoted by Hitzig, is not a real parallel; nor can the sentence, as it stands, be rendered, "Und dass die Scheu vor mir nicht an dich kam"); and renounce that which its consequences declare to be an evil course, instead of aggravating the evil of it by a new act of unfaithfulness.

For long ago didst thou break thy yoke, didst thou burst thy bonds, and saidst, I will not serve: for upon every high hill, and under each evergreen tree thou wert crouching in fornication (vv. 20-24). Such seems to be the best way of taking a verse which is far from clear as it stands in the Masoretic text. The prophet labours to bring home to his hearers a sense of the reality of the national sin; and he affirms once more (vv. 5, 7) that Israel's apostasy originated long ago, in the early period of its history, and implies that the taint thus contracted is a fact which can neither be denied nor obliterated. (The punctuators of the Hebrew text, having pointed the first two verbs as in the 1st pers. instead of the 2nd feminine, were obliged, further, to suggest the reading רוֹבֵעָא אֹל, "I will not transgress," for the original phrase אל רובעא "I will not serve;" a variant which is found in the Targum, and many MSS. and editions. "Serving" and "bearing the yoke" are equivalent expressions (xxvii. 11, 12); so that, if the first two verbs were really in the 1st pers., the sentence ought to be continued with, "And *I* said, *Thou* shalt not serve." But the purport of this verse is to justify the assertion of the last, as is evident from the introductory particle "for," יכ. The Syriac supports רובעא; and the LXX. and Vulg. have the two leading verbs in the 2nd pers., iv. 19.) The meaning is that Israel, like a stubborn ox, has broken the yoke imposed on him by Iahvah; a statement which is repeated in v. 5: "But these have altogether broken the yoke, they have burst the bonds" (cf. ver. 31, *infr.*; Hos. iv. 16; Acts xxvi. 14).

Yet I—I planted thee with (or, *as*) *noble vines, all of them genuine shoots; and· how hast thou turned Me thyself into the wild offshoots of a foreign vine?* (ver. 21). The thought seems to be borrowed from Isaiah's Song of the Beloved's Vineyard (Isa. v. 1 *sqq.*). The nation is addressed as a person, endowed with a continuity of moral existence from the earliest period. "The days of the life of a man may be numbered; but the days of Israel are innumerable" (Ecclus. xxxvii. 25). It was with the true seed of Abraham, the real Israel, that Iahvah had entered into covenant (Ex. xviii. 19; Rom. ix. 7); and this genuine offspring of the patriarch had its representatives in every succeeding generation, even in the worst of times (1 Kings xix. 18). But the prophet's argument seems to imply that the good plants had reverted to a wild state, and that the entire nation had become hopelessly degenerate; which was not far from the actual condition of things at the close of his career. The culmination of Israel's degeneracy, however, was seen in the rejection of Him to whom "gave all the prophets witness." The Passion of Christ sounded a deeper depth of sacred sorrow than the passion of any of

His forerunners. "O Jerusalem, Jerusalem! Thou that killest the prophets, and stonest them that are sent unto thee!"

> "Then on My head a crown of thorns I wear;
> For these are all the grapes Sion doth bear,
> Though I My vine planted and watered there:
> Was ever grief like Mine?"

For if thou wash with natron, and take thee much soap, spotted (crimsoned; Targ. Isa. i. 18: or written, recorded) is thy guilt before Me, saith My Lord Iahvah. Comparison with Isa. i. 18, "Though thy sins be as scarlet ... though they be red like crimson," suggests that the former rendering of the doubtful word (נִכְתָּם) is correct; and this idea is plainly better suited to the context than a reference to the Books of Heaven, and the Recording Angel; for the object of washing is to get rid of spots and stains.

How canst thou say, I have not defiled myself; after the Baals I have not gone: See thy way in the valley, know what thou hast done, O swift she-camel, running hither and thither (literally *intertwining* or *crossing her ways*) (ver. 23). The prophet anticipates a possible attempt at self-justification; just as in ver. 35 he complains of Israel's self-righteousness. Both here and there he is dealing with his own contemporaries in Judah; whereas the idolatry described in ver. 20 *sqq.* is chiefly that of the ruined kingdom of Ephraim (ch. iii. 24; 2 Kings xvii. 10). It appears that the worship of Baal proper only existed in Judah for a brief period in the reign of Ahaziah's usurping queen Athaliah, side by side with the worship of Iahvah (2 Chron. xxiii. 17); while on the high-places and at the local sanctuaries the God of Israel was honoured (2 Kings xviii. 22). So far as the prophet's complaints refer to old times, Judah could certainly boast of a relatively higher purity than the northern kingdom; and the manifold heathenism of Manasseh's reign had been abolished a whole year before this address was delivered (2 Chron. xxxiv. 3 *sqq.*). "The valley" spoken of as the scene of Judah's misdoings is that of Ben-Hinnom, south of Jerusalem, where, as the prophet elsewhere relates (vii. 31, xxxii. 35; 2 Kings xxiii. 10), the people sacrificed children by fire to the god Molech, whom he expressly designates as a *Baal* (xix. 5, xxxii. 35), using the term in its wider significance, which includes all the aspects of the Canaanite sun-god. And because Judah betook herself now to Iahvah, and now to Molech, varying, as it were, her capricious course from right to left and from left to right, and halting evermore between two opinions (1 Kings xviii. 21), the prophet calls her "a swift young she-camel,"—swift, that is, for evil—"intertwining, or crossing her ways." The hot zeal with which the people wantonly plunged into a sensual idolatry is aptly set forth in the figure of the next verse. *A wild ass, used to the wilderness* (Job xxiv. 5), *in the craving of her soul she snuffeth* up (xiv. 6) *the wind* (*not* "lässt sie kaum Athem genug finden, indem sie denselben vorweg vergeudet," as Hitzig; but, as a wild beast scenting prey, cf. xiv. 6, or food afar off, she scents companions at a distance); *her greedy lust, who can turn it back? None that seek her need weary themselves; in her month they find her.* While passion rages, animal instinct is too strong to be diverted from its purpose; it is idle to argue with blind appetite; it goes straight to its mark, like an arrow from a bow. Only when it has had its way, and the reaction of nature follows, does the influence of reason become possible. Such was Israel's passion for the false gods. They had no need to seek her (Hos. ii. 7; Ezek. xvi. 34); in the hour of her infatuation, she fell an easy victim to their passive allurements. (The "month" is the season when the sexual instinct is strong.) Warnings fell on deaf ears. *Keep back thy foot from bareness, and thy throat from thirst!* This cry of the prophets availed nothing: *Thou saidst, It is vain!* (*sc.* that thou urgest me.) *No, for I love the strangers and after them will I go!* The meaning of the admonition is not very clear. Some (*e.g.* Rosenmüller) have understood a reference to the shameless doings, and the insatiable cravings of lust. Others (as Gesenius) explain the words thus: "Do not pursue thy lovers in such hot haste, as to wear thy feet bare in the wild race!" Others, again, take the prohibition literally, and connect the barefootedness and the thirst with the orgies of Baal-worship (Hitz.), in which the priests leaped or rather limped with bare feet (what proof?) on the blazing âltar, as an act of religious mortification, shrieking the while till their throats were parched and dry (Ps. lxix. 4, יָנוֹגְ רֹחָן), in frenzied appeal to their lifeless god (cf. Ex. iii. 5; 2 Sam. xv. 30; 1 Kings xviii. 26). In this case, the command is, Cease this self-torturing and bootless worship! But the former sense seems to agree better with the context.

Like the shame of a thief, when he is detected, so are the house of Israel ashamed — *they, their kings, their princes, and their priests, and their prophets; in that they say* (are ever saying) *to the wood* (iii. 9 in Heb. masc.), *Thou art my father!* (iii. 4) *and to the stone* (in Heb. fem.), *Thou didst bring me forth! For they* (xxxii. 33) *have turned towards Me the back and not the face; but in the time of their trouble they say* (begin to say), *O rise and save us! But where are thy gods that thou madest for thyself? Let them arise, if they can save thee in the time of thy trouble; for numerous as thy cities are thy gods become, O Judah!* (vv. 26-28). "The Shame" (תשבה) is the well-known title of opprobrium which the prophets apply to Baal. Even in the histories, which largely depend on prophetic sources, we find such substitutions as Ishbosheth for Eshbaal, the "Man of Shame" for "Baal's Man." Accordingly, the point of ver. 26 *sqq.* is, that as Israel has served the Shame, the idol-gods, instead of Iahvah, shame has been and will be her reward: in the hour of bitter need, when she implores help from the One true God, she is put to shame by being referred back to her senseless idols. The "Israel" intended is the entire nation, as in ver. 3, and not merely the fallen kingdom of Ephraim. In ver. 28 the prophet specially addresses Judah, the surviving representative of the whole people. In the book of Judges (x. 10-14) the same idea of the attitude of Iahvah towards His faithless people finds historical illustration. Oppressed by the Ammonites they "cried unto the Lord, saying, We have sinned against Thee, in that we have both forsaken our own God, and have served the Baals;" but Iahvah, after reminding them of past deliverances followed by fresh apostasies, replies: "Go, and cry unto the gods which ye have chosen; let *them* save you in the time of your distress!" Here also we hear the echoes of a prophetic voice. The object of such ironical utterances was by no means to deride the self-caused miseries in which Israel was involved; but, as is evident from the sequel of the narrative in Judges, to deepen penitence and contrition, by making the people realize the full flagrancy of their sin, and the suicidal folly of their desertions of the God whom, in times of national distress, they recognised as the only possible Saviour. In the same way and with the same end in view, the prophetic psalmist of Deut. xxxii. represents the God of Israel as asking (ver. 37) "Where are their gods; the Rock in which they sought refuge? That used to eat the flesh of their sacrifices, that drank the wine of their libation? Let them arise and help you; let them be over you a shelter!" The purpose is to bring home to them a conviction of the utter vanity of idol-worship; for the poet continues: "See *now* that I even I am He"—the one God—"and there is no God beside Me" (with Me, sharing My sole attributes); "'Tis I that kill and save alive; I have crushed, and *I* heal." The folly of Israel is made conspicuous, first by the expression "Saying to the wood, Thou art my father, and to the stone, Thou didst bring me forth;" and secondly, by the statement, "Numerous as thy cities are thy gods become, O Judah!" In the former, we have a most interesting glimpse of the point of view of the heathen worshipper of the seventh century b.c., from which it appears that by a *god* he meant the original, *i.e.*, the real author of his own existence. Much has been written in recent years to prove that man's elementary notions of deity are of an altogether lower kind than those which find expression in the worship of a Father in heaven; but when we see that such an idea could subsist even in connexion with the most impure nature-worships, as in Canaan, and when we observe that it was a familiar conception in the religion of Egypt several thousand years previously, we may well doubt whether this idea of an Unseen Father of our race is not as old as humanity itself.

The sarcastic reference to the number of Judah's idols may remind us of what is recorded of classic Athens, in whose streets it was said to be easier to find a god than a man. The irony of the prophet's remark depends on the consideration that there is, or ought to be, safety in numbers. The impotence of the false gods could hardly be put in a stronger light in words as few as the prophet has used. In chap. xi. 13 he repeats the statement in an amplified form: "For numerous as thy cities have thy gods become, O Judah; and numerous as the streets of Jerusalem have ye made altars for The Shame, altars for sacrificing to the Baal." From this passage, apparently, the LXX. derived the words which it adds here: "And according to the number of the streets of Jerusalem did they sacrifice to the (image of) Baal" (ἔθυον τῇ Βάαλ).

Why contend ye with Me? All of you have rebelled against Me, saith Iahvah. (LXX. ἠσεβήσατε, καὶ πάντες ὑμεῖς ἠνομήσατε εἰς ἐμέ. "Ebenfalls authentisch" says Hitzig). *In vain have I smitten your sons; correction they* (i.e., the people; but LXX. ἐδέξασθε may be correct), *received not! your own sword hath eaten up your prophets, like a destroying lion. Generation that ye are! See the word of Iahvah! Is it a wilderness that I have been to Israel, or a land of deepest gloom? Why have My people said, We are free; we will come no more unto Thee? Doth a virgin forget her ornaments, a bride her bands* (or *garlands*, Rashi)? *yet My people hath forgotten Me days without number* (vv. 29-32). The question, "Why contend, or dispute ye (ובירת), or, as the LXX. has it, talk ye (ורבדת) towards or about Me (ילא)?" implies that the people murmured at the reproaches and menaces of the prophet (ver. 26 *sqq.*). He answers them by denying their right to complain. Their rebellion has been universal; no chastisement has reformed them; Iahvah has done nothing which can be alleged in excuse of their unfaithfulness; their sin is, therefore, a portentous anomaly, for which it is impossible to find a parallel in ordinary human conduct. In vain had "their sons," the young men of military age, fallen in battle (Amos iv. 10); the nation had stubbornly refused to see in such disasters a sign of Iahvah's displeasure, a token of Divine chastisement; or rather, while recognising the wrath of heaven, they had obstinately persisted in believing in false explanations of its motive, and refused to admit that the purpose of it was their religious and moral amendment. And not only had the nation refused warning, and despised instruction, and defeated the purposes of the Divine discipline. They had slain their spiritual monitors, the prophets, with the sword; the prophets who had founded upon the national disasters their rebukes of national sin, and their earnest calls to penitence and reform (1 Kings xix. 10; Neh. ix. 26; St. Matt. xxiii. 37). And so when at last the long deferred judgment arrived, it found a political system ready to go to pieces through the feebleness and corruption of the ruling classes; a religious system, of which the spirit had long since evaporated, and which simply survived in the interests of a venal priesthood, and its intimate allies, who made a trade of prophecy; and a kingdom and people ripe for destruction.

At the thought of this crowning outrage, the prophet cannot restrain his indignation. "Generation that ye are!" he exclaims, "behold the word of the Lord. Is it a wilderness that I have been to Israel, or a land of deepest gloom?" Have I been a thankless, barren soil, returning nothing for your culture? The question is more pointed in Hebrew than in English; for the same term (דבע ʿabad) means both to till the ground, and to serve and worship God. We have thus an emphatic repetition of the remonstrance with which the address opens: Iahweh has not been unmindful of Israel's service; Israel has been persistently ungrateful for Iahvah's gracious love. The cry "We are free!" (ונדר) implies that they had broken away from a painful yoke and a burdensome service (cf. ver. 20); the yoke being that of the Moral Law, and the service that perfect freedom which consists in subjection to Divine Reason. Thus sin always triumphs in casting away man's noblest prerogative; in trampling under foot that loyalty to the higher ideal which is the bridal adornment and the peculiar glory of the soul.

Why hurriest thou to seek thy love? (Lit. *why dost thou make good thy way?* somewhat as we say, "to make good way with a thing") (ver. 33). The key to the meaning here is supplied by ver. 36: *Why art thou in such haste to change thy way? In (Of) Egypt also thou shalt be disappointed, as thou wert in Assyria.* The "way" is that which leads to Egypt; and the "love" is that apostasy from Iahvah which invariably accompanies an alliance with foreign peoples (ver. 18). If you go to Assyria, you "drink the waters of the Euphrates," *i.e.*, you are exposed to all the malign influences of the heathen land. Elsewhere, also (iv. 30), Jeremiah speaks of the foreign peoples, whose connexion Israel so anxiously courted, as her "lovers"; and the metaphor is a common one in the prophets.

The words which follow are obscure. *Therefore the evil things also hast thou taught thy ways.* What "evil things"? Elsewhere the term denotes *misfortunes, calamities* (Lam. iii. 38); and so probably here (cf. iii. 5). The sense seems to be: Thou hast done evil, and in so doing hast taught Evil to dog thy steps! The term *evil* obviously suggests the two meanings of sin and the punishment of sin; as we say, "Be sure your *sin* will find you out!" Ver. 34 explains what was the special sin that followed and clung to Israel: *Also, in thy skirts*—the borders of thy garments—*are they* (the evil things) *found,* viz., *the life-blood of innocent helpless ones; not that thou didst find them house-breaking,* and so hadst excuse for slaying them (Exod. xxii. 2); *but for all these* warnings or, because of all these apostasies and dallyings with the heathen, which they denounced (cf. iii. 7), *thou slewest them.* The murder of the prophets (ver. 30) was the unatoned guilt which clung to the skirts of Israel.

And thou saidst, Certainly I am absolved! Surely His wrath is turned away from me! Behold I wilt reason with thee, because thou sayest, I sinned not! (ver. 35). This is what the people said when they murdered the prophets. They, and doubtless their false guides, regarded the national disasters as so much atonement for their sins. They believed that Iahvah's wrath had exhausted itself in the infliction of what they had already endured, and that they were now absolved from their offences. The prophets looked at the matter differently. To them, national disasters were warnings of worse to follow, unless the people would take them in that sense, and turn from their evil ways. The people preferred to think that their account with Iahvah had been balanced and settled by their misfortunes in war (ver. 30). Hence they slew those who never wearied of affirming the contrary, and threatening further woe, as false prophets (Deut. xviii. 20). The saying, "I sinned not!" refers to these cruel acts; they declared themselves guiltless in the matter of slaying the prophets, as if their blood was on their own heads. The only practical issue of the national troubles was that instead of reforming, they sought to enter into fresh alliances with the heathen, thus, from the point of view of the prophets, adding sin to sin. *Why art thou in such haste to change thy way?* (*i.e.* thy course of action, thy foreign policy). *Through Egypt also shalt thou be shamed, as thou hast been shamed through Assyria. Out of this affair also* (or, *from him,* as the country is perhaps personified as a lover of Judah;) *shalt thou go forth with thine hands upon thine head* (in token of distress, 2 Sam. xiii. 19: Tamar); *for Iahvah hath rejected the objects of thy trust, so that thou canst not be successful regarding them* (vv. 36, 37). The Egyptian alliance, like the former one with Assyria, was destined to bring nothing but shame and confusion to the Jewish people. The prophet urges past experience of similar undertakings, in the hope of deterring the politicians of the day from their foolish enterprise. But all that they had learnt from the failure and loss entailed by their intrigues with one foreign power was, that it was expedient to try another. So they made haste to "change their way," to alter the direction of their policy from Assyria to Egypt. King Hezekiah had renounced his vassalage to Assyria, in reliance, as it would seem, on the support of Taharka, king of Egypt and Ethiopia (2 Kings xviii. 7; cf. Isa. xxx. 1-5); and now again the nation was coquetting with the same power. As has been stated, an Egyptian force láy at this time on the confines of Judah, and the prophet may be referring to friendly advances of the Jewish princes towards its leaders.

In the Hebrew, ch. iii. opens with the word "saying" (רֵמאֹל). No real parallel to this can be found elsewhere, and the Sept. and Syriac omit the term. Whether we follow these ancient authorities, and do the same, or whether we prefer to suppose that the prophet originally wrote, as usually, "And the Word of Iahvah came unto me, saying," will not make much difference. One thing is clear; the division of the chapters is in this instance erroneous, for the short section, iii. 1-5, obviously belongs to and completes the argument of ch. ii. The statement of ver. 37, that Israel will not prosper in the negotiations with Egypt, is justified in iii. 1 by the consideration that prosperity is an outcome of the Divine favour, which Israel has forfeited. The rejection of Israel's "confidences" implies the rejection of the people themselves (vii. 29). *If a man divorce his wife and she go away from him* (וְהָלְכָה *de chez lui*), *and become another man's, doth he* (her former husband) *return unto her again? Would not that land be utterly polluted?* It is the case contemplated in the Book of the Law (Deut. xxiv. 1-4), the supposition being that the second husband may divorce the woman, or that the bond between them may be dissolved by his death. In either contingency, the law forbade reunion with the former husband, as "abomination before Iahvah;" and David's treatment of his ten wives, who had been publicly wedded by his rebel son Absalom, proves the antiquity of the usage in this respect (2 Sam. xx. 3). The relation of Israel to Iahvah is the relation to her former husband of the divorced wife who has married another. If anything it is worse. *And thou, thou hast played the harlot with many paramours; and shalt thou return unto Me? saith Iahvah.* The very idea of it is rejected with indignation. The Author of the law will not so flagrantly break the law. (With the Heb. form of the question, cf. the Latin use of the infin. "Mene incepto desistere victam?") The details of the unfaithfulness of Israel—the proofs that she belongs to others and not to Iahvah—are glaringly obvious; contradiction is impossible. *Lift up thine eyes upon the bare fells, and see!* cries the prophet; *where hast thou not been forced? By the roadsides thou satest for them like a Bedawi in the wilderness, and thou pollutedst the land with thy whoredom and with thine evil* (Hos. vi. 13). On every hill-top the evidence of Judah's sinful dalliance with idols was visible; in her eagerness to consort with the false gods, the objects of her infatuation, she was like a courtesan looking out for paramours by the wayside (Gen. xxxviii. 14), or an Arab lying in wait for the unwary traveller in the desert. (There may be a reference to the artificial *bamoth* or "high places" erected at the top of the streets, on which the wretched women, consecrated to the shameful rites of the Canaanite goddess Ashtoreth, were wont to sit plying their trade of temptation: 2 Kings xxiii. 8; Ezek. xvi. 25). We must never forget that, repulsive and farfetched as these comparisons of an apostate people to a sinful woman may seem to us, the ideas and customs of the time made them perfectly apposite. The worship of the gods of Canaan involved the practice of the foulest impurities; and by her revolt from Iahvah, her lord and husband, according to the common Semitic conception of the relation between a people and their god, Israel became a harlot in fact as well as in figure. The land was polluted with her "whoredoms," *i.e.*, her worship of the false gods, and her practice of their vile rites; and with her "evil," as instanced above (ii. 30, 35) in the murder of those who protested against these things (Num. xxxv. 33; Ps. cvi. 38). As a punishment for these grave offences, *the showers were withholden, and the spring rains fell not*; but the merciful purpose of this Divine chastisement was not fulfilled; the people were not stirred to penitence, but rather hardened in their sins: *but thou hadst a harlot's forehead; thou refusedst to be made ashamed*! And now the day of grace is past, and repentance comes too late. *Hast thou not but now called unto Me, My Father! Friend of my youth wert Thou? Will He retain His wrath for ever? or keep it without end?* (vv. 3, 5). The reference appears to be to the external reforms accomplished by the young king Josiah in his twelfth year—the year previous to the utterance of this prophecy; when, as we read in 2 Chron. xxxiv. 3, "He began to purge Judah and Jerusalem from the high places, and the Asherim, and the carven images, and the molten images." To all appearance, it was a return of the nation to its old allegiance; the return of the rebellious child to its father, of the erring wife to the husband of her youth. By those two sacred names which in her inexcusable fickleness and ingratitude she had lavished upon stocks and stones, Israel now seemed to be invoking the relenting compassion of her alienated God (ii. 27, ii. 2). But apart from the doubt attaching to the reality of reformations to order, carried out in obedience to a royal decree; apart from the question whether outward changes so easily and rapidly accomplished, in accordance with the will of an absolute monarch, were accompanied by any tokens of a genuine national repentance; the sin of Israel had gone too far, and been persisted in too long, for its terrible consequences to be averted. *Behold*—it is the closing sentence of the address; a sentence fraught with despair, and the certainty of coming ruin;—*Behold, thou hast planned and accomplished the evil* (ii. 33); *and thou hast prevailed!* The approaches of the people are met by the assurance that their own plans and doings, rather than Iahvah's wrath, are the direct cause of past and prospective adversity; ill doing is the mother of ill fortune. Israel inferred from her troubles that God was angry with her; and she is informed by His prophet that, had she been bent on bringing those troubles about, she could not have chosen any other line of conduct than that which she had actually pursued. The term "evils" again suggests both the false and impure worships, and their calamitous moral consequences. Against the will of Iahvah, His people *had wrought for its own ruin*, and had prevailed.

And now let us take a farewell look at the discourse in its entirety. Beginning at the beginning, the dawn of his people's life as a nation, the young prophet declares that in her early days, in the old times of simple piety and the uncorrupted life of the desert, Israel had been true to her God; and her devotion to her Divine spouse had been rewarded by guidance and protection. "Israel was a thing consecrated to Iahvah; whoever eat of it was held guilty, and evil came upon them" (ii. 1-3). This happy state of mutual love and trust between the Lord and His people began to change with the great change in outward circumstances involved in their conquest of Canaan and settlement among the aboriginal inhabitants as the ruling race. With the lands and cities of the conquered, the conquerors soon learned to adopt also their customs of worship, and the licentious merriment of their sacrifices and festivals. Gradually they lost all sense of any radical distinction between the God of Israel and the local deities at whose ancient sanctuaries they now worshipped Him. Soon they forgot their debt to Iahvah; His gracious and long-continued guidance in the Arabian steppes, and the loving care which had established them in the goodly land of orchards and vineyards and cornfields. The priests ceased to care about ascertaining and declaring His will; the princes openly broke His laws; and the popular prophets spoke in the name of the popular Baals (vv. 4-8). There was something peculiarly strange and startling in this general desertion of the national God and Deliverer; it was unparalleled among the surrounding heathen races. *They* were faithful to gods that were no gods; Israel actually exchanged her Glory, the living source of all her strength and well-being, for a useless, helpless idol. Her behaviour was as crazy as if she had preferred a cistern, all cracks and fissures, that could not possibly hold water, to a never-failing fountain of sweet spring water (vv. 9-13). The consequences were only too plain to such as had eyes to see. Israel, the servant, the favoured slave of Iahvah, was robbed and spoiled. The "lions," the fierce and rapacious warriors of Assyria had ravaged his land, and ruined his cities; while Egypt was proving but a treacherous friend, pilfering and plundering on the borders of Judah. It was all Israel's own doing; forsaking his God, he had forfeited the Divine protection. It was his own apostasy, his own frequent and flagrant revolts which were punishing him thus. Vain, therefore, utterly vain were his endeavours to find deliverance from trouble in an alliance with the great heathen powers of South or North (vv. 14-19). Rebellion was no new feature in the national history. No; for of old the people had broken the yoke of Iahvah, and burst the bonds of His ordinances, and said, I will not serve! and on every high hill, and under every evergreen tree, Israel had bowed down to the Baalim of Canaan, in spiritual adultery from her Divine Lord and Husband. The change was a portent; the noble vine-shoot had degenerated into a worthless wilding (vv. 20-21). The sin of Israel was inveterate and ingrained; nothing could wash out the stain of it. Denial of her guilt was futile; the dreadful rites in the valley of Hinnom witnessed against her. Her passion for the foreign worships was as insatiable and headstrong as the fierce lust of the camel or the wild ass. To protests and warnings her sole reply was: "It is in vain! I love the strangers, and them will I follow!" The outcome of all this wilful apostasy was the shame of defeat and disaster, the humiliation of disappointment, when the helplessness of the stocks and stones, which had supplanted her Heavenly Father, was demonstrated by the course of events. Then she bethought her of the God she had so lightly forsaken, only to hear in His silence a bitterly ironical reference to the multitude of her helpers, the gods of her own creation. The national reverses failed of the effect intended in the counsels of Providence. Her sons had fallen in battle; but instead of repenting of her evil ways, she slew the faithful prophets who warned her of the consequences of her misdeeds (vv. 20-30). It was the crowning sin; the cup of her iniquity was full to overflowing. Indignant at the memory of it, the prophet once more insists that the national crimes are what has put misfortune on the track of the nation; and chiefly, this heinous one of killing the messengers of God like housebreakers caught in the act; and then aggravating their guilt by self-justification, and by resorting to Egypt for that help, which they despaired of obtaining from an outraged God. All such negotiations, past or present, were doomed to failure beforehand; the Divine sentence had gone forth, and it was idle to contend against it (vv. 31-37). Idle also it was to indulge in hopes of the restoration of Divine favour. Just as it was not open to a discarded wife to return to her husband after living with another; so might not Israel be received back into her former position of the Bride of Heaven, after she had "played the harlot with many lovers." Doubtless of late she had given tokens of remembering her forgotten Lord, calling upon the Father who had been the guide of her youth, and deprecating the continuance of His wrath. But the time was long since past, when it was possible to avert the evil consequences of her misdoings. She had, as it were, steadily purposed and wrought out her own evils; both her sins and her sufferings past and to come: the iron sequence could not be broken; the ruin she had courted lay before her in the near future: she had "prevailed." All efforts such as she was now making to stave it off were like a deathbed repentance; in the nature of things, they could not annihilate the past, nor undo what had been done, nor substitute the fruit of holiness for the fruit of sin, the reward of faithfulness and purity for the wages of worldliness, sensuality, and forgetfulness of God.

Thus the discourse starts with impeachment, and ends with irreversible doom. Its tone is comminatory throughout; nowhere do we hear, as in other prophecies, the promise of pardon in return for penitence. Such preaching was necessary, if the nation was to be brought to a due sense of its evil; and the reformation of the eighteenth of Josiah, which was undoubtedly accompanied by a considerable amount of genuine repentance among the governing classes, was in all likelihood furthered by this and similar prophetic orations.[20]

III

ISRAEL AND JUDAH: A CONTRAST

Jeremiah iii. 6-iv. 2.

The first address of our prophet was throughout of a sombre cast, and the darkness of its close was not relieved by a single ray of hope. It was essentially a comminatory discourse, the purpose of it being to rouse a sinful nation to the sense of its peril, by a faithful picture of its actual condition, which was so different from what it was popularly supposed to be. The veil is torn aside; the real relations between Israel and his God are exposed to view; and it is seen that the inevitable goal of persistence in the course which has brought partial disasters in the past, is certain destruction in the imminent future. It is implied, but not said, that the only thing that can save the nation is a complete reversal of policies hitherto pursued, in Church and State and private life; and it is apparently taken for granted that the thing implied is no longer possible. The last word of the discourse was: "Thou hast purposed and performed the evils, and thou hast conquered" (iii. 5). The address before us forms a striking contrast to this dark picture. It opens a door of hope for the penitent. The heart of the prophet cannot rest in the thought of the utter rejection of his people; the harsh and dreary announcement that his people's woes are self-caused cannot be his last word. "His anger was only love provoked to distraction; here it has come to itself again," and holds out an offer of grace first to that part of the whole nation which needs it most, the fallen kingdom of Ephraim, and then to the entire people. The all Israel of the former discourse is here divided into its two sections, which are contrasted with each other, and then again considered as a united nation. This feature distinguishes the piece from that which begins chap. iv. 3, and which is addressed to "Judah and Jerusalem" rather than to Israel and Judah, like the one before us. An outline of the discourse may be given thus. It is shown that Judah has not taken warning by Iahvah's rejection of the sister kingdom (6-10); and that Ephraim may be pronounced less guilty than Judah, seeing that she had witnessed no such signal example of the Divine vengeance on hardened apostasy. She is, therefore, invited to repent and return to her alienated God, which will involve a return from exile to her own land; and the promise is given of the reunion of the two peoples in a restored Theocracy, having its centre in Mount Zion (11-19). All Israel has rebelled against God; but the prophet hears the cry of universal penitence and supplication ascending to heaven; and Iahvah's gracious answer of acceptance (iii. 20-iv. 2).

The opening section depicts the sin which had brought ruin on Israel, and Judah's readiness in following her example, and refusal to take warning by her fate. This twofold sin is aggravated by an insincere repentance. *And Iahvah said unto me, in the days of Josiah the king, Sawest thou what the Turncoat or Recreant Israel did? she would go up every high hill, and under every evergreen tree, and play the harlot there. And methought that after doing all this she would return to Me; but she returned not; and the Traitress, her sister Judah saw it. And I* [21] *saw that when for the very reason that she, the Turncoat Israel, had committed adultery, I had put her away, and given her her bill of divorce, the Traitress Judah, her sister, was not afraid, but she too went off and played the harlot. And so, through the cry* (cf. Gen. iv. 10, xviii. 20 *sq.*) *of her harlotry* (or read בר for לק, script. defect. through her manifold or abounding harlotry) *she polluted the land* (וַתֶּחֱנַף ver. 2), *in that she committed adultery with the Stone and with the Stock. And yet though she was involved in all this guilt* (lit. *and even in all this.* Perhaps the sin and the penalties of it are identified; and the meaning is: *And yet for all this liability*: cf. Isa. v. 25), *the Traitress Judah returned not unto Me with all her heart* (with a *whole* or *undivided* heart, with entire sincerity[22]) *but in falsehood saith Iahvah.* The example of the northern kingdom is represented as a powerful influence for evil upon Judah. This was only natural; for although from the point of view of religious development Judah is incomparably the more important of the sister kingdoms; the exact contrary is the case as regards political power and predominance. Under strong kings like Omri and Ahab, or again, Jeroboam II., Ephraim was able to assert itself as a first-rate power among the surrounding principalities; and in the case of Athaliah, we have a conspicuous instance of the manner in which Canaanite idolatry might be propagated from Israel to Judah. The prophet declares that the sin of Judah was aggravated by the fact that she had witnessed the ruin of Israel, and yet persisted in the same evil courses of which that ruin was the result. She sinned against light. The fall of Ephraim had verified the predictions of her prophets; yet "she was not afraid," but went on adding to the score of her own offences, and polluting the land with her unfaithfulness to her Divine Spouse. The idea that the very soil of her country was defiled by Judah's idolatry may be illustrated by reference to the well-known words of Ps. cvi. 38: "They shed innocent blood, even the blood of their sons and their daughters whom they sacrificed unto the idols of Canaan; and the land was defiled with the bloodshed." We may also remember Elohim's word to Cain: "The voice of thy brother's blood is crying unto Me from the ground!" (Gen. iv. 10). As Iahvah's special dwelling-place, moreover, the land of Israel was holy; and foreign rites desecrated and profaned it, and made it offensive in His sight. The pollution of it cried to heaven for vengeance on those who had caused it. To such a state had Judah brought her own land, and the very city of the sanctuary; "and yet in all this"—amid this accumulation of sins and liabilities—she turned not to her Lord with her whole heart. The reforms set on foot in the twelfth year of Josiah were but superficial and half-hearted; the people merely acquiesced in them, at the dictation of the court, and gave no sign of any inward change or deep-wrought repentance. The semblance without the reality of sorrow for sin is but a mockery of heaven, and a heinous aggravation of guilt. Hence the sin of Judah was of a deeper dye than that which had destroyed Israel. *And Iahvah said unto me, The Turncoat or Recreant Israel hath proven herself more righteous than the Traitress Judah.* Who could doubt it, considering that almost all the prophets had borne their witness in Judah; and that, in imitating her sister's idolatry, she had resolutely closed her eyes to the light of truth and reason? On this ground, that Israel has sinned less, and suffered more, the prophet is bidden to hold out to her the hope of Divine mercy. The greatness of her ruin, as well as the lapse of years since the fatal catastrophe, might tend to diminish in the prophet's mind the impression of her guilt; and his patriotic yearning for the restoration of the banished Ten Tribes, who, after all, were the near kindred of Judah, as well as the thought that they had borne their punishment, and thus atoned for their sin (Isa. xl. 2), might cooperate with the desire of kindling in his own countrymen a noble rivalry of repentance, in moving the prophet to obey the impulse which urged him to address himself to Israel. *Go thou, and cry these words northward* (toward the desolate land of Ephraim), *and say: Return, Turncoat or Recreant Israel, saith Iahvah; I will not let My countenance fall at the sight of you* (lit. *against you,* cf. Gen. iv. 5); *for I am loving, saith Iahvah, I keep not anger for ever. Only recognise thy guilt, that thou hast rebelled against Iahvah thy God, and hast scattered* (or *lavished*: Ps. cxii. 9) *thy ways to the strangers* (hast gone now in this direction, now in that, worshipping first one idol and then another; cf. ii. 23; and so, as it were, dividing up and dispersing thy devotion) *under every evergreen tree; but My voice ye have not obeyed, saith Iahvah.* The invitation, "Return Apostate Israel!"—[23]הבוש הבשמ שי—contains a play on words, which seems to suggest that the exile of the Ten Tribes was voluntary, or self-imposed; as if, when they turned their backs upon their true God, they had deliberately made choice of the inevitable consequence of that rebellion, and made up their minds to abandon their native land. So close is the connexion, in the prophet's view, between the misfortunes of his people and their sins.

Return, ye apostate children (again there is a play on words—ובוש סינב שובביס—*Turn back, ye back-turning sons*, or *ye sons that turn the back* to Me) *saith Iahvah; for it was I that wedded you* (ver. 14), and am, therefore, your proper lord. The expression is not stranger than that which the great prophet of the Return addresses to Zion: "Thy sons shall marry thee." But perhaps we should rather compare another passage of the book of Isaiah, where it is said: "Iahvah, our God! other lords beside Thee have had dominion over us" (וּנוּלָעְב Isa. xxvi. 13), and render: *For it is I that will be your lord*; or perhaps, *For it is I that have mastered you*, and put down your rebellion by chastisements; *and I will take you, one of a city and two of a clan, and will bring you to Zion*. As a "city" is elsewhere spoken of as a "thousand" (Mic. v. 1), and a "thousand" (ףלא) is synonymous with a "clan" (החפשמ), as providing a thousand warriors in the national militia; it is clear that the promise is that one or two representatives of each township in Israel shall be restored from exile to the land of their fathers. In other words, we have here Isaiah's doctrine of the remnant, which he calls a "tenth" (Isa. vi. 13), and of which he declared that "the survivors of the house of Judah that remain, shall again take root downwards, and bear fruit upwards" (Isa. xxxvii. 31). And as Zion is the goal of the returning exiles, we may see, as doubtless the prophets saw, a kind of anticipation and foreshadowing of the future in the few scattered members of the northern tribes of Asher, Manasseh and Zebulun, who "humbled themselves," and accepted Hezekiah's invitation to the passover (2 Chron. xxx. 11, 18); and, again, in the authority which Josiah is said to have exercised in the land of the Ten Tribes (2 Chron. xxxiv. 6; cf. 9). We must bear in mind that the prophets do not contemplate the restoration of every individual of the entire nation; but rather the return of a chosen few, a kind of "firstfruits" of Israel, who are to be a "holy seed" (Isa. vi. 13), from which the power of the Supreme will again build up the entire people according to its ancient divisions. So the holy Apostle in the Revelation hears that twelve thousand of each tribe are sealed as servants of God (Rev. vii.).

The happy time of restoration will also be a time of reunion. The estranged tribes will return to their old allegiance. This is implied by the promise, "I will bring you to Zion," and by that of the next verse: *And I will give you shepherds after My own heart; and they shall shepherd you with knowledge and wisdom*. Obviously, kings of the house of David are meant; the good shepherds of the future are contrasted with the "rebellious" ones of the past (ii. 8). It is the promise of Isaiah (i. 26): "And I will restore thy judges as at the first, and thy counsellors as at the beginning." In this connexion, we may recall the fact that the original schism in Israel was brought about by the folly of evil shepherds. The coming King will resemble not Rehoboam but David. Nor is this all; for *It shall come to pass, when ye multiply and become fruitful in the land, in those days, saith Iahvah, men shall not say any more, The ark of the covenant of Iahvah,* (or, as LXX., *of the Holy One of Israel); nor shall it* (the ark) *come to mind; nor shall men remember it, nor miss it; nor shall it be made any more* (pointing הֵעָשֶׂי although the verb may be impersonal. I do not understand why Hitzig asserts "Man wird keine andere machen (Movers) oder; sie wird nicht wieder gemacht (Ew., Graf) als wäre nicht von der geschichtlichen Lade die Rede, sondern von ihr begrifflich, können die Worte nicht bedeuten." But cf. Exod. xxv. 10; Gen. vi. 14; where the same verb עשה is used. Perhaps, however, the rendering of C. B. Michaelis, which he prefers, is more in accordance with what precedes: *nor shall all that be done any more,* Gen. xxix. 26, xli. 34. But דקפ does not mean *nachforschen*: cf. 1 Sam. xx. 6, xxv. 15). *In that time men will call Jerusalem the throne of Iahvah; and all the nations will gather into it* (Gen. i. 9), *for the name of Iahvah* [at Jerusalem: LXX. om.]; *and they* (the heathen) *will no longer follow the stubbornness of their evil heart* (vii. 24; Deut. xxix. 19).

In the new Theocracy, the true kingdom of God, the ancient symbol of the Divine presence will be forgotten in the realization of that presence. The institution of the New Covenant will be characterized by an immediate and personal knowledge of Iahvah in the hearts of all His people (xxxi. 31 *sq.*). The small object in which past generations had loved to recognise the earthly throne of the God of Israel, will be replaced by Jerusalem itself, the Holy City, not merely of Judah, nor of Judah and Israel, but of the world. Thither will all the nations resort "to the name of Iahvah;" ceasing henceforth "to follow the hardness (or callousness) of their own evil heart." That the more degraded kinds of heathenism have a hardening effect upon the heart; and that the cruel and impure worships of Canaan especially tended to blunt the finer sensibilities, to enfeeble the natural instincts of humanity and justice, and to confuse the sense of right and wrong, is beyond question. Only a heart rendered callous by custom, and stubbornly deaf to the pleadings of natural pity, could find genuine pleasure in the merciless rites of the Molech-worship; and they who ceased to follow these inhuman superstitions, and sought light and guidance from the God of Israel, might well be said to have ceased "to walk after the hardness of their own evil heart."[24] The more repulsive features of heathenism chime in too well with the worst and most savage impulses of our nature; they exhibit too close a conformity with the suggestions and demands of selfish appetite; they humour and encourage the darkest passions far too directly and decidedly, to allow us to regard as plausible any theory of their origin and permanence which does not recognise in them at once a cause and an effect of human depravity (cf. Rom. i.).

The repulsiveness of much that was associated with the heathenism with which they were best acquainted, did not hinder the prophets of Israel from taking a deep spiritual interest in those who practised and were enslaved by it. Indeed, what has been called the universalism of the Hebrew seers—their emancipation in this respect from all local and national limits and prejudices—is one of the clearest proofs of their divine mission. Jeremiah only reiterates what Micah and Isaiah had preached before him; that "in the latter days the mountain of Iahvah's House shall be established as the chief of mountains, and shall be exalted above the hills; and all the nations will flow unto it" (Isa. ii. 2). In ch. xvi. 19 *sq.* our prophet thus expresses himself upon the same topic. "Iahvah, my strength and my stronghold, and my refuge in the day of distress! unto Thee shall nations come from the ends of the earth, and shall say: Our forefathers inherited nought but a lie, vanity, and things among which is no helper. Shall a man make him gods, when they are no gods?" How largely this particular aspiration of the prophets of the seventh and eighth centuries b.c. has since been fulfilled in the course of the ages is a matter of history. The religion which was theirs has, in the new shape given it by our Lord and His Apostles, become the religion of one heathen people after another, until at this day it is the faith professed, not only in the land of its origin, but by the leading nations of the world. So mighty a fulfilment of hopes, which at the time of their first conception and utterance could only be regarded as the dreams of enthusiastic visionaries, justifies those who behold and realize it in the joyful belief that the progress of true religion has not been maintained for six and twenty centuries to be arrested now; and that these old-world aspirations are destined to receive a fulness of illustration in the triumphs of the future, in the light of which the brightest glories of the past will pale and fade away.

The prophet does not say, with a prophet of the New Covenant, that all *Israel shall be saved* (Rom. xi. 26). We may, however, fairly interpret the latter of the true Israel, *the remnant according to the election of grace*, rather than of *Israel according to the flesh*, and so both will be at one, and both at variance with the unspiritual doctrine of the Talmud, that *All Israel*, irrespective of moral qualifications, will have *a portion in the world to come*, on account of the surpassing merits of Abraham, Isaac and Jacob, and even of Abraham alone (cf. St. Matt. iii. 9; St. John viii. 33).

The reference to the ark of the covenant in the sixteenth verse is remarkable upon several grounds. This sacred symbol is not mentioned among the spoils which Nebuzaradan (Nabû-zir-iddin) took from the temple (lii. 17 *sqq.*); nor is it specified among the treasures appropriated by Nebuchadrezzar at the surrender of Jehoiachin. The words of Jeremiah prove that it cannot be included among "the vessels of gold" which the

Babylonian conqueror "cut in pieces" (2 Kings xxiv. 13). We learn two facts about the ark from the present passage: (1) that it no longer existed in the days of the prophet; (2) that people remembered it with regret, though they did not venture to replace the lost original by a new substitute. It may well have been destroyed by Manasseh, the king who did his utmost to abolish the religion of Iahvah. However that may be, the point of the prophet's allusion consists in the thought that in the glorious times of Messianic rule the idea of holiness will cease to be attached to things, for it will be realized in persons; the symbol will become obsolete, and its name and memory will disappear from the minds and affections of men, because the fact symbolized will be universally felt and perceived to be a present and self-evident truth. In that great epoch of Israel's reconciliation, all nations will recognise in Jerusalem the *throne of Iahvah*, the centre of light and source of spiritual truth; the Holy City of the world. Is it the earthly or the heavenly Jerusalem that is meant? It would seem, the former only was present to the consciousness of the prophet, for he concludes his beautiful interlude of promise with the words: *In those days will the house of Judah walk beside the house of Israel; and they will come together from the land of the North [and from all the lands: LXX add. cf. xvi. 15] unto the land that I caused your fathers to possess.* Like Isaiah (xi. 12 *sqq.*) and other prophets his predecessors, Jeremiah forecasts for the whole repentant and united nation a reinstatement in their ancient temporal rights, in the pleasant land from which they had been so cruelly banished for so many weary years.

"The letter killeth, but the spirit giveth life." If, when we look at the whole course of subsequent events, when we review the history of the Return and of the narrow religious commonwealth which was at last, after many bitter struggles, established on mount Sion; when we consider the form which the religion of Iahvah assumed in the hands of the priestly caste, and the half-religious, half-political sects, whose intrigues and conflicts for power constitute almost all we know of their period; when we reflect upon the character of the entire post-exilic age down to the time of the birth of Christ, with its worldly ideals, its fierce fanaticisms, its superstitious trust in rites and ceremonies; if, when we look at all this, we hesitate to claim that the prophetic visions of a great restoration found fulfilment in the erection of this petty state, this paltry edifice, upon the ruins of David's capital; shall we lay ourselves open to the accusation that we recognise no element of truth in the glorious aspirations of the prophets? I think not.

After all, it is clear from the entire context that these hopes of a golden time to come are not independent of the attitude of the people towards Iahvah. They will only be realized, if the nation shall truly repent of the past, and turn to Him with the whole heart. The expressions "at that time," "in those days" (vv. 17, 18), are only conditionally determinate; they mean the happy time of Israel's repentance, *if such a time should ever come.* From this glimpse of glorious possibilities, the prophet turns abruptly to the dark page of Israel's actual history. He has, so to speak, portrayed in characters of light the development as it might have been; he now depicts the course it actually followed. He restates Iahvah's original claim upon Israel's grateful devotion (ii. 2), putting these words into the mouth of the Divine Speaker: *And I indeed thought, How will I set thee among the sons* (of the Divine household), *and give thee a lovely land, a heritage the fairest among the nations! And methought, thou wouldst call Me 'My Father,' and wouldst not turn back from following Me.* Iahvah had at the outset adopted Israel, and called him from the status of a groaning bondsman to the dignity of a son and heir. When Israel was a child, He had loved him, and called His son out of Egypt (Hos. xi. 1), to give him a place and a heritage among nations. It was Iahvah, indeed, who originally assigned their holdings to all the nations, and separated the various tribes of mankind, *fixing the territories of peoples, according to the number of the sons of God* (Deut. xxxii. 8 Sept.). If He had brought up Israel from Egypt, He had also brought up the Philistines from Caphtor, and the Arameans from Kir (Amos ix. 7). But He had adopted Israel in a more special sense, which may be expressed in St. Paul's words, who makes it the chief advantage of Israel above the nations that *unto them were committed the oracles of God.* (Rom. iii. 2). What nobler distinction could have been conferred upon any race of men than that they should have been thus chosen, as Israel actually was chosen, not merely in the aspirations of prophets, but as a matter of fact in the divinely-directed evolution of human history, to become the heralds of a higher truth, the hierophants of spiritual knowledge, the universally recognised interpreters of God? Such a calling might have been expected to elicit a response of the warmest gratitude, the most enthusiastic loyalty and unswerving devotion. But Israel as a nation did not rise to the level of these lofty prophetic views of its vocation; it knew itself to be the people of Iahvah, but it failed to realize the moral significance of that privilege, and the moral and spiritual responsibilities which it involved. It failed to adore Iahvah as the Father, in the only proper and acceptable sense of that honourable name, the sense which restricts its application to one sole Being. Heathenism is blind and irrational as well as profane and sinful; and so it does not scruple to confer such absolutely individual titles as "God" and "Father" upon a multitude of imaginary powers.

Methought thou wouldst call Me 'My Father,' and wouldst not turn back from following Me. But (Zeph. iii. 7) *a woman is false to her fere; so were ye false to Me, O house of Israel, saith Iahvah.* The Divine intention toward Israel, God's gracious design for her everlasting good, God's expectation of a return for

His favour, and how that design was thwarted so far as man could thwart it, and that expectation disappointed hitherto; such is the import of the last two verses (19, 20). Speaking in the name of God, Jeremiah represents Israel's past as it appears to God. He now proceeds to shew dramatically, or as in a picture, how the expectation may yet be fulfilled, and the design realized. Having exposed the national guilt, he supposes his remonstrance to have done its work, and he overhears the penitent people pouring out its heart before God. Then a kind of dialogue ensues between the Deity and His suppliants. *Hark! upon the bare hills is heard the weeping of the supplications of the sons of Israel, that they perverted their way, forgot Iahvah their God.* The treeless hill-tops had been the scene of heathen orgies miscalled worship. There the rites of Canaan performed by Israelites had insulted the God of heaven (vv. 2 and 6). Now the very places which witnessed the sin, witness the national remorse and confession. The 'high-places' are not condemned even by Jeremiah as places of worship, but only as places of heathen and illicit worships. The solitude and quiet and purer air of the hill-tops, their unobstructed view of heaven and suggestive nearness thereto, have always made them natural sanctuaries both for public rites and private prayer and meditation: cf. 2 Sam. xv. 32; and especially St. Luke vi. 12.

In this closing section of the piece (iii. 19-iv. 2) 'Israel' means not the entire people, but the northern kingdom only, which is spoken of separately also in iii. 6-18, with the object of throwing into higher relief the heinousness of Judah's guilt. Israel—the northern kingdom—was less guilty than Judah, for she had no warning example, no beacon-light upon her path, such as her own fall afforded to the southern kingdom; and therefore the Divine compassion is more likely to be extended to her, even after a century of ruin and banishment, than to her callous, impenitent sister. Whether at the time Jeremiah was in communication with survivors of the northern Exile, who were faithful to the God of their fathers, and looked wistfully toward Jerusalem as the centre of the best traditions and the sole hope of Israelite nationality, cannot now be determined. The thing is not unlikely, considering the interest which the prophet afterwards took in the Judean exiles who were taken to Babylon with Jehoiachin (chap. xxix.) and his active correspondence with their leaders. We may also remember that "divers of Asher and Manasseh and Zebulun humbled themselves" and came to keep passover with king Hezekiah at Jerusalem. It cannot, certainly, be supposed, with any show of reason, that the Assyrians either carried away the entire population of the northern kingdom, or exterminated all whom they did not carry away. The words of the Chronicler who speaks of "a remnant ... escaped out of the hand of the kings of Assyria," are themselves perfectly agreeable to reason and the nature of the case, apart from the consideration that he had special historical sources at his command (2 Chron. xxx. 6, 11). We know that in the Maccabean and Roman wars the rocky fastnesses of the country were a refuge to numbers of the people, and the history of David shews that this had been the case from time immemorial (cf. Judg. vi. 2). Doubtless in this way not a few survived the Assyrian invasions and the destruction of Samaria (b.c. 721). But to return to the text. After the confession of the nation that they have *perverted their way* (that is, their mode of worship, by adoring visible symbols of Iahvah, and associating with Him as His compeers a multitude of imaginary gods, especially the local Baalim, ii. 23, and Ashtaroth), the prophet hears another voice, a voice of Divine invitation and gracious promise, responsive to penitence and prayer: *Return, ye apostate sons, let Me heal your apostasies!* or *If ye return, ye apostate sons, I will heal your apostasies!* It is an echo of the tenderness of an older prophet (Hos. xiv. 1, 4). And the answer of the penitents quickly follows: *Behold us, we are come unto Thee, for Thou art Iahvah our God.* The voice that now calls us, we know by its tender tones of entreaty, compassion and love to be the voice of Iahvah our own God; not the voice of sensual Chemosh, tempting to guilty pleasures and foul impurities, not the harsh cry of a cruel Molech, calling for savage rites of pitiless bloodshed. Thou, Iahvah—not these nor their fellows—art our true and only God.

Surely, in vain (for nought, bootlessly, 1 Sam. xxv. 21; chap. v. 2, xvi. 19) *on the hills did we raise a din* (lit. 'hath one raised'; reading תּוֹעֵבַּג and מִירָה); *surely, in Iahvah our God is the safety of Israel!* The Hebrew cannot be original as it now stands in the Masoretic text, for it is ungrammatical. The changes I have made will be seen to be very slight, and the sense obtained is much the same as Ewald's *Surely in vain from the hills is the noise, from the mountains* (where every reader must feel that *from the mountains* is a forcible-feeble addition which adds nothing to the sense). We might also perhaps detach the *mem* from the term for 'hills,' and connect it with the preceding word, thus getting the meaning: *Surely, for Lies are the hills, the uproar of the mountains!* (מִירָה וָמֶה ... מִירְקָשֶׁל); that is to say, the high-places are devoted to delusive nonentities, who can do nothing in return for the wild orgiastic worship bestowed on them; a thought which contrasts very well with the second half of the verse: *Surely, in Iahvah our God is the safety of Israel!*

The confession continues: *And as for the Shame*—the shameful idol, the Baal whose worship involved shameful rites (chap. xi. 13; Hos. ix. 10), and who put his worshippers to shame, by disappointing them of help in the hour of their need (ii. 8, 26, 27)—*as for the Shame*—in contrast with Iahvah, the Safety of Israel, who gives all, and requires little or nothing of this kind in return—*it devoured the labour of our fathers from our youth, their flocks and their herds, their sons and their daughters.* The allusion is to the insatiable greed of the idol-priests, and the lavish expense of perpetually recurring feasts and sacrifices, which constituted a serious drain upon the resources of a pastoral and agricultural community; and to the bloody rites which, not content with animal offerings, demanded human victims for the altars of an appalling superstition. *Let us lie down in our shame, and let our infamy cover us! for toward Iahvah our God we trespassed, we and our fathers, from our youth even unto this day, and obeyed not the voice of Iahvah our God.* A more complete acknowledgment of sin could hardly be conceived; no palliating circumstances are alleged, no excuses devised, of the kind with which men usually seek to soothe a disturbed conscience. The strong seductions of Canaanite worship, the temptation to join in the joyful merriment of idol-festivals, the invitation of friends and neighbours, the contagion of example,—all these extenuating facts must have been at least as well known to the prophet as to modern critics, but he is expressively silent on the point of mitigating circumstances in the case of a nation to whom such light and guidance had come, as came to Israel. No, he could discern no ground of hope for his people except in a full and unreserved admission of guilt, an agony of shame and contrition before God, a heartfelt recognition of the truth that from the outset of their national existence to the passing day they had continually sinned against Iahvah their God and resisted His holy Will.

Finally, to this cry of penitents humbled in the dust, and owning that they have no refuge from the consequences of their sin but in the Divine Mercy, comes the firm yet loving answer: *If thou wilt return, O Israel, saith Iahvah, unto Me wilt return, and if thou wilt put away thine Abominations [out of thy mouth and, LXX.] out of My Presence, and sway not to and fro* (1 Kings xiv. 15), *but wilt swear 'By the Life of Iahvah!' in good faith, justice, and righteousness; then shall the nations bless themselves by Him, and in Him shall they glory* (iv. 1, 2). Such is the close of this ideal dialogue between God and man. It is promised that if the nation's repentance be sincere—not half-hearted like that of Judah (iii. 10; 2 Chron. xxxiv. 33)—and if the fact be demonstrated by a resolute and unwavering rejection of idol-worship, evinced by the disuse of their names in oaths, and the expulsion of their symbols *from the Presence*, that is, out of the sanctuaries and domain of Iahvah, and by adhering to the Name of the God of Israel in oaths and compacts of all kinds, and by a scrupulous loyalty to such engagements (Ps. xv. 4; Deut. x. 20; Isa. xlviii. 1); then the ancient oracle of blessing will be fulfilled, and Israel will become a proverb of felicity, the pride and boast of mankind, the glorious ideal of perfect virtue and perfect happiness (Gen. xii. 3; Isa. lxv. 16). Then, *all the nations will gather together unto Jerusalem for the Name of Iahvah* (iii. 17); they will recognise in the religion of Iahvah the answer to their highest longings and spiritual necessities, and will take Israel for what Iahvah intended him to be, their example and priest and prophet.

Jeremiah could hardly have chosen a more extreme instance for pointing the lesson he had to teach than the long-since ruined and depopulated kingdom of the Ten Tribes. Hopeless as their actual condition must have seemed at the time, he assures his own countrymen in Judah and Jerusalem that even yet, if only the moral requirements of the case were fulfilled, and the heart of the poor remnant and of the survivors in banishment aroused to a genuine and permanent repentance, the Divine promises would be accomplished in a people whose sun had apparently set in darkness for ever. And so he passes on to address his own people directly in tones of warning, reproof, and menace of approaching wrath (iv. 3-vi. 30.)

IV
THE SCYTHIANS AS THE SCOURGE OF GOD

Jeremiah iv. 3-vi. 30.

If we would understand what is written here and elsewhere in the pages of prophecy, two things would seem to be requisite. We must prepare ourselves with some knowledge of the circumstances of the time, and we must form some general conception of the ideas and aims of the inspired writer, both in themselves, and in their relation to passing events. Of the former, a partial and fragmentary knowledge may suffice, provided it be true so far as it goes; minuteness of detail is not necessary to general accuracy. Of the latter, a very full and complete conception may be gathered from a careful study of the prophetic discourses.

The chapters before us were obviously composed in the presence of a grave national danger; and what that danger was is not left uncertain, as the discourse proceeds. An invasion of the country appeared to be imminent; the rumour of approaching war had already made itself heard in the capital; and all classes were terror-stricken at the tidings.

As usual in such times of peril, the country people were already abandoning the uncalled towns and villages, to seek refuge in the strong places of the land, and, above all, in Jerusalem, which was at once the capital and the principal fortress of the kingdom. The evil news had spread far and near; the trumpet-signal of alarm was heard everywhere; the cry was, *Assemble yourselves, and let us go into the fenced cities!* (iv. 5).

The ground of this universal terror is thus declared: *The lion is gone up from his thicket, and the destroyer of nations is on his way, is gone forth from his place; to make thy land a desolation, that thy cities be laid waste, without inhabitant* (ver. 7). *A hot blast over the bare hills in the wilderness, on the road to the daughter of my people, not for winnowing, nor for cleansing; a full blast from those hills cometh at My beck* (ver. 11). *Lo, like clouds he cometh up, and, like the whirlwind, his chariots; swifter than vultures are his horses. Woe unto us! We are verily destroyed* (ver. 13). *Besiegers* (lit. *watchmen*, Isa. i. 8) *are coming from the remotest land, and they utter their cry against the cities of Judah. Like keepers of a field become they against her on every side* (vv. 16-17). At the same time, the invasion is still only a matter of report; the blow has not yet fallen upon the trembling people. *Behold, I am about to bring upon you a nation from afar, O house of Israel, saith Iahvah; an inexhaustible nation it is, a nation of old time it is, a nation whose tongue thou knowest not, nor understandest* (lit. *hearest*) *what it speaketh. Its quiver is like an opened grave; they all are heroes. And it will eat up thine harvest and thy bread, which thy sons and thy daughters should eat; it will eat up thy flock and thine herd; it will eat up thy vine and thy figtree; it will shatter thine embattled cities, wherein thou art trusting, with the sword* (v. 15-17). *Thus hath Iahvah said: Lo, a people cometh from a northern land, and a great nation is awaking from the uttermost parts of earth. Bow and lance they hold; savage it is, and pitiless; the sound of them is like the sea, when it roareth; and on horses they ride; he is arrayed as a man for battle, against thee, O daughter of Zion. We have heard the report of him; our hands droop; anguish hath taken hold of us, throes, like hers that travaileth* (vi. 22 sq.). With the graphic force of a keen observer, who is also a poet, the priest of Anathoth has thus depicted for all time the collapse of terror which befel his contemporaries, on the rumoured approach of the Scythians in the reign of Josiah. And his lyric fervour carries him beyond this; it enables him to see with the utmost distinctness the havoc wrought by these hordes of savages; the surprise of cities, the looting of houses, the flight of citizens to the woods and the hills at the approach of the enemy; the desertion of the country towns, the devastation of fields and vineyards, confusion and desolation everywhere, as though primeval chaos had returned; and he tells it all with the passion and intensity of one who is relating an actual personal experience. *In my vitals, my vitals, I quake, in the walls of my heart! My heart is murmuring to me; I cannot hold my peace; for my soul is listening to the trumpet-blast, the alarm of war! Ruin on ruin is cried, for all the land is ravaged; suddenly are my tents ravaged, my pavilions in a moment! How long must I see the standards, must I listen to the trumpet-blast?* (iv. 19-21). *I look at the earth, and lo, 'tis chaos: at the heavens, and their light is no more. I look at the mountains, and lo, they rock, and all the hills sway to and fro. I look, and lo, man is no more, and the birds of the air are gone, I look, and lo, the fruitful soil is wilderness, and all the cities of it are overthrown* (iv. 23-26). *At the noise of horseman and archer all the city is in flight! They are gone into the thickets, and up the rocks they have clomb: all the city is deserted* (ver. 29). His eye follows the course of devastation until it reaches Jerusalem: Jerusalem, the proud, luxurious capital, now isolated on her hills, bereft of all her daughter cities, abandoned, even betrayed, by her foreign allies. *And thou, that art doomed to destruction, what canst thou do? Though thou clothe thee in scarlet, though thou deck thee with decking of gold, though thou broaden thine eyes with henna, in vain dost thou make thyself fair; the lovers have scorned thee, thy life are they seeking.* [25] The "lovers"—the false foreigners—have turned against her in the time of her need; and the strange gods, with whom she dallied in the days of prosperity, can bring her no help. And now, while she witnesses, but cannot avert, the slaughter of her children, her shrieks ring in the prophet's ear: *A cry, as of one in travail, do I hear; pangs as of her that beareth her firstborn; the cry of the daughter of Zion, that panteth, that spreadeth out her hands: Woe's me! my soul swooneth for the slayers!* (vv. 30, 31).

Even the strong walls of Jerusalem are no sure defence; there is no safety but in flight. *Remove your goods, ye sons of Benjamin, from within Jerusalem! And in Tekoah* (as if Blaston or Blowick or Trumpington) *blow a trumpet-blast, and upon Beth-hakkérem raise a signal* (or *beacon*)! *for evil hath looked forth from the north, and mighty ruin* (vi. 1, 2). The two towns mark the route of the fugitives, making for the wilderness of the south; and the trumpet-call, and the beacon-light, muster the scattered companies at these rallying points or haltingplaces. *The beautiful and the pampered one will I destroy—the daughter of Sion.* (Perhaps: *The beautiful and the pampered woman art thou like, O daughter of Sion!* 3rd fem. sing. in *-i.*) *To her come the shepherds and their flocks; they pitch the tents upon her round about; they graze each at his own side* (*i.e.* on the ground nearest him). The figure changes, with lyric abruptness, from the fair woman, enervated by luxury (ver. 2) to the fair pasture-land, on which the nomad shepherds encamp, whose flocks soon eat the herbage down, and leave the soil stripped bare (ver. 3); and then, again, to an army beleaguering the fated city, whose cries of mutual cheer, and of impatience at all delay, the poet-prophet hears and rehearses. *Hallow ye war against her! Arise ye, let us go up* (to the assault) *at noontide! Unhappy we! the day hath turned; the shadows of eventide begin to lengthen! Arise ye, and let us go up in the night, to destroy her palaces!* (vv. 4, 5).

As a fine example of poetical expression, the discourse obviously has its own intrinsic value. The author's power to sketch with a few bold strokes the magical effect of a disquieting rumour; the vivid force with which he realizes the possibilities of ravage and ruin which are wrapped up in those vague, uncertain tidings; the pathos and passion of his lament over his stricken country, stricken as yet to his perception only; the tenderness of feeling; the subtle sweetness of language; the variety of metaphor; the light of imagination illuminating the whole with its indefinable charm; all these characteristics indicate the presence and power of a master-singer. But with Jeremiah, as with his predecessors, the poetic expression of feeling is far from being an end in itself. He writes with a purpose to which all the endowments of his gifted nature are freely and resolutely subordinated. He values his powers as a poet and orator solely as instruments which conduce to an efficient utterance of the will of Iahvah. He is hardly conscious of these gifts as such. He exists to "declare in the house of Jacob and to publish in Judah" the word of the Lord.

It is in this capacity that he now comes forward, and addresses his terrified countrymen, in terms not calculated to allay their fears with soothing suggestions of comfort and reassurance, but rather deliberately chosen with a view to heightening those fears, and deepening them to a sense of approaching judgment. For, after all, it is not the rumoured coming of the Scythian hordes that impels him to break silence. It is his consuming sense of the moral degeneracy, the spiritual degradation of his countrymen, which flames forth into burning utterance. *Whom shall I address and adjure, that they may hear? Lo, their ear is uncircumcised, and they cannot hearken; lo, the word of Iahvah hath become to them a reproach; they delight not therein. And of the fury of Iahvah I am full; I am weary of holding it in.* Then the other voice in his heart answers: *Pour thou it forth upon the child in the street, and upon the company of young men together!* (vi. 10, 11). It is the righteous indignation of an offended God that wells up from his heart, and overflows at his lips, and cries woe, irremediable woe, upon the land he loves better than his own life.

He begins with encouragement and persuasion, but his tone soon changes to denunciation and despair (iv. 3 *sq.*). *Thus hath Iahvah said to the men of Judah and to Jerusalem, Break you up the fallows, and sow not into thorns! Circumcise yourselves to Iahvah, and remove the foreskins of your heart, ye men of Judah, and ye inhabitants of Jerusalem! lest My fury come forth like fire, and burn with none to quench it, because of the evil of your doings.* Clothed with the Spirit, as Semitic speech might express it, his whole soul enveloped in a garment of heavenly light—a magical garment whose virtues impart new force as well as new light—the prophet sees straight to the heart of things, and estimates with God-given certainty the real state of his people, and the moral worth of their seeming repentance. The first measures of Josiah's reforming zeal have been inaugurated; at least within the limits of the capital, idolatry in its coarser and more repellent forms has been suppressed; there is a shew of return to the God of Israel. But the popular heart is still wedded to the old sanctuaries, and the old sensuous rites of Canaan; and, worse than this, the priests and prophets, whose centre of influence was the one great sanctuary of the Book of the Law, the temple at Jerusalem, have simply taken advantage of the religious reformation for their own purposes of selfish aggrandisement. *From the youngest to the oldest of them, they all ply the trade of greed; and from prophet to priest, they all practice lying. And they have repaired the ruin of* [*the daughter*] *of my people in light fashion, saying, It is well, it is well! though it be not well* (vi. 13, 14). The doctrine of the one legitimate sanctuary, taught with disinterested earnestness by the disciples of Isaiah, and enforced by that logic of events which had demonstrated the feebleness of the local holy places before the Assyrian destroyers, had now come to be recognised as a convenient buttress of the private gains of the Jerusalem priesthood and the venal prophets who supported their authority. The strong current of national reform had been utilized for the driving of their private machinery; and the sole outcome of the self-denying efforts and sufferings of the past appeared to be the enrichment of these grasping and unscrupulous worldlings who sat, like an incubus, upon the heart of the national church. So long as money flowed steadily into their coffers, they were eager enough to reassure the doubting, and to dispel all misgivings by their deceitful oracle that all was well. So long as the sacrifices, the principal source of the priestly revenue, abounded, and the festivals ran their yearly round, they affirmed that Iahweh was satisfied, and that no harm could befal the people of His care. This trading in things Divine, to the utter neglect of the higher obligations of the moral law, was simply appalling to the sensitive conscience of the true prophet of that degenerate age. *A strange and a startling thing it is, that is come to pass in the land. The prophets, they have prophesied in the Lie, and the priests, they tyrannise under their direction; and My people, they love it thus; and what will ye do for the issue thereof?* (v. 30, 31.) For such facts must have an issue; and the present moral and spiritual ruin of the nation points with certainty to impending ruin in the material and political sphere. The two things go together; you cannot have a decline of faith, a decay of true religion, and permanent outward prosperity; *that* issue is incompatible with the eternal laws which regulate the life and progress of humanity. One sits in the heavens, over all things from the beginning, to whom all stated worship is a hideous offence when accompanied by hypocrisy and impurity and fraud and violence in the ordinary relations of life. *What good to me is incense that cometh from Sheba, and the choice calamus from a far country? your burnt offerings* (holocausts) *are not acceptable, and your sacrifices are not sweet unto Me.* Instead of purchasing safety, they will ensure perdition: *Therefore thus hath Iahvah said: Lo, I am about to lay for this people stumblingblocks, and they shall stumble upon them, fathers and sons together, a neighbour and his friend; and they shall perish* (vi. 20 sq.).

In the early days of reform, indeed, Jeremiah himself appears to have shared in the sanguine views associated with a revival of suspended orthodoxy. The tidings of imminent danger were a surprise to him, as to the zealous worshippers who thronged the courts of the temple. So then, after all, "the burning anger of Iahvah was not turned away" by the outward tokens of penitence, by the lavish gifts of devotion; this unexpected and terrifying rumour was a call for the resumption of the garb of mourning and for the renewal of those public fasts which had marked the initial stages of reformation (iv. 8). The astonishment and the disappointment of the man assert themselves against the inspiration of the prophet, when, contemplating the helpless bewilderment of kings and princes, and the stupefaction of priests and prophets in face of the national calamities, he breaks out into remonstrance with God. *And I said, Alas, O Lord Iahvah! of a truth, Thou hast utterly beguiled this people and Jerusalem, saying, It shall be well with you; whereas the sword will reach to the life.* The allusion is to the promises contained in the Book of the Law, the reading of which had so powerfully conduced to the movement for reform. That book had been the text of the prophet-preachers, who were most active in that work; and the influence of its ideas and language upon Jeremiah himself is apparent in all his early discourses.

The prophet's faith, however, was too deeply rooted to be more than momentarily shaken; and it soon told him that the evil tidings were evidence not of unfaithfulness or caprice in Iahvah, but of the hypocrisy and corruption of Israel. With this conviction upon him, he implores the populace of the capital to substitute an inward and real for an outward and delusive purification. *Break up the fallows!* Do not dream that any adequate reformation can be superinduced upon the mere surface of life: *Sow not among thorns!* Do not for one moment believe that the word of God can take root and bear fruit in the hard soil of a heart that desires only to be secured in the possession of present enjoyments, in immunity for self-indulgence, covetousness, and oppression of the poor. *Wash thine heart from wickedness, O Jerusalem! that thou mayst be saved. How long shall the schemings of thy folly lodge within thee? For hark! one declareth from Dan, and proclaimeth folly from the hills of Ephraim* (iv. 14 *sq.*). The "folly" (*'awen*) is the foolish hankering after the gods which are nothing in the world but a reflexion of the diseased fancy of their worshippers; for it is always true that man makes his god in his own image, when he *does* make him, and does not receive the knowledge of him by revelation. It was a folly inveterate and, as it would seem, hereditary in Israel, going back to the times of the Judges, and recalling the story of Micah the Ephraimite and the Danites who stole his images. That ancient sin still cried to heaven for vengeance; for the apostatizing tendency, which it exemplified, was still active in the heart of Israel.[26] The nation had "rebelled against" the Lord, for it was foolish and had never really known Him; the people were silly children, and lacked insight; skilled only in doing wrong, and ignorant of the way to do right (iv. 22). Like the things they worshipped, they had eyes, but saw not; they had ears, but heard not. Enslaved to the empty terrors of their own imaginations, they, who cowered before dumb idols, stood untrembling in the awful presence of Him whose laws restrained the ocean within due limits, and upon whose sovereign will the fall of the rain and increase of the field depended (v. 21-24). The popular blindness to the claims of the true religion, to the inalienable rights of the God of Israel, involved a corresponding and ever-increasing blindness to the claims of universal morality, to the rights of man. Competent observers have often called attention to the remarkable influence exercised by the lower forms of heathenism in blunting the moral sense; and this influence was fully illustrated in the case of Jeremiah's contemporaries. So complete, so universal was the national decline that it seemed impossible to find one good man within the bounds of the capital. Every aim in life found illustration in those gay, crowded streets, in the bazaars, in the palaces, in the places by the gate where law was administered, except the aim of just and righteous and merciful dealing with one's neighbour. God was ignored or misconceived of, and therefore man was wronged and oppressed. Perjury, even in the Name of the God of Israel, whose eyes regard faithfulness and sincerity, and whose favour is not to be won by professions and presents; a self-hardening against both Divine chastisement and prophetic admonition; a fatal inclination to the seductions of Canaanite worship and the violations of the moral law, which that worship permitted and even encouraged as pleasing to the gods; these vices characterized the entire population of Jerusalem in that dark period. *Run ye to and fro in the streets of Jerusalem, and see now, and know, and seek ye in the broad places thereof, if ye can find a man, if indeed there be one that doeth justice, that seeketh sincerity; that I may pardon her. And if they say, By the life of Iahvah! even so they swear falsely. Iahvah, are not thine eyes toward sincerity? Thou smotest them, and they trembled not; Thou consumedst them, they refused to receive instruction; they made their faces harder than a rock, they refused to repent. And for me, I said* (methought), *These are but poor folk; they behave foolishly, because they know not the way of Iahvah, the justice* (ver. 1) *of their God: let me betake myself to the great, and speak with them; for they at least know the way of Iahvah, the justice of their God: but these with one consent had broken the yoke, had burst the bonds in sunder* (v. 1-5).

Then, as now, the debasement of the standard of life among the ruling classes was a far more threatening symptom of danger to the commonwealth than laxity of principle among the masses, who had never enjoyed the higher knowledge and more thorough training which wealth and rank, as a matter of course, confer. If the crew turn drunken and mutinous, the ship is in unquestionable peril; but if they who have the guidance of the vessel in their hands, follow the vices of those whom they should command and control, wreck and ruin are assured.

The profligacy allowed by heathenism, against which the prophets cried in vain, is forcibly depicted in the words: *Why should I pardon thee? Thy sons have forsaken Me, and have sworn by them that are no gods: though I had bound them* (to Me) *by oath,* [27] *they committed* (spiritual) *adultery, and into the house of the Fornicatress* (the idol's temple, where the harlot priestess sat for hire) *they would flock. Stallions roaming at large were they; neighing each to his neighbour's wife. Shall I not punish such offences, saith Iahvah; and shall not My soul avenge herself on such a nation as this?* The cynical contempt of justice, the fraud and violence of those who were in haste to become rich, are set forth in the following: *Among My people are found godless men; one watcheth, as birdcatchers lurk; they have set the trap, they catch men. Like a cage filled with birds, so are their houses filled with fraud: therefore they are become great, and have amassed wealth. They are become fat, they are sleek; also they pass over* (Isa. xl. 27) *cases* (Ex. xxii. 9, xxiv. 14; cf. also 1 Sam. x. 2) *of wickedness—neglect to judge heinous crimes; the cause they judge not, the cause of the fatherless, to make it succeed; and the right of the needy they vindicate not* (v. 26-28).

She is the city doomed to be punished! she is all oppression within. As a spring poureth forth its waters, so she poureth forth her wickedness; violence and oppression resound in her; before Me continually is sickness and wounds (vi. 6, 7). There would seem to be no hope for such a people and such a city. The prophet, indeed, cannot forget the claims of kindred, the thousand ties of blood and feeling that bind him to this perverse and sinful nation. Thrice, even in this dark forecast of destruction, he mitigates severity with the promise, *yet will I not make a full end.* The door is still left open, on the chance that some at least may be won to penitence. But the chance was small. The difficulty was, and the prophet's yearning tenderness towards his people could not blind him to the fact, that all the lessons of God's providence were lost upon this reprobate race: *They have belied the Lord, and said, it is not He; neither shall evil come upon us; neither shall we see sword and famine.* The prophets, they insisted, were wrong both in the significance which they attributed to occasional calamities, and in the disasters, which they announced as imminent: *The prophets will become wind, and the Word of God is not in them; so will it turn out with them.* It was, therefore, wholly futile to appeal to their better judgment against themselves: *Thus said Iahvah, Stop on the ways, and consider, and ask after the eternal paths, where is the good way, and walk therein, and find rest for your soul: and they said, We will not walk therein. And I will set over you watchmen* (the prophets); *hearken ye to the call of the trumpet!* (the warning note of prophecy) *and they said We will not hearken.* From such wilful hardness and impenitence, disdaining correction and despising reproof, God appeals to the heathen themselves, and to the dumb earth, to attest the justice of His sentence of destruction against this people: *Therefore, hear, O ye nations, and know, and testify what is among them! Hear, O earth! Lo, I am about to bring evil upon this people, the fruit of their own devisings; for unto My words they have not hearkened, and as for Mine instruction, they have rejected it.* Their doom was inevitable, for it was the natural and necessary consequence of their own doings: *Thine own way and thine Own deeds have brought about these evils for thee; this is thine own evil; verily, it is bitter, verily, it reacheth unto thine heart.* The discourse ends with a despairing glance at the moral reprobation of Israel. *An assayer did I make thee among My people, a refiner* (reading *mecārēf*, Mal. iii. 2, 3), *that thou mightest know and assay their kind* (lit. *way*). Jeremiah's call had been to "sit as a refiner and purifier of silver" in the name of his God: in other words, to separate the good elements from the bad in Israel, and to gather around himself the nucleus of a people "prepared for Iahvah." But his work had been vain. In vain had the prophetic fire burnt within him; in vain had the vehemency of the spirit fanned the flame; the Divine word—that solvent of hearts—had been expended in vain; no good metal could come of an ore so utterly base. *They are all the worst* (1 Ki. xx. 43) *of rebels* (or, *deserters to the rebels*), *going about with slander; they are brass and iron; they all deal corruptly.* [28] *The bellows blow; the lead* (used for fining the ore) *is consumed by the fire; in vain do they go on refining* (or, *does the refiner refine* [29]); *and the wicked are not separated. Refuse silver are they called, for Iahvah hath refused them.*

V
POPULAR AND TRUE RELIGION

Jeremiah vii.-x., xxvi.

In the four chapters which we are now to consider we have what is plainly a finished whole. The only possible exception (x. 1-16) shall be considered in its place. The historical occasion of the introductory prophecy (vii. 1-15), and the immediate effect of its delivery, are recorded at length in the twenty-sixth chapter of the book, so that in this instance we are happily not left to the uncertainties of conjecture. We are there told that it was *in the beginning of the reign of Jehoiakim son of Josiah, king of Judah,* that Jeremiah received the command to stand in the fore-court of Iahvah's house, and to declare *to all the cities of Judah that were come to worship* there, that unless they repented and gave ear to Iahvah's servants the prophets, He would make the temple like Shiloh, and Jerusalem itself a curse to all the nations of the earth. The substance of the oracle is there given in briefer form than here, as was natural, where the writer's object was principally to relate the issue of it as it affected himself. In neither case is it probable that we have a verbatim report of what was actually said, though the leading thoughts of his address are, no doubt, faithfully recorded by the prophet in the more elaborate composition (chap. vii.). Trifling variations between the two accounts must not, therefore, be pressed.

Internal evidence suggests that this oracle was delivered at a time of grave public anxiety, such as marked the troubled period after the death of Josiah, and the early years of Jehoiakim. *All Judah, or all the cities of Judah* (xxvi. 2), that is to say, the people of the country towns as well as the citizens of Jerusalem, were crowding into the temple to supplicate their God (vii. 2). This indicates an extraordinary occasion, a national emergency affecting all alike. Probably a public fast and humiliation had been ordered by the authorities, on the reception of some threatening news of invasion. "The opening paragraphs of the address are marked by a tone of controlled earnestness, by an unadorned plainness of statement, without passion, without exclamation, apostrophe, or rhetorical device of any kind; which betokens the presence of a danger which spoke too audibly to the general ear to require artificial heightening in the statement of it. The position of affairs spoke for itself" (Hitzig). The very words with which the prophet opens his message, *Thus said Iahvah Sabaoth, the God of Israel, Make good your ways and your doings, that I may cause you to dwell (permanently) in this place!* (ver. 3, cf. ver. 7) prove that the anxiety which agitated the popular heart and drove it to seek consolation in religious observances, was an anxiety about their political stability, about the permanence of their possession of the fair land of promise. The use of the expression *Iahvah Sabaoth* "Iahvah (the God) of Hosts" is also significant, as indicating that war was what the nation feared; while the prophet reminds them thus that all earthly powers, even the armies of heathen invaders, are controlled and directed by the God of Israel for His own sovereign purposes. A particular crisis is further suggested by the warning: *Trust ye not to the lying words, 'The Temple of Iahvah, the Temple of Iahvah, the Temple of Iahvah, is this!'* The fanatical confidence in the inviolability of the temple, which Jeremiah thus deprecates, implies a time of public danger. A hundred years before this time the temple and the city had really come through a period of the gravest peril, justifying in the most palpable and unexpected manner the assurances of the prophet Isaiah. This was remembered now, when another crisis seemed imminent, another trial of strength between the God of Israel and the gods of the heathen. Only part of the prophetic teachings of Isaiah had rooted itself in the popular mind — the part most agreeable to it. The sacrosanct inviolability of the temple, and of Jerusalem for its sake, was an idea readily appropriated and eagerly cherished. It was forgotten that all depended on the will and purposes of Iahvah himself; that the heathen might be the instruments with which He executed his designs, and that an invasion of Judah might mean, not an approaching trial of strength between His omnipotence and the impotency of the false gods, but the judicial outpouring of His righteous wrath upon His own rebellious people.

Jeremiah, therefore, affirms that the popular confidence is ill-founded; that his countrymen are lulled in a false security; and he enforces his point, by a plain exposure of the flagrant offences, which render their worship a mockery of God.

Again, it may be supposed that the startling word, *Add your burnt-offerings to your* (ordinary) *offerings, and eat the flesh (of them)* (vii. 21), implies a time of unusual activity in the matter of honouring the God of Israel with the more costly offerings of which the worshippers did not partake, but which were wholly consumed on the altar; which fact also might point to a season of special danger.

And, lastly, the references to taking refuge behind the walls of 'defenced cities' (viii. 14; x. 17), as we know that the Rechabites and doubtless most of the rural populace took refuge in Jerusalem on the approach of the third and last Chaldean expedition, seem to prove that the occasion of the prophecy was the first Chaldean invasion, which ended in the submission of Jehoiakim to the yoke of Babylon (2 Kings xxiv. 1). Already the northern frontier had experienced the destructive onslaught of the invaders, and rumour announced that they might soon be expected to arrive before the walls of Jerusalem (viii. 16, 17).

The only other historical occasion which can be suggested with any plausibility is the Scythian invasion of Syria-Palestine, to which the previous discourse was assigned. This would fix the date of the prophecy at some point between the thirteenth and the eighteenth years of Josiah (b.c. 629-624). But the arguments for this view do not seem to be very strong in themselves, and they certainly do not explain the essential identity of the oracle summarized in chap. xxvi. 1-6, with that of vii. 1-15. The "undisguised references to the prevalence of idolatry in Jerusalem itself (vii. 17; cf. 30, 31), and the unwillingness of the people to listen to the prophet's teaching, (vii. 27)," are quite as well accounted for by supposing a religious or rather an irreligious reaction under Jehoiakim—which is every way probable considering the bad character of that king (2 Kings xxiii. 37; Jer. xxii. 13 sqq.), and the serious blow inflicted upon the reforming party by the death of Josiah; as by assuming that the prophecy belongs to the years before the extirpation of idolatry in the eighteenth year of the latter sovereign.

And now let us take a rapid glance at the salient points of this remarkable utterance. The people are standing in the outer court, with their faces turned toward the court of the priests, in which stood the holy house itself (Ps. v. 7). The prophetic speaker stands facing them, "in the gate of the Lord's house," the entry of the upper or inner court, the place whence Baruch was afterwards to read another of his oracles to the people (xxxvi. 10). Standing here, as it were between his audience and the throne of Iahvah, Jeremiah acts as visible mediator between them and their God. His message to the worshippers who throng the courts of Iahvah's sanctuary is not one of approval. He does not congratulate them upon their manifest devotion, upon the munificence of their offerings, upon their ungrudging and unstinted readiness to meet an unceasing drain upon their means. His message is a surprise, a shock to their self-satisfaction, an alarm to their slumbering consciences, a menace of wrath and destruction upon them and their holy place. His very first word is calculated to startle their self-righteousness, their misplaced faith in the merit of their worship and service. *Amend your ways and your doings!* Where was the need of amendment? they might ask. Were they not at that moment engaged in a function most grateful to Iahvah? Were they not keeping the law of the sacrifices, and were not the Levitical priesthood ministering in their order, and receiving their due share of the offerings which poured into the temple day by day? Was not all this honour enough to satisfy the most exacting of deities? Perhaps it was, had the deity in question been merely as one of the gods of Canaan. So much lip-service, so many sacrifices and festivals, so much joyous revelling in the sanctuary, might be supposed to have sufficiently appeased one of the common Baals, those half-womanish phantoms of deity whose delight was imagined to be in feasting and debauchery. Nay, so much zeal might have propitiated the savage heart of a Molech. But the God of Israel was not as these, nor one of these; though His ancient people were too apt to conceive thus of Him, and certain modern critics have unconsciously followed in their wake.

Let us see what it was that called so loudly for amendment, and then we may become more fully aware of the gulf that divided the God of Israel from the idols of Canaan, and His service from all other service. It is important to keep this radical difference steadily before our minds, and to deepen the impression of it, in days when the effort is made by every means to confuse Iahvah with the gods of heathendom, and to rank the religion of Israel with the lower surrounding systems.

Jeremiah accuses his countrymen of flagrant transgression of the universal laws of morality. Theft, murder, adultery, perjury, fraud and covetousness, slander and lying and treachery (vii. 9, ix. 3-8), are charged upon these zealous worshippers by a man who lived amongst them, and knew them well, and could be contradicted at once if his charges were false.

He tells them plainly that, in virtue of their frequenting it, the temple is become a den of robbers.

And this trampling upon the common rights of man has its counterpart and its climax in treason against God, in *burning incense to the Baal, and walking after other gods whom they know not* (vii. 9); in an open and shameless attempt to combine the worship of the God who had from the outset revealed Himself to their prophets as a "jealous," *i.e.*, an exclusive God, with the worship of shadows who had not revealed themselves at all, and could not be "known," because devoid of all character and real existence. They thus ignored the ancient covenant which had constituted them a nation (vii. 23).

In the cities of Judah, in the streets of the very capital, the cultus of Ashtōreth, the Queen of Heaven, the voluptuous Canaanite goddess of love and dalliance, was busily practised by whole families together, in deadly provocation of the God of Israel. The first and great commandment said, Thou shalt love Iahvah thy God, and Him only shalt thou serve. And they loved and served and followed and sought after and worshipped the sun and the moon and the host of heaven, the objects adored by the nation that was so soon to enslave them (viii. 2). Not only did a worldly, covetous and sensual priesthood connive in the restoration of the old superstitions which associated other gods with Iahvah, and set up idol symbols and altars within the precincts of His temple, as Manasseh had done (2 Kings xxi. 4-5); they went further than this in their "syncretism," or rather in their perversity, their spiritual blindness, their wilful misconception of the God revealed to their fathers. They actually confounded Him—the Lord *who exercised loving kindness, justice, and righteousness, and delighted in* the exhibition of these qualities by His worshippers (ix. 24)—with the dark and cruel sun-god of the Ammonites. They *rebuilt the high-places of the Tophet, in the valley of ben Hinnom,* on the north side of Jerusalem, *to burn their sons and their daughters in the fire;* if by means so revolting to natural affection they might win back the favour of heaven—means which Iahvah *commanded not, neither came they into His mind* (vii. 31). Such fearful and desperate expedients were doubtless first suggested by the false prophets and priests in the times of national adversity under king Manasseh. They harmonized only too well with the despair of a people, who saw in a long succession of political disasters the token of Iahvah's unforgiving wrath. That these dreadful rites were not a "survival" in Israel, seems to follow from the horror which they excited in the allied armies of the two kingdoms, when the king of Moab, in the extremity of the siege, offered his eldest son as a burnt-offering on the wall of his capital before the eyes of the besiegers. So appalled were the Israelite forces by this spectacle of a father's despair, that they at once raised the blockade, and retreated homeward (2 Kings iii. 27). It is probable, then, that the darker and bloodier aspects of heathen worship were of only recent appearance among the Hebrews, and that the rites of Molech had not been at all frequent or familiar, until the long and harassing conflict with Assyria broke the national spirit and inclined the people, in their trouble, to welcome the suggestion that costlier sacrifices were demanded, if Iahvah was to be propitiated and His wrath appeased. Such things were not done, apparently, in Jeremiah's time; he mentions them as the crown of the nation's past offences; as sins that still cried to heaven for vengeance, and would surely entail it, because the same spirit of idolatry which had culminated in these excesses, still lived and was active in the popular heart. It is the persistence in sins of the same character which involves our drinking to the dregs the cup of punishment for the guilty past. The dark catalogue of forgotten offences witnesses against us before the Unseen Judge, and is only obliterated by the tears of a true repentance, and by the new evidence of a change of heart and life. Then, as in some palimpsest, the new record covers and conceals the old; and it is only if we fatally relapse, that the erased writing of our misdeeds becomes visible again before the eye of Heaven. Perhaps also the prophet mentions these abominations because at the time he saw around him unequivocal tendencies to the renewal of them. Under the patronage or with the connivance of the wicked king Jehoiakim, the reactionary party may have begun to set up again the altars thrown down by Josiah, while their religious leaders advocated both by speech and writing a return to the abolished cultus. At all events, this supposition gives special point to the emphatic assertion of Jeremiah, that Iahvah had *not* commanded nor even thought of such hideous rites. The reference to the false labours of the scribes (chap. viii. 8) lends colour to this view. It may be that some of the interpreters of the sacred law actually anticipated certain writers of our own day, in putting this terrible gloss upon the precept, *The firstborn of thy sons shalt thou give unto Me* (Ex. xxii. 29).

The people of Judah were misled, but they were willingly misled. When Jeremiah declares to them, *Lo, ye are trusting, for your part, upon the words of delusion, so that ye gain no good!* (vii. 8) it is perhaps not so much the smooth prophecies of the false prophets as the fatal attitude of the popular mind, out of which those misleading oracles grew, and which in turn they aggravated, that the speaker deprecates. He warns them that an absolute trust in the *præsentia Numinis* is delusive; a trust, cherished like theirs independently of the condition of its justification, viz., a walk pleasing to God. *What! will ye break all My laws, and then come and stand with polluted hands before Me in this house* (Isa. i. 15), *which is named after Me 'Iahvah's House'*, (Isa. iv. 1), *and reassure yourselves with the thought, We are absolved from the consequences of all these abominations?* (vv. 9-10. Lit. *We are saved, rescued, secured, with regard to having done all these abominations*: cf. ii. 35. But perhaps, with Ewald, we should point the Hebrew term differently, and read, "Save us!" *to do all these abominations*, as if that were the express object of their petition, which would really ensue, if their prayer were granted: a fine irony. For the form of the verb, cf. Ezek. xiv. 14.) They thought their formal devotions were more than enough to counterbalance any breaches of the decalogue; they laid that flattering unction to their souls. They could make it up with God for setting His moral law at nought. It was merely a question of compensation. They did not see that the moral law is as immutable as laws physical; and that the consequences of violating or keeping it are as inseparable from it as pain from a blow, or death from poison. They did not see that the moral law is simply the law of man's health and wealth, and that the transgression of it is sorrow and suffering and death.

"If men like you," argues the prophet, "dare to tread these courts, it must be because you believe it a proper thing to do. But that belief implies that you hold the temple to be something other than what it really is; that you see no incongruity in making the House of Iahvah a meeting-place of murderers (*spelunca latronum*: Matt. xxi. 13). That you have yourselves made it, in the full view of Iahvah, whose seeing does not rest there, but involves results, such as the present crisis of public affairs; the national danger is proof that He has seen your heinous misdoings." For Iahvah's seeing brings a vindication of right, and vengeance upon evil (2 Chron. xxiv. 22; Ex. iii. 7). He is the watchman that never slumbers nor sleeps; the eternal Judge, Who ever upholds the law of righteousness in the affairs of man, nor suffers the slightest infringement of that law to go unpunished. And this unceasing watchfulness, this perpetual dispensation of justice, is really a manifestation of Divine mercy; for the purpose of it is to save the human race from self-destruction, and to raise it ever higher in the scale of true well-being, which essentially consists in the knowledge of God and obedience to His laws.

Jeremiah gives his audience further ground for conviction. He points to a striking instance in which conduct like theirs had involved results such as his warning holds before them. He establishes the probability of chastisement by an historical parallel. He offers them, so to speak, ocular demonstration of his doctrine. *I also, lo, I have seen, saith Iahvah!* Your eyes are fixed on the temple; so are Mine, but in a different way. You see a national palladium; *I* see a desecrated sanctuary, a shrine polluted and profaned. This distinction between God's view and yours is certain: *for, go ye now to My place which was at Shiloh, where I caused My Name to abide at the outset* (of your settlement in Canaan); *and see the thing that I have done to it, because of the wickedness of My people Israel* (the northern kingdom). *There* is the proof that Iahvah seeth not as man seeth; there, in that dismantled ruin, in that historic sanctuary of the more powerful kingdom of Ephraim, once visited by thousands of worshippers like Jerusalem to-day, now deserted and desolate, a monument of Divine wrath.

The reference is not to the tabernacle, the sacred Tent of the Wanderings, which was first set up at Nob (1 Sam. xxi. 22) and then removed to Gibeon (2 Chron. i. 3), but obviously to a building more or less like the temple, though less magnificent. The place and its sanctuary had doubtless been ruined in the great catastrophe, when the kingdom of Samaria fell before the power of Assyria (721 b.c.).

In the following words (vv. 13-15) the example is applied. *And now—* stating the conclusion—*because of your having done all these deeds* (*saith Iahvah,* LXX. omits), *and because I spoke unto you* (*early and late,* LXX. omits), *and ye hearkened not, and I called you and ye answered not* (Prov. i. 24): *I will do unto the house upon which My Name is called, wherein ye are trusting, and unto the place which I gave to you and to your fathers—as I did unto Shiloh.*

Some might think that if the city fell, the holy house would escape, as was thought by many like-minded fanatics when Jerusalem was beleaguered by the Roman armies seven centuries later: but Jeremiah declares that the blow will fall upon both alike; and to give greater force to his words, he makes the judgment begin at the house of God. (The Hebrew reader will note the dramatic effect of the disposition of the accents. The principal pause is placed upon the word "fathers," and the reader is to halt in momentary suspense upon that word, before he utters the awful three which close the verse: *as I—did to—Shiloh.* The Massorets were masters of this kind of emphasis.)

And I will cast you away from My Presence, as I cast (*all*: LXX. omits[30]) *your kinsfolk, all the posterity of Ephraim* (2 Kings xvii. 20). Away from My Presence: far beyond the bounds of that holy land where I have revealed Myself to priests and prophets, and where My sanctuary stands; into a land where heathenism reigns, and the knowledge of God is not; into the dark places of the earth, that lie under the blighting shadow of superstition, and are enveloped in the moral midnight of idolatry. *Projiciam vos a facie mea.* The knowledge and love of God—heart and mind ruled by the sense of purity and tenderness and truth and right united in an Ineffable Person, and enthroned upon the summit of the universe—these are light and life for man; where these are, there is His Presence. They who are so endowed behold the face of God, in Whom is no darkness at all. Where these spiritual endowments are non-existent; where mere power, or superhuman force, is the highest thought of God to which man has attained; where there is no clear sense of the essential holiness and love of the Divine Nature; there the world of man lies in darkness that may be felt; there bloody rites prevail; there harsh oppression and shameless vices reign: for the dark places of the earth are full of the habitations of cruelty.

And thou, pray thou not for this people (xviii. 20), *and lift not up for them outcry nor prayer, and urge not Me, for I hear thee not. Seest thou not what they do in the cities of Judah and in the streets of Jerusalem? The children gather sticks, and the fathers light the fire, and the women knead dough, to make sacred buns* (xliv. 19) *for the Queen of Heaven, and to pour libations to other gods, in order to grieve Me* (Deut. xxxii. 16, 21). *Is it Me that they grieve? saith Iahvah; is it not themselves* (rather), *in regard to the shame of their own faces* (16-19).

From one point of view, all human conduct may be said to be *indifferent* to God; He is αὐτάρκης, self-sufficing, and needs not our praises, our love, our obedience, any more than He needed the temple ritual and the sacrifices of bulls and goats. Man can neither benefit nor injure God; he can only affect his own fortunes in this world and the next, by rebellion against the laws upon which his welfare depends, or by a careful observance of them. In this sense, it is true that wilful idolatry, that treason against God, does not "provoke" or "grieve" the Immutable One. Men do such things to their own sole hurt, to the shame of their own faces: that is, the punishment will be the painful realization of the utter groundlessness of their confidence, of the folly of their false trust; the mortification of disillusion, when it is too late. That Jeremiah should have expressed himself thus is sufficient answer to those who pretend that the habitual anthropomorphism of the prophetic discourses is anything more than a mere accident of language and an accommodation to ordinary style.

In another sense, of course, it is profoundly true to say that human sin provokes and grieves the Lord. God is Love; and love may be pained to its depths by the fault of the beloved, and stirred to holy indignation at the disclosure of utter unworthiness and ingratitude. Something corresponding to these emotions of man may be ascribed, with all reverence, to the Inscrutable Being who creates man "in His own image," that is, endowed with faculties capable of aspiring towards *Him*, and receiving the knowledge of His being and character.

Pray not thou for this people ... for I hear thee not! Jeremiah was wont to intercede for his people (xi. 14, xviii. 20, xv. 1; cf. 1 Sam. xii. 23). The deep pathos which marks his style, the minor key in which almost all his public utterances are pitched, proves that the fate which he saw impending over his country, grieved him to the heart. "Our sweetest songs are those which tell of saddest thought;" and this is eminently true of Jeremiah. A profound melancholy had fallen like a cloud upon his soul; he had seen the future, fraught as it was with suffering and sorrow, despair and overthrow, slaughter and bitter servitude; a picture in which images of terror crowded one upon another, under a darkened sky, from which no ray of blessed hope shot forth, but only the lightnings of wrath and extermination. Doubtless his prayers were frequent, alive with feeling, urgent, imploring, full of the convulsive energy of expiring hope. But in the midst of his strong crying and tears, there arose from the depths of his consciousness the conviction that all was in vain. *Pray not thou for this people, for I will not hear thee.* The thought stood before him, sharp and clear as a command; the unuttered sound of it rang in his ears, like the voice of a destroying angel, a messenger of doom, calm as despair, sure as fate. He knew it was the voice of God.

In the history of nations as in the lives of individuals there are times when repentance, even if possible, would be too late to avert the evils which long periods of misdoing have called from the abyss to do their penal and retributive work. Once the dike is undermined, no power on earth can hold back the flood of waters from the defenceless lands beneath. And when a nation's sins have penetrated and poisoned all social and political relations, and corrupted the very fountains of life, you cannot avert the flood of ruin that must come, to sweep away the tainted mass of spoiled humanity; you cannot avert the storm that must break to purify the air, and make it fit for men to breathe again.

Therefore—because of the national unfaithfulness—*thus said the Lord Iahvah, Lo, Mine anger and My fury are being poured out toward this place—upon the men, and upon the cattle, and upon the trees of the field, and upon the fruit of the ground; and it will burn, and not be quenched!* (vii. 20). The havoc wrought by war, the harrying and slaying of man and beast, the felling of fruit trees and firing of the vineyards, are intended; but not so as to exclude the ravages of pestilence and droughts (chap. xiv.) and famine. All these evils are manifestations of the wrath of Iahvah. Cattle and trees and "the fruit of the ground," *i.e.* of the cornlands and vineyards, are to share in the general destruction (cf. Hos. iv. 3), not, of course, as partakers of man's guilt, but only by way of aggravating his punishment. The final phrase is worthy of consideration, because of its bearing upon other passages. *It will burn and not be quenched,* or *it will burn unquenchably.* The meaning is not that the Divine wrath once kindled will go on burning for ever; but that once kindled, no human or other power will be able to extinguish it, until it has accomplished its appointed work of destruction.

Thus said Iahvah Sabaoth, the God of Israel: Your holocausts add ye to your common sacrifices, and eat ye flesh! that is, Eat flesh in abundance, eat your fill of it! Stint not yourselves by devoting any portion of your offerings wholly to Me. I am as indifferent to your "burnt-offerings," your more costly and splendid gifts, as to the ordinary sacrifices, over which you feast and make merry with your friends (1 Sam. i. 4, 13). The holocausts which you are now burning on the altar before Me will not avail to alter My settled purpose. *For I spake not with your fathers, nor commanded them, in the day that I brought them forth out of the land of Egypt, concerning matters of holocaust and sacrifice, but this matter commanded I them, "Hearken ye unto My voice, so become I God to you, and you—ye shall become to Me a people; and walk ye in all the way that I shall command you, that it may go well with you!"* (22-23) cf. Deut. vi. 3. Those who believe that the entire priestly legislation as we now have it in the Pentateuch is the work of Moses, may be content to find in this passage of Jeremiah no more than an extreme antithetical expression of the truth that to obey is better than sacrifice. There can be no question that from the outset of its history, Israel, in common with all the Semitic nations, gave outward expression to its religious ideas in the form of animal sacrifice. Moses cannot have originated the institution, he found it already in vogue, though he may have regulated the details of it. Even in the Pentateuch, the term "sacrifice" is nowhere explained; the general understanding of the meaning of it is taken for granted (see Ex. xii. 27, xxiii. 18). Religious customs are of immemorial use, and it is impossible in most cases to specify the period of their origin. But while it is certain that the institution of sacrifice was of extreme antiquity in Israel as in other ancient peoples, it is equally certain, from the plain evidence of their extant writings, that the prophets before the Exile attached no independent value either to it or to any other part of the ritual of the temple. We have already seen how Jeremiah could speak of the most venerable of all the symbols of the popular faith (iii. 16). Now he affirms that the traditional rules for the burnt-offerings and other sacrifices were not matters of special Divine institution, as was popularly supposed at the time. The reference to the Exodus may imply that already in his day there were written narratives which asserted the contrary; that the first care of the Divine Saviour after He had led His people through the sea was to provide them with an elaborate system of ritual and sacrifice, identical with that which prevailed in Jeremiah's day. The important verse already quoted (viii. 8) seems to glance at such pious fictions of the popular religious teachers: *How say ye, We are wise, and the instruction* (A. V. "law") *of Iahvah is with us? But behold for lies hath it wrought—the lying pen of the scribes!*

It is, indeed, difficult to see how Jeremiah or any of his predecessors could have done otherwise than take for granted the established modes of public worship, and the traditional holy places. The prophets do not seek to alter or abolish the externals of religion as such; they are not so unreasonable as to demand that stated rites and traditional sanctuaries should be disregarded, and that men should worship in the spirit only, without the aid of outward symbolism of any sort, however innocent and appropriate to its object it might seem. They knew very well that rites and ceremonies were necessary to public worship; what they protested against was the fatal tendency of their time to make these the whole of religion, to suppose that Iahvah's claims could be satisfied by a due performance of these, without regard to those higher moral requirements of His law which the ritual worship might fitly have symbolized but could not rightly supersede. It was not a question with Hosea, Amos, Micah, Isaiah, Jeremiah, whether or not Iahvah could be better honoured with or without temples and priests and sacrifices. The question was whether these traditional institutions actually served as an outward expression of that devotion to Him and His holy law, of that righteousness and holiness of life, which is the only true worship, or whether they were looked upon as in themselves comprising the whole of necessary religion. Since the people took this latter view, Jeremiah declares that their system of public worship is futile.

Hearken unto My voice: not as giving regulations about the ritual, but as inculcating moral duty by the prophets, as is explained immediately (ver. 25), and as is clear also from the statement that *they walked in the schemes of their own evil heart* [omit: *in the stubbornness*, with LXX., and read *mô˙ açôth* stat. constr.], *and fell to the rear and not the front.* As they did not advance in the knowledge and love of the spiritual God, who was seeking to lead them by His prophets, from Moses downwards (Deut. xviii. 15), they steadily retrograded and declined in moral worth, until they had become hopelessly corrupt and past correction. (Lit. *and they became back and not face*, which may mean, they turned their backs upon Iahvah and His instruction.) This steady progress in evil is indicated by the words, *and they hardened their neck, they did worse than their fathers* (ver. 26). It is implied that this was the case with each successive generation, and the view of Israel's history thus expressed is in perfect harmony with common experience. Progress, one way or the other, is the law of character; if we do not advance in goodness, we go back, or, what is the same thing, we advance in evil.

Finally, the prophet is warned that his mission also must fail, like that of his predecessors, unless indeed the second clause of ver. 27, which is omitted by the Septuagint, be really an interpolation. At all events, the failure is implied if not expressed, for he is to pronounce a sentence of reprobation upon his people. *And thou shalt speak all these words unto them [and they will not hearken unto thee, and thou shalt call unto them, and they will not answer thee: LXX. omits]. And thou shalt say unto them, This is the nation that hearkened not unto the voice of Iahvah its God, and received not correction: Good faith is perished and cut off from their mouth* (cf. ix. 3 *sq.*). The charge is remarkable. It is one which Jeremiah reiterates: see ver. 9, vi. 13, viii. 5, ix. 3 *sqq.*, xii. 1. His fellow-countrymen are at once deceivers and deceived. They have no regard for truth and honour in their mutual dealings; grasping greed and lies and trickery stamp their everyday intercourse with each other; and covetousness and fraud equally characterise the behaviour of their religious leaders. Where truth is not prized for its own sake, there debased ideas of God and lax conceptions of morality creep in and spread. Only he who loves truth comes to the light; and only he who does God's will sees that truth is divine. False belief and false living in turn beget each other; and as a matter of experience it is often impossible to say which was antecedent to the other.

In the closing section of this first part of his long address (vv. 29-viii. 3), Jeremiah apostrophizes the country, bidding her bewail her imminent ruin. *Shear thy tresses* (coronal of long hair) *and cast them away, and lift upon the bare hills a lamentation!*—sing a dirge over thy departed glory and thy slain children, upon those unhallowed mountain-tops which were the scene of thine apostasies (iii. 21); *for Iahvah hath rejected and forsaken the generation of His wrath.* The hopeless tone of this exclamation (cf. also vv. 15, 16, 20) seems to agree better with the times of Jehoiakim, when it had become evident to the prophet that amendment was beyond hope, than with the years prior to Josiah's reformation. His own contemporaries are 'the generation of Iahvah's wrath,' *i.e.* upon which His wrath is destined to be poured out, for the day of grace is past and gone; and this, because of the desecration of the temple itself by such kings as Ahaz and Manasseh, but especially because of the horrors of the child-sacrifices in the valley of ben Hinnom (2 Kings xvi. 3, xxi. 3-6), which those kings had been the first to introduce in Judah. *Therefore behold days are coming, saith Iahvah, and it shall no more be called the Tophet* (an obscure term, probably meaning something like *Pyre* or *Burningplace*: cf. the Persian *tab-idan* "to burn," and the Greek θάπτω, ταφ-εῖν "to bury," strictly "to burn" a corpse; also τύφω, "to smoke," Sanskrit *dhûp*: to suppose a reproachful name like "Spitting" = "Object of loathing," is clearly against the context: the honourable name is to be exchanged for one of dishonour), *and the Valley of ben Hinnom, but the Valley of Slaughter, and people shall bury in [the] Tophet for want of room (elsewhere)!* A great battle is contemplated, as is evident also from Deut. xxviii. 25, 26, the latter verse being immediately quoted by the prophet (ver. 33). The Tophet will be defiled for ever by being made a burial place; but many of the fallen will be left unburied, a prey to the vulture and the jackal. In that fearful time, all sounds of joyous life will cease in the cities of Judah and in the capital itself, *for the land will become a desolation.* And the scornful enemy will not be satisfied with wreaking his vengeance upon the living; he will insult the dead, by breaking into the sepulchres of the kings and grandees, the priests and prophets and people, and haling their corpses forth to lie rotting in face of the sun, moon and stars, which they had so sedulously worshipped in their lifetime, but which will be powerless to protect their dead bodies from this shameful indignity. And as for the survivors, *death will be preferred to life in the case of all the remnant that remain of this evil tribe, in all the places whither I shall have driven them, saith Iahvah Sabaoth* (omit the second *that remain*, with LXX. as an accidental repetition from the preceding line, and as breaking the construction). The prophet has reached the conviction that Judah will be driven into banishment; but the details of the destruction which he contemplates are obviously of an imaginative and rhetorical character. It is, therefore, superfluous to ask whether a great battle was actually fought afterwards in the valley of ben Hinnom, and whether the slain apostates of Judah were buried there in heaps, and whether the conquerors violated the tombs. Had the Chaldeans or any of their allies done this last, in search of treasure for instance, we should expect to find some notice of it in the historical chapters of Jeremiah. But it was probably known well enough to the surrounding peoples that the Jews were not in the habit of burying treasure in their tombs. The prophet's threat however, curiously corresponds to what Josiah is related to have done at Bethel and elsewhere, by way of irreparably polluting the high places (2 Kings xxiii. 16 *sqq.*); and it is probable that his recollection of that event, which he may himself have witnessed, determined the form of Jeremiah's language here.[31]

In the second part of this great discourse (viii. 4-23) we have a fine development of thoughts which have already been advanced in the opening piece, after the usual manner of Jeremiah. The first half (or strophe) is mainly concerned with the sins of the nation (vv. 4-13), the second with a despairing lament over the punishment (14-23 = ix. 1). *And thou shalt say unto them: Thus said Iahvah, Do men fall and not rise again? Doth a man turn back, and not return? Why doth Jerusalem make this people to turn back with an eternal* (or perfect, utter, absolute) *turning back? Why clutch they deceit, refuse to return?* (The LXX. omits "Jerusalem," which is perhaps only a marginal gloss. We should then have to read בבוש *shobab* for הבבוש *shobebah*, as "this people" is masc. The He has been written twice by inadvertence. The verb, however, is transitive in l. 19; Isa. xlvii. 10, etc.; and I find no certain instance of the intrans. form besides Ezek. xxxviii. 8, participle.) *I listened and heard; they speak not aright* (Ex. x. 29; Isa. xvi. 6); *not a man repenteth over his evil, saying* (or thinking), *"What have I done?" They all* (lit. *all of him, i.e.* the people) *turn back into their courses* (plur. Heb. text; sing. Heb. marg.), *like the rushing horse into the battle.*

There is something unnatural in this obstinate persistence in evil. If a man happens to fall he does not remain on the ground, but quickly rises to his feet again; and if he turn back on his way for some reason or other, he will usually return to that way again. There is a play on the word 'turn back' or 'return,' like that in iii. 12, 14. The term is first used in the sense of turning back or away from Iahvah, and then in that of returning to Him, according to its metaphorical meaning "to repent." Thus the import of the question is: Is it natural to apostatize and never to repent of it? (Perhaps we should rather read, after the analogy of iii. 1, "Doth a man *go away* (הֲלֵיָה) on a journey, and not return?")

Others interpret: *Doth a man return, and not return?* That is, if he return, he does it, and does not stop midway; whereas Judah only pretends to repent, and does not really do so. This, however, does not agree with the parallel member, nor with the following similar questions.

It is very noticeable how thoroughly the prophets, who, after all, were the greatest of practical moralists, identify religion with right aims and right conduct. The beginning of evil courses is turning away from Iahvah; the beginning of reform is turning back to Iahvah. For Iahvah's character as revealed to the prophets is the ideal and standard of ethical perfection; He does and delights in love, justice and equity (ix. 23). If a man look away from that ideal, if he be content with a lower standard than the Will and Law of the All-Perfect, then and thereby he inevitably sinks in the scale of morality. The prophets are not troubled by the idle question of medieval schoolmen and sceptical moderns. It never occurred to them to ask the question whether God is good because God wills it, or whether God wills good because it is good. The dilemma is, in truth, no better than a verbal puzzle, if we allow the existence of a personal Deity. For the idea of God is the idea of a Being who is absolutely good, the *only* Being who is such; perfect goodness is understood to be realized nowhere else but in God. It is part of His essence and conception; it is the aspect under which the human mind apprehends Him. To suppose goodness existing apart from Him, as an independent object which He may choose or refuse, is to deal in empty abstractions. We might as well ask whether convex can exist apart from concave in nature, or motion apart from a certain rate of speed. The human spirit can apprehend God in His moral perfections, because it is, at however vast a distance, akin to Him—a *divinæ particula auræ*; and it can strive towards those perfections by help of the same grace which reveals them. The prophets know of no other origin or measure of moral endeavour than that which Iahvah makes known to them. In the present instance, the charge which Jeremiah makes against his contemporaries is a radical falsehood, insincerity, faithlessness: *they clutch* or *cling to deceit, they speak what is not right* or *honest, straightforward* (Gen. xlii. 11, 19). Their treason to God and their treachery to their fellows are opposite sides of the same fact. Had they been true to Iahvah, that is, to His teachings through the higher prophets and their own consciences, they would have been true to one another. The forbearing love of God, His tender solicitude to hear and save, are illustrated by the words: *I listened and heard ... not a man repented over his evil, saying, What have I done?* (The feeling of the stricken conscience could hardly be more aptly expressed than by this brief question.) But in vain does the Heavenly Father wait for the accents of penitence and contrition: *they all return*—go back again and again (Ps. xxiii. 6)—*into their own race or courses, like a horse rushing* (lit. *pouring forth*: of rushing waters, Ps. lxxviii. 20) *into the battle*. The eagerness with which they follow their own wicked desires, the recklessness with which they "give their sensual race the rein," in set defiance of God, and wilful oblivion of consequences, is finely expressed by the simile of the warhorse rushing in headlong eagerness into the fray (Job xxxix. 25). *Also* (or *even*) *the stork in the heavens knoweth her appointed times, and turtledove, swift and crane observe the season of their coming; but My people know not the ordinance of Iahvah*—what He has willed and declared to be right for man (His Law; *jus divinum, relligio divina*). The dullest of wits can hardly fail to appreciate the force of this beautiful contrast between the regularity of instinct and the aberrations of reason. All living creatures are subject to laws upon obedience to which their well-being depends. The life of man is no exception; it too is subject to a law—a law which is as much higher than that which regulates mere animal existence, as reason and conscience and spiritual aspiration are higher than instinct and sexual impulse. But whereas the lower forms of life are obedient to the laws of their being, man rebels against them, and dares to disobey what he knows to be for his good; nay, he suffers himself to be so blinded by lust and passion and pride and self-will that at last he does not even recognise the Law—the ordinance of the Eternal—for what it really is, the organic law of his true being, the condition at once of his excellence and his happiness.

The prophet next meets an objection. He has just alleged a profound moral ignorance—a culpable ignorance—against the people. He supposes them to deny the accusation, as doubtless they often did in answer to his remonstrances (cf. xvii. 15, xx. 7 sq.) *How can ye say, "We are wise"—* morally wise—*"and the teaching of Iahvah is with us!"* [*but behold*: LXX. omits: either term would be sufficient by itself] *for the Lie hath the lying pen of the scribes made it!* The reference clearly is to what Jeremiah's opponents call "the teaching (or *law: torah*) of Iahvah"; and it is also clear that the prophet charges the "scribes" of the opposite party with falsifying or tampering with the teaching of Iahvah in some way or other. Is it meant that they misrepresented the terms of a written document, such as the Book of the Covenant, or Deuteronomy? But they could hardly do this without detection, in the case of a work which was not in their exclusive possession. Or does Jeremiah accuse them of misinterpreting the sacred law, by putting false glosses upon its precepts, as might be done in a legal document wherever there seemed room for a difference of opinion, or wherever conflicting traditional interpretations existed side by side? (Cf. my remarks on vii. 31.) The Hebrew may indicate this, for we may translate: *But lo, into the lie the lying pen of the scribes hath made it!* which recalls St. Paul's description of the heathen as changing the truth of God into a lie (Rom. i. 26). The construction is the same as in Gen. xii. 2; Isa. xliv. 17. Or, finally, does he boldly charge these abettors of the false prophets with forging supposititious law-books, in the interest of their own faction, and in support of the claims and doctrines of the worldly priests and prophets? This last view is quite admissible, so far as the Hebrew goes, which, however, is not free from ambiguity. It might be rendered, *But behold, in vain*, or *bootlessly* (iii. 23) *hath the lying pen of the scribes laboured*; taking the verb in an absolute sense, which is not a common use (Ruth ii. 19). Or we might transpose the terms for "pen" and "lying," and render, *But behold, in vain hath the pen of the scribes fabricated falsehood*. In any case, the general sense is the same: Jeremiah charges not only the speakers, but the writers, of the popular party with uttering their own inventions in the name of Iahvah. These scribes were the spiritual ancestors of those of our Saviour's time, who "made the word of God of none effect for the sake of their traditions" (Matt. xv. 6). *For the Lie* means, to maintain the popular misbelief. (It might also be rendered, *for falsehood, falsely*, as in the phrase *to swear falsely*, i.e., for deceit; Lev. v. 24.) It thus appears that conflicting and competing versions of the law were current in that age. Has the Pentateuch preserved elements of both kinds, or is it homogeneous throughout? Of the scribes of the period we, alas! know little beyond what this passage tells us. But Ezra must have had predecessors, and we may remember that Baruch, the friend and amanuensis of Jeremiah, was also a scribe (xxxvi. 26).

The "wise" will blush, they will be dismayed and caught! Lo, the word of Iahvah they rejected, and wisdom of what sort have they? (vi. 10). The whole body of Jeremiah's opponents, the populace as well as the priests and prophets, are intended by *the wise*, that is, the wise in their own conceits (ver. 8); there is an ironical reference to their own assumption of the title. These self-styled wise ones, who preferred their own wisdom to the guidance of the prophet, will be punished by the mortification of discovering their folly when it is too late. Their folly will be the instrument of their ruin, for "He taketh the wise in their own craftiness" as in a snare (Prov. v. 22).

They who reject Iahvah's word, in whatever form it comes to them, have no other light to walk by; they must needs walk in darkness, and stumble at noonday. For Iahvah's word is the only true wisdom, the only true guide of man's footsteps. And this is the kind of wisdom which the Holy Scriptures offer us; not a merely speculative wisdom, not what is commonly understood by the terms science and art, but the priceless knowledge of God and of His will concerning us; a kind of knowledge which is beyond all comparison the most important for our well-being here and hereafter. If this Divine wisdom, which relates to the proper conduct of life and the right education of the highest faculties of our being, seem a small matter to any man, the fact argues spiritual blindness on his part; it cannot diminish the glory of heavenly wisdom.

Some well-meaning but mistaken people are fond of maintaining what they call "the scientific accuracy of the Bible," meaning thereby an essential harmony with the latest discoveries, or even the newest hypotheses, of physical science. But even to raise such a preposterous question, whether as advocate or as assailant, is to be guilty of a crude anachronism, and to betray an incredible ignorance of the real value of the Scriptures. That value I believe to be inestimable. But to discuss "the scientific accuracy of the Bible" appears to me to be as irrelevant to any profitable issue, as it would be to discuss the meteorological precision of the Mahabharata, or the marvellous chemistry of the Zendavesta, or the physiological revelations of the Koran, or the enlightened anthropology of the Nibelungenlied.

A man may reject the word of Iahvah, he may reject Christ's word, because he supposes that it is not sufficiently attested. He may urge that the proof that it is of GOD breaks down, and he may flatter himself that he is a person of superior discernment, because he perceives a fact to which the multitude of believers are apparently blind. But what kind of proof would he have? Does he demand more than the case admits of? Some portent in earth or sky or sea, which in reality would be quite foreign to the matter in hand, and could have none but an accidental connexion with it, and would, in fact, be no proof at all, but itself a mystery requiring to be explained by the ordinary laws of physical causation? To demand a kind of proof which is irrelevant to the subject is a mark not of superior caution and judgment, but of ignorance and confusion of thought. The plain truth is, and the fact is abundantly illustrated by the teachings of the prophets and, above all, of our Divine Lord, that moral and spiritual truths are self-attesting to minds able to realize them; and they no more need supplementary corroboration than does the ultimate testimony of the senses of a sane person.

Now the Bible as a whole is an unique repertory of such truths; this is the secret of its age-long influence in the world. If a man does not care for the Bible, if he has not learned to appreciate this aspect of it, if he does not *love* it precisely on this account, I, in turn, care very little for his opinion about the Bible. There may be much in the Bible which is otherwise valuable, which is precious as history, as tradition, as bearing upon questions of interest to the ethnologist, the antiquarian, the man of letters. But these things are the shell, *that* is the kernel; these are the accidents, *that* is the substance; these are the bodily vesture, *that* is the immortal spirit. A man who has not felt this, has yet to learn what the Bible is.

In his text as we now have it, Jeremiah proceeds to denounce punishment on the priests and prophets, whose fraudulent oracles and false interpretations of the Law ministered to their own greedy covetousness, and who smoothed over the alarming state of things by false assurances that all was well (vv. 10-12). The Septuagint, however, omits the whole passage after the words, *Therefore I will give their wives to others, their fields to conquerors!* and as these words are obviously an abridgment of the threat, vi. 12 (cf. Deut. xxviii. 30), while the rest of the passage agrees verbatim with vi. 13-15, it may be supposed that a later editor inserted it in the margin here, as generally apposite (cf. vi. 10 with ver. 9), whence it has crept into the text. It is true that Jeremiah himself is fond of repetition, but not so as to interrupt the context, as the "therefore" of ver. 10 seems to do. Besides, the "wise" of ver. 8 are the self-confident people; but if this passage be in place here, "the wise" of ver. 9 will have to be understood of their false guides, the prophets and priests. Whereas, if the passage be omitted, there is manifest continuity between the ninth verse and the thirteenth: *"I will sweep, sweep them away," saith Iahvah; no grapes on the vine, and no figs on the fig tree, and the foliage is withered, and I have given them destruction* (or *blasting*).

The opening threat is apparently quoted from the contemporary prophet Zephaniah (i. 2, 3). The point of the rest of the verse is not quite clear, owing to the fact that the last clause of the Hebrew text is undoubtedly corrupt. We might suppose that the term "laws" (מִיקֶּח) had fallen out, and render, *and I gave them laws which they transgress* (cf. v. 22, xxxi. 35). The Vulgate has an almost literal translation, which gives the same sense: "et dedi eis quæ praetergressa sunt."[32] The Septuagint omits the clause, probably on the ground of its difficulty. It may be that bad crops and scarcity are threatened (cf. chap. xiv., v. 24, 25). In that case, we may correct the text in the manner suggested above מִירְבָּשׁ or וְשׁוֹהָב ׳xvii. 18, for מוּרְבָעִי; or וְזִּפְדָשׁ Amos iv. 9, for the מוּדְבָעִי of other MSS.. Others understand the verse in a metaphorical sense. The language seems to be coloured by a reminiscence of Micah vii. 1, 2; and the "grapes" and "figs" and "foliage" may be the fruits of righteousness, and the nation is like Isaiah's unfruitful vineyard (Isa. v.) or our Lord's barren fig tree (Matt. xxi. 19), fit only for destruction (cf. also vi. 9 and ver. 20). Another passage which resembles the present is Hab. iii. 17: "For the fig tree will not blossom, and there will be no yield on the vines; the produce of the olive will disappoint, and the fields will produce no food." It was natural that tillage should be neglected upon the rumour of invasion. The country-folk would crowd into the strong places, and leave their vineyards, orchards and cornfields to their fate (ver. 14). This would, of course, lead to scarcity and want, and aggravate the horrors of war with those of dearth and famine. I think the passage of Habakkuk is a precise parallel to the one before us. Both contemplate a Chaldean invasion, and both anticipate its disastrous effects upon husbandry.

It is possible that the original text ran: *And I have given (will give) unto them their own work* (*i.e.*, the fruit of it, מְתָדְבָע: used of field-work, Ex. i. 14; of the earnings of labour, Isa. xxxii. 17). This, which is a frequent thought in Jeremiah, forms a very suitable close to the verse. The objection is that the prophet does not use this particular term for "work" elsewhere. But the fact of its only once occurring might have caused its corruption. (Another term, which would closely resemble the actual reading, and give much the same sense as this last, is תְּרוּבֵע "their produce." This, too, as a very rare expression, only known from Josh. v. 11, 12, might have been misunderstood and altered by an editor or copyist. It is akin to the Aramaic רוּבַע, and there are other Aramaisms in our prophet.) One thing is certain; Jeremiah cannot have written what now appears in the Masoretic text.

It is now made clear what the threatened evil is, in a fine closing strophe, several expressions of which recall the prophet's magnificent alarm upon the coming of the Scythians (cf. iv. 5 with viii. 14; iv. 15 with viii. 16; iv. 19 with viii. 18). Here, however, the colouring is darker, and the prevailing gloom of the picture unrelieved by any ray of hope. The former piece belongs to the reign of Josiah, this to that of the worthless Jehoiakim. In the interval between the two, moral decline and social and political disintegration had advanced with fearfully accelerated speed, and Jeremiah knew that the end could not be far off.

The fatal news of invasion has come, and he sounds the alarm to his countrymen. *Why are we sitting still* (in silent stupefaction)? *assemble yourselves, that we may go into the defenced cities, and be silent* (or *amazed, stupefied,* with terror) *there! for Iahvah our God hath silenced us* (with speechless terror) *and given us water of gall to drink; for we trespassed toward Iahvah. We looked for peace* (or, *weal, prosperity*), *and there is no good; for a time of healing, and behold panic fear!* So the prophet represents the effect of the evil tidings upon the rural population. At first they are taken by surprise; then they rouse themselves from their stupor to take refuge in the walled cities. They recognise in the trouble a sign of Iahvah's anger. Their fond hopes of returning prosperity are nipped in the bud; the wounds of the past are not to be healed; the country has hardly recovered from one shock, before another and more deadly blow falls upon it. The next verse describes more particularly the nature of the bad news; the enemy, it would seem, had actually entered the land, and given no uncertain indication of what the Judeans might expect, by his ravages on the northern frontier. *From Dan was heard the snorting of his horses; at the sound of the neighings of his chargers all the land did quake: and they came in* (into the country) *and eat up the land and the fulness thereof, a city and them that dwelt therein.* This was what the invaders did to city after city, once they had crossed the border; ravaging its domain, and sacking the place itself. Perhaps, however, it is better to take the perfects as prophetic, and to render: "From Dan shall be heard ... shall quake: and they shall come and eat up the land," etc. This makes the connexion easier with the next verse, which certainly has a future reference: *For behold I am about to send* (or simply, *I send*) *against you serpents, basilisks* (Isa. xi. 8, the *çif·oni* was a small but very poisonous snake; Aquila βασιλίσκος, Vulg. regulus), *for whom there is no charm, and they will bite you! saith Iahvah.* If the tenses be supposed to describe what has already happened, then the connexion of thought may be expressed thus: all this evil that you have heard of has happened, not by mere ill fortune, but by the Divine will: Iahvah Himself has done it, and the evil will not stop there, *for* He purposes to send these destroying serpents into your very midst (cf. Num. xxi. 6).

The eighteenth verse begins in the Hebrew with a highly anomalous word, which is generally supposed to mean "my source of comfort" (יתגילבמ).

But both the strangeness of the form itself, which can hardly be paralleled in the language, and the indifferent sense which it yields, and the uncertainty of the Hebrew MSS., and the variations of the old versions, indicate that we have here another corruption of the text. Some Hebrew copies divide the word, and this is supported by the Septuagint and the Syro-Hexaplar version, which treat the verse as the conclusion of ver. 17, and render "and they shall bite you *incurably, with pain of your perplexed heart*" (Syro-Hex. "without cure"). But if the first part of the word is "without" (יְלִבְמ "for lack of" ...), what is the second? No such root as the existing letters imply is found in Hebrew or the cognate languages. The Targum does not help us: *Because they were scoffing* (וְיִגַעלְמ) *against the prophets who prophesied unto them, sorrow and sighing will I bring* (יתיא) *upon them on account of their sins: upon them, saith the prophet, my heart is faint.* It is evident that this is no better than a kind of punning upon the words of the Masoretic text.[33] I incline to read "How shall I cheer myself? Upon me is sorrow; upon me my heart is sick." (The prophet would write עַל not יַלְע for "against," without a suffix. Read הָמ וֹזִי יַלְע הָגִילְבָא Job ix. 27, x. 20; Ps. xxxix. 14.) The passage is much like iv. 19.

Another possible emendation is: "Iahvah causeth sorrow to flash forth upon me" (הוהי גילבמ; after the archetype of Amos v. 9); but I prefer the former.

Jeremiah closes the section with an outpouring of his own overwhelming sorrow at the heart-rending spectacle of the national calamities. No reader endued with any degree of feeling can doubt the sincerity of the prophet's patriotism, or the willingness with which he would have given his own life for the salvation of his country. This one passage alone says enough to exonerate its author from the charge of indifference, much more of treachery to his fatherland. He imagines himself to hear the cry of the captive people, who have been carried away by the victorious invader into a distant land: *Hark! the sound of the imploring cry of the daughter of my people from a land far away! "Is Iahvah not in Sion? or is not her King in her?"* (cf. Mic. iv. 9). Such will be the despairing utterance of the exiles of Judah and Jerusalem; and the prophet hastens to answer it with another question, which accounts for their ruin by their disloyalty to that heavenly King; *O why did they vex Me with their graven images, with alien vanities?* Compare a similar question and answer in an earlier discourse (v. 19). It may be doubted whether the pathetic words which follow — *The harvest is past, the fruit-gathering is finished, but as for us, we are not delivered!* — are to be taken as a further complaint of the captives, or as a reference by the prophet himself to hopes of deliverance which had been cherished in vain, month after month, until the season of campaigns was over. In Palestine, the grain crops are harvested in April and May, the ingathering of the fruit falls in August. During all the summer months,

Jehoiakim, as a vassal of Egypt, may have been eagerly hoping for some decisive interference from that quarter. That he was on friendly terms with that power at the time appears from the fact that he was allowed to fetch back refugees from its territory (xxvi. 22 *sq.*). A provision for the extradition of offenders is found in the far more ancient treaty between Ramses II. and the king of the Syrian Chetta (fourteenth cent. b.c.). But perhaps the prophet is alluding to one of those frequent failures of the crops, which inflicted so much misery upon his people (cf. vers. 13, iii. 3, v. 24, 25), and which were a natural incident of times of political unsettlement and danger. In that case, he says, the harvest has come and gone, and left us unhelped and disappointed. I prefer the political reference, though our knowledge of the history of the period is so scanty, that the particulars cannot be determined.

It is clear enough from the lyrical utterance which follows (vv. 21-23), that heavy disasters had already befallen Judah: *For the shattering of the daughter of my people am I shattered; I am a mourner; astonishment hath seized me!* This can hardly be pure anticipation. The next two verses may be a fragment of one of the prophet's elegies (*qinoth*). At all events, they recall the metre of Lam. iv. and v.:

> *Doth balm in Gilead fail?*
> *Fails the healer there?*
> *Why is not bound up*
> *My people's deadly wound?*
>
> *O that my head were springs,*
> *Mine eye a fount of tears!*
> *To weep both day and night*
> *Over my people's slain.*

It is not impossible that these two quatrains are cited from the prophet's elegy upon the last battle of Megiddo and the death of Josiah. Similar fragments seem to occur below (ix. 17, 18, 20) in the instructions to the mourning-women, the professional singers of dirges over the dead.

The beauty of the entire strophe, as an outpouring of inexpressible grief, is too obvious to require much comment. The striking question "Is there no balm in Gilead, is there no physician there?" has passed into the common dialect of religious aphorism; and the same may be said of the despairing cry, "The harvest is past, the summer is ended, and we are not saved!"

The wounds of the state are past healing; but how, it is asked, can this be? Does nature yield a balm which is sovereign for bodily hurts, and is there nowhere a remedy for those of the social organism? Surely that were something anomalous, strange and unnatural (cf. viii. 7). *Is there no balm in*

Gilead? Yes, it is found nowhere else (cf. Plin., *Hist. Nat.,* xii. 25 *ad init.* "Sed omnibus odoribus præfertur balsamum, *uni terrarum Judææ concessum"*). Then has Iahvah mocked us, by providing a remedy for the lesser evil, and leaving us a hopeless prey to the greater? The question goes deep down to the roots of faith. Not only is there an analogy between the two realms of nature and spirit; in a sense, the whole physical world is an adumbration of things unseen, a manifestation of the spiritual. Is it conceivable that order should reign everywhere in the lower sphere, and chaos be the normal state of the higher? If our baser wants are met by provisions adapted in the most wonderful way to their satisfaction, can we suppose that the nobler—those cravings by which we are distinguished from irrational creatures—have not also their satisfactions included in the scheme of the world? To suppose it is evidence either of capricious unreason, or of a criminal want of confidence in the Author of our being.

Is there no balm in Gilead? Is there no healer there? There is a panacea for Israel's woes—the "law" or teaching of Iahvah; there is a Healer in Israel, Iahvah Himself (iii. 22, xvii. 14), who has declared of Himself, *I wound and I heal* (Deut. xxxii. 39; chap. xxx. 17, xxxiii. 6). *Why then is no bandage applied to the daughter of my people?* This is like the cry of the captives, *Is Iahvah not in Sion, is not her King in her?* (ver. 19). The answer there is, Yes! it is not that Iahvah is wanting; it is that the national guilt is working out its own retribution. He leaves this to be understood here; having framed his question so as to compel people, if it might be, to the right inference and answer.

The precious balsam is the distinctive glory of the mountain land of Gilead, and the knowledge of Iahvah is the distinctive glory of His people Israel. Will no one, then, apply the true remedy to the hurt of the state? No, for priests and prophets and people *know not—they have refused to know* Iahvah (ver. 5). The nation will not look to the Healer and live. It is their misfortunes that they hate, not their sins. There is nothing left for Jeremiah but to sing the funeral song of his fatherland.

While weeping over their inevitable doom, the prophet abhors with his whole soul his people's wickedness, and longs to fly from the dreary scene of treachery and deceit. *O that I had in the wilderness a lodging-place of wayfaring men*—some lonely khan on a caravan track, whose bare, unfurnished walls, and blank almost oppressive stillness, would be a grateful exchange for the luxury and the noisy riot of Judah's capital—*that I might leave my people and go away from among them!* The same feeling finds expression in the sigh of the psalmist, who is perhaps Jeremiah himself: *O for the wings of a dove!* (Ps. lv. 6 *sqq.*) The same feeling has often issued in actual withdrawal from the world. And under certain circumstances, in certain states of religion and society, the solitary life has its peculiar advantages. The life of towns is doubtless busy, practical, intensely real; but its business is not always of the ennobling sort, its practice in the strain and struggle of selfish competition is often distinctly hostile to the growth and play of the best instincts of human nature; its intensity is often the mere result of confining the manifold energies of the mind to one narrow channel, of concentrating the whole complex of human powers and forces upon the single aim of self-advancement and self-glorification; and its reality is consequently an illusion, phenomenal and transitory as the unsubstantial prizes which absorb all its interest, engross its entire devotion, and exhaust its whole activity. It is not upon the broad sea, nor in the lone wilderness, that men learn to question the goodness, the justice, the very being of their Maker. Atheism is born in the populous wastes of cities, where human beings crowd together, not to bless but to prey upon each other; where rich and poor dwell side by side, but are separated by the gulf of cynical indifference and social disdain; where selfishness in its ugliest forms is rampant, and is the rule of life with multitudes:—the selfishness which grasps at personal advantage and is deaf to the cries of human pain; the selfishness which calls all manner of fraud and trickery lawful means for the achievement of its sordid ends; and the selfishness of flagrant vice, whose activity is not only earthly and sensual but also devilish, as directly involving the degradation and ruin of human souls. No wonder that they whose eyes have been blinded by the god of this world, fail to see evidence of any other God; no wonder that they in whose hearts a coarse or a subtle self-worship has dried the springs of pity and love can scoff at the very idea of a compassionate God; no wonder that a soul, shaken to its depths by the contemplation of this bewildering medley of heartlessness and misery, should be tempted to doubt whether there is indeed a Judge of all the earth, who doeth right.

There is no truth, no honour in their dealings with one another; falsehood is the dominant note of their social existence: *They are all adulterers, a throng of traitors!* The charge of adultery is no metaphor (chap. v. 7, 8). Where the sense of religious sanctions is weakened or wanting, the marriage tie is no longer respected; and that which perhaps lust began, is ended by lust, and man and woman are faithless to each other, because they are faithless to God.

And they bend their tongue, their bow, falsely.[34] The tongue is as a bow of which words are the arrows. Evildoers "stretch their arrow, the bitter word, to shoot in ambush at the blameless man" (Ps. lxiv. 4; cf. Ps. xi. 2). The metaphor is common in the language of poetry; we have an instance in Longfellow's "I shot an arrow into the air," and Homer's familiar ἔπεα πτερόεντα, "winged words," is a kindred expression. (Others render, *and they bend their tongue as their bow of falsehood*, as though the term *sheqer, mendacium*, were an epithet qualifying the term for "bow." I have taken it adverbially, a use justified by Pss. xxxviii. 20, lxix. 5, cxix. 78, 86.) In colloquial English a man who exaggerates a story is said to "draw the long bow."

Their tongue is a bow with which they shoot lies at their neighbours, *and it is not by truth*—faithfulness, honour, integrity—*that they wax mighty in the land*; their riches and power are the fruit of craft and fraud and overreaching. As was said in a former discourse, "their houses are full of deceit, therefore they become great, and amass wealth" (v. 27). *By truth*, or more literally *unto truth, according to the rule or standard of truth* (cf. Isa. xxxii. 1, "according to right;" Gen. i. 11, "according to its kind"). With the idea of the verb, we may compare Ps. cxii. 2: "Mighty in the land shall his seed become" (cf. also Gen. vii. 18, 19). The passage chap. v. 2, 3, is essentially similar to the present, and is the only one besides where we find the term "by truth" (הנומאל *le'emunah*). The idiom seems certain, and the parallel passages, especially v. 27, appear to establish the translation above given; otherwise one might be tempted to render: *they stretch their tongue, their bow, for lying* (רקשל, v. 2), *and it is not for truth that they are strong in the land.* "Noblesse oblige" is no maxim of theirs; they use their rank and riches for unworthy ends.

For out of evil unto evil they go forth—they go from one wickedness to another, adding sin to sin. Apparently, a military metaphor. What they have and are is evil, and they go forth to secure fresh conquests of the same kind. Neither good nor evil is stationary; progress is the law of each—*and Me they know not, saith Iahvah*—they know not that I am truth itself, and therefore irreconcilably opposed to all this fraud and falsehood.

Beware ye, every one of his companion, and in no brother confide ye; for every brother will surely play the Jacob,—and every companion will go about slandering. And they deceive each his neighbour, and truth they speak not: they have trained their tongue to speak falsehood, to pervert (their way, iii. 21) *they toil* (chap. xx. 9; cf. Gen. xix. 11). *Thine inhabiting is in the midst of deceit; through deceit they refuse to know Me, saith Iahvah* (3-5).[35] As Micah had complained before him (Mic. vii. 5), and as bitter experience had taught our prophet (xi. 18 sqq., xii. 6), neither friend nor brother was to be trusted; and that this was not merely the melancholy characteristic of a degenerate age, is suggested by the reference to the unbrotherly intrigues of the far-off ancestor of the Jewish people, in the traditional portrait of whom the best and the worst features of the national character are reflected with wonderful truth and liveliness.[36] *Every brother will not fail to play the Jacob* (Gen. xxv. 29 sqq., xxvii. 36; Hos. xii. 4), to outwit, defraud, supplant; cunning and trickery will subserve acquisitiveness. But though an inordinate love of acquisition may still seem to be specially characteristic of the Jewish race, as in ancient times it distinguished the Canaanite and Semitic nations in general, the tendency to cozen and overreach one's neighbour is so far from being confined to it, that some modern ethical speculators have not hesitated to assume this tendency to be an original and natural instinct of humanity. The fact, however, for which those who would account for human nature upon purely "natural" grounds are bound to supply some rational explanation, is not so much that aspect of it which has been well-known to resemble the instincts of the lower animals ever since observation began, but the aspect of revolt and protest against those lower impulses which we find reflected so powerfully in the documents of the higher religion, and which makes thousands of lives a perpetual warfare.

Jeremiah presents his picture of the universal deceit and dissimulation of his own time as something peculiarly shocking and startling to the common sense of right, and unspeakably revolting in the sight of God, the Judge of all. And yet the difficulty to the modern reader is to detect any essential difference between human nature then and human nature now—between those times and these. It is still true that avarice and lust destroy natural affection; that the ties of blood and friendship are no protection against a godless love of self. The work of slander and misrepresentation is not left to avowed enemies; your own acquaintance will gratify their envy, spite, or mere ill-will in this unworthy way. A simple child may tell the truth; but tongues have to be trained to expertness in lying, whether in commerce or in diplomacy, in politics or in the newspaper press, in the art of the salesman or in that of the agitator and the demagogue. Men still make a toil of perverting their way, and spend as much pains in becoming accomplished villains as honest folk take to excel in virtue. Deceit is still the social atmosphere and environment, and *through deceit* men *refuse to know Iahvah*. The knowledge, the recognition, the steady recollection of what Iahvah is, and what His law requires, does not suit the man of lies; his objects oblige him to shut his eyes to the truth. Men *do not will* and *will not*, to know the moral impediments that lie in the way of self-seeking and self-pleasing. Sinning is always a matter of choice, not of nature, nor of circumstances alone. To desire to be delivered from moral evil is, so far, a desire to know God.

Thine inhabiting is in the midst of deceit: who that ever lifts an eye above the things of time, has not at times felt thus? "This is a Christian country." Why? Because the majority are as bent on self-pleasing, as careless of God, as heartlessly and systematically forgetful of the rights and claims of others, as they would have been had Christ never been heard of? A Christian country? Why? Is it because we can boast of some two hundred forms or fashions of supposed Christian belief, differentiated from each other by heaven knows what obscure shibboleths, which in the lapse of time have become meaningless and obsolete; while the old ill-will survives, and the old dividing lines remain, and Christians stand apart from Christians in a state of dissension and disunion that does despite and dishonour to Christ, and must be very dear to the devil? Some people are bold enough to defend this horrible condition of things by raising a cry of Free Trade in Religion. But religion is not a trade, not a thing to make a profit of, except with Simon Magus and his numerous followers both inside and outside of the Church.

A Christian country! But the rage of avarice, the worship of Mammon, is not less rampant in London than in old Jerusalem. If the more violent forms of oppression and extortion are restrained among us by the more complete organization of public justice, the fact has only developed new and more insidious modes of attack upon the weak and the unwary. Deceit and fraud have been put upon their mettle by the challenge of the law, and thousands of people are robbed and plundered by devices which the law can hardly reach or restrain. Look where the human spider sits, weaving his web of guile, that he may catch and devour men! Look at the wonderful baits which the company-monger throws out day by day to human weakness and cupidity! Do you call him shrewd and clever and enterprising? It is a sorry part to play in life, that of Satan's decoy, tempting one's fellow-creatures to their ruin. Look at the lying advertisements, which meet your eyes wherever you turn, and make the streets of this great city almost as hideous from the point of view of taste as from that of morality! What a degrading resource! To get on by the industrious dissemination of lies, by false pretences, which one knows to be false! And to trade upon human misery — to raise hopes that can never be fulfilled — to add to the pangs of disease the smart of disappointment and the woe of a deeper despair, as countless quacks in this Christian country do!

A Christian country: where God is denied on the platform and through the press; where a novel is certain of widespread popularity, if its aim be to undermine the foundations of the Christian faith; where atheism is mistaken for intelligence, and an inconsistent Agnosticism for the loftiest outcome of logic and reason; where flagrant lust walks the streets unrebuked, unabashed; where every other person you meet is a gambler in one form or another, and shopmen and labourers and loafers and errand boys are all eager about the result of races, and all agog to know the forecasts of some wily tipster, some wiseacre of the halfpenny press!

A Christian country: where the rich and noble have no better use for profuse wealth than horse-training, and no more elevating mode of recreation than hunting and shooting down innumerable birds and beasts; where some must rot in fever-dens, clothed in rags, pining for food, stifling for lack of air and room; while others spend thousands of pounds upon a whim, a banquet, a party, a toy for a fair woman. I am not a Socialist; I do not deny a man's right to do what he will with his own, and I believe that state interference would be in the last degree disastrous to the country. But I affirm the responsibility before God of the rich and great; and I deny that they who live and spend for themselves alone are worthy of the name of Christian.

A Christian country: where human beings die, year after year, in the unspeakable, unimaginable agonies of canine madness, and dogs are kept by the thousand in crowded cities, that the sacrifice to the fiend of selfishness and the mocking devil of vanity may never lack its victims! There is a more than Egyptian worship of Anubis, in the silly infatuation which lavishes tenderness upon an unclean brute, and credulously invests instinct with the highest attributes of reason; and there is a worse than heathenish besottedness in the heart that can pamper a dog, and be utterly indifferent to the helplessness and the sufferings of the children of the poor. And people will go to church, and hear what the preacher has to say, and "think he said what he ought to have said," or not, as the case may be, and return to their own settled habits of worldly living, as a matter of course. Oh yes! it is a Christian country—the name of Christ has been named in it for fifteen centuries past; and for that reason Christ will judge it.

Therefore, thus said Iahvah Sabaoth: Lo, I am about to melt them and put them to proof (Job xii. 11; Judg. xvii. 4; ch. vi. 25.); *for how am I to deal in face of* [*the wickedness of,* LXX: the term has fallen out of the Heb. text: cf. iv. 4, vii. 12] *the daughter of My people?* This is the meaning of the disasters that have fallen and are even now falling upon the country. Iahvah will melt and assay this rough, intractable human ore, in the fiery furnace of affliction; the strain of insincerity that runs through it, the base earthy nature, can only thus be separated and purged away (Isa. xlviii. 10). *A deadly arrow* [LXX. a *wounding* one, *i.e.*, one which does not miss, but hits and kills] *is their tongue; deceit it spake: with his mouth peace with his companion he speaketh, and inwardly he layeth his ambush* (Ps. lv. 22). The verse again specifies the wickedness complained of, and justifies our restoration of that word in the previous verse.

Perhaps, with the Peshito Syriac and the Targum, we ought rather to render: *a sharp arrow is their tongue.* There is an Arabic saying quoted by Lane, "Thou didst sharpen thy tongue against us," which seems to present a kindred root[37] (cf. Ps. lii. 3, lvii. 4; Prov. xxv. 18). The Septuagint may be right, with its probable reading: *deceit are the words of his mouth.* This certainly improves the symmetry of the verse.

For such things (emphatic) *shall I not*—or *should I not*, with an implied *ought*—*shall I not punish them, saith Iahvah, or on such a nation shall not My soul avenge herself?* (v. 9, 29, after which the LXX. omits *them* here.) These questions, like the previous one, *How am I to deal*—or, *how could I act*—*in face of the wickedness of the daughter of My people?* imply the moral necessity of the threatened evils. If Iahweh be what He has taught man's conscience that He is, national sin must involve national suffering, and national persistence in sin must involve national ruin. Therefore He will *melt and try* this people, both for their punishment and their reformation, if it may be so. For punishment is properly retributive, whatever may be alleged to the contrary. Conscience tells us that we *deserve* to suffer for ill-doing, and conscience is a better guide than ethical or sociological speculators who have lost faith in God. But God's chastisements as known to our experience, that is to say, in the present life, are reformatory as well as retributive; they compel us to recollect, they bring us, like the Prodigal, back to ourselves, out of the distractions of a sinful career, they humble us with the discovery that we have a Master, that there is a Power above ourselves and our apparently unlimited capacity to choose evil and to do it: and so by Divine grace we may become contrite and be healed and restored.

The prophet thus, perhaps, discerns a faint glimmer of hope, but his sky darkens again immediately. The land is already to a great extent desolate, through the ravages of the invaders, or through severe droughts (cf. iv. 25, viii. 20(?), xii. 4). *Upon the mountains will I lift up weeping and wailing, and upon the pastures of the prairie a lamentation, for they have been burnt up* (ii. 15; 2 Kings xxii. 13), *so that no man passeth over them, and they have not heard the cry of the cattle: from the birds of the air to the beasts, they are fled, are gone* (iv. 25). The perfects may be prophetic and announce what is certain to happen hereafter. The next verse, at all events, is unambiguous in this respect: *And I will make Jerusalem into heaps, a haunt of jackals; and the cities of Judah will I make a desolation without inhabitant.* Not only the country districts, but the fortified towns, and Jerusalem itself, the heart and centre of the nation, will be desolated. Sennacherib boasts that he took forty-six strong cities, and "little towns without number," and carried off 200,150 male and female captives, and an immense booty in cattle, before proceeding to invest Jerusalem itself; a state which shews how severe the sufferings of Judah might be, before the enemy struck at its vitals.

In the words *I will make Jerusalem heaps*, there is not necessarily a change of subject. Jeremiah was authorized to "root up and pull down and destroy" in the name of Iahvah.

He now challenges the popular wise men (viii. 8, 9) to account for what, on their principles, must appear an inexplicable phenomenon. *Who is the (true) wise man, so that he understands this* (Hos. xiv. 9), *and who is he to whom the mouth of Iahvah hath spoken, so that he can explain it [unto you?* LXX.]. *Why is the land undone, burnt up like the prairie, without a passer by?* Both to Jeremiah and to his adversaries the land was Iahvah's land; what befel it must have happened by His will, or at least with His consent. Why had He suffered the repeated ravages of foreign invaders to desolate His own portion, where, if anywhere on earth, He must display His power and the proof of His deity? Not for lack of sacrifices, for these were not neglected. Only one answer was possible, to those who recognised the validity of the Book of the Law, and the binding character of the covenant which it embodied. The people and their wise men cannot account for the national calamities; Jeremiah himself can only do so, because he is inwardly taught by Iahvah himself (ver. 12): *And Iahvah said.* It may be supposed that ver. 11 states the popular dilemma, the anxious question which they put to the official prophets, whose guidance they accepted. The prophets could give no reasonable or satisfying answer, because their teaching hitherto had been that Iahvah could be appeased "with thousands of rams, and ten thousand torrents of oil" (Mic. vi. 7). On such conditions they had promised peace, and their teaching had been falsified by events. Therefore Jeremiah gives the true answer for Iahvah. But why did not the people cease to believe those whose word was thus falsified? Perhaps the false prophets would reply to objectors, as the refugees in Egypt answered Jeremiah's reproof of their renewed worship of the Queen of Heaven: "It was in the years that followed the abolition of this worship that our national disasters began" (xliv. 18). It is never difficult to delude those whose evil and corrupt hearts make them desire nothing so much as to be deluded.

And Iahvah said: Because they forsook (lit. *upon* = on account of *their forsaking*) *"My Law which I set before them"* (Deut. iv. 18), *and they hearkened not unto My voice* (Deut. xxviii. 15), *and walked not therein* (in My Law; LXX. omits the clause); *and walked after the obstinacy of their own* (*evil:* LXX.) *heart, and after the Baals* (Deut. iv. 3) *which their fathers taught them*—instead of teaching them the laws of Iahvah (Deut. xi. 19). Such were, and had always been, the terms of the answer of Iahvah's true prophets. Do you ask *upon what ground* (`al mah*) misfortune has overtaken you? Upon the ground of your having forsaken Iahvah's "law" or instruction, His doctrine concerning Himself and your consequent obligations towards Him. They had this teaching in the Book of the Law, and had solemnly undertaken to observe it, in that great national assembly of the eighteenth year of Josiah. And they had had it from the first in the living utterances of the prophets.

This, then, is the reason why the land is waste and deserted. And *therefore*—because past and present experience is an index of the future, for

Iahvah's character and purpose are constant—therefore the desolation of the cities of Judah and of Jerusalem itself, will ere long be accomplished. *Therefore thus said Iahvah Sabaoth, the God of Armies and the God of Israel; Lo, I am about to feed them*—or, *I continue to feed them*—to wit, *this people* (an epexegetical gloss omitted by the LXX.) *with wormwood, and I will give them to drink waters of gall* (Deut. xxix. 17. An Israelite inclining to foreign gods is "a root bearing wormwood and gall"—bearing a bitter harvest of defeat, a cup of deadly disaster for his people; cf. Am. vi. 12), *and I will "scatter them among the nations," "whom they and their fathers knew not"* (Deut. xxviii. 36, 64). The last phrase is remarkable as evidence of the isolation of Israel, whose country lay off the beaten track between the Trans-Euphratean empires and Egypt, which ran along the sea-coast. They knew not Assyria, until Tiglath Pileser's intervention (circ. 734), nor Babylon till the times of the New Empire. In Hezekiah's day, Babylon is still "a far country" (2 Kings xx. 14). Israel was in fact an agricultural people, trading directly with Phenicia and Egypt, but not with the lands beyond the Great River. The prophets heighten the horror of exile by the strangeness of the land whither Israel is to be banished.

And I will send after them the sword, until I have consumed them. The survivors are to be cut off (cf. viii. 3); there is no reserve, as in iv. 27, v. 10, 18; a "full end" is announced; which, again, corresponds to the aggravation of social and private evils in the time of Jehoiakim, and the prophet's despair of reform.

The judgment of Judah is the ruin of her cities, the dispersion of her people in foreign lands, and extermination by the sword. Nothing is left for this doomed nation but to sing its funeral song; to send for the professional wailing women, that they may come and chant their dirges, not over the dead but over the living who are condemned to die: *Thus said Iahvah Sabaoth* (here as in ver. 6, LXX. omits the expressive *Sabaoth*), *Mark ye well* the present crisis, and what it implies (cf. ii. 10; LXX. wrongly omits this emphatic term), *and summon the women that sing dirges, that they come, and unto the skilful women send ye, that they come* [LXX. omits], *and hasten* [LXX. *and speak and*] *to lift up the death-wail over us, that our eyes may run down with tears, and our eyelids pour down waters.* The "singing women" of 2 Chron. xxxv. 25, or the "minstrels" of St. Matt. ix. 23, are intended. The reason assigned for thus inviting them assumes that the prophet's forecast is already fulfilled. Already, as in viii. 19, Jeremiah hears the loud wailing of the captives as they are driven away from their ruined homes: *For the sound of the death-wail is heard from Sion, "How are we undone! We are sore ashamed"*—of our false confidence and foolish security and deceitful hopes—*"for, after all, we have left the land, for our dwellings have cast (us) out!"* The last two lines appear to be parallels, which is against the rendering, *For men have cast down our dwellings.* Cf. Lev. xviii. 25; chap. xxii. 28. From the wailing women, the address now seems to turn to the Judean women generally; but perhaps the former are still intended, as their peculiar calling was probably hereditary and passed on from mother to daughter: *For hear, ye women, the word of Iahvah, and let your ear take in the word of His mouth! and teach ye your daughters the death-wail, and each her companion the lamentation; for*

> "*Death scales our lattices,*
> *Enters our palaces,*
> *To cut off boy without,*
> *The young men from the streets.*"

And the corpses of men will fall—the tense certifies the future reference of the others—*like dung* (viii. 2) *on the face of the field* (2 Kings ix. 37, of Jezebel's corpse)—left without burial rites to rot and fatten the soil—*and like the corn-swath behind the reaper, and none shall gather (them).* The quatrain (ver. 20) is possibly quoted from some familiar elegy; and the allusion seems to be to a mysterious visitation like the plague, which used to be known in Europe as "the Black Death" (cf. xv. 2, xviii. 21, xliii. 11). In this time of closed gates and barred doors, death is represented as entering the house, not by the door, but "climbing up some other way" like a thief (Joel ii. 9; St. John x. 1). Bars and bolts will be futile against such an invader. The figure is not continued in the second half of the stanza.[38] The point of the closing comparison seems to be that whereas the corn-swaths are gathered up in sheaves and taken home, the bodies will lie where the reaper Death cuts them down.

Thus said Iahvah: Let not a wise man glory in his wisdom, and let not the mighty man glory in his might! Let not a rich man glory in his riches, but in this let him glory that glorieth, in being prudent and knowing Me (LXX. omits pronoun, cf. Gen. i. 4), *that I, Iahvah, do lovingkindness (and: LXX. and Orientals), justice and righteousness upon the earth; for in these I delight, saith Iahvah.*

It is not easy, at first sight, to see the connexion of this, one of the finest and deepest of Jeremiah's oracles, with the sentence of destruction which precedes it. It is not satisfactory to regard it as stating "the only means of escape and the reason why it is not used" (the latter being set forth in vv. 24, 25); for the leading idea of the whole composition, from vii. 13 to ix. 22, is that retribution is coming, and no escape, not even that of a remnant, is contemplated. The passage looks like an appendix to the previous pieces, such as the prophet might have added at a later period when the crisis was over, and the country had begun to breathe again, after the shock of invasion had rolled away. And this impression is confirmed by its contents. We have no details about the first interference of the new Chaldean power in Judah; we only read that in Jehoiakim's days *Nebuchadrezzar the king of Babylon came up, and Jehoiakim became his servant three years: then he turned and rebelled against him* (2 Kings xxiv. 1). But before this, for some two or three years, Jehoiakim was the vassal of the king of Egypt to whom he owed his crown, and Nebuchadrezzar had to reduce Necho before he could attend to Jehoiakim. It may be, therefore, that the worst apprehensions of the time not having been realized, in the year or two of lull which followed, the politicians of Judah began to boast of their foresight and the caution and sagacity of their measures for the public safety, instead of ascribing the respite to God; the warrior class might vaunt the bravery which it had exhibited or intended to exhibit in the service of the country; and the rich nobles might exult in the apparent security of their treasures and the new lease of enjoyment accorded to themselves. To these various classes, who would not be slow to ridicule his dark forebodings as those of a moody and unpatriotic pessimist (xx. 7, xxvi. 11, xxix. 26, xxxvii. 13), Jeremiah now speaks, to remind them that if the danger is over for the present, it is the lovingkindness and the righteous government of Iahvah which has removed it, and to declare that it is only suspended and postponed, not abolished for ever: *Behold, days are coming, saith Iahvah, when I will visit* (his guilt) *upon every one that is circumcised in foreskin* (only, and not *in heart* also): *upon Egypt and upon Judah, and upon Edom and upon the benê Ammon and upon Moab, and upon all the tonsured folk that dwell in the wilderness: For all the nations are uncircumcised, and all the house of Israel are uncircumcised in heart.* Egypt is mentioned first, as the leading nation, to which at the time the petty states of the west looked for help in their struggle against Babylon (cf. xxvii. 3). The prophet numbers Judah with the rest, not only as a member of the same political group, but as standing upon the same level of unspiritual life. Like Israel, Egypt also practised circumcision, and both the context here requires and their kinship with the Hebrews makes it probable that the other peoples mentioned observed the same custom (Herod., ii. 36, 104), which is actually portrayed in a wall-painting at Karnak. The "tonsured folk" or "cropt-heads" of the wilderness are north Arabian nomads like the Kedarenes (xlix. 28, 32), and the tribes of Dedan, Tema and Buz (xxv. 23), whose ancestor was the circumcised Ishmael (Gen. xxv. 13 *sqq.*, xvii. 23). Herodotus records their custom of shaving the temples all round, and leaving a tuft of hair on the top of the head (Herod., iii. 8), which practice, like circumcision, had a religious significance, and was forbidden to the Israelites (Lev. xix. 27, xxi. 5).

Now why does Jeremiah mention circumcision at all? The case is, I think, parallel to his mention of another external distinction of the popular religion, the Ark of the Covenant (iii. 15). Just as in that place God promises *shepherds according to Mine heart which shall shepherd* the restored Israel *with knowledge and prudence,* and then directly adds that, in the light and truth of those days, the ark will be forgotten (iii. 15, 16); so here, he bids the ruling classes, the actual shepherds of the nation, not to trust in their own wisdom or valour or wealth (cf. xvii. 5 *sqq.*), but in *being prudent and knowing Iahvah,* and then adds that the outward sign of circumcision, upon which the people prided themselves as the mark of their dedication to Iahvah, was in itself of no value, apart from a "circumcised heart," *i.e.,* a heart purified of selfish aims and devoted to the will and glory of God (iv. 4). So far as Iahvah is concerned, all Judah's heathen neighbours are uncircumcised, in spite of their observance of the outward rite. The Jews themselves would hardly admit the validity of heathen circumcision, because the manner of it was different, just as at this day the Muhammadan method differs from the Jewish. But Jeremiah puts "all the house of Israel," who were circumcised in the orthodox manner, on a level with the imperfectly circumcised heathen peoples around them. All alike are uncircumcised before God; those who have the orthodox rite, and those who have but an inferior semblance of it; and all alike will in the day of judgment be visited for their sins (cf. Amos i.).

With the increasing carelessness of moral obligations, an increasing importance would be attached to the observance of such a rite as circumcision, which was popularly supposed to devote a man to Iahvah in such sense that the tie was indissoluble. Jeremiah says plainly that this is a mistaken view. The outward sign must have an inward and spiritual grace corresponding thereto; else the Judeans are no better than those whose circumcision they despise as defective. His meaning is that of the Apostle, "Circumcision verily profiteth, *if thou keep the law;* but if thou be a breaker of law, thy circumcision hath become uncircumcision" (Rom. ii. 25). "Circumcision is nothing, and uncircumcision is nothing, *but the keeping of the commandments of God,"* scil. is everything (1 Cor. vii. 19). It is "faith working by love," it is the "new creature" that is essential in spiritual religion (Gal. v. 6, vi. 15).

Hæc dicit Dominus: Non glorietur sapiens in sapientia sua. Glancing back over the whole passage, we discern an inward relation between these verses and the preceding discourse. It is not the outward props of state-craft, and strong battalions, and inexhaustible wealth, that really and permanently uphold a nation; not these, but the knowledge of Iahvah, a just insight into the true nature of God, and a national life regulated in all its departments by that insight. At the outset of this third section of his discourse (ix. 3-6), Jeremiah declared that corrupt Israel *knew not* and *refused to know* its God. At the beginning of the entire piece (vii. 3 *sq.*), he urged his countrymen to *amend their ways and their doings,* and not go on trusting in *lying words* and doing the opposite of *lovingkindness and justice and righteousness,* which alone are pleasing to Iahvah (Mic. vi. 8), Who *delighteth in lovingkindness and not sacrifice, and in the knowledge of God more than in burnt-offerings* (Hos. vi. 6). And just as in the opening section the sacrificial worship was disparaged, taken as an "opus operatum," so here at the close circumcision is declared to have no independent value as a means of securing Divine favour (ix. 25). Thus the entire discourse is rounded off by the return of the end to the beginning; and the main thought of the whole, which Jeremiah has developed and enforced with so much variety of feeling and oratorical and poetical ornament, is the eternally true thought that a service of God which is purely external is no service at all, and that rites without a loving obedience are an insult to the Majesty of Heaven.

x. 17-25. The latter part of chap. x. resumes the subject suspended at ix. 22. It evidently contemplates the speedy departure of the people into banishment. *Away out of the land with thy pack* (or *thy goods*; LXX. ὑπόστασις, "property," Targ. "merchandise," the Heb. term, which is related to "Canaan," occurs here only), *O thou that sittest in distress!* (or *abidest in the siege*: lii. 5; 2 Kings xxiv. 10). Sion is addressed, and bidden to prepare her scanty bundle of bare necessaries for the march into exile. So Egypt is bidden to "make for herself vessels of exile," xlvi. 19. Some think that Sion is warned to withdraw her goods from the open country to the protection of her strong walls, before the siege begins, as in viii. 14; but we have passed that stage in the development of the piece, and the next verse seems to shew the meaning: *For thus hath Iahvah said, Lo, I am about to sling forth the inhabitants of the land this time*—as opposed to former occasions, when the enemy retired unsuccessful (2 Kings xvi. 5, xix. 36), or went off satisfied with plunder or an indemnity, like the Scythians (see also 2 Kings xiv. 14)—*and I will distress them that they may find out* the truth, which now they refuse to see. The aposiopesis *that they may find out!* is very striking. The Vulgate renders the verb in the passive: "Tribulabo eos ita ut inveniantur." This, however, does not give so good a sense as the Masoretic pointing, and Ewald's reference of the term to the goods of the panic-stricken fugitives seems flat and tasteless ("the inhabitants of the land will this time ... not be able to hide their goods from the enemy!"). The best comment on the phrase is supplied by a later oracle: *Lo, I am about to make them know this time—I will make them know My hand and My might; that they may know that My name is Iahvah* (xvi. 21). Cf. also xvii. 9; Eccles. viii. 17.

The last verse (17) resembles a poetical quotation; and this one looks like the explication of it. There the population is personified as a woman; here we have instead the plain prose expression, "inhabitants of the land." The figurative, "I will sling them forth" or "cast them out," explains the bidding of Sion to *pack up her bundle* or *belongings*—there seems to be a touch of contempt in this isolated word, as much as to signify that the people must go forth into exile with no more of their possessions than they can carry like a beggar in a bundle. The expression, "I will distress them," seems to shew that "thou that sittest in the distress" is proleptic, or to be rendered "thou that art to sit in distress," which comes to the same thing.

And now the prophet imagines the distress and the remorse of this forlorn mother, as it will manifest itself when her house is ruined and her children are gone and she realizes the folly of the past (cf. iv. 31):—

> "Woe's me for my wound!
> Fatal is my stroke!"

(perhaps quoted from a familiar elegy). *And yet I—I thought* (chap. xxii. 21; Ps. xxx. 7), *Only this*—no more than this—*is my sickness: I can bear it!* (ילח הו דא נאשא; LXX. σου, Vulg. *mea*). The people had never fully realized the threatenings of the prophets, until they began to be accomplished. When they heard them, they had said, half-incredulously, half-mockingly, Is that all? Their false guides, too, had treated apparent danger as a thing of little moment, assuring them that their half reforms, and zealous outward worship, were sufficient to turn away the Divine displeasure (vi. 14). And so they said to themselves, as sinners are still in the habit of saying, "If the worst come to the worst, I can bear it. Besides, God is merciful, and things may turn out better for frail humanity than your preachers of wrath and woe predict. Meanwhile—I shall do as I please, and take my chance of the issue."

The lament of the mourning mother continues: *My tent is laid waste and all my cords are broken; My sons went forth of me* (to battle) *and are not; There is none to spread my tent any more, And to set up my curtains* (cf. Amos ix. 11). Overhearing, as it were, this sorrowful lamentation (*qinah*), the prophet interposes with the reason of the calamity: *For the shepherds became brutish* or *behaved foolishly,* stulte egerunt (Vulg.)—the leaders of the nation shewed themselves as insensate and silly as cattle—*and Iahvah they sought not* (ii. 8); *Therefore*—as they had no regard for Divine counsel—*they dealt not wisely* (iii. 15, ix. 23, xx. 11), *and all their flock was scattered abroad.*

Once more, and for the last time, the prophet sounds the alarm: *Hark! a rumour! lo, it cometh! and a great uproar from the land of the north; to make the cities of Judah a desolation, a haunt of jackals!* It is not likely that the verse is to be regarded as spoken by the mourning country; she contemplates the evil as already done, whereas here it is only imminent (cf. iv. 6, vi. 22, i. 15). The piece concludes with a prayer (vv. 23-25), which may be considered either as an intercession by the prophet on behalf of the nation (cf. xviii. 20), or as a form of supplication which he suggests as suitable to the existing crisis.

I know, Iahvah, that man's way is not his own; That it pertaineth not to a man to walk and direct his own steps: Correct me, Iahvah, but with justice; Not in Thine anger, lest Thou make me small! (Partly quoted, Ps. vi. 1, xxxviii. 1.) *Pour out Thy fury upon the nations that know Thee not, And upon tribes that have not called upon Thy name; For they have devoured Jacob [and will devour him], [and consumed him], and his pasture they have desolated!* (Ps. lxxix. 6, 7, quoted from this place. In Jer. the LXX. omits "and will devour him;" while the psalm omits both of the bracketed expressions.)

The Vulgate renders ver. 23: "Scio, Domine, quia non est hominis via ejus; nec viri est ut ambulet, et dirigat gressus suos." I think this indicates the correct reading of the Hebrew text (וְיֵכֵהוּ דְלֹה; cf. ix. 23, where two infinitives absolute are used in a similar way). The Septuagint also must have had the same text, for it translates, "nor will (= can) a man walk and direct his own walking." The Masoretic punctuation is certainly incorrect; and the best that can be made of it is Hitzig's version, which, however, disregards the accents, although their authority is the same as that of the vowel points: *I know Iahvah that not to man belongeth his way, not to a perishing* (lit. "going," "departing") *man—and to direct his steps*. Any reader of Hebrew may see at once that this is a very unusual form of expression. (For the thought, cf. Prov. xvi. 9, xix. 21; Ps. xxxvii. 23.)

The words express humble submission to the impending chastisement. The penitent people does not deprecate the penalty of its sins, but only prays that the measure of it may be determined by right rather than by wrath (cf. xlvi. 27, 28). The very idea of right and justice implies a limit, whereas wrath, like all passions, is without limit, blind and insatiable. "In the Old Testament, justice is opposed, not to mercy, but to high-handed violence and oppression, which recognise no law but subjective appetite and desire. The just man owns the claims of an objective law of right."

Non est hominis via ejus. Neither individuals nor nations are masters of their own fortunes in this world. Man has not his fate in his own hands; it is controlled and directed by a higher Power. By sincere submission, by a glad, unswerving loyalty, which honours himself as well as its Object, man may co-operate with that Power, to the furtherance of ends which are of all possible ends the wisest, the loftiest, the most beneficial to his kind. Self-will may oppose those ends, it cannot thwart them; at the most it can but momentarily retard their accomplishment, and exclude itself from a share in the universal blessing.

Israel now confesses, by the mouth of his best and truest representative, that he has hitherto loved to choose his own path, and to walk in his own strength, without reference to the will and way of God. Now, the overwhelming shock of irresistible calamity has brought him to his senses, has revealed to him his powerlessness in the hands of the Unseen Arbiter of events, has made him see, as he never saw, that mortal man can determine neither the vicissitudes nor the goal of his journey. Now he sees the folly of the mighty man glorying in his might, and the rich man glorying in his riches; now he sees that the *how* and the *whither* of his earthly course are not matters within his own control; that all human resources are nothing *against* God, and are only helpful when used *for* and *with* God. Now he sees that the path of life is not one which we enter upon and traverse of our own motion, but a path along which we are led; and so, resigning his former pride of independent choice, he humbly prays, "Lead Thou me on!" Lead me whither Thou wilt, in the way of trouble and disaster and chastisement for my sins; but remember my human frailty and weakness, and let not Thy wrath destroy me! Finally, the suppliant ventures to remind God that others are guilty as well as he, and that the ruthless destroyers of Israel are themselves fitted to be objects as well as instruments of Divine justice. They are such (i) because they have not "known" nor "called upon" Iahvah; and (ii) because they have "devoured Jacob" who was a thing consecrated to Iahvah (ii. 3), and therefore are guilty of sacrilege (cf. l. 28, 29).

It has never been our lot to see our own land overrun by a barbarous invader, our villages burnt, our peasantry slaughtered, our towns taken and sacked with all the horrors permitted or enjoined by a non-Christian religion. We read of but hardly realize the atrocities of ancient warfare. If we did realize them, we might even think a saint justified in praying for vengeance upon the merciless destroyers of his country. But apart from this, I see a deeper meaning in this prayer. The justice of this terrible visitation upon Judah is admitted by the prophet. Yet in Judah many righteous were involved in the general calamity. On the other hand, Jeremiah knew something of the vices of the Babylonians, against which his contemporary Habakkuk inveighs so bitterly. They "knew not" nor "called upon" Iahvah; but a base polytheism reflected and sanctioned the corruption of their lives. A kind of moral dilemma, therefore, is proposed here. If the purpose of this outpouring of Divine wrath be to bring Israel to "find out" (ver. 18) and to acknowledge the truth of God and his own guiltiness, can wrath persist, when that result is attained? Does not justice demand that the torrent of destruction be diverted upon the proud oppressor? So prayer, the forlorn hope of poor humanity, strives to overcome and compel and prevail with God, and to wrest a blessing even from the hand of Eternal Justice.

VI

THE IDOLS OF THE HEATHEN
AND THE GOD OF ISRAEL

Jeremiah x. 1-16.

This fine piece is altogether isolated from the surrounding context, which it interrupts in a very surprising manner. Neither the style nor the subject, neither the idioms nor the thoughts expressed in them, agree with what we easily recognise as Jeremiah's work. A stronger contrast can hardly be imagined than that which exists between the leading motive of this oracle as it stands, and that of the long discourse in which it is embedded with as little regard for continuity as an aerolite exhibits when it buries itself in a plain. In what precedes, the prophet's fellow-countrymen have been accused of flagrant and defiant idolatry (vii. 17 *sqq.*, 30 *sqq.*); the opening words of this piece imply a totally different situation. *To the way of the nations become not accustomed, and of the signs of heaven be not afraid; for the nations are afraid of them.* [39] Jeremiah would not be likely to warn inveterate apostates not to "accustom themselves" to idolatry. The words presuppose, not a nation whose idolatry was notorious, and had just been the subject of unsparing rebuke and threats of imminent destruction; they presuppose a nation free from idolatry, but exposed to temptation from surrounding heathenism. The entire piece contains no syllable of reference to past or present unfaithfulness on the part of Israel. Here at the outset, and throughout, Israel is implicitly contrasted with "the nations" (τὰ ἔθνη) as the servant of Iahvah with the foolish worshippers of lifeless gods. There is a tone of contempt in the use of the term *goyim*—"To the way of the *goyim* accustom not yourselves ... for the *goyim* are afraid of them" (of the signs of heaven); or as the Septuagint puts it yet more strongly, "for *they* (the besotted *goyim*) are afraid (*i.e.*, worship) before them;" as though that alone—the sense of Israel's superiority—should be sufficient to deter Israelites from any bowings in the house of Rimmon.[40] Neither this contemptuous use of the term *goyim*, "Gentiles," nor the scathing ridicule of the false gods and their devotees, is in the manner of Jeremiah. Both are characteristic of a later period. The biting scorn of image-worship, the intensely vivid perception of the utter incommensurableness of Iahvah, the Creator of all things, with the handiwork of the carpenter and the silversmith, are well-known and distinctive features of the great prophets of the Exile (see especially Isa. xl.-lxvi.). There are plenty of allusions to idolatry in Jeremiah; but they are expressed in a tone of fervid indignation, not of ridicule. It was the initial offence, which issued in a hopeless degradation of public and private morality, and would have for its certain consequence the rejection and ruin of the nation (ii. 5-13, 20-28, iii. 1-9, 23 *sqq.*). All the disasters, past and present, which had befallen the country, were due to it (vii. 9, 17 *sqq.*, 30 *sqq.*, viii. 2 etc.). The people are urged to repent and return to Iahvah with their whole heart (iii. 12 *sqq.*, iv. 3 *sqq.*, v. 21 *sqq.*, vi. 8), as the only means of escape from deadly peril. The Baals are things that cannot help or save (ii. 8, 11); but the prophet does not say, as here (x. 5), "Fear them not; they cannot harm you!" The piece before us breathes not one word about Israel's apostasy, the urgent need of repentance, the impending ruin. Taken as a whole, it neither harmonizes with Jeremiah's usual method of argument, nor does it suit the juncture of affairs implied by the language which precedes and follows (vii. 1-ix. 26, x. 17-25). For let us suppose that this oracle occupies its proper place here, and was actually written by Jeremiah at the crisis which called forth the preceding and following utterances. Then the warning cry, "Be not afraid of the signs of heaven!" can only mean "Be not afraid of the Powers under whose auspices the Chaldeans are invading your country; Iahvah, the true and living God, will protect you!" But consolation of this kind would be diametrically opposed to the doctrine which Jeremiah shares with all his predecessors; the doctrine that Iahvah Himself is the prime cause of the coming trouble, and that the heathen invaders are His instruments of wrath (v. 9 *sq.*, vi. 6); it would imply assent to that fallacious confidence in Iahvah, which the prophet has already done his utmost to dissipate (vi. 14, vii. 4 *sq.*).

The details of the idolatry satirized in the piece before us point to Chaldea rather than to Canaan. We have here a zealous worship of wooden images overlaid and otherwise adorned with silver and gold, and robed in rich garments of violet and purple (cf. Josh. vii. 21). This does not agree with what we know of Judean practice in Jeremiah's time, when, besides the worship of the Queen of Heaven, the people adored "stocks and stones;" probably the wooden symbols of the goddess Asherah and rude sun-pillars, but hardly works of the costly kind described in the text, which indicate a wealthy people whose religion reflected an advanced condition of the arts and commerce. The designation of the objects of heathen worship as "the signs of heaven," and the gibe at the custom of carrying the idol-statues in procession (Isa. xlvi. 1, 7), also point us to Babylon, "the land of graven images" (1. 38), and the home of star-worship and astrological superstition (Isa. xlvii. 13).

From all these considerations, it would appear that not Israel in Canaan but Israel in Chaldea is addressed in this piece by some unknown prophet, whose leaflet has been inserted among the works of Jeremiah. In that case, the much disputed eleventh verse, written in Aramaic, and as such unique in the volume of the prophets proper, may really have belonged to the original piece. Aramaic was the common language of intercourse between East and West both before and during the captivity (cf. 2 Kings xviii. 26); and the suggestion that the tempted exiles should answer in this dialect the heathen who pressed them to join in their worship, seems suitable enough. The verse becomes very suspicious, if we suppose that the whole piece is really part and parcel of Jeremiah's discourse, and as such addressed to the Judeans in the reign of Jehoiakim. Ewald, who maintains this view upon grounds that cannot be called convincing, thinks the Aramaic verse was originally a marginal annotation on verse 15, and suggests that it is a quotation from some early book similar to the book of Daniel. At all events, it is improbable that the verse proceeded from the pen of Jeremiah, who writes Aramaic nowhere else, not even in the letter to the exiles of the first Judean captivity (chap. xxix.).

But might not the piece be an address which Jeremiah sent to the exiles of the Ten Tribes, who were settled in Assyria, and with whom it is otherwise probable that he cultivated some intercourse? The expression "House of *Israel*" (ver. 1) has been supposed to indicate this. That expression, however, occurs in the immediately preceding context (ix. 26), as does also that of "the nations"; facts which may partially explain why the passage we are discussing occupies its present position. The unknown author of the Apocryphal Letter of Jeremiah and the Chaldee Targumist appear to have held the opinion that Jeremiah wrote the piece for the benefit of the exiles carried away with Jehoiachin in the first Judean captivity. The Targum introduces the eleventh verse thus: "This is a copy of the letter which Jeremiah the prophet sent to the remnant of the elders of the captivity which was in Babylon. And if the peoples among whom ye are shall say unto you, Fear the Errors, O house of Israel! thus shall ye answer and thus shall ye say unto them: The Errors whom ye fear are (but) errors, in which there is no profit: they from the heavens are not able to bring down rain, and from the earth they cannot make fruits to spring: they and those who fear them will perish from the earth, and will be brought to an end from under these heavens. And thus shall ye say unto them: We fear Him that maketh the earth by His power," etc. (ver. 12). The phrase "the *remnant of the elders of the captivity which was* (or *who were*) *in Babylon"* is derived from Jer. xxix. 1. But how utterly different are the tone and substance of that message from those of the one before us! Far from warning his captive countrymen against the state-worship of Babylon, far from satirizing its absurdity, Jeremiah bids the exiles be contented in their new home, and to pray for the peace of the city. The false prophets who appear at Babylon prophesy in Iahvah's name (vv. 15, 21), and in denouncing them Jeremiah says not a word about idolatry. It is evident from the whole context that he did not fear it in the case of the exiles of Jehoiachin's captivity. (See also the simile of the Good and Bad Figs, chap. xxiv., which further illustrates the prophet's estimation of the earlier body of exiles.)

The Greek Epistle of Jeremiah, which in MSS. is sometimes appended to Baruch, and which Fritzsche refers to the Maccabean times, appear to be partially based upon the passage we are considering. Its heading is: "Copy of a letter which Jeremiah sent unto those who were about to be carried away captives to Babylon, by the king of the Babylonians; to announce to them as was enjoined him by God." It then begins thus: "On account of your sins which ye have sinned before God ye will be carried away to Babylon as captives by Nabuchodonosor king of the Babylonians. Having come, then, into Babylon, ye will be there many years, and a long time, until seven generations; but after this I will bring you forth from thence in peace. But now ye will see in Babylon gods, silvern and golden and wooden, borne upon shoulders, shewing fear (an object of fear) to the nations. Beware then, lest ye also become like unto the nations, and fear take you at them, when ye see a multitude before and behind them worshipping them. But say ye in the mind: Thee it behoveth us to worship, O Lord! For Mine angel is with you, and He is requiring your lives." The whole epistle is well worth reading as a kind of paraphrase of our passage. "For their tongue is carven (or polished) by a carpenter, and themselves are overlaid with gold and silver, but lies they are and they cannot speak." "They *being cast about with purple apparel* have their face wiped on account of the dust from the house, which is plentiful upon them" (13). "But he holds a dagger with right hand and an axe, but *himself from war and robbers he will not* (= cannot) *deliver"* (15), cf. Jer. x. 15. "*He is like one of the house-beams"* (20, cf. Jer. x. 8, and perhaps 5). "Upon their body and upon their head alight bats, swallows, and the birds, likewise also the cats; whence ye will know that they are not gods; therefore fear them not" (cf. Jer. x. 5). "At all cost are they purchased, in which there is no spirit" (25; cf. Jer. x. 9, 14). "*Footless, upon shoulders they are carried*, displaying their own dishonour to men" (26). "Neither if they suffer evil from any one, nor if good, will they be able to recompense" (34; cf. ver. 5). "But they that serve them will be ashamed" (39; cf. ver. 14). "By carpenters and goldsmiths are they prepared; they become nothing but what the craftsmen wish them to become. And the very men that prepare them cannot last long; how then are the things prepared by them likely to do so? for they left lies and a reproach to them that come after. For whenever war and evils come upon them, the priests consult together where to hide with them. How then is it possible not to perceive that they are not gods, who neither save themselves from war nor from evils? For being of wood and overlaid with gold and silver they will be known hereafter, that they are lies. To all the nations and to the kings it will be manifest that they are not gods but works of men's hands, and no work of God is in them" (45-51; cf. Jer. x. 14-15). "*A wooden pillar in a palace* is more useful than the false gods" (59). "*Signs* among nations they will not shew *in heaven*, nor yet will they shine like the sun, nor give light as the moon" (67). "*For as a scarecrow in a cucumber-bed guarding nothing, so their gods are wooden and overlaid with gold and with silver*" (70; cf. Jer. x. 5). The mention of the sun, moon and stars, the lightning, the wind, the clouds, and fire "sent forth from above," as totally unlike the idols in "forms and powers," seems to shew that the author had verses 12, 13 before him.

When we turn to the Septuagint, we are immediately struck by its remarkable omissions. The four verses 6-8 and 10 do not appear at all in this oldest of the versions; while the ninth is inserted between the first clause and the remainder of the fifth verse. Now, on the one hand, it is just the verses which the LXX. translates, which both in style and matter contrast so strongly with Jeremiah's authentic work, and are plainly incongruous with the context and occasion; while, on the other hand, the omitted verses contain nothing which points positively to another author than Jeremiah, and, taken by themselves, harmonise very well with what may be supposed to have been the prophet's feeling at the actual juncture of affairs.

"There is none at all like Thee, O Iahvah!
Great art Thou, and great is Thy Name in might!
Who should not fear Thee, O King of the nations? for 'tis
Thy due
For among all the wise of the nations and in all their
kingdom there is none at all like Thee.
And in one thing they are brute-like and dull;
In the doctrine of Vanities, which are wood!
But Iahvah Elohim is truth;
He is a living God, and an eternal King:
At His wrath the earth quaketh,
And nations abide not His indignation."

As Hitzig has observed, it is natural that now, as the terrible decision approaches, the prophet should seek and find comfort in the thought of the all-overshadowing greatness of the God of Israel. If, however, we suppose these verses to be Jeremiah's, we can hardly extend the same assumption to verses 12-16, in spite of one or two expressions of his which occur in them; and, upon the whole, the linguistic argument seems to weigh decisively against Jeremiah's authorship of this piece (see Naegelsbach).

It may be true enough that "the basis and possibility of the true prosperity and the hope of the genuine community are unfolded in these strophes" (Ewald); but that does not prove that they belong to Jeremiah. Nor can I see much force in the remark that "didactic language is of another kind than that of pure prophecy." But when the same critic affirms that "the description of the folly of idolatry ... is also quite new, and clearly serves as a model for the much more elaborate ones, Isa. xl. 19-24 (20), xli. 7, xliv. 8-20, xlvi. 5-7;" he is really giving up the point in dispute. Verses 12-16 are repeated in the prophecy against Babylon (li. 15-19); but this hardly proves that "the later prophet, chap. l.-li., found *all these words* in our piece;" it is only evidence, so far as it goes, for those verses themselves.

The internal connexion which Ewald assumes, is not self-evident. There is no proof that "the thought that the gods of the heathen might again rule" occurred for one moment to Jeremiah on this occasion; nor the thought that "the maintenance of the ancient true religion in conflict with the heathen must produce the regeneration of Israel." There is no reference throughout the disputed passage to the spiritual condition of the people, which is, in fact, presupposed to be good; and the return in verses 17-25 "to the main subject of the discourse" is inexplicable on Ewald's theory that the whole chapter, omitting verse 11, is one homogeneous structure.

Hear ye the word that Iahvah spake upon you, O house of Israel! Thus said Iahvah. The terms imply a particular crisis in the history of Israel, when a Divine pronouncement was necessary to the guidance of the people. Iahvah speaks indeed in all existence and in all events, but His voice becomes audible, is recognised as His, only when human need asserts itself in some particular juncture of affairs. Then, in view of the actual emergency, the mind of Iahweh declares itself by the mouth of His proper spokesmen; and the prophetic *Thus said Iahvah* contrasts the higher point of view with the lower, the heavenly and spiritual with the earthly and the carnal; it sets forth the aspect of things as they appear to God, in the sharpest antithesis to the aspect of things as they appear to the natural unilluminated man. *Thus said Iahvah*: This is the thought of the Eternal, this is His judgment upon present conditions and passing events, whatever *your* thought and your judgment may happen or incline to be! Such, I think, is the essential import of this *vox solennis*, this customary formula of the dialect of prophecy.

On the present occasion, the crisis in view of which a prophet declares the mind of Iahvah is not a political emergency but a religious temptation. The day for the former has long since passed away, and the depressed and scattered communities of exiled Israelites are exposed among other trials to the constant temptation to sacrifice to present expediency the only treasure which they have saved from the wreck of their country, the faith of their fathers, the religion of the prophets. The uncompromising tone of this isolated oracle, the abruptness with which the writer at once enters *in medias res*, the solemn emphasis of his opening imperatives, proves that this danger pressed at the time with peculiar intensity. *Thus said Iahvah: Unto the way of the nations use not yourselves, And of the signs of heaven stand not in awe, for that the nations stand in awe of them!* (cf. Lev. xviii. 3; Ezek. xx. 18). The "way" of the nations is their religion, the mode and manner of their worship (v. 4, 5); and the exiles are warned not to suffer themselves to be led astray by example, as they had been in the land of Canaan; they are not to adore the signs of heaven, simply because they see their conquerors adoring them. The "signs of heaven" would seem to be the sun, moon and stars, which were the objects of Babylonian worship; although the passage is unhappily not free from ambiguity. Some expositors have preferred to think of celestial phenomena such as eclipses and particular conjunctions of the heavenly bodies, which in those days were looked upon as portents, foreshadowing the course of national and individual fortunes. That there is really a reference to the astrological observation of the stars, is a view which finds considerable support in the words addressed to Babylon on the eve of her fall, by a prophet, who, if not identical was at least contemporary with him whose message we are discussing. In the forty-seventh chapter of the book of Isaiah, it is said to Babylon: "Let now them that parcel out the heavens, that gaze at the stars, arise and save thee, prognosticating month by month the things that will come upon thee" (Isa. xlvii. 13). The *signs of heaven* are, in this case, the supposed indications of coming events furnished by the varying appearances of the heavenly bodies; and one might even suppose that the immediate occasion of our prophecy was some eclipse of the sun or moon, or some remarkable conjunction of the planets which at the time was exciting general anxiety among the motley populations of Babylonia. The prophecy then becomes a remarkable instance of the manner in which an elevated spiritual faith, free from all the contaminating and blinding influences of selfish motives and desires, may rise superior to universal superstition, and boldly contradict the suggestions of what is accounted the highest wisdom of the time, anticipating the results though not the methods nor the evidence of science, at an epoch when science is as yet in the mythological stage. And the prophet might well exclaim in a tone of triumph, *Among all the wise of the nations none at all is like unto thee, O Lord,* as a source of true wisdom and understanding for the guidance of life (ver. 7).

The inclusion of eclipses and comets among the signs of heaven here spoken of has been thought to be barred by the considerations that these are sometimes alleged by the prophets themselves as signs of coming judgment exhibited by the God of Israel; that, as a matter of fact, they were as mysterious and awful to the Jews as to their heathen neighbours; and that what is here contemplated is not the terror inspired by rare occasional phenomena of this kind, but an habitual superstition in relation to some ever-present causes. It is certain that in another prophecy against Babylon, preserved in the book of Isaiah, it is declared that, as a token of the impending destruction, "the stars of heaven and the Orions thereof shall not give their light: the sun shall be darkened in his going forth, and the moon shall not cause his light to shine" (Isa. xiii. 10); and the similar language of the prophet Joel is well known (Joel ii. 2, 10, 30, 31, iii. 15). But these objections are not conclusive, for what our author is denouncing is the heathen association of "the signs of the heavens," whatever may be intended by that expression, with a false system of religious belief. It is a special kind of idolatry that he contemplates, as is clear from the immediate context. Not only does the parallel clause "Unto the way of the nations use not yourselves" imply a gradual conformity to a heathen religion; not only is it the fact that the Hebrew phrase rendered in our versions "Be not dismayed!" may imply religious awe or worship (Mal. ii. 5), as indeed terms denoting fear or dread are used by the Semitic languages in general; but the prophet at once proceeds to an exposure of the absurdity of image-worship: *For the ordinances* (established modes of worship; 2 Kings xvii. 8; here, established objects of worship) *of the peoples are a mere breath* (*i.e.,* nought)! *for it* (the idol) *is a tree, which out of the forest one felled* (so the accents); *the handiwork of the carpenter with the bill. With silver and with gold one adorneth it* (or, *maketh it bright*); *with nails and with hammers they make them fast, that one sway not* (or, *that there be no shaking*). *Like the scarecrow of a garden of gourds are they, and they cannot speak; they are carried and carried, for they cannot take a step* (or, *march*): *be not afraid of them, for they cannot hurt, neither is it in their power to benefit!* "Be not afraid of them!" returns to the opening charge: "Of the signs of heaven stand not in awe!" (cf. Gen. xxxi. 42, 53; Isa. viii. 12, 13). Clearly, then, the *signa cœli* are the idols against whose worship the prophet warns his people; and they denote "the sun, the moon, the constellations (of the Zodiac), and all the host of heaven" (2 Kings xxiii. 5). We know that the kings of Judah, from Ahaz onwards, derived this worship from Assyria, and that its original home was Babylon, where in every temple the exiles would see images of the deities presiding over the heavenly bodies, such as Samas (the sun) and his consort Aa (the moon) at Sippara, Merodach (Jupiter) and his son Nebo (Mercurius) at Babylon and Borsippa, Nergal (Mars) at Cutha, daily served with a splendid and attractive ritual, and honoured with festivals and processions on the most costly and magnificent scale. The prophet looks through all this outward display to the void within, he draws no subtle distinction between the symbol and the thing symbolized; he accepts the popular confusion of the god with his image, and identifies all the deities of the heathen with the materials out of which their statues are made by the hands of men. And he is justified in doing this, because there can be but one god in his sense of the word; a multitude of *gods* is a contradiction in terms. From this point of view, he exposes the absurdity of the splendid idolatry which his captive countrymen see all around them. Behold that thing, he cries, which they call a god, and before which they tremble with religious fear! It is nothing but a tree trunk hewn in the forest, and trimmed into shape by the carpenter, and plated with silver and gold, and fixed on its pedestal with hammer and nails, for fear it should fall! Its terrors are empty terrors, like those of the palm-trunk, rough-hewn into human shape, and set up among the melons to frighten the birds away.

> "Olim truncus eram ficulnus, inutile lignum,
> Cum faber, incertus scamnum faceretne Priapum,
> Maluit esse deum. Deus inde ego, furum ariumque
> Maxima formido." (Hor., *Sat.* i. 8, 1, *sqq.*)

Though the idol has the outward semblance of a man, it lacks his distinguishing faculty of speech; it is as dumb as the scarecrow, and as powerless to move from its place; so it has to be borne about on men's shoulders (a mocking allusion to the grand processions of the gods, which distinguished the Babylonian festivals). Will you then be afraid of things that can do neither good nor harm? asks the prophet; in terms that recall the challenge of another, or perchance of himself, to the idols of Babylon: *Do good or do evil, that we may look at each other and see it together* (Isa. xli. 23).

In utter contrast with the impotence, the nothingness of all the gods of the nations, whether Israel's neighbours or his invaders, stands for ever the God of Israel. *There is none at all like Thee, O Iahweh! great art Thou, and great is Thy Name in might!* With different vowel points, we might render, *Whence* (cometh) *Thy like, O Iahvah?* This has been supported by reference to chap. xxx. 7: *Alas! for great is that day. Whence* (is one) *like it?* (*me`ayin?*); but there too, as here, we may equally well translate, *there is none like it.*

The interrogative, in fact, presupposes a negative answer; and the Hebrew particle usually rendered *there is not, are not* (`*ayin*, `*ên*) has been explained as originally identical with the interrogative *where?* (`*ayin*, implied in *me`ayin*, "from where?" "whence?" cf. Job. xiv. 10: *where is he? = he is not*). The idiom of the text expresses a more emphatic negation than the ordinary form would do; and though rare, is by no means altogether unparalleled (see Isa. xl. 17, xli. 24; and other references in Gesenius). *Great art Thou and great is Thy Name in might*; that is to say, Thou art great in Thyself, and great in repute or manifestation among men, in respect of *might*, virile strength or prowess (Ps. xxi. 14). Unlike the do-nothing idols, Iahvah reveals His strength in deeds of strength (cf. Exod. xv. 3 *sqq.*). *Who should not fear Thee, Thou King of the nations?* (cf. v. 22) *for Thee it beseemeth* (= it is Thy due, and Thine only): *for among all the wise of the nations and in all their realm, there is none at all* (as in ver. 6) *like Thee*. Religious fear is instinctive in man; but, whereas the various nations lavish reverence upon innumerable objects utterly unworthy of the name of deity, rational religion sees clearly that there can be but One God, working His supreme will in heaven and earth; and that this Almighty being is the true "King of the nations," and disposes their destinies as well as that of His people Israel, although they know Him not, but call other imaginary beings their *kings* (a common Semitic designation of a national god: Ps. xx. 9; Isa. vi. 5, viii. 21). He, then, is the proper object of the instinct of religious awe; all the peoples of the earth owe Him adoration, even though they be ignorant of their obligation; worship is His unshared prerogative.

Among all the wise of the nations and in all their realm, not one is like Thee! Who are the wise thus contrasted with the Supreme God? Are the false gods the reputed wise ones, giving pretended counsel to their deluded worshippers through the priestly oracle? The term "kingdom" seems to indicate this view, if we take "their kingdom" to mean the kingdom of the wise ones of the nations, that is, the countries whose "kings" they are, where they are worshipped as such. The heathen in general, and the Babylonians in particular, ascribed wisdom to their gods. But there is no impropriety from an Old Testament point of view in comparing Iahvah's wisdom with the wisdom of man. The meaning of the prophet may be simply this, that no earthly wisdom, craft or political sagacity, not even in the most powerful empires such as Babylon, can be a match for Iahvah the All-wise, or avail to thwart His purposes (Isa. xxxi. 1, 2). "Wise" and "sagacious" are titles which the kings of Babylon continually assert for themselves in their extant inscriptions; and the wisdom and learning of the Chaldeans was famous in the ancient world. Either view will agree with what follows: *But in one thing they*—the nations, or their wise men—*will turn out brutish and besotted*: (in) *the teaching of Vanities which are wood*. The verse is difficult; but the expression "the teaching (or doctrine) of Vanities" may perhaps be regarded as equivalent to *the idols taught of*; and then the second half of the verse is constructed like the first member of ver. 3: *The ordinances of the peoples are Vanity*, and may be rendered, *the idols taught of are mere wood* (cf. ver. 3 *b*, ii. 27, iii. 9). It is possible also that the right reading is "foundation" (*mûsad*) not "doctrine" (*mûsar*): *the foundation* (basis, substratum, substance) *of idols is wood*. (The term "Vanities"—*habalim*—is used for "idols," viii. 19, xiv. 22; Ps. xxxi. 7). And, lastly, I think, the clause might be rendered: *a doctrine of Vanities, of mere wood, it*—their religion—*is*![41] This supreme folly is the "one thing" that discredits all the boasted wisdom of the Chaldeans; and their folly will hereafter be demonstrated by events (ver. 14).

The body of the idol is wood, and outwardly it is decorated with silver and gold and costly apparel; but the whole and every part of it is the work of man. *Silver plate* (lit. *beaten out*) *from Tarshish*—from far away Tartessus in Spain—*is brought, and gold from Uphaz* (Dan. x. 5), *the work of the smith, and of the hands of the founder*—who have beaten out the silver and smelted the gold: *blue and purple is their clothing* (Ex. xxvi. 31, xxviii. 8): *the work of the wise*—of skilled artists (Isa. xl. 20)—*is every part of them*. Possibly the verse might better be translated: *Silver to be beaten out*—argentum malleo diducendum—*which is brought from Tarshish, and gold* which is brought *from Uphaz*, are *the work of the smith and of the hands of the smelter; the blue and purple* which are *their clothing*, are *the work of the wise all of them*. At all events, the point of the verse seems to be that, whether you look at the inside or the outside of the idol, his heart of wood or his casing of gold and silver and his gorgeous robes, the whole and every bit of him as he stands before you is a manufactured article, the work of men's hands. The supernatural comes in nowhere. In sharpest contrast with this lifeless fetish, *Iahvah is a God that is truth*, *i.e.*, a true God (cf. Prov. xxii. 21), or *Iahvah is God in truth*—is really God—*He is a living God, and an eternal King*; the sovereign whose rule is independent of the vicissitudes of time, and the caprices of temporal creatures: *at His wrath the earth quaketh, and nations cannot abide His indignation*: the world of nature and the world of man are alike dependent upon His Will, and He exhibits His power and his righteous anger in the disturbances of the one and the disasters of the other.

According to the Hebrew punctuation, we should rather translate: *But Iahvah Elohim* (the designation of God in the second account of creation, Gen. ii. 4-iii. 24) *is truth*, *i.e.*, reality; as opposed to the falsity and nothingness of the idols; or *permanence, lastingness* (Ps. xix. 10), as opposed to their transitoriness (vv. 11-15).

The statement of the tenth verse respecting the eternal power and godhead of Iahvah is confirmed in the twelfth and thirteenth by instances of His creative energy and continual activity as exhibited in the world of nature. *The Maker of the earth by His power, Establishing the habitable world by His wisdom, And by His insight He did stretch out the heavens: At the sound of His giving voice* (Ps. lxxvii. 18; *i.e.*, thundering) *there is an uproar of waters in the heavens, And He causeth the vapours to rise from the end of the earth; Lightnings for the rain He maketh, And causeth the wind to go forth out of His treasuries.* There is no break in the sense between these sentences and the tenth verse. The construction resembles that of Amos v. 8, ix. 5, 6, and is interrupted by the eleventh verse, which in all probability was, to begin with, a marginal annotation.

The solid earth is itself a natural symbol of strength and stability. The original creation of this mighty and enduring structure argues the omnipotence of the Creator; while the "establishing" or "founding" of it upon the waters of the great deep is a proof of supreme wisdom (Ps. xxiv. 2; cxxxvi. 6), and the "spreading out" of the visible heavens or atmosphere like a vast canopy or tent over the earth (Ps. civ. 2; Isa. xl. 22), is evidence of a perfect insight into the conditions essential to the existence and wellbeing of man.

It is, of course, clear enough that physical facts and phenomena are here described in popular language as they appear to the eye, and by no means with the severe precision of a scientific treatise. It is not to be supposed that this prophet knew more about the actual constitution of the physical universe than the wise men of his time could impart. But such knowledge was not necessary to the enforcement of the spiritual truths which it was his mission to proclaim; and the fact that his brief oracle presents those truths in a garb which we can only regard as poetical, and which it would argue a want of judgment to treat as scientific prose, does not affect their eternal validity, nor at all impair their universal importance. The passage refers us to God as the ultimate source of the world of nature. It teaches us that the stability of things is a reflexion of His eternal being; that the persistence of matter is an embodiment of His strength; that the indestructibility which science ascribes to the materials of the physical universe is the seal which authenticates their Divine original. Persistence, permanence, indestructibleness, are properly sole attributes of the eternal Creator, which He communicates to His creation. Things are indestructible as regards man, not as regards the Author of their being.

Thus the wisdom enshrined in the laws of the visible world, all its strength and all its stability, is a manifestation of the Unseen God. Invisible in themselves, the eternal power and godhead of Iahvah become visible in His creation. And, as the Hebrew mode of expression indicates, His activity is never suspended, nor His presence withdrawn. The conflict of the elements, the roar of the thunder, the flash of the lightning, the downpour of waters, the rush of the stormwind, are His work; and not less His work, because we have found out the "natural" causes, that is, the established conditions of their occurrence; not less His work, because we have, in the exercise of faculties really though remotely akin to the Divine Nature, discovered how to imitate, or rather mimic, even the more awful of these marvellous phenomena. Mimicry it cannot but appear, when we compare the overwhelming forces that rage in a tropical storm with our electric toys. The lightnings in their glory and terror are still God's arrows, and man cannot rob His quiver.

Nowadays more is known about the machinery of the world, but hardly more of the Intelligence that contrived it, and keeps it continually in working order, nay, lends it its very existence. More is known about means and methods, but hardly more about aims and purposes. The reflexion, how few are the master-conceptions which modern speculation has added to the treasury of thought, should suggest humility to the vainest and most self-confident of physical inquirers. In the very dawn of philosophy the human mind appears to have anticipated as it were by sudden flashes of insight some of the boldest hypotheses of modern science, including that of Evolution itself.

The unchangeable or invariable laws of nature, that is to say, the uniformity of sequence which we observe in physical phenomena, is not to be regarded as a thing that explains itself. It is only intelligible as the expression of the unchanging will of God. The prophet's word is still true. It is God who "causes the vapours to rise from the end of the earth," drawing them up into the air from oceans and lakes by the simple yet beautiful and efficient action of the solar heat; it is God who "makes lightnings for the rain," charging the clouds with the electric fluid, to burst forth in blinding flashes when the opposing currents meet. It is God who "brings the wind out of His treasuries." In the prophet's time the winds were as great a mystery as the thunder and lightning; it was not known whence they came nor whither they went. But the knowledge that they are but currents of air due to variations of temperature does not really deprive them of their wonder. Not only is it impossible, in the last resort, to comprehend what heat is, what motion is, what the thing moved is. A far greater marvel remains, which cries aloud of God's wisdom and presence and sovereignty over all; and that is the wonderful consilience of all the various powers and forces of the natural world in making a home for man, and enabling so apparently feeble a creature as he to live and thrive amidst the perpetual interaction and collision of the manifold and mighty elements of the universe.

The true author of all this magnificent system of objects and forces, to the wonder and the glory of which only custom can blind us, is the God of the prophet. This sublime, this just conception of God was possible, for it was actually realized, altogether apart from the influence of Hellenic philosophy and modern European science. But it was by no means as common to the Semitic peoples. In Babylon, which was at the time the focus of all earthly wisdom and power, in Babylon the ancient mother of sciences and arts, a crude polytheism stultified all the wisdom of the wise, and lent its sanction to a profound moral corruption. Rapid and universal conquests, enormous wealth accruing from the spoils and tributes of all nations, only subserved the luxury and riotous living which issued in a general effeminacy and social enervation; until the great fabric of empire, which Nabopalassar and Nebuchadrezzar had reared by their military and political genius, sank under the weight of its own vices.

Looking round upon this spectacle of superstitious folly, the prophet declares that *all men are become too brute-like for knowledge*; too degraded to appreciate the truth, the simplicity of a higher faith; too besotted with the worship of a hundred vain idols, which were the outward reflexion of their own diseased imaginations, to receive the wisdom of the true religion, and to perceive especially the truth just enunciated, that it is Iahvah who gives the rain and upon whom all atmospheric changes depend (cf. xiv. 22): and thus, in the hour of need, *every founder blushes for the image, because his molten figure is a lie, and there is no breath in them*; because the lifeless idol, the work of his hands, can lend no help. Perhaps both clauses of the verse rather express a prophecy: *All men will be proven brutish, destitute of knowledge; every founder will blush for the graven image.* Wise and strong as the Babylonians supposed themselves to be, the logic of events would undeceive them. They were doomed to a rude awakening; to discover in the hour of defeat and surrender that the molten idol was a delusion, that the work of their hands was an embodied lie, void of life, powerless to save. *Vanity*—a mere breath, nought—*are they, a work of knaveries* (a term recurring only in li. 18; the root seems to mean "to stammer," "to imitate"); *in the time of their visitation they will perish!* or simply *they perish!*—in the burning temples, in the crash of falling shrines.

It has happened so. At this day the temples of cedar and marble, with their woodwork overlaid with bronze and silver and gold, of whose glories the Babylonian sovereigns so proudly boast in their still existing records, as "shining like the sun, and like the stars of heaven," are shapeless heaps or rather mountains of rubbish, where Arabs dig for building materials and treasure trove, and European explorers for the relics of a civilisation and a superstition which have passed away for ever. "Vana sunt, et opus risu dignum." In the revolutions of time, which are the outward measures of the eternally self-unfolding purposes of God, the word of the Judean prophets has been amply fulfilled. Babylon and her idols are no more.

All other idols, too, must perish in like manner. *Thus shall ye say of them: The gods who the* heavens *and earth did not make, perish from the earth and from under the heavens shall these!* The assertion that the idols of Babylon were doomed to destruction, was not the whole of the prophetic message. It is connected with and founded upon the antithetic assertion of the eternity of Iahvah. They will perish, but He endures. The one eternal is El Elyon, the Most High God, the Maker of heaven and earth. But heaven and earth and whatever partakes only of their material nature are also doomed to pass away. And in that day of the Lord, when the elements melt with fervent heat, and the earth and the works that are therein shall be burnt up (2 Pet. iii. 10), not only will the idols of the heathen world, and the tawdry dolls which a degenerate church suffers to be adored as a kind of magical embodiment of the Mother of God, but all other idols which the sensebound heart of man makes to itself, vanish into nothingness before that overwhelming revelation of the supremacy of God.

There is something amazing in the folly of worshipping man, whether in the abstract form of the cultus of "Humanity," or in any of the various forms of what is called "Hero-worship," or in the vulgar form of self-worship, which is the religion of the selfish and the worldly. To ascribe infallibility to any mortal, whether Pope or politician, is to sin in the spirit of idolatry. The Maker of heaven and earth, and He alone, is worthy of worship. "Where wast thou when I laid the foundations of the earth? declare, if thou hast understanding" (Job xxxviii. 4). No human wisdom nor power presided there; and to produce the smallest of asteroids is still a task which lies infinitely beyond the combined resources of modern science. Man and all that man has created is nought in the scale of God's creation. He and all the mighty works with which he amazes, overshadows, enslaves his little world, will perish and pass away; only that will survive which he builds of materials which are imperishable, fabrics of spiritual worth and excellence and glory (1 Cor. iii. 13). A Nineveh, a Babylon, a London, a Paris, may disappear; *but he that doeth the will of God abideth for ever* (1 John ii. 17). *Not like these* (cf. verse 11 *ad fin.*) *is Jacob's Portion, but the Maker and Moulder of the All—He is his heritage; Iahvah Sabaoth is His name!* (Both here and at li. 19 = xxviii. 19 the LXX. omits: *and Israel is the tribe*, which seems to have been derived from Deut. xxxii. 9. Israel is elsewhere called *Iahvah's heritage*, Ps. xxxiii. 12, and *portion*, Deut. xxxii. 9; but that thought hardly suits the connexion here.)

Not like these: for He is the Divine Potter who moulded all things, including the signs of heaven, and the idols of wood and metal, and their foolish worshippers. And he is *Jacob's portion*; for the knowledge and worship of Him was, in the Divine counsels, originally assigned to Israel (cf. Deut. iv. 19; and xxxii. 8, according to the true reading, preserved in the LXX.); and therefore Israel alone knows Him and His glorious attributes. *Iahvah Sabaoth is His name*: the Eternal, the Maker and Master of the hosts of heaven and earth, is the aspect under which He has revealed Himself to the true representatives of Israel, His servants the prophets.

The portion of Israel is his God—his abiding portion; of which neither the changes of time nor the misconceptions of man can avail to rob him. When all that is accidental and transitory is taken away, this distinction remains: Israel's portion is his God. Iahvah was indeed the national God of the Jews, argue some of our modern wise ones; and therefore He cannot be identified with the universal Deity. He has been developed, expanded, into this vast conception; but originally He was but the private god of a petty tribe, the Lar of a wandering household. Now herein is a marvellous thing. How was it that this particular household god thus grew to infinite proportions, like the genius emerging from the unsealed jar of Arab fable, until, from His prime foothold on the tent-floor of a nomad family, He towered above the stars and His form overshadowed the universe? How did it come to pass that His prophet could ask in a tone of indisputable truth, recognised alike by friend and foe, "Do not I fill heaven and earth, saith Iahvah"? (Jer. xxiii. 24). How, that this immense, this immeasurable expansion took place in this instance, and not in that of any one of the thousand rival deities of surrounding and more powerful tribes and nations? How comes it that we to-day are met to adore Iahvah, and not rather one of the forgotten gods of Canaan or Egypt or Babylon? Merodach and Nebo have vanished, but Iahvah is the Father of our Lord Jesus Christ. It certainly looks very much as if the Hebrew prophets were right; as if Iahvah were really the God of the creation as well as the Portion of Jacob.

The portion of Jacob. Is His relation to that one people a stumbling-block? Can we see no eternal truth in the statement of the Psalmist that *the Lord's portion is His people*? Who can find fault with the enthusiastic faith of holy men thus exulting in the knowledge and love of God? It is a characteristic of all genuine religion, this sweet, this elevating consciousness that God is *our* God; this profound sense that He has revealed Himself to us in a special and peculiar and individual manner. But the actual historical results, as well as the sacred books, prove that the sense of possessing God and being possessed by Him was purer, stronger, deeper, more effectual, more abiding, in Israel than in any other race of the ancient world.

One must tread warily upon slippery ground; but I cannot help thinking that many of the arguments alleged against the probability of God revealing Himself to man at all or to a single nation in particular, are sufficiently met by the simple consideration that He has actually done so. Any event whatever may be very improbable until it has happened; and assuming that God has *not* revealed Himself, it may perhaps be shewn to be highly improbable that He would reveal Himself. But, meanwhile, all religions and all faith and the phenomena of conscience and the highest intuitions of reason presuppose this improbable event as the fact apart from which they are insoluble riddles. This is not to say that the precise manner of revelation—the contact of the Infinite with the Finite Spirit—is definable. There are many less lofty experiences of man which also are indefinable and mysterious, but none the less actual and certain. Facts are not explained by denial, which is about the most barren and feeble attitude a man can take up in the presence of a baffling mystery. Nor is it for man to prescribe conditions to God. He who made us and knows us far better than we know ourselves, knows also how best to reveal Himself to His creatures.

The special illumination of Israel, however, does not imply that no light was vouchsafed elsewhere. The religious systems of other nations furnish abundant evidence to the contrary. God "left not Himself without witness," the silent witness of that beneficent order of the natural world, which makes it possible for man to live, and to live happily. St. Paul did not scruple to compliment even the degenerate Athenians of his own day on the ground of their attention to religious matters, and he could cite a Greek poet in support of his doctrine that man is the offspring of the one God and Father of all.

We may see in the fact a sufficient indication of what St. Paul would have said, had the nobler non-Christian systems fallen under his cognisance; had heathenism become known to him not in the heterogeneous polytheism of Hellas, which in his time had long since lost what little moral influence it had ever possessed, nor in the wild orgiastic nature worships of the Lesser Asia, which in their thoroughly sensuous basis did dishonour alike to God and to man; but in the sublime tenets of Zarathustra, with their noble morality and deep reverence for the One God, the Spirit of all goodness and truth, or in the reformed Brahmanism of Gautama the Buddha, with its grand principle of self-renunciation and universal charity.

The peculiar glories of Bible religion are not dimmed in presence of these other lights. Allowing for whatever is valuable in these systems of belief, we may still allege that Bible religion comprises all that is good in them, and has, besides, many precious features peculiar to itself; we may still maintain that their excellences are rather testimonies to the truth of the biblical teachings about God, than difficulties in the way of a rational faith; that it would be far more difficult to a thoughtful mind to accept the revelation of God conveyed in the Bible, if it were the fact that no rays of Divine light had cheered the darkness of the millions of struggling mortals beyond the pale of Judaism, than it is under the actual circumstances of the case: in short, that the truths implicated in imperfect religions, isolated from all contact with Hebrew or Christian belief, are a witness to and a foreshadowing of the truths of the gospel.

Our prophet declares that Jacob's portion—the God of Israel—is not like the gods of contemporary peoples. How, then, does he conceive of Him? Not as a metaphysical entity—a naked, perhaps empty abstraction of the understanding. Not as the Absolute and Infinite Being, who is out of all relation to space and time. His language—the language of the Old Testament—possesses no adjectives like "Infinite," "Absolute," "Eternal," "Omniscient," "Omnipresent," nor even "Almighty," although that word so often appears in our venerable Authorized Version. It is difficult for us, who are the heirs of ages of thought and intellectual toil, and whose thinking is almost wholly carried on by means of abstract ideas, to realize a state of mind and a habit of thought so largely different from our own as that of the Hebrew people and even of the Hebrew prophets. Yet unless we make an effort to realize it, however inadequately, unless we exert ourselves, and strive manfully to enter through the gate of an instructed imagination into that far-off stage of life and thought which presents so many problems to the historical student, and hides in its obscurity so many precious truths; we must inevitably fail to appreciate the full significance, and consequently fail of appropriating the full blessing of those wonderful prophecies of ancient Israel, which are not for an age but for all time.

Let us, then, try to apprehend the actual point of view from which the inspired Israelite regarded his God. In the first place, that point of view was eminently practical. As a recent writer has forcibly remarked, "The primitive mind does not occupy itself with things of no practical importance, and it is only in the later stages of society that we meet with traditional beliefs nominally accepted by every one but practically regarded by none; or with theological speculations which have an interest for the curious, but are not felt to have a direct bearing on the concerns of life."

The pious Israelite could not indulge a morbidly acute and restlessly speculative intellect with philosophical or scientific theories about the Deity, His nature in Himself, His essential and accidental attributes, His relation to the visible world. Neither did such theories then exist ready made to his hand, nor did his inward impulses and the natural course of thought urge him to pry into such abstruse matters, and with cold irreverence to subject his idea of God to critical analysis. Could he have been made to understand the attitude and the demands of some modern disputants, he would have been apt to exclaim, "Canst thou by searching find out God? Canst thou find out Shaddai unto perfection? It is as high as heaven, what canst thou do? deeper than hell, what canst thou know?" To find out and to know God as the understanding finds out and knows, how can that ever become possible to man? Such knowledge depends entirely upon processes of comparison; upon the perception of similarity between the object investigated and other known objects; upon accurate naming and classification. But who can dream of successfully referring the Deity to a class? "To what will ye liken God, or what likeness will ye compare unto Him?" In the brief prophecy before us, as in the fortieth chapter of Isaiah, with which it presents so many points of contact, we have a splendid protest against all attempts at bringing the Most High within the limitations of human cognition, and reducing God to the category of things known and understood. Directed in the first instance against idolatry—against vain efforts to find an adequate likeness of the Supreme in some one of the numberless creations of His hand, and so to compare and gauge and comprehend Himself,—that protest is still applicable, and with even greater force, against the idolatrous tendencies of the present age: when one school of devotees loudly declares,

"Thou, Nature, art our goddess; to thy law
Our services are bound: wherefore should we
Stand in the plague of custom?"

and another is equally loud in asserting that it has found the true god in man himself; and another proclaims the divinity of brute force, and feels no shame in advocating the sovereignty of those gross instincts and passions which man shares with the beasts that perish. It is an unworthy and an inadequate conception of God, which identifies Him with Nature; it is a deplorably impoverished idea, the mere outcome of philosophic despair, which identifies him with Humanity; but what language can describe the grovelling baseness of that habit of thought which knows of nothing higher than the sensual appetite, and seeks nothing better than its continual indulgence; which sees the native impress of sovereignty on the brow of passing pleasure, and recognises the image and likeness of God in a temporary association of depraved instincts?

It is to this last form of idolatry, this utter heathenism in the moral life, that all other forms really converge, as St. Paul has shewn in the introduction of his Epistle to the Romans, where, in view of the unutterable iniquities which were familiar occurrences in the world of his contemporaries, he affirms that moral decadence of the most appalling character is ultimately traceable to a voluntary indulgence of those idolatrous tendencies which ignore God's revelation of Himself to the heart and reason, and prefer to find their deity in something less awful in purity and holiness, less averse to the defilements of sin, less conversant with the secrets of the soul; and so, not liking to retain the true and only God in knowledge, change His truth into a lie, and worship and serve the creature more than the Creator: changing the glory of the incorruptible God into an image made like unto corruptible man, or even to birds and fourfooted beasts and creeping things.

VII
THE BROKEN COVENANT

Jeremiah xi., xii.

There is no visible break between these two chapters. They seem to summarize the history of a particular episode in the prophet's career. At the same time, the style is so peculiar, that it is not so easy, as it might appear at a first glance, to determine exactly what it is that the section has to tell us. When we come to take a closer look at it, we find a thoroughly characteristic mixture of direct narrative and soliloquy, of statement of facts and reflexion upon those facts, of aspiration and prayer and prophecy, of self-communing and communing with God. Careful analysis may perhaps furnish us with a clue to the disentanglement of the general sense and drift of this characteristic medley. We may thus hope to get a clearer insight into the bearing of this old-world oracle upon our own needs and perplexities, our sins and the fruit of our sins, what we have done and what we may expect as the consequence of our doings. For the Word of God is "quick and powerful." Its outward form and vesture may change with the passing of time; but its substance never changes. The old interpreters die, but the Word lives, and its life is a life of power. By that Word men live in their successive generations; it is at once creative and regulative; it is the seed of life in man, and it is the law of that life. Apart from the Divine Word, man would be no more than a brute gifted with understanding, but denied all answer to the higher cravings of soul and spirit; a being whose conscious life was a mere mockery; a self-tormentor, tantalized with vain surmises, tortured with ever-recurring problems; longing for light, and beset with never-lifting clouds of impenetrable darkness; the one sole instance, among the myriads of sentient beings, of a creature whose wants Nature refuses to satisfy, and whose lot it is to consume for ever in the fires of hopeless desire.

The sovran Lord, who is the Eternal Wisdom, has not made such a mistake. He provides satisfaction for all His creatures, according to the varying degrees of their capacity, according to their rank in the scale of being, so that all may rejoice in the fulness and the freedom of a happy life for their allotted time. Man is no exception to the universal rule. His whole constitution as God has fashioned it is such that he can find his perfect satisfaction in the Word of the Lord. And the depth of his dissatisfaction, the poignancy and the bitterness of his disappointment and disgust at himself and at the world in which he finds himself, are the strongest evidence that he has sought satisfaction in things that cannot satisfy; that he has foolishly endeavoured to feed his soul upon ashes, to still the cravings of his spirit with something other than that Word of God which is the Bread of Life.

You will observe that the discourse we are to consider, is headed: "*The word that fell to Jeremiah from Iahvah* (lit. *from with,* that is, *from the presence of* the Eternal), *saying.*" I think that expression "saying" covers all that follows, to the end of the discourse. The prophet's preaching the Law, and the consequences of that preaching as regarded himself; his experience of the stubbornness and treachery of the people; the varying moods of his own mind under that bitter experience; his reflexions upon the condition of Judah, and the condition of Judah's ill-minded neighbours; his forecasts of the after-course of events as determined by the unchanging will of a righteous God; all these things seem to be included in the scope of that "Word from the presence of Iahvah," which the prophet is about to put on record. You will see that it is not a single utterance of a precise and definite message, which he might have delivered in a few moments of time before a single audience of his countrymen. The Word of the Lord is progressively revealed; it begins with a thought in the prophet's mind, but its entire content is unfolded gradually, as he proceeds to act upon that thought or Divine impulse; it is, as it were, evolved as the result of collision between the prophet and his hearers; it emerges into clear light out of the darkness of storm and conflict; a conflict both internal and external; a conflict within, between his own contending emotions and impulses and sympathies; and a conflict without, between an unpopular teacher, and a wayward and corrupt and incorrigible people. *From with Iahvah.* There may be strife and tumult and the darkness of ignorance and passion upon earth; but the star of truth shines in the firmament of heaven, and the eye of the inspired man sees it. This is his difference from his fellows.

Hear ye the words of this covenant, and speak ye unto the men of Judah, and upon the dwellers in Jerusalem! And say thou unto them, Thus saith Iahvah, the God of Israel, Accursed are the men that hear not the words of this covenant, which I lay on your fathers, in the day that I brought them forth from the land of Egypt, from the furnace of iron, saying, Hearken unto My voice, and do these things, according to all that I shall charge you: that ye may become for Me a people, and that I Myself may become for you a God. That I may make good (מיקהל vid. infr.) *the oath which I sware to your forefathers, that I would give them a land flowing with milk and honey, as it now is* (or simply, *to-day*). *And I answered and said, Amen, Iahvah!* (xi. 1-5). "Hear ye ... speak ye unto the men of Judah!"

The occasion referred to is that memorable crisis in the eighteenth year of king Josiah, when Hilkiah the high priest had "found the book of the law in the house of the Lord" (2 Kings xxii. 8 *sqq.*), and the pious king had read in the hearing of the assembled people those fervid exhortations to obedience, those promises fraught with all manner of blessing, those terrible denunciations of wrath and ruin reserved for rebellion and apostasy, which we may still read in the closing chapters of the book of Deuteronomy (Deut. xxvii. *sq.*). Jeremiah is recalling the events of his own ministry, and passes in rapid review from the time of his preaching upon the Book of the Law, to the Chaldean invasion in the reign of Jehoiachin (xiii. 18 *sqq.*). He recalls the solemn occasion when king and people bound themselves by oath to observe the law of their God; when "the king stood upon the platform, and made the covenant before Iahvah, that he would follow Iahvah, and keep his commandments, and his laws and his statutes, with whole heart and with whole soul; to make good (מִקְהֵל) the words of this covenant, that were written upon this roll; and all the people stood to the covenant" (2 Kings xxiii. 3). At or soon after this great meeting, the prophet gives, in the name of Iahvah, an emphatic approval to the public undertaking; and bids the leaders in the movement not to rest contented with this good beginning, but to impress the obligation more deeply upon the community at large, by sending a mission of properly qualified persons, including himself, which should at once enforce the reforms necessitated by the covenant of strict obedience to the Law, and reconcile the people both of the capital and of the rural towns and hamlets to the sudden and sweeping changes demanded of them, by shewing their entire consonance with the Divine precepts. "Hear *ye*"—princes and priests—"the words of this covenant; and speak *ye* unto the men of Judah!" Then follows, in brief, the prophet's own commission, which is to reiterate, with all the force of his impassioned rhetoric, the awful menaces of the Sacred Book: *Cursed be the men that hear not the words of this covenant!* Now again, in these last years of their national existence, the chosen people are to hear an authoritative proclamation of that Divine Law upon which all their weal depends; the Law given them at the outset of their history, when the memory of the great deliverance was yet fresh in their minds; the Law which was the condition of their peculiar relation to the Universal God. At Sinai they had solemnly undertaken to observe that Law; and Iahweh had fulfilled His promise to their "fathers"—to Abraham, Isaac, and Jacob—and had given them a goodly land, in which they had now been established for at least six hundred years. The Divine truth and righteousness were manifest upon a retrospect of this long period of eventful history; and Jeremiah could not withhold his inward assent, in the formula prescribed by the Book of the Law (Deut. xxvii. 15 *sqq.*), to the perfect justice of the sentence: "Cursed be the men that hear not the words of this covenant." *And I answered and said, Amen, Iahvah!* [42] So to this true Israelite, thus deeply communing with his own spirit, two things had become clear as day. The one was the absolute righteousness of God's entire dealing with Israel, from first to last; the righteousness of disaster and overthrow as well as of victory and prosperity: the other was his own present duty to bring this truth home to the hearts and consciences of his fellow-countrymen. This is how he states the fact: *And Iahvah said unto me, Proclaim thou all these words in the cities of Judah and in the streets of Jerusalem, saying, Hear ye the words of this covenant and do them. For I earnestly adjured your fathers, when I brought them up from the land of Egypt (and I have done so continually) even unto this very day, saying, Obey ye My voice! And they obeyed not, nor inclined their ear; and they walked, each and all, in the hardness of their wicked heart. So I brought upon them all the threats* (lit. *words) of this covenant, which I had charged them to keep, and they kept it not.* (xi. 6-8). God is always self-consistent; man is often inconsistent with himself; God is eternally true, man is ever giving fresh proofs of his natural faithlessness. God is not only just in keeping His promises; He is also merciful, in labouring ever to induce man to be self-consistent, and true to moral obligations. And Divine mercy is revealed alike in the pleadings of the Holy Spirit by the mouth of prophets, by the voice of conscience, and in the retribution that overtakes persistence in evil. The Divine Law is life and health to them that keep it; it is death to them that break it. "Thou, Lord, art merciful; for thou rewardest every man according to his works."

The relation of the One God to this one people was neither accidental nor arbitrary. It is sometimes spoken of as a thing glaringly unjust to the other nations of the ancient world, that the Father of all should have chosen Israel only to be the recipient of His special favours. Sometimes it is demanded, as an unanswerable dilemma, How *could* the Universal God be the God of the Jews, in the restricted sense implied by the Old Testament histories? But difficulties of this kind rest upon misunderstanding, due to a slavishly literal interpretation of certain passages, and inability to take a comprehensive view of the general drift and tenor of the Old Testament writings as they bear upon this subject. God's choice of Israel was proof of His love for mankind. He did not select one people, because He was indifferent or hostile to all other peoples; but because He wished to bring all the nations of the earth to the knowledge of Himself, and the observance of His law. The words of our prophet shew that he was profoundly convinced that the favour of Iahvah had from the outset depended upon the obedience of Israel: *Hearken unto My voice, and do these things ... that ye may become for Me a people, and that I Myself may become for you a God.* How strangely must such words have sounded in the ears of people who believed, as the masses both in town and country appear for the most part to have done, that Iahvah as the ancestral god was bound by an indissoluble tie to Israel, and that He could not suffer the nation to perish without incurring irreparable loss, if not extinction, for Himself! It is as if the prophet had said: You call yourselves the people of God; but it is not so much that you *are* His people, as that you may become such by doing His will. You suppose that Iahvah, the Eternal, the Creator, is to you what Chemosh is to Moah, or Molech to Ammon, or Baal to Tyre; but that is just what He is not. If you entertain such ideas of Iahvah, you are worshipping a figment of your own carnal imaginations; your god is not the Universal God but a gross unspiritual idol. It is only upon your fulfilment of His conditions, only upon your yielding an inward assent to His law, a hearty acceptance to His rule of life, that He Himself—the One only God— can truly become your God. In accepting His law, you accept Him, and in rejecting His law, you reject Him; for His law is a reflexion of Himself; a revelation, so far as such can be made to a creature like man, of His essential being and character. Therefore think not that you can worship Him by mere external rites; for the true worship is "righteousness, and holiness of life."

The progress of the reforming movement, which was doubtless powerfully stimulated by the preaching of Jeremiah, is briefly sketched in the chapter of the book of Kings, to which I have already referred (2 Kings xxiii.). That summary of the good deeds of king Josiah records apparently a very complete extirpation of the various forms of idolatry, and even a slaughter of the idol-priests upon their own altars. Heathenism, it would seem, could hardly have been practised again, at least openly, during the twelve remaining years of Josiah. But although a zealous king might enforce outward conformity to the Law, and although the earnest preaching of prophets like Zephaniah and Jeremiah might have considerable effect with the better part of the people, the fact remained that those whose hearts were really open to the word of the Lord were still, as always, a small minority; and the tendency to apostasy, though checked, was far from being rooted up. Here and there the forbidden rites were secretly observed; and the harsh measures which had accompanied their public suppression may very probably have intensified the attachment of many to the local forms of worship. Sincere conversions are not effected by violence; and the martyrdom of devotees may give new life even to degraded and utterly immoral superstitions. The transient nature of Josiah's reformation, radical as it may have appeared at the time to the principal agents engaged in it, is evident from the testimony of Jeremiah himself. *And Iahvah said unto me, There exists a conspiracy among the men of Judah, and among the inhabitants of Jerusalem. They have returned to the old sins of their fathers, who refused to hear My words; and they too have gone away after other gods, to serve them: the house of Israel and the house of Judah have broken My covenant, which I made with their forefathers. Therefore thus saith Iahvah, Behold I am about to bring unto them an evil from which they cannot get forth; and they will cry unto Me, and I will not listen unto them. And the cities of Judah and the inhabitants of Jerusalem will go and cry unto the gods to whom they burn incense* (i.e., now; ptcp.); *and they will yield them no help at all in the time of their evil. For many as thy cities are thy gods become, O Judah! and many as the streets of Jerusalem have ye appointed altars to the Shame, altars for burning incense to the Baal. And as for thee, intercede thou not for this people, nor lift up for them outcry* (i.e., mourning) *and intercession; for I intend not to hearken, in the time when they call unto Me, in the time of their evil* (so read: cf. vers. 12, תעב instead of דעב) (vv. 9-14). All this appears to indicate the course of the prophet's reflexion, after it had become clear to him that the reformation was illusory, and that his own labours had failed of their purpose. He calls the relapse of the people a plot or conspiracy; thereby suggesting, perhaps, the secrecy with which the prohibited worships were at first revived, and the intrigues of the unfaithful nobles and priests and prophets, in order to bring about a reversal of the policy of reform, and a return to the old system; and certainly suggesting that the heart of the nation, as a whole, was disloyal to its Heavenly King, and that its renewed apostasy was a wicked disavowal of lawful allegiance, and an act of unpardonable treason against God.

But the word further signifies that a bond has been entered into, a bond which is the exact antithesis of the covenant with Iahvah; and it implies that this bond has about it a fatal strength and permanence, involving as its necessary consequence the ruin of the nation. Breaking covenant with Iahvah meant making a covenant with other gods; it was impossible to do the one thing without the other. And that is as true now, under totally different conditions, as it was in the land of Judah, twenty-four centuries ago. If you have broken faith with God in Christ, it is because you have entered into an agreement with another; it is because you have foolishly taken the tempter at his word, and accepted his conditions, and surrendered to his proposals, and preferred his promises to the promises of God. It is because, against all reason, against conscience, against the Holy Spirit, against the witness of God's Word, against the witness of His Saints and Confessors in all ages, you have believed that a Being less than the Eternal God could ensure your weal and make you happy. And now your heart is no longer at unity in itself, and your allegiance is no longer single and undivided. *Many as thy cities are thy gods become, O Judah!* The soul that is not unified and harmonized by the fear of the One God, is torn and distracted by a thousand contending passions: and vainly seeks peace and deliverance by worship at a thousand unholy shrines. But Mammon and Belial and Ashtaroth and the whole rout of unclean spirits, whose seductions have lured you astray, will fail you at last; and in the hour of bitter need, you will learn too late that there is no god but God, and no peace nor safety nor joy but in Him.

It is futile to pray for those who have deliberately cast off the covenant of Iahvah, and made a covenant with His adversary. *Intercede not for this people, nor lift up outcry and intercession for them!* Prayer cannot save, nothing can save, the impenitent; and there is a state of mind, in which one's own prayer is turned into sin; the state of mind in which a man prays, merely to appease God, and escape the fire, but without a thought of forsaking sin, without the faintest aspiration after holiness. There is a degree of guilt upon which sentence is already passed, which is "unto death," and for which intercession is interdicted alike by the Apostle of the New as to the prophet of the Old Covenant.

What availeth it My beloved, that she fulfilleth her intent in Mine house? Can vows and hallowed flesh make thine evil to pass from thee? Then mightest thou indeed rejoice [43] (ver. 15). Such appears to be the true sense of this verse, the only difficult one in the chapter. The prophet had evidently the same thought in his mind as in ver. 11: *I will bring unto them an evil, from which they cannot get forth; and they will cry unto Me, and I will not hearken unto them.* The words also recall those of Isaiah (Isa. i. 11 *sqq.*): "For what to Me are your many sacrifices, saith Iahvah? When ye enter in to see My face, who hath sought this at your hand, to trample My courts? Bring no more a vain oblation; loathly incense it is to Me!" The term which I have rendered "intent," usually denotes an evil intention; so that, like Isaiah, our prophet implies that the popular worship is not only futile but sinful. So true it is that "He that turneth away his ear from hearing the law, even his prayer is an abomination" (Prov. xxviii. 9); or, as the Psalmist puts the same truth, "If I incline unto wickedness with my heart, the Lord will not hear me."

"A flourishing olive, fair with shapely fruit, did Iahvah call thy name. To the sound of a great uproar will He set her on fire; and his hanging boughs will crackle (in the flames). And Iahvah Sabaoth, that planted thee, Himself hath pronounced evil upon thee; because of the evil of the house of Israel and the house of Judah, which they have done to themselves (iv. 18, vii. 19) *in provoking Me, in burning incense to the Baal"* (vers. 16-17). The figure of the olive seems a very natural one (cf. Rom. xi. 17), when we remember the beauty and the utility for which that tree is famous in Eastern lands. *Iahvah called thy name*; that is, called thee into determinate being; endowed thee at thine origin with certain characteristic qualities. Thine original constitution, as thou didst leave thy Maker's hand, was fair and good. Israel among the nations was as beautiful to the eye as the olive among trees; and his "fruit," his doings, were a glory to God and a blessing to men, like that precious oil, for "which God and man honour"

the olive (Judg. ix. 9). (Zech. iv. 3; Hos. xiv. 7; Ps. lii. 10.) But now the noble stock had degenerated; the "green olive tree," planted in the very court of Iahvah's house, had become no better than a barren wilding, fit only for the fire. The thought is essentially similar to that of an earlier discourse: "I planted thee a noble vine, wholly a right seed; how then hast thou turned into the degenerate plant of a strange vine unto Me?" (ii. 21). Here, there is an abrupt transition, which forcibly expresses the *suddenness* of the destruction that must devour this degenerate people: *To the sound of a great uproar*—the din of invading armies—*he will set her* (the beloved, symbolized by the tree) *on fire; and his* (the olive's) *hanging boughs will crackle in the flames.* And this fierce work of a barbarous soldiery is no chance calamity; it is the execution of a Divine judgment: *Iahvah Sabaoth ... Himself hath pronounced evil upon thee.* And yet further, it is the nation's own doing; the two houses of Israel have persistently laboured for their own ruin; they have brought it upon themselves. Man is himself the author of his own weal and woe; and they who are not "working out their own salvation," are working out their own destruction.

And it was Iahvah that gave Me knowledge, so that I well knew; at that time, Thou didst shew me their doings. But, for myself, like a favourite (lit. tame, friendly, gentle: iii. 4) *lamb that is led to the slaughter, I wist not that against me they had laid a plot. 'Let us fell the tree in its prime,* [44] *and let us cut him off out of the land of the living, that his name be remembered no more.' 'Yea, but Iahvah* [45] *Sabaoth judgeth righteously, trieth reins and heart. I shall see Thy vengeance on them; for unto Thee have I laid bare my cause.' Therefore thus said Iahvah; Upon the men of Anathoth that were seeking thy life, saying, Thou shalt not prophesy in the name of Iahvah, that thou die not by our hand:—therefore thus said Iahvah Sabaoth, Behold I am about to visit it upon them: the young men will die by the sword; their sons and their daughters will die by the famine. And a remnant they shall not have: for I will bring an evil unto the men of Anathoth, the year of their visitation* (vv. 18-23).

The prophet, it would seem, had made the round of the country places, and come to Anathoth, on his return journey to Jerusalem. Here, in his native town, he proclaimed to his own people that same solemn message which he had delivered to the country at large. It is very probable that the preceding verses (9-17) contain the substance of his address to his kinsfolk and acquaintance; an address which stirred them, not to repentance towards God but to murderous wrath against His prophet. A plot was laid for Jeremiah's life by his own neighbours and even his own family (xii. 6); and he owed his escape to some providential circumstance, some "lucky accident," as men might say, which revealed to him their unsuspected perfidy. What the event was which thus suddenly disclosed the hidden danger, is not recorded; and the whole episode is rather alluded to than described. But it is clear that the prophet knew nothing about the plot, until it was ripe for execution. He was as wholly unconscious of the death prepared for him, as a petted lamb on the way to the altar. "Then" — when his fate seemed sure — then it was that something happened by which "Iahvah gave him knowledge," and "shewed him their doings." The thought or saying attributed to his enemies, "Let us fell the tree(s) in the prime thereof!" may contain a sarcastic allusion really made to the prophet's own warning (ver. 16): "A flourishing olive, fair with shapely fruit, did Iahvah call thy name: to the noise of a great uproar will He set it on fire, and the branches thereof shall crackle in the flames." The words that follow (ver. 20), "yea, but (or, and yet) Iahvah Sabaoth judgeth righteously; trieth reins and heart" (cf. xx. 12), is the prophet's reply, in the form of an unexpressed thought, or a hurried ejaculation upon discovering their deadly malice. The timely warning which he had received, was fresh proof to him of the truth that human designs are, after all that their authors can do, dependent on the will of an Unseen Arbiter of events; and the Divine justice, thus manifested towards himself, inspired a conviction that those hardened and bloodthirsty sinners would, sooner or later, experience in their own destruction that display of the same Divine attribute which was necessary to its complete manifestation. It was this conviction, rather than personal resentment, however excusable under the circumstances that feeling would have been, which led Jeremiah to exclaim: "I shall see Thy vengeance on them, for unto Thee have I laid bare my cause."

He had appealed to the Judge of all the earth, that doeth right; and he knew the innocency of his own heart in the quarrel. He was certain, therefore, that his cause would one day be vindicated, when that ruin overtook his enemies, of which he had warned them in vain. Looked at in this light, his words are a confident assertion of the Divine justice, not a cry for vengeance. They reveal what we may perhaps call the *human* basis of the formal prophecy which follows; they shew by what steps the prophet's mind was led on to the utterance of a sentence of destruction upon the men of Anathoth. That Jeremiah's invectives and threatenings of wrath and ruin should provoke hatred and opposition was perhaps not wonderful. Men in general are slow to recognise their own moral shortcomings, to believe evil of themselves; and they are apt to prefer advisers, whose optimism, though ill-founded and misleading, is pleasant and reassuring and confirmatory of their own prejudices. But it does seem strange that it should have been reserved for the men of his own birthplace, his own "brethren and his father's house," to carry opposition to the point of meditated murder. Once more Jeremiah stands before us, a visible type of Him whose Divine wisdom declared that a prophet finds no honour in his own country, and whose life was attempted on that Sabbath day at Nazareth (St. Luke iv. 24 *sqq.*).

The sentence was pronounced, but the cloud of dejection was not at once lifted from the soul of the seer. He knew that justice must in the end overtake the guilty; but, in the meantime, "his enemies lived and were mighty," and their criminal designs against himself remained unnoticed and unpunished. The more he brooded over it, the more difficult it seemed to reconcile their prosperous immunity with the justice of God. He has given us the course of his reflections upon this painful question, ever suggested anew by the facts of life, never sufficiently answered by toiling reason. *Too righteous art Thou, Iahvah, for me to contend with Thee: I will but lay arguments before Thee* (i.e., argue the case forensically). *Wherefore doth the way of the wicked prosper? Wherefore are they undisturbed, all that deal very treacherously? Thou plantest them, yea, they take root; they grow ever, yea, they bear fruit: Thou art nigh in their mouth, and far from their reins. And Thou, Iahvah, knowest me; Thou seest me, and triest mine heart in Thy mind. Separate them like sheep for the slaughter, and consecrate them for the day of killing! How long shall the land mourn, and the herbage of all the country wither? From the evil of the dwellers therein, beasts and birds perish: for they have said* (or, *thought*), *He cannot see our end* (xii. 1-4). It is not merely that his would-be murderers thrive; it is that they take the holy Name upon their unclean lips; it is that they are hypocrites combining a pretended respect for God, with an inward and thorough indifference to God. He is nigh in their mouth and far from their reins. They "honour Him with their lips, but have removed their heart far from Him; and their worship of Him is a mere human commandment, learned by rote" (Isa. xxix. 13). They swear by His Name, when they are bent on deception (ch. v. 2). It is all this which especially rouses the prophet's indignation; and contrasting therewith his own conscious integrity and faithfulness to the Divine law, he calls upon Divine Justice to judge between himself and them: *Pull them out like sheep for slaughter, and consecrate them* (set them apart—from the rest of the flock) *for the day of killing!* It has been said that Jeremiah throughout this whole paragraph speaks not as a prophet but as a private individual; and that in this verse especially he "gives way to the natural man, and asks the life of his enemies" (1 Kings iii. 11; Job xxxi. 30). This is perhaps a tenable opinion. We have to bear in mind the difference of standpoint between the writers of the Old Covenant and those of the New. Not much is said by the former about the forgiveness of injuries, about withholding the hand from vengeance. The most ancient law, indeed, contained a noble precept, which pointed in this direction: "If thou meet thine enemy's ox or his ass going astray, thou shalt surely bring it back to him again. If thou see the ass of him that hateth thee lying under his burden, and wouldest forbear to help him, thou shalt surely help with him" (Ex. xxiii. 4, 5). And in the book of Proverbs we read: "Rejoice not when thine enemy falleth, And let not thine heart be glad when he is overthrown." But the impression of magnanimity thus produced is somewhat diminished by the reason which is added immediately: "Lest the Lord see it and it displease Him, *And He turn away His wrath from him:*" a motive of which the best that can be said is that it is characteristic of the imperfect morality of the time (Prov. xxiv. 17 *sq.*). The same objection may be taken to that other famous passage of the same book: "If thine enemy be hungry, give him bread to eat; And if he be thirsty, give him water to drink: *For thou shalt heap coals of fire upon his head,* And the Lord shall reward thee" (Prov. xxv. 21 *sq.*). The reflexion that the relief of his necessities will mortify and humiliate an enemy to the utmost, which is what seems to have been originally meant by "heaping coals of fire upon his head," however practically useful in checking the wild impulses of a hot-blooded and vindictive race, such as the Hebrews were, and such as their kindred the Bedawi Arabs have remained to this day under a system of faith which has *not* said, "Love your enemies"; and however capable of a new application in the more enlightened spirit of Christianity (Rom. xii. 19 *sqq.*); is undoubtedly a motive marked by the limitations of Old Testament ethical thought. And edifying as they may prove to be, when understood in that purely spiritual and universal sense, to which the Church has lent her authority, how many of the psalms were, in their primary intention, agonizing cries for vengeance; prayers that the human victim of oppression and wrong might "see his desire upon his enemies"? All this must be borne in mind; but there are other considerations also which must not be omitted, if we would get at the exact sense of our prophet in the passage before us.

We must remember that he is laying a case before God. He has admitted at the outset that God is absolutely just, in spite of and in view of the fact that his murderous enemies are prosperous and unpunished. When he pleads his own sincerity and purity of heart, in contrast with the lip-service of his adversaries, it is perhaps that God may grant, not so much *their* perdition, as the salvation of the country from the evils they have brought and are bringing upon it. Ascribing the troubles already present and those which are yet to come, the desolations which he sees and those which he foresees, to their steady persistence in wickedness, he asks, How long must this continue? Would it not be better, would it not be more consonant with Divine wisdom and righteousness to purify the land of its fatal taint by the sudden destruction of those heinous and hardened offenders, who scoff at the very idea of a true forecast of their "end" (ver. 4)? But this is not all. There would be more apparent force in the allegation we are discussing if it were. The cry to heaven for an immediate act of retributive justice is not the last thing recorded of the prophet's experience on this occasion. He goes on to relate, for our satisfaction, the Divine answer to his questionings, which seems to have satisfied his own troubled mind. *If thou hast run but with footracers, and they have wearied thee, how then wilt thou compete with the coursers? And if thy confidence be in a land of peace* (or, *a quiet land*), *how then wilt thou do in the thickets (jungles) of Jordan?* [46] *For even thine own brethren and thy father's house, even they will deal treacherously with thee; even they will cry aloud after thee: trust thou not in them, though they speak thee fair!* (xii. 5, 6). The metaphors convey a rebuke of impatience and premature discouragement. Hitzig aptly quotes Demosthenes: "If they cannot face the candle, what will they do when they see the sun?" (*Plut. de vitioso pudore*, c. 5.) It is "the voice of the prophet's better feeling, and of victorious self-possession," adds the critic; and we, who earnestly believe that, of the two voices which plead against each other in the heart of man, the voice that whispers good is the voice of God, find it not hard to accept his statement in that sense. The prophet is giving us the upshot of his reflexion upon the terrible danger from which he had been mercifully preserved; and we see that his thoughts were guided to the conclusion that, having once accepted the Divine Call, it would be unworthy to abdicate his mission on the first signal of danger. Great as that danger had been, he now, in his calmer hour, perceives that, if he is to fulfil his high vocation, he must be prepared to face even worse things. With serious irony he asks himself, if a runner who is overcome in a footrace can hope to outstrip horses? or how a man, who is only bold where no danger is, will face the perils that lurk in the jungles of the Jordan? He remembers that he has to fight a more arduous battle and on a greater scene. Jerusalem is more than Anathoth; and "the kings of Judah and the princes thereof" are mightier adversaries than the conspirators of a country town. And his present escape is an earnest of deliverance on the wider field: *They shall fight against thee, but they shall not prevail against thee: for I am with thee, said Iahvah, to deliver thee* (see i. 17-19). But to a deeply affectionate and sensitive nature like Jeremiah's, the thought of being forsaken by his own kindred might well appear as a trial worse than death. This is the "contending with horses," the struggle that is almost beyond the powers of man to endure; this is the deadly peril, like that of venturing into the lion-haunted thickets of Jordan, which he clearly foresees as awaiting him: *For even thine own brethren and thy father's house, even they will deal treacherously with thee.*[47] It would seem that the prophet, with whose "timidity" some critics have not hesitated to find fault, had to renounce all that man holds dear, as a condition of faithfulness to his call. Again we are reminded of One, of whom it is recorded that "Neither did His brethren believe in Him" (St. John vii. 5), and that "His friends went out to lay hold on Him, for they said, He is beside Himself" (St. Mark iii. 21). The closeness of the parallel between type and antitype, between the sorrowful prophet and the Man of Sorrows, is seen yet further in the words, "Even they will cry aloud after thee" (lit. *with full cry*). The meaning may be: They will join in the hue and cry of thy pursuers, the mad shouts of "Stop him!" or "Strike him down!" such as may perhaps have rung in the prophet's ears as he fled from Anathoth. But we may also understand a metaphorical description of the efforts of his family to recall him from the unpopular path on which he had entered; and this perhaps agrees better with the warning: "Trust them not, though they speak thee fair." And understood in this sense, the words coincide with what is told us in the Gospel of the attempt of our Lord's nearest kin to arrest the progress of His Divine mission, when His mother and His brethren "standing without, sent unto Him, calling Him" (St. Mark iii. 31).

The lesson for ourselves is plain. The man who listens to the Divine call, and makes God his portion, must be prepared to surrender everything else. He must be prepared, not only to renounce much which the world accounts good; he must be prepared for all kinds of opposition, passive and active, tacit and avowed; he may even find, like Jeremiah, that his foes are the members of his own household (St. Matt. x. 36). And, like the prophet, his acceptance of the Divine call binds him to close his ears against entreaties and flatteries, against mockery and menace; and to act upon his Master's word: "If any man would come after Me, let him deny himself, and take up his cross, and follow Me. For whosoever would save his life shall lose it; and whosoever shall lose his life for My sake and the gospel's shall save it" (St. Mark viii. 34 *sq.*). "If any man come unto Me, and hate not his father and mother and wife and children and brethren and sisters, yea and his own life also, he cannot be My disciple" (St. Luke xiv. 26). A great prize is worth a great risk; and eternal life is a prize infinitely great. It is therefore worth the hazard and the sacrifice of all (St. Luke xviii. 29 *sq.*).

The section which follows (vv. 7-17) has been supposed to belong to the time of Jehoiakim, and consequently to be out of place here, having been transposed from its original context, because the peculiar Hebrew term which is rendered "dearly beloved" (ver. 7), is akin to the term rendered "My beloved," chap. xi. 15. But this supposition depends on the assumption that the "historical basis of the section" is to be found in the passage 2 Kings xxiv. 2, which relates briefly that in Jehoiakim's time plundering bands of Chaldeans, Syrians, Moabites and Ammonites overran the country. The prophecy concerning Iahvah's "evil neighbours" is understood to refer to these marauding inroads, and is accordingly supposed to have been uttered between the eighth and the eleventh years of Jehoiakim (Hitzig). It has, however, been pointed out (Naegelsbach) that the prophet does not once name the Chaldeans in the present discourse; which "he invariably does in all discourses subsequent to the decisive battle of Carchemish in the fourth year of Jehoiakim," which gave the Chaldeans the sovereignty of Western

Asia. This discourse must, therefore, be of earlier date, and belong either to the first years of Jehoiakim, or to the time immediately subsequent to the eighteenth of Josiah. The history as preserved in Kings and Chronicles is so incomplete, that we are not bound to connect the reference to "evil neighbours" with what is so summarily told in 2 Kings xxiv. 2. There may have been other occasions when Judah's jealous and watchful enemies profited by her internal weakness and dissensions to invade and ravage the land; and throughout the whole period the country was exposed to the danger of plundering raids by the wild nomads of the eastern and southern borders. It is possible, however, that vv. 14-17 are a later postscript, added by the prophet when he wrote his book in the fifth or sixth year of Jehoiakim (xxxvi. 9, 32).

There is, in reality, a close connexion of thought between ver. 7 *sqq.* and what precedes. The relations of the prophet to his own family are made to symbolise the relations of Iahvah to His rebellious people; just as a former prophet finds in his own merciful treatment of a faithless wife a parable of Iahvah's dealings with faithless Israel. *I have forsaken My house, I have cast away My domain; I have given My soul's love into the grasp of her foes. My domain hath become to Me like the lion in the wood; she hath given utterance with her voice against Me; therefore I hate her.* It is Iahvah who still speaks, as in ver. 6; the "house" is His holy house,[48] the temple; the domain is His domain, the land of Judah; His "soul's love," is the Jewish people. Yet the expressions, "my house," "my domain," "my soul's love," equally suit the prophet's own family and their estate; the mention of the "lion in the wood" and its threatening roar, and the enmity provoked thereby, recalls what was said about the "wilds of the Jordan" in ver. 5, and the full outcry of his kindred after the prophet in ver. 6; and the solemn words "I have forsaken Mine house, I have cast away My domain" ... "I hate her," clearly correspond with the sentence of destruction upon Anathoth, ch. xi. 21 *sqq.* The double reference of the language becomes intelligible when we remember that in rejecting His messengers, Israel, nay mankind, rejects God; and that words and deeds done and uttered by Divine authority may be ascribed directly to God Himself. And regarded in the light of the prophet's commission "to pluck up and to break down, and to destroy and to overthrow, to build and to plant" nations and kingdoms (i. 10), all that is here said may be taken to be the prophet's own deliverance concerning his country. This, at all events, is the case with verses 12, 13.

What! do I see my domain (all) *vultures* (and) *hyenas?* [49] *Are vultures all around her? Go ye, assemble all the beasts of the field! Bring them to devour* (ver. 9). The questions express astonishment at an unlooked-for and unwelcome spectacle. The loss of Divine favour has exposed Judah to the active hostility of man; and her neighbours eagerly fall upon her, like birds and beasts of prey, swarming over a helpless quarry. It is—so the prophet puts it—it is as if a proclamation had gone forth to the wolves and jackals of the desert, bidding them come and devour the fallen carcase.[50] In another oracle he speaks of the heathen as "devouring Jacob" (x. 25). The people of Iahvah are their natural prey (Ps. xiv. 4: "who eat up My people as they eat bread"); but they are not suffered to devour them, until they have forfeited His protection.

The image is now exchanged for another, which approximates more nearly to the fact pourtrayed. *Many shepherds have marred My vineyard; they have trodden down My portion; they have turned My pleasant portion into a desolate wilderness. He* (the foe, the instrument of this ruin) *hath made it a desolation; it mourneth against Me, being desolate; desolated is all the land, for there is no man that giveth heed* (vv. 10, 11). As in an earlier discourse, ch. vi. 3, the invaders are now compared to hordes of nomad shepherds, who enter the land with their flocks and herds, and make havoc of the crops and pastures. From time immemorial the wandering Bedawis have been a terror to the settled peasantry of the East, whose way of life they despise as ignoble and unworthy of free men. Of this traditional enmity we perhaps hear a far-off echo in the story of Cain the tiller of the ground and Abel the keeper of sheep; and certainly in the statement that "every shepherd was an abomination unto the Egyptians" (Gen. xlvi. 34). The picture of utter desolateness, which the prophet suggests by a fourfold repetition, is probably sketched from a scene which he had himself witnessed; if it be not rather a representation of the actual condition of the country at the time of his writing. That the latter is the case might naturally be inferred from a consideration of the whole passage; and the twelfth verse seems to lend much support to this view: *Over all bare hills in the wilderness have come ravagers; for Iahvah hath a devouring sword: from land's end to land's end no flesh hath peace.*[51] The language indeed recalls that of ch. iv. 10, 11; and the entire description might be taken as an ideal picture of the ruin that must ensue upon Iahvah's rejection of the land and people, especially if the closing verses (14-17) be considered as a later addition to the prophecy, made in the light of accomplished facts. But, upon the whole, it would seem to be more probable that the prophet is here reading the moral of present or recent experience. He affirms (ver. 11) that the affliction of the country is really a punishment for the religious blindness of the nation: *there is no man that layeth to heart* the Divine teaching of events as interpreted by himself (cf. ver. 4). The fact that we are unable, in the scantiness of the records of the time, to specify the particular troubles to which allusion is made, is no great objection to this view, which is at least effectively illustrated by the brief statement of 2 Kings xxiv. 2. The reflexion appended in ver. 13 points in the same direction: *They have sown wheat, and have reaped thorns; they have put themselves to pain* (or, *exhausted themselves*) *without profit,* (or, *made themselves sick with unprofitable toil); and they are ashamed of their* [52] *produce (ingatherings), through the heat of the wrath of Iahvah.* When the enemy had ravaged the crops, thorns would naturally spring up on the wasted lands; and "the heat of the wrath of Iahvah" appears to have been further manifested in a parching drought, which ruined what the enemy had left untouched (ver. 4, ch. xiv.).

Thus, then, Jeremiah receives the answer to his doubts in a painfully visible demonstration of what the wrath of Iahvah means. It means drought and famine; it means the exposure of the country, naked and defenceless, to the will of rapacious and vindictive enemies. For Iahvah's wrongs are far deeper and more bitter than the prophet's. The misdeeds of individuals are lighter in the balance than the sins of a nation; the treachery of a few persons on a particular occasion is as nothing beside the faithlessness of many generations. The partial evils, therefore, under which the country groans, can only be taken as indications of a far more complete and terrible destruction reserved for final impenitence. The perception of this truth, we may suppose, sufficed for the time to silence the prophet's complaints; and in the revulsion of feeling inspired by the awful vision of the unimpeded outbreak of Divine wrath, he utters an oracle concerning his country's destroyers, in which retributive justice is tempered by compassion and mercy. *Thus hath Jehovah said, Upon all Mine evil neighbours, who touch the heritage which I caused My people Israel to inherit: Lo I am about to uproot* (i. 10) *them from off their own land, and the house of Judah will I uproot from their midst. And after I have uprooted them, I will have compassion on them again, and will restore them each to their own heritage and their own land. And if they truly learn the ways of My people, to swear by My name, 'as Iahvah liveth!' even as they taught My people to swear by the Baal; they shall be rebuilt in the midst of My people. And if they will not hear, I will uproot that nation, utterly and fatally; it is an oracle of Iahvah* (14-17). The preceding section (vv. 7-14), as we have seen, rapidly yet vividly sketches the calamities which have ensued and must further ensue upon the Divine desertion of the country. Iahvah has forsaken the land, left her naked to her enemies, for her causeless, capricious, thankless revolt against her Divine Lord. In this forlorn, defenceless condition, all manner of evils befall her; the vineyards and cornfields are ravaged, the goodly land is desolated, by hordes of savage freebooters pouring in from the eastern deserts. These invaders are called Iahvah's "evil neighbours;" an expression which implies, not individuals banded together for purposes of brigandage, but hostile nations.[53] Upon these nations also will the justice of God be vindicated; for that justice is universal in its operation, and cannot therefore be restricted to Israel. Judgment must "begin at the house of God;" but it will not end there. The "evil neighbours," the surrounding heathen kingdoms, have been Iahvah's instruments for the chastisement of His rebellious people; but they are not on that account exempted from recompense. They too must reap what they have sown. They have insulted Iahvah, by violating His territory; they have indulged their malice and treachery and rapacity, in utter disregard of the rights of neighbours, and the moral claims of kindred peoples. As they have done, so shall it be done unto them: Δράσαντι παθεῖν. They have laid hands on the possessions of their neighbour, and their own shall be taken from them; *I am about to uproot them from off their own land* (cf. Amos i. 3-ii. 3). And not only so, but *the house of Judah will I pluck up from their midst*. The Lord's people shall be no more exposed to their unneighbourly ill-will; the butt of their ridicule, the victim of their malice, will be removed to a foreign soil as well as they; but oppressed and oppressors will no longer be together; their new settlements will lie far apart; under the altered state of things, under the shadow of the great conqueror of the future, there will be no opportunity for the old injurious dealings. All alike, Judah and the enemies of Judah, will be subject to the will of the foreign lord. But that is not the end. The Judge of all the earth is merciful as well as just. He is loth to blot whole peoples out of existence, even though they have merited destruction by grievous and prolonged transgression of His laws. Therefore banishment will be followed by restoration, not in the case of Judah only, but of all the expatriated peoples. After enduring the Divine probation of adversity, they will be brought again, by the Divine compassion, "each to their own heritage and their own land." And then, if they will profit by the teaching of Iahvah's prophets, and "learn the ways," that is, the religion of His people, making their supreme appeal to Iahvah, as the fountain of all truth and the sovran vindicator of right and justice, as hitherto they have appealed to the Baal, and misled Israel into the same profane and futile course; then "they shall be built up," or rebuilt, or brought to great and ever-growing prosperity, "in the midst of My people." Such is to be the blessing of the Gentiles; they shall share in the glorious future that awaits repentant Israel. The present condition of things is to be completely reversed: now Judah sojourns in *their* midst; then *they* will be surrounded on every side by the emancipated and triumphant people of God: now *they* beset Judah with jealousies, suspicions, enmities; then Judah will embrace them all with the arms of an unselfish and protecting love. A last word of warning is added. The doom of the nation that will not accept the Divine teaching will be utter and absolute extermination.

The forecast is plainly of a Messianic nature; it recognises in Iahvah the Saviour, not of a nation, but of the world. It perceives that the disunion and mutual hatred of peoples, as of individuals, is a breach of Divine law; and it proclaims a general return to God, and submission to His guidance in all political as well as private affairs, as the sole cure for the numberless evils that flow from that hatred and disunion. It is only when men have learnt that God is their common Father and Lord, that they come to see with the clearness and force of practical conviction that they themselves are all members of one family, bound as such to mutual offices of kindness and charity; it is only when there is a conscious identity of interest with all our fellows, based upon the recognition that all alike are children of God and heirs of eternal life, that true freedom and universal brotherhood become possible for man.

VIII
THE FALL OF PRIDE

Jeremiah xiii.

This discourse is a sort of appendix to the preceding; as is indicated by its abrupt and brief beginning with the words "Thus said Iahvah unto me," without the addition of any mark of time, or other determining circumstance. It predicts captivity, in retribution for the pride and ingratitude of the people; and thus suitably follows the closing section of the last address, which announces the coming deportation of Judah and her evil neighbours. The recurrence here (ver. 9) of the peculiar term rendered "swelling" or "pride" in our English versions (ch. xii. 5), points to the same conclusion. We may subdivide it thus: It presents us with (i) a symbolical action, or acted parable, with its moral and application (vv. 1-11); (ii) a parabolic saying and its interpretation, which leads up to a pathetic appeal for penitence (vv. 12-17); (iii) a message to the sovereigns (vv. 18, 19); and (iv) a closing apostrophe to Jerusalem—the gay and guilty capital, so soon to be made desolate for her abounding sins (vv. 20-27).

In the first of these four sections, we are told how the prophet was bidden of God to buy a linen girdle, and after wearing it for a time, to bury it in a cleft of the rock at a place whose very name might be taken to symbolize the doom awaiting his people. A long while afterwards he was ordered to go and dig it up again, and found it altogether spoiled and useless. The significance of these proceedings is clearly enough explained. The relation between Israel and the God of Israel had been of the closest kind. Iahvah had chosen this people, and bound it to Himself by a covenant, as a man might bind a girdle about his body; and as the girdle is an ornament of dress, so had the Lord intended Israel to display His glory among men (ver. 11). But now the girdle is rotten; and like that rotten girdle will He cause the pride of Judah to rot and perish (vv. 9, 10).

It is natural to ask, whether Jeremiah really did as he relates; or whether the narrative about the girdle be simply a literary device intended to carry a lesson home to the dullest apprehension. If the prophet's activity had been confined to the pen; if he had not been wont to labour by word and deed for the attainment of his purposes; the latter alternative might be accepted. For mere readers, a parabolic narrative might suffice to enforce his meaning. But Jeremiah, who was all his life a man of action, probably did the thing he professes to have done, not in thought nor in word only, but in deed and to the knowledge of certain competent witnesses. There was nothing novel in this method of attracting attention, and giving greater force and impressiveness to his prediction. The older prophets had often done the same kind of things, on the principle that deeds may be more effective than words. What could have conveyed a more vivid sense of the Divine intention, than the simple act of Ahijah the Shilonite, when he suddenly caught away the new mantle of Solomon's officer, and rent it into twelve pieces, and said to the astonished courtier, "Take thee ten pieces! for thus said Iahvah, the God of Israel, Behold I am about to rend the kingdom out of the hand of Solomon, and will give the ten tribes to thee"? (1 Kings xi. 29 *sqq*.) In like manner, when Ahab and Jehoshaphat, dressed in their robes of state, sat enthroned in the gateway of Samaria, and "all the prophets were prophesying before them" about the issue of their joint expedition to Ramoth-gilead, Zedekiah, the son of a Canaanitess—as the writer is careful to add of this false prophet—"made him horns of iron and said, Thus said Iahvah, With these shalt thou butt the Arameans, until thou make an end of them" (1 Kings xxii. 11). Isaiah, Hosea, and Ezekiel, record similar actions of symbolical import. Isaiah for a time walked half-clad and barefoot, as a sign that the Egyptians and Ethiopians, upon whom Judah was inclined to lean, would be led away captive, in this comfortless guise, by the king of Assyria (Isa. xx.). Such actions may be regarded as a further development of those significant gestures, with which men in what is called a state of nature are wont to give emphasis and precision to their spoken ideas. They may also be compared with the symbolism of ancient law. "An ancient conveyance," we are told, "was not written but acted. Gestures and words took the place of written technical phraseology, and any formula mispronounced, or symbolical act omitted, would have vitiated the proceeding as fatally as a material mistake in stating the uses or setting out the remainders would, two hundred years ago, have vitiated an English deed." (Maine, *Ancient Law*, p. 276.) Actions of a purely symbolical nature surprise us, when we first encounter them in Religion or Law, but that is only because they are survivals. In the ages when they originated, they were familiar occurrences in all transactions between man and man. And this general consideration tends to prove that those expositors are wrong who maintain that the prophets did not really perform the symbolical actions of which they speak. Just as it is argued that the visions which they describe, are merely a literary device; so the reality of these symbolical actions has needlessly enough been called in question. The learned Jews Abenezra and Maimonides in the twelfth century, and David Kimchi in the thirteenth, were the first to affirm this opinion. Maimonides held that all such actions passed in vision before the prophets; a view which has found a modern advocate in Hengstenberg: and Stäudlin, in the last century, affirmed that they had neither an objective nor a subjective reality, but were simply a "literary device." This, however, is only true, if true at all, of the declining period of prophecy, as in the case of the visions. In the earlier period, while the prophets were still accustomed to an oral delivery of their discourses, we may be quite sure that they suited the action to the word in the way that they have themselves recorded; in order to stir the popular imagination, and to create a more vivid and lasting impression. The narratives of the historical books leave no doubt about the matter. But in later times, when spoken addresses had for the most part become a thing of the past, and when prophets published their convictions in manuscript, it is possible that they were content with the description of symbolical doings, as a sort of parable, without any actual performance of them. Jeremiah's hiding his girdle in a cleft of the rock at "Euphrates" has been regarded by some writers as an instance of such purely ideal symbolism. And certainly it is difficult to suppose that the prophet made the long and arduous journey from Jerusalem to the Great River for such a purpose. It is, however, a highly probable conjecture that the place whither he was directed to repair was much nearer home; the addition of a single letter to the name rendered "Euphrates" gives the far preferable reading "Ephrath," that is to say, Bethlehem in Judah (Gen. xlviii. 7). Jeremiah may very well have buried his girdle at Bethlehem, a place only five miles or so to the south of Jerusalem; a place, moreover, where he would have no trouble in finding a "cleft of the rock," which would hardly be the case upon the alluvial banks of the Euphrates. If not accidental, the difference may be due to the intentional employment of an unusual form of the name, by way of hinting at the source whence the ruin of Judah was to flow. The enemy "from the north" (ver. 20) is of course the Chaldeans.

The mention of the queen-mother (ver. 18) along with the king appears to point unmistakably to the reign of Jehoiachin or Jechoniah. The allusion is compared with the threat of ch. xxii. 26: "I will cast thee out, and thy mother that bare thee into another country." Like Josiah, this king was but eight years old when he began to reign (2 Chron. xxxvi. 9, after which 2 Kings xxiv. 8 must be corrected); and he had enjoyed the name of king only for the brief period of three months, when the thunderbolt fell, and Nebuchadrezzar began his first siege of Jerusalem. The boy-king can hardly have had much to do with the issue of affairs, when "he and his mother and his servants and his princes and his eunuchs" surrendered the city, and were deported to Babylon, with ten thousand of the principal inhabitants

(2 Kings xxiv. 12 *sqq.*). The date of our discourse will thus be the beginning of the year b.c. 599, which was the eighth year of Nebuchadrezzar (2 Kings xxiv. 12).

It is asserted, indeed, that the difficult verse 21 refers to the revolt from Babylon as an accomplished fact; but this is by no means clear from the verse itself. *What wilt thou say,* demands the prophet, *when He shall appoint over thee—albeit, thou thyself hast instructed them against thyself;—lovers to be thy head?* The term "lovers" or "lemans" applies best to the foreign idols, who will one day repay the foolish attachment of Iahvah's people by enslaving it (cf. ch. iii. 4, where Iahvah himself is called the "lover" of Judah's youthful days); and this question might as well have been asked in the days of Josiah, as at any later period. At various times in the past Israel and Judah had courted the favour of foreign deities. Ahaz had introduced Aramean and Assyrian novelties; Manasseh and Amon had revived and aggravated his apostasy. Even Hezekiah had had friendly dealings with Babylon, and we must remember that in those times friendly intercourse with a foreign people implied some recognition of their gods, which is probably the true account of Solomon's chapels for Tyrian and other deities.

The queen of ver. 18 might conceivably be Jedidah, the mother of Josiah, for that king was only eight at his accession, and only thirty-nine at his death (2 Kings xxii. 1). And the message to the sovereigns (ver. 18) is not couched in terms of disrespect nor of reproach: it simply declares the imminence of overwhelming disaster, and bids them lay aside their royal pomp, and behave as mourners for the coming woe. Such words might perhaps have been addressed to Josiah and his mother, by way of deepening the impression produced by the Book of the Law, and the rumoured invasion of the Scythians. But the threat against "the kings that sit on David's throne" (ver. 13) is hardly suitable on this supposition; and the ruthless tone of this part of the address--*I will dash them in pieces, one against another, both the fathers and the sons together: I will not pity, nor spare, nor relent from destroying them*—considered along with the emphatic prediction of an utter and entire captivity (ver. 19), seems to indicate a later period of the prophet's ministry, when the obduracy of the people had revealed more fully the hopelessness of his enterprise for their salvation. The mention of the enemy "from the north" will then be a reference to present circumstances of peril, as triumphantly vindicating the prophet's former menaces of destruction from that quarter. The carnage of conquest and the certainty of exile are here threatened in the plainest and most direct style; but nothing is said by way of heightening the popular terror of the coming destroyer. The prophet seems to take it for granted that the nature of the evil which hangs over their heads, is well known to the people, and does not need to be dwelt upon or amplified with the lyric fervour of former utterances (see ch. iv., v. 15 *sqq.*, vi. 22 *sqq.*). This appears quite natural, if we suppose that the first invasion of the Chaldeans was now a thing of the past; and that the nation was awaiting in trembling uncertainty the consequences of Jehoiakim's breach of faith with his Babylonian suzerain (2 Kings xxiv. i. 10). The prophecy may therefore be assigned with some confidence to the short reign of Jehoiachin, to which perhaps the short section, ch. x. 17-25, also belongs; a date which harmonizes better than any other with the play on the name Euphrates in the opening of the chapter. It agrees, too, with the emphatic *Iahvah hath spoken!* (ver. 15), which seems to be more than a mere assertion of the speaker's veracity, and to point rather to the fact that the course of events had reached a crisis; that something had occurred in the political world, which suggested imminent danger; that a black cloud was looming up on the national horizon, and signalling unmistakably to the prophet's eye the intention of Iahvah. What other view so well explains the solemn tone of warning, the vivid apprehension of danger, the beseeching tenderness, that give so peculiar a stamp to the three verses in which the address passes from narrative and parable, to direct appeal? *Hear ye and give ear: be not proud: for Iahvah hath spoken! Give glory to Iahvah your God*—the glory of confession, of avowing your own guilt and His perfect righteousness (Josh. vii. 19; St. John ix. 24); of recognising the due reward of your deeds in the destruction that threatens you; the glory involved in the cry, "God be merciful to me a sinner!"—*Give glory to Iahvah your God, before the darkness fall, and before your feet stumble upon the twilight mountains; and ye wait for dawn, and He make it deepest gloom, He turn it to utter darkness.* The day was declining; the evening shadows were descending and deepening; soon the hapless people would be wandering bewildered in the twilight, and lost in the darkness, unless, ere it had become too late, they would yield their pride, and throw themselves upon the pity of Him who "maketh the seven stars and Orion, and turneth the deepest gloom into the morning" (Amos v. 8).

The verbal allusiveness of the opening section does not, according to Oriental taste, diminish the solemnity of the speaker; on the contrary, it tends to deepen the impression produced by his words. And perhaps there is a psychological reason for the fact, beyond the peculiar partiality of Oriental peoples for such displays of ingenuity. It is, at all events, remarkable that the greatest of all masters of human feeling has not hesitated to make a dying prince express his bitter and desponding thoughts in what may seem an artificial toying and trifling with the suggestiveness of his own familiar name; and when the king asks: "Can sick men play so nicely with their names?" the answer is: "No, misery makes sport to mock itself." (Rich. II., Act 2, Sc. i., 72 *sqq.*) The Greek tragedian, too, in the earnestness of bitter sport, can find a prophecy in a name. *"Who* was for naming her thus, with truth so entire? (Was it One whom we see not, wielding tongue happily with full foresight of what was to be?) the Bride of Battles, fiercely contested *Helen*: seeing that, in full accord with her name, *haler* of ships, *haler* of men, *haler* of cities, forth of the soft and precious tapestries away she sailed, under the gale of the giant West" (Æsch., *Ag.*, 681 *sqq.*). And so, to Jeremiah's ear, Ephrath is prophetic of Euphrates, upon whose distant banks the glory of his people is to languish and decay. "I to Ephrath, and you to Phrath!" is his melancholy cry. Their doom is as certain as if it were the mere fulfilment of an old-world prophecy, crystallized long ages ago in a familiar name; a word of destiny fixed in this strange form, and bearing its solemn witness from the outset of their history until now concerning the inevitable goal.

There is nothing so very surprising, as Ewald seems to have thought, in the suggestion that the *Perath* of the Hebrew text may be the same as Ephrath. But perhaps the valley and spring now called *Furāh* (or *Furāt*) which lies at about the same distance N.E. of Jerusalem, is the place intended by the prophet. The name, which means *fresh* or *sweet water* is identical with the Arabic name of the Euphrates (*Furāt*,), which again is philologically identical with the Hebrew Perath. It is obvious that this place would suit the requirements of the text quite as well as the other, while the coincidence of name enables us to dispense with the supposition of an unusual form or even a corruption of the original; but *Furāt* or *Forāh* is not mentioned elsewhere in the Old Testament. The old versions send the prophet to the river Euphrates, which Jeremiah calls simply "The River" in one place (ii. 18), and *"The river* of Perath" in three others (xlvi. 2, 6, 10); while the rare "Perath," without any addition, is only found in the second account of the Creation (Gen. ii. 14), in 2 Chron. xxxv. 20, and in a passage of this book which does not belong, nor profess to belong, to Jeremiah (li. 63). We may, therefore, conclude that "Perath" in the present passage means not the great river of that name, but a place near Jerusalem, although that place was probably chosen with the intention, as above explained, of alluding to the Euphrates.

I cannot assent to the opinion which regards this narrative of the spoiled girdle as founded upon some accidental experience of the prophet's life, in which he afterwards recognised a Divine lesson. The precision of statement, and the nice adaptation of the details of the story to the moral which the prophet wished to convey, rather indicate a symbolical course of action, or what may be called an acted parable. The whole proceeding appears to have been carefully thought out beforehand. The intimate connexion between Iahvah and Israel is well symbolized by a girdle—that part of an Eastern dress which "cleaves to the loins of a man," that is, fits closest to the body, and is most securely attached thereto. And if the nations be represented by the rest of the apparel, as the girdle secures and keeps that in its place, we may see an implication that Israel was intended to be the chain that bound mankind to God. The girdle was of *linen*, the material of the priestly dress, not only because Jeremiah was a priest, but because Israel was called to be "a kingdom of priests," or the Priest among nations (Ex. xix. 6). The significance of the command to wear the girdle, but not to put it into water, seems to be clear enough. The unwashed garment which the prophet continues to wear for a time represents the foulness of Israel; just as the order to bury it at Perath indicates what Iahvah is about to do with His polluted people.

The exposition begins with the words, *Thus will I mar the great pride of Judah and of Jerusalem!* The spiritual uncleanness of the nation consisted in the proud self-will which turned a deaf ear to the warnings of Iahvah's prophets, and obstinately persisted in idolatry (ver. 10). It continues: *For as the girdle cleaveth to the loins of a man, so made I the whole house of Israel and the whole house of Judah to cleave unto Me, saith Iahvah; that they might become to Me for a people, and for a name, and for a praise, and for an ornament* (Ex. xxviii. 2). Then their becoming morally unclean, through the defilements of sin, is briefly implied in the words, *And they obeyed not* (ver. 11).

It is not the pride of the tyrant king Jehoiakim that is here threatened with destruction. It is the *national* pride which had all along evinced itself in rebellion against its heavenly King—*the great pride of Judah and Jerusalem;* and this pride, inasmuch as it "trusted in man and made flesh its arm" (xvii. 5), and boasted in a carnal wisdom, and material strength and riches (ix. 23, xxi. 13), was to be brought low by the complete extinction of the national autonomy, and the reduction of a high-spirited and haughty race to the status of humble dependents upon a heathen power.

2. A parabolic saying follows, with its interpretation. *And say thou unto them this word: Thus said Iahvah, the God of Israel: Every jar is wont to be filled* (or *shall be filled*) *with wine. And if they say unto thee, Are we really not aware that every jar is wont to be filled with wine? say thou unto them, Thus said Iahvah, Lo, I am about to fill all the inhabitants of this land, and the kings that sit for David upon his throne, and the priests and the prophets, and all the inhabitants of Jerusalem, with drunkenness; and I will dash them in pieces against one another, and the fathers and the sons together, saith Iahvah: I will not forbear nor spare nor pity, so as not to mar them* (cf. vv. 7, 9).

The individual members of the nation, of all ranks and classes, are compared to earthenware jars, not "skins," as the LXX. gives it, for they are to be *dashed in pieces,* "like a potter's vessel" (Ps. ii. 9; cf. ver. 14).[54]

Regarding them all as ripe for destruction, Jeremiah exclaims, "Every jar is filled with wine," in the ordinary course of things; that is its destiny. His hearers answer with the mocking question, "Do you suppose that we don't know that?" They would, of course, be aware that a prophet's figure, however homely, covered an inner meaning of serious import; but derision was their favourite retort against unpopular truths (xvii. 15, xx. 7, 8). They would take it for granted that the thing suggested was unfavourable, from their past experience of Jeremiah. Their ill-timed banter is met by the instant application of the figure. They, and *the kings* then sitting oñ David's throne, *i.e.*, the young Jehoiachin and the queen-mother Nehushta (who probably had all the authority if not the title of a regent), and the priests and prophets who fatally misled them by false teachings and false counsels, are the wine-jars intended, and the wine that is to fill them is the wine of the wrath of God (Ps. lxxv. 8; Jer. xxv. 15; cf. li. 7; Rev. xvi. 19; Isa. xix. 14, 15). The effect is intoxication—a fatal bewilderment, a helpless lack of decision, an utter confusion and stupefaction of the faculties of wisdom and foresight, in the very moment of supreme peril (cf. Isa. xxviii. 7; Ps. lx. 5). Like drunkards, they will reel against and overthrow each other. The strong term *I will dash them in pieces* is used, to indicate the deadly nature of their fall, and because the prophet has still in his mind the figure of the wine-jars, which were probably amphoræ, pointed at the end, like those depicted in Egyptian mural paintings, so that they could not stand upright without support. By their fall they are to be utterly "marred" (the term used of the girdle, ver. 9).

But even yet one way of escape lies open. It is to sacrifice their pride, and yield to the will of Iahvah. *Hear ye, and give ear, be not haughty! for Iahvah hath spoken: give ye to Iahvah your God the glory, before it grow dark (or He cause darkness), and before your feet stumble upon mountains of twilight; and ye wait for the dawn, and He make it gloom, turning it to cloudiness!* (Isa. v. 30, viii. 20, 22; Amos viii. 9). It is very remarkable, that even now, when the Chaldeans are actually in the country, and blockading the strong places of southern Judah (ver. 19), which was the usual preliminary to an advance upon Jerusalem itself (2 Chron. xii. 4, xxxii. 9; Isa. xxxvi. 1, 2), Jeremiah should still speak thus; assuring his fellow-citizens that confession and self-humiliation before their offended God might yet deliver them from the bitterest consequences of past misdoing. Iahvah had indeed spoken audibly enough, as it seemed to the prophet, in the calamities that had already befallen the country; these were an indication of more and worse to follow, unless they should prove efficacious in leading the people to repentance. If they failed, nothing would be left for the prophet but to mourn in solitude over his country's ruin (ver. 17). But Jeremiah was fully persuaded that the Hand that had stricken could heal; the Power that had brought the invaders into Judah, could cause them to "return by the way that they had come" (Isa. xxxvii. 34). Of course such a view is unintelligible from the standpoint of unbelief; but then the standpoint of the prophets is faith.

3. After this general appeal for penitence, the discourse turns to the two exalted persons whose position and interest in the country were the highest of all, the youthful king, and the empress or queen-mother. They are addressed in a tone which, though not disrespectful, is certainly despairing. They are called upon, not so much to set the example of penitence (cf. Jonah iii. 6), as to take up the attitude of mourners (Job ii. 13; Isa. iii. 26; Lam. ii. 10; Ezek. xxvi. 16) in presence of the public disasters. *Say thou to the king and to the empress, Sit ye low on the ground!* (lit. *make low your seat!* cf. Isa. vii. for the construction) *for it is fallen from your heads* [55] *—your beautiful crown!* (Lam. v. 16). *The cities of the south are shut fast, and there is none that openeth* (Josh. vi. 1): *Judah is carried away captive all of her, she is wholly carried away.* There is no hope; it is vain to expect help; nothing is left but to bemoan the irreparable. The siege of the great fortresses of the south country and the sweeping away of the rural population were sure signs of what was coming upon Jerusalem. The embattled cities themselves may be suggested by the fallen crown of beauty; Isaiah calls Samaria "the proud crown of the drunkards of Ephraim" (Isa. xxviii. 1), and cities are commonly represented in ancient art by female figures wearing mural crowns. In that case, both verses are addressed to the sovereigns, and the second is exegetical of the first.

As already observed, there is here no censure, but only sorrowful despair over the dark outlook. In the same way, Jeremiah's utterance (xxii. 20 *sqq.*) about the fate of Jehoiachin is less a malediction than a lament. And when we further consider his favourable judgment of the first body of exiles, who were carried away with this monarch soon after the time of the present oracle (chap. xxiv.), we may perhaps see reason to conclude that the surrender of Jerusalem to the Chaldeans on this occasion was partly due to his advice. The narrative of Kings, however, is too brief to enable us to come to any certain decision about the circumstances of Jehoiachin's submission (2 Kings xxiv. 10-12).

4. From the sovereigns, the prophet turns to Jerusalem. *Lift up thine eyes (O Jerusalem* [56]*), and behold them that came from the north! Where is the flock that was given to thee, thy beautiful sheep? What wilt thou say when He shall appoint over thee—nay, thou thyself hast spurred them against thyself!—lovers* (iii. 4, xi. 19) *for head? Will not pangs take thee, as a woman in travail?* Jerusalem sits upon her hills, as a beautiful shepherdess. The country towns and unwalled villages lay about her, like a fair flock of sheep and goats entrusted to her

care and keeping. But now these have been destroyed and their pastures are made a silent solitude, and the destroyer is advancing against herself. What pangs of shame and terror will be hers, when she recognises in the enemy triumphing over her grievous downfall the heathen "friends" whose love she had courted so long! Her sin is to be her scourge. She shall be made the thrall of her foreign lovers. Iahvah will "appoint them over her" (xv. 3, li. 27); they will become the "head," and she the "tail" (Lam. i. 5; Deut. xxviii. 44). Yet this will, in truth, be her own doing, not Iahvah's; she has herself "accustomed them to herself" (x. 2), or "instructed" or "spurred them on" against herself (ii. 33, iv. 18). The revolt of Jehoiakim, his wicked breach of faith with Nebuchadrezzar, had turned friends to enemies (iv. 30). But the chief reference seems to be more general—the continual craving of Judah for foreign alliances and foreign worships. *And if thou say in thine heart, "Wherefore did these things befall me?" through the greatness of thy guilt were thy skirts uncovered, thine heels violated* (Nah. iii. 5) or *exposed. Will a Cushite change his skin, or a leopard his spots? ye, too, are ye able to do good, O ye that are wont to do evil?* If amid the sharp throes of suffering Jerusalem should still fail to recognise the moral cause of them (v. 19), she may be assured beforehand that her unspeakable dishonour is the reward of her sins; *that* is why "the virgin daughter of Sion" is surprised and ravished by the foe (a common figure: Isa. xlvii. 1-3). Sin has become so ingrained in her, that it can no more be eradicated than the blackness of an African skin, or the spots of a leopard's hide. The habit of sinning has become "a second nature," and, like nature, is not to be expelled (cf. viii. 4-7).

The effect of use and wont in the moral sphere could hardly be expressed more forcibly, and Jeremiah's comparison has become a proverb. Custom binds us all in every department of life; it is only by enlisting this strange influence upon the side of virtue, that we become virtuous. Neither virtue nor vice can be pronounced perfect, until the habit of either has become fixed and invariable. It is the tendency of habitual action of any kind to become automatic; and it is certain that sin may attain such a mastery over the active powers of a man that its indulgence may become almost an unconscious exercise of his will, and quite a matter of course. But this fearful result of evil habits does not excuse them at the bar of common sense, much less at the tribunal of God. The inveterate sinner, the man totally devoid of scruple, whose conscience is, as it were, "seared with a hot iron," is not on that account excused by the common judgment of his kind; the feeling he excites is not forbearance, but abhorrence; he is regarded not as a poor victim of circumstances over which he has no control, but as a monster of iniquity. And justly so; for if he has lost control of his passions, if he is no longer master of himself, but the slave of vice, he is responsible for the long course of self-indulgence which has made him what he is. The prophet's comparison cannot be applied in support of a doctrine of immoral fatalism. The very fact that he makes use of it, implies that he did not intend it to be understood in such a sense. *"Will a Cushite change his skin, or a leopard his spots? Ye also*—supposing such a change as that—*will be able to do good, O ye that are taught*—trained, accustomed—*to do evil!"* (perhaps the preferable rendering).

Not only must we abstain from treating a rhetorical figure as a colourless and rigorous proposition of mathematical science; not only must we allow for the irony and the exaggeration of the preacher: we must also remember his object, which is, if possible, to shock his hearers into a sense of their condition, and to awaken remorse and repentance even at the eleventh hour. His last words (ver. 27) prove that he did not believe this result, improbable as it was, to be altogether impossible. Unless some sense of sin had survived in their hearts, unless the terms, "good" and "evil," had still retained a meaning for his countrymen, Jeremiah would hardly have laboured still so strenuously to convince them of their sin.

For the present, when retribution is already at the doors, when already the Divine wrath has visibly broken forth, his prevailing purpose is not so much to suggest a way of escape, as to bring home to the heart and conscience of the nation the true meaning of the public calamities. They are the consequence of habitual rebellion against God. *And I will scatter them like stubble passing away to* (= before: cf. xix. 10) *the wind of the wilderness. This is thy lot* (fem. thine, O Jerusalem), *the portion of thy measures* (others: lap) *from Me, saith Iahvah; because thou forgattest Me, and didst trust in the Lie. And I also—I will surely strip thy skirts to thy face, and thy shame shall be seen!* (Nah. iii. 5). *Thine adulteries and thy neighings, the foulness of thy fornications upon the hills in the field* (iii. 2-6)—*I have seen thine abominations!* (For the construction, compare Isa. i. 13.) *Woe unto thee, O Jerusalem! After how long yet wilt thou not become clean?* (2 Kings v. 12, 13). That which lies before the citizens in the near future is not deliverance, but dispersion in foreign lands. The onset of the foe will sweep them away, as the blast from the desert drives before it the dry stubble of the corn-fields (cf. iv. 11, 12). This is no chance calamity, but a recompense allotted and meted out by Iahvah to the city that forgot Him and "trusted in the Lie" of Baal-worship and the associated superstitions. The city that dealt shamefully in departing from her God, and dallying with foul idols, shall be put to shame by Him before all the world (ver. 26 recurring to the thought of ver. 22, but ascribing the exposure directly to Iahvah). Woe—certain woe—awaits Jerusalem; and it is but a faint and far-off glimmer of hope that is reflected in the final question, which is like a weary sigh: *After how long yet wilt thou not become clean?* How long must the fiery process of cleansing go on, ere thou be purged of thine inveterate sins? It is a recognition that the punishment will not be exterminative; that God's chastisements of His people can no more fail at last than His promises; that the triumph of a heathen power and the disappearance of Iahvah's Israel from under His heaven cannot be the final phase of that long eventful history which began with the call of Abraham.

IX
THE DROUGHT AND ITS MORAL IMPLICATIONS

Jeremiah xiv., xv. (xvii.?).

Various opinions have been expressed about the division of these chapters. They have been cut up into short sections, supposed to be more or less independent of each other;[57] and they have been regarded as constituting a well-organized whole, at least so far as the eighteenth verse of chap. xvii. The truth may lie between these extremes. Chapters xiv., xv. certainly hang together; for in them the prophet represents himself as twice interceding with Iahvah on behalf of the people, and twice receiving a refusal of his petition (xiv. 1-xv. 4), the latter reply being sterner and more decisive than the first. The occasion was a long period of drought, involving much privation for man and beast. The connexion between the parts of this first portion of the discourse is clear enough. The prophet prays for his people, and God answers that He has rejected them, and that intercession is futile. Thereupon, Jeremiah throws the blame of the national sins upon the false prophets; and the answer is that both the people and their false guides will perish. The prophet then soliloquises upon his own hard fate as a herald of evil tidings, and receives directions for his own personal guidance in this crisis of affairs (xv. 10-xvi. 9). There is a pause but no real break at the end of chap. xv. The next chapter resumes the subject of directions personally affecting the prophet himself; and the discourse is then continuous so far as xvii. 18, although, naturally enough, it is broken here and there by pauses of considerable duration, marking transitions of thought, and progress in the argument.

The heading of the entire piece is marked in the original by a peculiar inversion of terms, which meets us again, chap. xlvi. 1, xlvii. 1, xlix. 34, but which, in spite of this recurrence, wears a rather suspicious look. We might render it thus: "What fell as a word of Iahvah to Jeremiah, on account of the droughts" (the plural is intensive, or it signifies the long continuance of the trouble—as if one rainless period followed upon another). Whether or not the singular order of the words be authentic, the recurrence at chap. xvii. 8 of the remarkable term for "drought" (Heb. *baccóreth* of which *baccaróth* here is plur.) favours the view that that chapter is an integral portion of the present discourse. The exordium (xiv. 1-9) is a poetical sketch of the miseries of man and beast, closing with a beautiful prayer. It has been said that this is not "a word of Iahvah to Jeremiah," but rather the reverse. If we stick to the letter, this no doubt is the case; but, as we have seen in former discourses, the phrase "Iahvah's word" meant in prophetic use very much more than a direct message from God, or a prediction uttered at the Divine instigation. Here, as elsewhere, the prophet evidently regards the course of his own religious reflexion as guided by Him who "fashioneth the hearts of men," and "knoweth their thoughts long before;" and if the question had suggested itself, he would certainly have referred his own poetic powers— the tenderness of his pity, the vividness of his apprehension, the force of his passion,—to the inspiration of the Lord who had called and consecrated him from the birth, to speak in His Name.

There lies at the heart of many of us a feeling, which has lurked there, more or less without our cognisance, ever since the childish days when the Old Testament was read at the mother's knee, and explained and understood in a manner proportioned to the faculties of childhood. When we hear the phrase "The Lord spake," we instinctively think, if we think at all, of an actual voice knocking sensibly at the door of the outward ear. It was not so; nor did the sacred writer mean it so. A knowledge of Hebrew idiom—the modes of expression usual and possible in that ancient speech—assures us that this statement, so startlingly direct in its unadorned simplicity, was the accepted mode of conveying a meaning which we, in our more complex and artificial idioms, would convey by the use of a multitude of words, in terms far more abstract, in language destitute of all that colour of life and reality which stamps the idiom of the Bible. It is as though the Divine lay farther off from us moderns; as though the marvellous progress of all that new knowledge of the measureless magnitude of the world, of the power and complexity of its machinery, of the surpassing subtlety and the matchless perfection of its laws and processes, had become an impassable barrier, at least an impenetrable veil, between our minds and God. We have lost the sense of His nearness, of His immediacy, so to speak; because we have gained, and are ever intensifying, a sense of the nearness of the world with which He environs us. Hence, when we speak of Him, we naturally cast about either for poetical phrases and figures, which must always be more or less vague and undefined, or for highly abstract expressions, which may suggest scientific exactness, but are, in truth, scholastic formulæ, dry as the dust of the desert, untouched by the breath of life; and even if they affirm a Person, destitute of all those living characters by which we instinctively and without effort recognise Personality. We make only a conventional use of the language of the sacred writers, of the prophets and prophetic historians, of the psalmists, and the legalists of the Old Testament; the language which is the native expression of a peculiar intensity of religious faith, realizing the Unseen as the Actual and, in truth, the only Real.

"Judah mourneth and the gates thereof languish,
They are clad in black down to the ground;
And the cry of Jerusalem hath gone up.
And their nobles have sent their lesser folk for water;
They have been to the pits, and found no water:
Their vessels have come back empty;
Ashamed and confounded, they have covered their heads.

"Because the ground is chapt, for there hath not been rain
in the land,
The plowmen are ashamed, they have covered their heads.

"For even the hind in the field hath yeaned and forsaken
her fawn,
For there is no grass.
And the wild asses stand on the bare fells;
They snuff the wind like jackals;
Their eyes fail, for there is no pasturage.

"If our sins have answered against us,
Iahweh, act for Thine own Name sake;
For our relapses are many;
Against Thee have we trespassed.

"Hope of Israel, that savest him in time of trouble,
Wherefore wilt Thou be as a stranger in the land,
And as a traveller that leaveth the road but for the night?
Wherefore wilt Thou be as a man o'erpowered with sleep,
As a warrior that cannot rescue?

"Sith Thou art in our midst, O Iahvah,
And Thy Name upon us hath been called;
Cast us not down!"

How beautiful both plaint and prayer! The simple description of the effects of the drought is as lifelike and impressive as a good picture. The whole country is stricken; the city-gates, the place of common resort, where the citizens meet for business and for conversation, are gloomy with knots of mourners robed in black from head to foot, or, as the Hebrew may also imply, sitting on the ground, in the garb and posture of desolation (Lam. ii. 10, iii. 28). The magnates of Jerusalem send out their retainers to find water;

and we see them returning with empty vessels, their heads muffled in their cloaks, in sign of grief at the failure of their errand (cf. 1 Kings xviii. 5, 6). The parched ground everywhere gapes with fissures;[58] the yeomen go about with covered heads in deepest dejection. The distress is universal, and affects not man only, but the brute creation. Even the gentle hind, that proverb of maternal tenderness, is driven by sorest need to forsake the fruit of her hard travail; her starved dugs are dry, and she flies from her helpless offspring. The wild asses of the desert, fleet, beautiful and keen-eyed creatures, scan the withered landscape from the naked cliffs, and snuff the wind, like jackals scenting prey; but neither sight nor smell suggests relief. There is no moisture in the air, no glimpse of pasture in the wide sultry land.

The prayer is a humble confession of sin, an unreserved admission that the woes of man evince the righteousness of God. Unlike certain modern poets, who bewail the sorrows of the world as the mere infliction of a harsh and arbitrary and inevitable Destiny, Jeremiah makes no doubt that human sufferings are due to the working of Divine justice. "Our sins have answered against our pleas at Thy judgment seat; our relapses are many; against Thee have we trespassed," against Thee, the sovereign Disposer of events, the Source of all that happens and all that is. If this be so, what plea is left? None, but that appeal to the Name of Iahvah, with which the prayer begins and ends. "Act for Thine own Name sake."... "Thy Name upon us hath been called." Act for Thine own honour, that is, for the honour of Mercy, Compassion, Truth, Goodness; which Thou hast revealed Thyself to be, and which are parts of Thy glorious Name (Ex. xxxiv. 6). Pity the wretched, and pardon the guilty; for so will Thy glory increase amongst men; so will man learn that the relentings of love are diviner affections than the ruthlessness of wrath and the cravings of vengeance.

There is also a touching appeal to the past. The very name by which Israel was sometimes designated as "the people of Iahvah," just as Moab was known by the name of its god as "the people of Chemosh" (Num. xxi. 29), is alleged as proof that the nation has an interest in the compassion of Him whose name it bears; and it is implied that, since the world knows Israel as Iahvah's people, it will not be for Iahvah's honour that this people should be suffered to perish in their sins. Israel had thus, from the outset of its history, been associated and identified with Iahvah; however ill the true nature of the tie has been understood, however unworthily the relation has been conceived by the popular mind, however little the obligations involved in the call of their fathers have been recognised and appreciated. God must be true, though man be false. There is no weakness, no caprice, no vacillation in God. In bygone "times of trouble" the "Hope of Israel" had saved Israel over and over again; it was a truth admitted by all—even by the prophet's enemies. Surely then He will save His people once again, and vindicate His Name of Saviour. Surely He who has dwelt in their midst so many changeful centuries, will not now behold their trouble with the lukewarm feeling of an alien dwelling amongst them for a time, but unconnected with them by ties of blood and kin and common country; or with the indifference of the traveller who is but coldly affected by the calamities of a place where he has only lodged one night. Surely the entire past shews that it would be utterly inconsistent for Iahvah to appear now as a man so buried in sleep that He cannot be roused to save His friends from imminent destruction (cf. 1 Kings xviii. 27) (St. Mark iv. 38). He who had borne Israel and carried him as a tender nurseling all the days of old (Isa. lxiii. 9) could hardly without changing His own unchangeable Name, His character and purposes, cast down His people and forsake them at last.

Such is the drift of the prophet's first prayer. To this apparently unanswerable argument his religious meditation upon the present distress has brought him. But presently the thought returns with added force, with a sense of utmost certitude, with a conviction that it is Iahvah's Word, that the people have wrought out their own affliction, that misery is the hire of sin.

"Thus hath Iahvah said of this people:
Even so have they loved to wander,
Their feet they have not refrained;
And as for Iahvah, He accepteth them not;

"He now remembereth their guilt,
And visiteth their trespasses.
And Iahvah said unto me,
Intercede thou not for this people for good!
If they fast, I will not hearken unto their cry;
And if they offer whole-offering and oblation,
I will not accept their persons;
But by the sword, the famine, and the plague, will I
consume them.

"And I said, Ah, Lord Iahvah!
Behold the prophets say to them, Ye shall not see sword,
And famine shall not befall you;
For peace and permanence will I give you in this place.

"And Iahvah said unto me:
Falsehood it is that the prophets prophesy in My Name.
I sent them not, and I charged them not, and I spake not
unto them.

A vision of falsehood and jugglery and nothingness, and
the guile of their own heart,
They, for their part, prophesy you.

"Therefore thus said Iahvah:
Concerning the prophets who prophesy in My Name, albeit
I sent them not,
And of themselves say, Sword and famine there shall not
be in this land;
By the sword and by the famine shall those prophets be
fordone.
And the people to whom they prophesy shall lie thrown
out in the streets of Jerusalem,
Because of the famine and the sword,
With none to bury them, —
Themselves, their wives, and their sons and their
daughters:
And I will pour upon them their own evil.
And thou shalt say unto them this word:
Let mine eyes run down with tears, night and day,
And let them not tire;
For with mighty breach is broken
The virgin daughter of my people—
With a very grievous blow.
If I go forth into the field,
Then behold! the slain of the sword;
And if I enter the city,
Then behold! the pinings of famine:
For both prophet and priest go trafficking about the land,
And understand not."[59]

It has been supposed that this whole section is misplaced, and that it
would properly follow the close of chap. xiii. The supposition is due to a
misapprehension of the force of the pregnant particle which introduces the
reply of Iahvah to the prophet's intercession. "*Even so* have they loved to
wander;" *even so*, as is naturally implied by the severity of the punishment of
which thou complainest. The dearth is prolonged; the distress is widespread
and grievous. *So* prolonged, *so* grievous, *so* universal, has been their rebellion
against Me. The penalty corresponds to the offence. It is really "their own
evil" that is being poured out upon their guilty heads (ver. 16; cf. iv. 18).
Iahvah cannot accept them in their sin; the long drought is a token that their
guilt is before His mind, unrepented, unatoned. Neither the supplications
of another, nor their own fasts and sacrifices, avail to avert the visitation.

So long as the disposition of the heart remains unaltered; so long as man hates, not his darling sins, but the penalties they entail, it is idle to seek to propitiate Heaven by such means as these. And not only so. The droughts are but a foretaste of worse evils to come; *by the sword, the famine, and the plague will I consume them.* The condition is understood, If they repent and amend not. This is implied by the prophet's seeking to palliate the national guilt, as he proceeds to do, by the suggestion that the people are more sinned against than sinning, deluded as they are by false prophets; as also by the renewal of his intercession (ver. 19). Had he been aware in his inmost heart that an irreversible sentence had gone forth against his people, would he have been likely to think either excuses or intercessions availing? Indeed, however absolute the threats of the prophetic preachers may sound, they must, as a rule, be qualified by this limitation, which, whether expressed or not, is inseparable from the object of their discourses, which was the moral amendment of those who heard them.

Of the "false," that is, the common run of prophets, who were in league with the venal priesthood of the time, and no less worldly and self-seeking than their allies, we note that, as usual, they foretell what the people wishes to hear; "Peace (Prosperity), and Permanence," is the burden of their oracles. They knew that invectives against prevailing vices, and denunciations of national follies, and forecasts of approaching ruin, were unlikely means of winning popularity and a substantial harvest of offerings. At the same time, like other false teachers, they knew how to veil their errors under the mask of truth; or rather, they were themselves deluded by their own greed, and blinded by their covetousness to the plain teaching of events. They might base their doctrine of "Peace and Permanence in this place!" upon those utterances of the great Isaiah, which had been so signally verified in the lifetime of the seer himself; but their keen pursuit of selfish ends, their moral degradation, caused them to shut their eyes to everything else in his teachings, and, like his contemporaries, they "regarded not the work of Iahvah, nor the operation of His hand." Jeremiah accuses them of "lying visions;" visions, as he explains, which were the outcome of magical ceremonies, by aid of which, perhaps, they partially deluded themselves, before deluding others, but which were, none the less, "things of nought," devoid of all substance, and mere fictions of a deceitful and self-deceiving mind (ver. 14). He expressly declares that they have no mission; in other words, their action is not due to the overpowering sense of a higher call, but is inspired by purely ulterior considerations of worldly gain and policy. They prophesy to order; to the order of man, not of God. If they visit the country districts, it is with no spiritual end in view; priest and prophet alike make a trade of their sacred profession, and, immersed in their sordid pursuits, have no eye for truth, and no perception of the dangers hovering over their country. Their misconduct and misdirection of affairs are certain to bring destruction upon themselves and upon those whom they mislead. War and its attendant famine will devour them all.

But the day of grace being past, nothing is left for the prophet himself but to bewail the ruin of his people (ver. 17). He will betake himself to weeping, since praying and preaching are vain. The words which announce this resolve may portray a sorrowful experience, or they may depict the future as though it were already present (vv. 17, 18). The latter interpretation would suit ver. 17, but hardly the following verse, with its references to "going forth into the field," and "entering into the city." The way in which these specific actions are mentioned seems to imply some present or recent calamity; and there is apparently no reason why we may not suppose that the passage was written at the disastrous close of the reign of Josiah, in the troublous interval of three months, when Jehoahaz was nominal king in Jerusalem, but the Egyptian arms were probably ravaging the country, and striking terror into the hearts of the people. In such a time of confusion and bloodshed, tillage would be neglected, and famine would naturally follow; and these evils would be greatly aggravated by drought. The only other period which suits is the beginning of the reign of Jehoiakim;[60] but the former seems rather to be indicated by chap. xv. 6-9.

Heartbroken at the sight of the miseries of his country, the prophet once more approaches the eternal throne. His despairing mood is not so deep and dark as to drown his faith in God. He refuses to believe the utter rejection of Judah, the revocation of the covenant. (The measure is Pentameter).

"Hast Thou indeed cast off Judah?
Hath Thy soul revolted from Sion?
Why hast Thou smitten us, past healing?
Waiting for peace, and no good came,
For a time of healing, and behold terror!

"We know, Iahvah, our wickedness, our fathers' guilt;
For we have trespassed toward Thee.
Scorn Thou not, for Thy Name sake,
Disgrace not Thy glorious throne!Remember, break not,
Thy covenant with us!

"Are there, in sooth, among the Nothings of the nations
senders of rain?
And is it the heavens that bestow the showers?
Is it not Thou, Iahvah our God?

And we wait for Thee,
For Thou it was that madest the world."[61]

To all this the Divine answer is stern and decisive. *And Iahvah said unto me: If Moses and Samuel were to stand* (pleading) *before Me, My mind would not be towards this people: send them away from before Me* (dismiss them from My Presence), *that they may go forth!* After ages remembered Jeremiah as a mighty intercessor, and the brave Maccabeus could see him in his dream as a grey-haired man "exceeding glorious" and "of a wonderful and excellent majesty," who "prayed much for the people and for the holy city" (2 Macc. xv. 14). And the beauty of the prayers which lie like scattered pearls of faith and love among the prophet's soliloquies is evident at a glance. But here Jeremiah himself is conscious that his prayers are unavailing; and that the office to which God has called him is rather that of pronouncing judgment than of interceding for mercy. Even a Moses or a Samuel, the mighty intercessors of the old heroic times, whose pleadings had been irresistible with God, would now plead in vain (Ex. xvii. 11 *sqq.*, xxxii. 11 *sqq.*; Num. xiv. 13 *sqq.* for Moses; 1 Sam. vii. 9 *sqq.*, xii. 16 *sqq.*; Ps. xcix. 6; Ecclus. xlvi. 16 *sqq.* for Samuel). The day of grace has gone, and the day of doom is come. His sad function is to "send them away" or "let them go" from Iahvah's Presence; to pronounce the decree of their banishment from the holy land where His temple is, and where they have been wont to "see His face." The main part of his commission was "to root out, and to pull down, and to destroy, and to overthrow" (i. 10). *And if they say unto thee, Whither are we to go forth? Thou shalt say unto them, thus hath Iahvah said: They that belong to the Death* (*i.e.* the Plague; as the Black Death was spoken of in medieval Europe) *to death; and they that belong to the Sword, to the sword; and they that belong to the Famine, to famine; and they that belong to Captivity, to captivity!* The people were to "go forth" out of their own land, which was, as it were, the Presence-chamber of Iahvah, just as they had at the outset of their history gone forth out of Egypt, to take possession of it. The words convey a sentence of exile, though they do not indicate the place of banishment. The menace of woe is as general in its terms as that lurid passage of the Book of the Law upon which it appears to be founded (Deut. xxviii. 21-26). The time for the accomplishment of those terrible threatenings "is nigh, even at the doors." On the other hand, Ezekiel's "four sore judgments" (Ezek. xiv. 21) were suggested by this passage of Jeremiah.

The prophet avoids naming the actual destination of the captive people, because captivity is only one element in their punishment. The horrors of war—sieges and slaughters and pestilence and famine—must come first. In what follows, the intensity of these horrors is realized in a single touch. The slain are left unburied, a prey to the birds and beasts. The elaborate care of the ancients in the provision of honourable resting places for the dead is a measure of the extremity thus indicated. In accordance with the feeling of his age, the prophet ranks the dogs and vultures and hyenas that drag and disfigure and devour the corpses of the slain, as three "kinds" of evil equally appalling with the sword that slays. The same feeling led our Spenser to write:

> "To spoil the dead of weed
> Is sacrilege, and doth all sins exceed."

And the destruction of Moab is decreed by the earlier prophet Amos, "because he burned the bones of the king of Edom into lime," thus violating a law universally recognised as binding upon the conscience of nations (Amos ii. 1). Cf. also Gen. xxiii.

Thus death itself was not to be a sufficient expiation for the inveterate guilt of the nation. Judgment was to pursue them even after death. But the prophet's vision does not penetrate beyond this present scene. With the visible world, so far as he is aware, the punishment terminates. He gives no hint here, nor elsewhere, of any further penalties awaiting individual sinners in the unseen world. The scope of his prophecy indeed is almost purely national, and limited to the present life. It is one of the recognised conditions of Old Testament religious thought.

And the ruin of the people is the retribution reserved for what Manasseh did in Jerusalem. To the prophet, as to the author of the book of Kings, who wrote doubtless under the influence of his words, the guilt contracted by Judah under that wicked king was unpardonable. But it would convey a false impression if we left the matter here; for the whole course of his after-preaching—his exhortations and promises, as well as his threats—prove that Jeremiah did not suppose that the nation could not be saved by genuine repentance and permanent amendment. What he intends rather to affirm is that the sins of the fathers will be visited upon children, who are partakers of their sins. It is the doctrine of St. Matt. xxiii. 29 *sqq.*; a doctrine which is not merely a theological opinion, but a matter of historical observation.

And I will set over them four kinds—It is an oracle of Iahvah—the sword to slay, and the dogs to hale, and the fowls of the air, and the beasts of the earth, to devour and to destroy. And I will make them a sport for all the realms of earth; on account of Manasseh ben Hezekiah king of Judah, for what he did in Jerusalem.

Jerusalem!—the mention of that magical name touches another chord in the prophet's soul; and the fierce tones of his oracle of doom change into a dirge-like strain of pity without hope.

"For who will have compassion on Thee, O Jerusalem?
And who will yield thee comfort?
And who will turn aside to ask of thy welfare?
'Twas thou that rejectedst Me (it is Iahvah's word);
Backward wouldst thou wend:
So I stretched forth My hand against thee and destroyed
thee;
I wearied of relenting.
And I winnowed them with a fan in the gates of the land;
I bereaved, I undid My people:
Yet they returned not from their own ways.
His widows outnumbered before Me the sand of seas:
I brought them against the Mother of Warriors a harrier at
high noon;
I threw upon her suddenly anguish and horrors.
She that had borne seven sons did pine away;
She breathèd out her soul.
Her sun did set, while it yet was day;
He blushed and paled.
But their remnant will I give to the sword
Before their foes: (It is Iahvah's word)."

The fate of Jerusalem would strike the nations dumb with horror; it would not inspire pity, for man would recognise that it was absolutely just. Or perhaps the thought rather is, In proving false to Me, thou wert false to thine only friend: Me thou hast estranged by thy faithlessness; and from the envious rivals, who beset thee on every side, thou canst expect nothing but rejoicing at thy downfall (Ps. cxxxvi.; Lam. ii. 15-17; Obad. 10 *sqq.*). The peculiar solitariness of Israel among the nations (Num. xxiii. 9) aggravated the anguish of her overthrow.

In what follows, the dreadful past appears as a prophecy of the yet more terrible future. The poet-seer's pathetic monody moralizes the lost battle of Megiddo—that fatal day when the sun of Judah set in what seemed the high day of her prosperity, and all the glory and the promise of good king Josiah vanished like a dream in sudden darkness. Men might think—doubtless Jeremiah thought, in the first moments of despair, when the news of that overwhelming disaster was brought to Jerusalem, with the corpse of the good king, the dead hope of the nation—that this crushing blow was proof that Iahvah had rejected His people, in the exercise of a sovereign caprice, and without reference to their own attitude towards Him. But, says or chants the prophet, in solemn rhythmic utterance,

> "'Twas thou that rejectedst Me;
> Backward wouldst thou wend:
> So I stretched forth My hand against thee, and wrought
> thee hurt;
> I wearied of relenting."

The cup of national iniquity was full, and its baleful contents overflowed in a devastating flood. "In the gates of the land"—the point on the north-west frontier where the armies met—Iahvah "winnowed His people with a fan," separating those who were doomed to fall from those who were to survive, as the winnowing fan separates the chaff from the wheat in the threshing-floor. There He "bereaved" the nation of their dearest hope, "the breath of their nostrils, the Lord's Anointed" (Lam. iv. 20); there He multiplied their widows. And after the lost battle He brought the victor in hot haste against the "Mother" of the fallen warriors, the ill-fated city, Jerusalem, to wreak vengeance upon her for her ill-timed opposition. But, for all this bitter fruit of their evil doings, the people "turned not back from their own ways"; and therefore the strophe of lamentation closes with a threat of utter extermination: "Their remnant"—the poor survival of these fierce storms—"Their remnant will I give to the sword before their foes."[62]

If the thirteenth and fourteenth verses be not a mere interpolation in this chapter (see xvii. 3, 4), their proper place would seem to be here, as continuing and amplifying the sentence upon the residue of the people. The text is unquestionably corrupt, and must be amended by help of the other passage, where it is partially repeated. The twelfth verse may be read thus:

> "Thy wealth and thy treasures will I make a prey,
> For the sin of thine high places in all thy borders."[63]

Then the fourteenth verse follows, naturally enough, with an announcement of the Exile:

> "And I will enthral thee to thy foes
> In a land thou knowest not:
> 'For a fire is kindled in Mine anger,
> 'That shall burn for evermore!"[64]

The prophet has now fulfilled his function of judge by pronouncing upon his people the extreme penalty of the law. His strong perception of the national guilt and of the righteousness of God has left him no choice in the matter. But how little this duty of condemnation accorded with his own individual feeling as a man and a citizen is clear from the passionate outbreak of the succeeding strophe.

"Woe's me, my mother," he exclaims, "that thou barest me,
A man of strife and a man of contention to all the country!
Neither lender nor borrower have I been;
Yet all of them do curse me."

A desperately bitter tone, evincing the anguish of a man wounded to the heart by the sense of fruitless endeavour and unjust hatred. He had done his utmost to save his country, and his reward was universal detestation. His innocence and integrity were requited with the odium of the pitiless creditor who enslaves his helpless victim, and appropriates his all; or the fraudulent borrower who repays a too ready confidence with ruin.[65]

The next two verses answer this burst of grief and despair:

"Said Iahvah, Thine oppression shall be for good;
I will make the foe thy suppliant in time of evil and in time
of distress.
Can one break iron,
Iron from the north, and brass?"

In other words, faith counsels patience, and assures the prophet that all things work together for good to them that love God. The wrongs and bitter treatment which he now endures will only enchance his triumph, when the truth of his testimony is at last confirmed by events, and they who now scoff at his message, come humbly to beseech his prayers. The closing lines refer, with grave irony, to that unflinching firmness, that inflexible resolution, which, as a messenger of God, he was called upon to maintain. He is reminded of what he had undertaken at the outset of his career, and of the Divine Word which made him "a pillar of iron and walls of brass against all the land" (i. 18). Is it possible that the pillar of iron can be broken, and the walls of brass beaten down by the present assault?

There is a pause, and then the prophet vehemently pleads his own cause with Iahvah. Smarting with the sense of personal wrong, he urges that his suffering is for the Lord's own sake; that consciousness of the Divine calling has dominated his entire life, ever since his dedication to the prophetic office; and that the honour of Iahvah requires his vindication upon his heartless and hardened adversaries.

"*Thou* knowest, Iahvah!
Remember me, and visit me, and avenge me on my
persecutors.
Take me not away in thy longsuffering;
Regard my bearing of reproach for Thee.

"Thy words were found, and I did eat them,
And it became to me a joy and mine heart's gladness;
For I was called by Thy Name, O Iahvah, God of Sabaoth!

"I sate not in the gathering of the mirthful, nor rejoiced;
Because of Thine hand I sate solitary,
For with indignation Thou didst fill me.

"Why hath my pain become perpetual,
And my stroke malignant, incurable?
Wilt Thou indeed become to me like a delusive stream,
Like waters which are not lasting?"

The pregnant expression, "*Thou* knowest, Iahvah!" does not refer specially to anything that has been already said; but rather lays the whole case before God in a single word. The *Thou* is emphatic; Thou, Who knowest all things, knowest my heinous wrongs: Thou knowest and seest it all, though the whole world beside be blind with passion and self-regard and sin (Ps. x. 11-14). Thou knowest how pressing is my need; therefore *Take me not away in Thy longsuffering*: sacrifice not the life of Thy servant to the claims of forbearance with his enemies and Thine. The petition shews how great was the peril in which the prophet perceived himself to stand: he believes that if God delay to strike down his adversaries, that longsuffering will be fatal to his own life.

The strength of his case is that he is persecuted, because he is faithful; he bears reproach for God. He has not abused his high calling for the sake of worldly advantage; he has not prostituted the name of prophet to the vile ends of pleasing the people, and satisfying personal covetousness. He has not feigned smooth prophecies, misleading his hearers with flattering falsehood; but he has considered the privilege of being called a prophet of Iahvah as in itself an all-sufficient reward; and when the Divine Word came to him, he has eagerly received, and fed his inmost soul upon that spiritual aliment, which was at once his sustenance and his deepest joy. Other joys, for the Lord's sake, he has abjured. He has withdrawn himself even from harmless mirth, that in silence and solitude he might listen intently to the inward Voice, and reflect with indignant sorrow upon the revelation of his people's corruption. *Because of Thine Hand*—under Thy influence; conscious of the impulse and operation of Thy informing Spirit;—*I sate solitary; for with indignation Thou didst fill me*. The man whose eye has caught a glimpse of eternal Truth, is apt to be dissatisfied with the shows of things; and the lighthearted merriment of the world rings hollow upon the ear that listens for the Voice of God. And the revelation of sin—the discovery of all that ghastly evil which lurks beneath the surface of smooth society—

the appalling vision of the grim skeleton hiding its noisome decay behind the mask of smiles and gaiety; the perception of the hideous incongruity of revelling over a grave; has driven others, besides Jeremiah, to retire into themselves, and to avoid a world from whose evil they revolted, and whose foreseen destruction they deplored.

The whole passage is an assertion of the prophet's integrity and consistency, with which, it is suggested, that the failure which has attended his efforts, and the serious peril in which he stands, are morally inconsistent, and paradoxical in view of the Divine disposal of events. Here, in fact, as elsewhere, Jeremiah has freely opened his heart, and allowed us to see the whole process of his spiritual conflict in the agony of his moments of doubt and despair. It is an argument of his own perfect sincerity; and, at the same time, it enables us to assimilate the lesson of his experience, and to profit by the heavenly guidance he received, far more effectually, than if he had left us ignorant of the painful struggles at the cost of which that guidance was won.

The seeming injustice or indifference of Providence is a problem which recurs to thoughtful minds in all generations of men.

> "O, goddes cruel, that govérne
> This world with byndyng of youre word eterne ...
> What governance is in youre prescience
> That gilteles tormenteth innocence?...
> Alas! I see a serpent or a theif,
> That many a trewé man hath doon mescheit,
> Gon at his large, and wher him luste may turne;
> But I moste be in prisoun."

That such apparent anomalies are but a passing trial, from which persistent faith will emerge victorious in the present life, is the general answer of the Old Testament to the doubts which they suggest. The only sufficient explanation was reserved, to be revealed by Him, who, in the fulness of time, "brought life and immortality to light."

The thought which restored the failing confidence and courage of Jeremiah was the reflexion that such complaints were unworthy of one called to be a spokesman for the Highest; that the supposition of the possibility of the Fountain of Living Waters failing like a winter torrent, that runs dry in the summer heats, was an act of unfaithfulness that merited reproof; and that the true God could not fail to protect His messenger, and to secure the triumph of truth in the end.

> *"To this Iahvah said thus:*
> If thou come again,

I will make thee again to stand before Me;
And if thou utter that is precious rather than that is vile,
As My mouth shalt thou become:
They shall return unto thee,
But Thou shalt not return unto them.

"And I will make thee to this people an embattled wall of
brass;
And they shall fight against thee, but not overcome thee,
For I will be with thee to help thee and to save thee;
It is Iahvah's word.
And I will save thee out of the grasp of the wicked,
And will ransom thee out of the hand of the terrible."

In the former strophe, the inspired poet set forth the claims of the psychic man, and poured out his heart before God. Now he recognises a Word of God in the protest of his better feeling. He sees that where he remains true to himself, he will also stand near to his God. Hence springs the hope, which he cannot renounce, that God will protect His accepted servant in the execution of the Divine commands. Thus the discords are resolved; and the prophet's spirit attains to peace, after struggling through the storm.

It was an outcome of earnest prayer, of an unreserved exposure of his inmost heart before God. What a marvel it is—that instinct of prayer! To think that a being whose visible life has its beginning and its end, a being who manifestly shares possession of this earth with the brute creation, and breathes the same air, and partakes of the same elements with them for the sustenance of his body; who is organized upon the same general plan as they, has the same principal members discharging the same essential functions in the economy of his bodily system; a being who is born and eats and drinks and sleeps and dies like all other animals;—that this being and this being only of all the multitudinous kinds of animated creatures, should have and exercise a faculty of looking off and above the visible which appears to be the sole realm of actual existence, and of holding communion with the Unseen! That, following what seems to be an original impulse of his nature, he should stand in greater awe of this Invisible than of any power that is palpable to sense; should seek to win its favour, crave its help in times of pain and conflict and peril; should professedly live, not according to the bent of common nature and the appetites inseparable from his bodily structure, but according to the will and guidance of that Unseen Power! Surely there is here a consummate marvel. And the wonder of it does not diminish, when it is remembered that this instinct of turning to an unseen Guide and Arbiter of events, is not peculiar to any particular section of the human race. Wide and manifold as are the differences which characterize and divide the families of man, all races possess in common the apprehension of the Unseen and the instinct of prayer. The oldest records of humanity bear witness to its primitive activity, and whatever is known of human history combines with what is known of the character and workings of the human mind to teach us that as prayer has never been unknown, so it is never likely to become obsolete.

May we not recognise in this great fact of human nature a sure index of a great corresponding truth? Can we avoid taking it as a clear token of the reality of revelation; as a kind of immediate and spontaneous evidence on the part of nature that there is and always has been in this lower world some positive knowledge of that which far transcends it, some real apprehension of the mystery that enfolds the universe? a knowledge and an apprehension which, however imperfect and fragmentary, however fitful and fluctuating, however blurred in outline and lost in infinite shadow, is yet incomparably more and better than none at all. Are we not, in short, morally driven upon the conviction that this powerful instinct of our nature is neither blind nor aimless; that its Object is a true, substantive Being; and that this Being has discovered, and yet discovers, some precious glimpses of Himself and His essential character to the spirit of mortal man? It must be so, unless we admit that the soul's dearest desires are a mocking illusion, that her aspirations towards a truth and a goodness of superhuman perfection are moonshine and madness. It cannot be nothingness that avails to evoke the deepest and purest emotions of our nature; not mere vacuity and chaos, wearing the semblance of an azure heaven. It is not into a measureless waste of outer darkness that we reach forth trembling hands.

Surely the spirit of denial is the spirit that fell from heaven, and the best and highest of man's thoughts aim at and affirm something positive, something that is, and the soul thirsts after God, the Living God.

We hear much in these days of our physical nature. The microscopic investigations of science leave nothing unexamined, nothing unexplored, so far as the visible organism is concerned. Rays from many distinct sources converge to throw an ever-increasing light upon the mysteries of our bodily constitution. In all this, science presents to the devout mind a valuable subsidiary revelation of the power and goodness of the Creator. But science cannot advance alone one step beyond the things of time and sense; her facts belong exclusively to the material order of existence; her cognition is limited to the various modes and conditions of force that constitute the realm of sight and touch; she cannot climb above these to a higher plane of being. And small blame it is to science, that she thus lacks the power of overstepping her natural boundaries. The evil begins when the men of science venture, in her much-abused name, to ignore and deny realities not amenable to scientific tests, and immeasurably transcending all merely physical standards and methods.

Neither the natural history nor the physiology of man, nor both together, are competent to give a complete account of his marvellous and many-sided being. Yet some thinkers appear to imagine that when a place has been assigned him in the animal kingdom, and his close relationship to forms below him in the scale of life has been demonstrated; when every tissue and structure has been analysed, and every organ described and its function ascertained; then the last word has been spoken, and the subject exhausted. Those unique and distinguishing faculties by which all this amazing work of observation, comparison, reasoning, has been accomplished, appear either to be left out of the account altogether, or to be handled with a meagre inadequacy of treatment that contrasts in the strongest manner with the fulness and the elaboration which mark the other discussion. And the more this physical aspect of our composite nature is emphasized; the more urgently it is insisted that, somehow or other, all that is in man and all that comes of man may be explained on the assumption that he is the natural climax of the animal creation, a kind of educated and glorified brute—that and nothing more;—the harder it becomes to give any rational account of those facts of his nature which are commonly recognised as spiritual, and among them of this instinct of prayer and its Object.

Under these discouraging circumstances, men are fatally prone to seek escape from their self-involved dilemma, by a hardy denial of what their methods have failed to discover and their favourite theories to explain. The soul and God are treated as mere metaphysical expressions, or as popular designations of the unknown causes of phenomena; and prayer is declared to be an act of foolish superstition which persons of culture have long since outgrown. Sad and strange this result is; but it is also the natural outcome of an initial error, which is none the less real because unperceived. Men "seek the living among the dead"; they expect to find the soul by *post mortem* examination, or to see God by help of an improved telescope. They fail and are disappointed, though they have little right to be so, for "spiritual things are discerned spiritually," and not otherwise.

In speculating on the reasons of this lamentable issue, we must not forget that there is such a thing as an unpurified intellect as well as a corrupt and unregenerate heart. Sin is not restricted to the affections of the lower nature; it has also invaded the realm of thought and reason. The very pursuit of knowledge, noble and elevating as it is commonly esteemed, is not without its dangers of self-delusion and sin. Wherever the love of self is paramount, wherever the object really sought is the delight, the satisfaction, the indulgence of self, no matter in which of the many departments of human life and action, there is sin. It is certain that the intellectual consciousness has its own peculiar pleasures, and those of the keenest and most transporting character; certain that the incessant pursuit of such pleasures may come to absorb the entire energies of a man, so that no room is left for the culture of humility or love or worship. Everything is sacrificed to what is called the pursuit of truth, but is in sober fact a passionate prosecution of private pleasure. It is not truth that is so highly valued; it is the keen excitement of the race, and not seldom the plaudits of the spectators when the goal is won. Such a career may be as thoroughly selfish and sinful and alienated from God as a career of common wickedness. And thus employed or enthralled, no intellectual gifts, however splendid, can bring a man to the discernment of spiritual truth. Not self-pleasing and foolish vanity and arrogant self-assertion, but a self-renouncing humility, an inward purity from idols of every kind, a reverence of truth as divine, are indispensable conditions of the perception of things spiritual.

The representation which is often given is a mere travesty. Believers in God do *not* want to alter His laws by their prayers—neither His laws physical, nor His laws moral and spiritual. It is their chief desire to be brought into submission or perfect obedience to the sum of His laws. They ask their Father in heaven to lead and teach them, to supply their wants in His own way, because He *is* their Father; because "It is He that made us, and His we are." Surely, a reasonable request, and grounded in reason.

To a plain man, seeking for arguments to justify prayer may well seem like seeking a justification of breathing, or eating and drinking and sleeping, or any other natural function. Our Lord never does anything of the kind, because His teaching takes for granted the ultimate prevalence of common sense, in spite of all the subtleties and airspun perplexities, in which a speculative mind delights to lose itself. So long as man has other wants than those which he can himself supply, prayer will be their natural expression.

If there be a spiritual as distinct from a material world, the difficulty to the ordinary mind is not to conceive of their contact but of their absolute isolation from each other. This is surely the inevitable result of our own individual experience, of the intimate though not indissoluble union of body and spirit in every living person.

How, it may be asked, can we really think of his Maker being cut off from man, or man from his Maker? God were not God, if He left man to himself. But not only are His wisdom, justice and love manifested forth in the beneficent arrangements of the world in which we find ourselves; not only is He "kind to the unjust and the unthankful." In pain and loss He quickens our sense of Himself (cf. xiv. 19-22). Even in the first moments of angry surprise and revolt, that sense is quickened; we rebel, not against an inanimate world or an impersonal law, but against a Living and Personal Being, whom we acknowledge as the Arbiter of our destinies, and whose wisdom and love and power we affect for the time to question, but cannot really gainsay. The whole of our experience tends to this end—to the continual rousing of our spiritual consciousness. There is no interference, no isolated and capricious interposition or interruption of order within or without us. Within and without us, His Will is always energizing, always manifesting forth His Being, encouraging our confidence, demanding our obedience and homage.

Thus prayer has its Divine as well as its human side; it is the Holy Spirit drawing the soul, as well as the soul drawing nigh unto God. The case is like the action and reaction of the magnet and the steel. And so prayer is not a foolish act of unauthorised presumption, not a rash effort to approach unapproachable and absolutely isolated Majesty. Whenever man truly prays, his Divine King has already extended the sceptre of His mercy, and bidden him speak.

xvi.-xvii. After the renewal of the promise there is a natural pause, marked by the formula with which the present section opens. When the prophet had recovered his firmness, through the inspired and inspiring reflexions which took possession of his soul after he had laid bare his inmost heart before God (xv. 20, 21), he was in a position to receive further guidance from above. What now lies before us is the direction, which came to him as certainly Divine, for the regulation of his own future behaviour as the chosen minister of Iahvah at this crisis in the history of his people. "And there fell a word of Iahvah unto me, saying: Thou shalt not take thee a wife; that thou get not sons and daughters in this place." Such a prohibition reveals, with the utmost possible clearness and emphasis, the gravity of the existing situation. It implies that the "peace and permanence," so glibly predicted by Jeremiah's opponents, will never more be known by that sinful generation. "This place," the holy place which Iahvah had "chosen, to establish His name there," as the Book of the Law so often describes it; "this place," which had been inviolable to the fierce hosts of the Assyrian in the time of Isaiah (Isa. xxxvii. 33), was now no more a sure refuge, but doomed to utter and speedy destruction. To beget sons and daughters there was to prepare more victims for the tooth of famine, and the pangs of pestilence, and the devouring sword of a merciless conqueror. It was to fatten the soil with unburied carcases, and to spread a hideous banquet for birds and beasts of prey. Children and parents were doomed to perish together; and

Iahvah's witness was to keep himself unencumbered by the sweet cares of husband and father, that he might be wholly free for his solemn duties of menace and warning, and be ready for every emergency.

> "For thus hath Iahvah said:
> Concerning the sons and concerning the daughters that are
> born in this place,
> And concerning their mothers that bear them,
> And concerning their fathers that beget them, in this land:
> By deaths of agony shall they die;
> They shall not be mourned nor buried;
> For dung on the face of the ground shall they serve;
> And by the sword and by the famine shall they be fordone:
> And their carcase shall serve for food
> To the fowls of the air and to the beasts of the earth" (xvi.
> 3-4).

The "deaths of agony" seem to indicate the pestilence, which always ensued upon the scarcity and vile quality of food, and the confinement of multitudes within the narrow bounds of a besieged city (see Josephus' well-known account of the last siege of Jerusalem).

The attitude of solitary watchfulness and strict separation, which the prophet thus perceived to be required by circumstances, was calculated to be a warning of the utmost significance, among a people who attached the highest importance to marriage, and the permanence of the family.

It proclaimed more loudly than words could do, the prophet's absolute conviction that offspring was no pledge of permanence; that universal death was hanging over a condemned nation. But not only this. It marks a point of progress in the prophet's spiritual life. The crisis, through which we have seen him pass, has purged his mental vision. He no longer repines at his dark lot; no longer half envies the false prophets, who may win the popular love by pleasing oracles of peace and well-being; no longer complains of the Divine Will, which has laid such a burden upon him. He sees now that his part is to refuse even natural and innocent pleasures for the Lord's sake; to foresee calamity and ruin; to denounce unceasingly the sin he sees around him; to sacrifice a tender and affectionate heart to a life of rigid asceticism; and he manfully accepts his part. He knows that he stands alone—the last fortress of truth in a world of falsehood; and that for truth it becomes a man to surrender his all.

That which follows tends to complete the prophet's social isolation. He is to give no sign of sympathy in the common joys and sorrows of his kind.

"For thus hath Iahvah said:
Enter thou not into the house of mourning,
Nor go to lament, nor comfort thou them:
For I have taken away My friendship from this people ('Tis
Iahvah's utterance!)
The lovingkindness and the compassion;
And old and young shall die in this land,
They shall not be buried, and men shall not wail for them;
Nor shall a man cut himself, nor make himself bald, for
them:
Neither shall men deal out bread to them in mourning,
To comfort a man over the dead;
Nor shall they give them to drink the cup of consolation,
Over a man's father and over his mother.

"And the house of feasting thou shalt not enter,
To sit with them to eat and to drink.
For thus hath Iahvah Sabaoth, the God of Israel, said:
Lo, I am about to make to cease from this place,
Before your own eyes and in your own days,
Voice of mirth and voice of gladness,
The voice of the bridegroom and the voice of the bride."

Acting as prophet, that is, as one whose public actions were symbolical of a Divine intent, Jeremiah is henceforth to stand aloof, on occasions when natural feeling would suggest participation in the outward life of his friends and acquaintance. He is to quell the inward stirrings of affection and sympathy, and to abstain from playing his part in those demonstrative lamentations over the dead, which the immemorial custom and sentiment of his country regarded as obligatory; and this, in order to signify unmistakably that what thus appeared to be the state of his own feelings, was really the aspect under which God would shortly appear to a nation perishing in its guilt. "Enter not into the house of mourning ... *for* I have taken away My friendship from this people, the lovingkindness and the compassion." An estranged and alienated God would view the coming catastrophe with the cold indifference of exact justice. And the consequence of the Divine aversion would be a calamity so overwhelming, that the dead would be left without those rites of burial, which the feeling and conscience of all races of mankind have always been careful to perform. There should be no burial, much less ceremonial lamentation, and those more serious modes of evincing grief by disfigurement of the person,[66] which, like tearing the hair and rending the garments, are natural tokens of the first distraction of bereavement. Not for wife or child (מַת: see Gen. xxiii. 3), nor for father or mother should the funeral feast be held; for men's hearts would grow hard at the daily spectacle of death, and at last there would be no survivors.

In like manner, the prophet is forbidden to enter as guest "the house of feasting." He is not to be seen at the marriage-feast,—that occasion of highest rejoicing, the very type and example of innocent and holy mirth; to testify by his abstention that the day of judgment was swiftly approaching, which would desolate all homes, and silence for evermore all sounds of joy and gladness in the ruined city. And it is expressly added that the blow will fall "before your own eyes and in your own days;" shewing that the hour of doom was very near, and would no more be delayed.

In all this, it is noticeable that the Divine answer appears to bear special reference to the peculiar terms of the prophet's complaint. In despairing tones he had cried (xv. 10), "Woe's me, my mother, that thou didst bear me!" and now he is himself warned not to take a wife, and seek the blessing of children. The outward connexion here may be: "Let it not be that thy children speak of thee, as thou hast spoken of thy mother!"[67] But the inner link of thought may rather be this, that the prophet's temporary unfaithfulness evinced in his outcry against God and his lament that ever he was born is punished by the denial to him of the joys of fatherhood—a penalty which would be severe to a loving, yearning nature like his, but which was doubtless necessary to the purification of his spirit from all worldly taint, and to the discipline of his natural impatience and tendency to repine under the hand of God. His punishment, like that of Moses, may appear disproportionate to his offence; but God's dealings with man are not regulated by any mechanical calculation of less and more, but by His perfect knowledge of the needs of the case; and it is often in truest mercy that His hand strikes hard. "As gold in the furnace doth He try them"; and the purest metal comes out of the hottest fire.

Further, it is not the least prominent but the leading part of a man's nature that most requires this heavenly discipline, if the best is to be made of it that can be made. The strongest element, that which is most characteristic of the person, that which constitutes his individuality, is the chosen field of Divine influence and operation; for here lies the greatest need. In Jeremiah this master element was an almost feminine tenderness; a warmly affectionate disposition, craving the love and sympathy of his fellows, and recoiling almost in agony from the spectacle of pain and suffering. And therefore it was that the Divine discipline was specially applied to this element in the prophet's personality. In him, as in all other men, the good was mingled with evil, which, if not purged away, might spread until it spoiled his whole nature. It is not virtue to indulge our own bent, merely because it pleases us to do so; nor is the exercise of affection any great matter to an affectionate nature. The involved strain of selfishness must be separated, if any naturally good gift is to be elevated to moral worth, to become acceptable in the sight of God. And so it was precisely here, in his most susceptible point, that the sword of trial pierced the prophet through. He was saved from all hazard of becoming satisfied with the love of wife and children, and forgetting in that earthly satisfaction the love of his God. He was saved from absorption in the pleasures of friendly intercourse with neighbours, from passing his days in an agreeable round of social amenities; at a time when ruin was impending over his country, and well nigh ready to fall. And the means which God chose for the accomplishment of this result were precisely those of which the prophet had complained (xv. 17); his social isolation, which though in part a matter of choice, was partly forced upon him by the irritation and ill-will of his acquaintance. It is now declared that this trial is to continue. The Lord does not necessarily remove a trouble, when entreated to do it. He manifests His love by giving strength to bear it, until the work of chastening be perfected.

An interruption is now supposed, such as may often have occurred in the course of Jeremiah's public utterances. The audience demands to know why all this evil is ordained to fall upon them. *What is our guilt and what our trespass, that we have trespassed against Iahvah our God?* The answer is a twofold accusation. Their fathers were faithless to Iahvah, and they have outdone their fathers' sin; and the penalty will be expulsion and a foreign servitude.

> "Because your fathers forsook Me (It is Iahvah's word!)
> And went after other gods, and served them, and bowed
> down to them,
> And Me they forsook, and My teaching they observed not:
> And ye yourselves (or, as for you) have done worse than
> your fathers;
> And lo, ye walk each after the stubbornness of his evil
> heart,
> So as not to hearken unto Me.
> Therefore will I hurl you from off this land,
> On to the land that ye and your fathers knew not;
> And ye may serve there other gods, day and night,
> Since I will not grant you grace."

The damning sin laid to Israel's charge is idolatry, with all the moral consequences involved in that prime transgression. That is to say, the offence consisted not barely in recognising and honouring the gods of the nations along with their own God, though that were fault enough, as an act of treason against the sole majesty of Heaven; but it was aggravated enormously by the moral declension and depravity, which accompanied this apostasy. They and their fathers forsook Iahvah *"and kept not His teaching;"* a reference to the Book of the Law, considered not only as a collection of ritual and ceremonial precepts for the regulation of external religion, but as a guide of life and conduct. And there had been a progress in evil; the nation had gone from bad to worse with fearful rapidity: so that now it could be said of the existing generation that it paid no heed at all to the monitions which Iahvah uttered by the mouth of His prophet, but walked simply in stubborn self-will and the indulgence of every corrupt inclination. And here too, as in so many other cases, the sin is to be its own punishment. The Book of the Law had declared that revolt from Iahvah should be punished by enforced service of strange gods in a strange land (Deut. iv. 28, xxviii. 36, 64); and Jeremiah repeats this threat, with the addition of a tone of ironical concession: there, in your bitter banishment, you may have your wish to the full; you may serve the foreign gods, and that without intermission (implying that the service would be a slavery).

The whole theory of Divine punishment is implicit in these few words of the prophet. They who sin persistently against light and knowledge are at last given over to their own hearts' lust, to do as they please, without the gracious check of God's inward voice. And then there comes a strong delusion, so that they believe a lie, and take evil for good and good for evil, and hold themselves innocent before God, when their guilt has reached its climax; so that, like Jeremiah's hearers, if their evil be denounced, they can ask in astonishment: "What is our iniquity? or what is our trespass?"

They are so ripe in sin that they retain no knowledge of it as sin, but hold it virtue.

> "And they, so perfect is their misery,
> Not once perceive their foul disfigurement,
> But boast themselves more comely than before."

And not only do we find in this passage a striking instance of judicial blindness as the penalty of sin. We may see also in the penalty predicted for the Jews a plain analogy to the doctrine that the permanence of the sinful state in a life to come is the penalty of sin in the present life. "He that is unjust, let him be unjust still; and he that is filthy, let him be filthy still!" and know himself to be what he is.

The prophet's dark horizon is here apparently lit up for a moment by a gleam of hope. The fourteenth and fifteenth verses, however, with their beautiful promise of restoration, really belong to another oracle, whose prevailing tones are quite different from the present gloomy forecast of retribution (xxiii. 7 *sqq.*). Here they interrupt the sense, and make a cleavage in the connexion of thought, which can only be bridged over artificially, by the suggestion that the import of the two verses is primarily not consolatory but minatory; that is to say, that they threaten Exile rather than promise Return; a mode of understanding the two verses which does manifest violence to the whole form of expression, and, above all, to their obvious force in the original passage from which they have been transferred hither. Probably some transcriber of the text wrote them in the margin of his copy, by way of palliating the otherwise unbroken gloom of this oracle of coming woe. Then, at some later time, another copyist, supposing the marginal note indicated an omission, incorporated the two verses in his transcription of the text, where they have remained ever since. (See on xxiii. 7, 8.)

After plainly announcing in the language of Deuteronomy the expulsion of Judah from the land which they had desecrated by idolatry, the prophet develops the idea in his own poetic fashion; representing the punishment as universal, and insisting that it *is* a punishment, and not an unmerited misfortune.

> "Lo, I am about to send many fishers (It is Iahvah's word!)
> And they shall fish them;
> And afterwards will I send many hunters,
> And they shall hunt them,
> From off every mountain,
> And from off every hill,
> And out of the clefts of the rocks."

Like silly fish, crowding helplessly one over another into the net,[68] when the fated moment arrives, Judah will fall an easy prey to the destroyer. And "afterwards," to ensure completeness, those who have survived this first disaster will be hunted like wild beasts, out of all the dens and caves in the mountains, the Adullams and Engedis, where they have found a refuge from the invader.

There is clearly reference to two distinct visitations of wrath, the latter more deadly than the former; else why the use of the emphatic note of time "afterwards"? If we understand by the "fishing" of the country the so-called first captivity, the carrying away of the boy-king Jehoiachin and his mother and his nobles and ten thousand principal citizens, by Nebuchadrezzar to Babylon (2 Kings xxiv. 10 *sqq.*); and by the "hunting" the final catastrophe in the time of Zedekiah; we get, as we shall see, a probable explanation of a difficult expression in the eighteenth verse, which cannot otherwise be satisfactorily accounted for. The next words (ver. 17) refute an assumption, implied in the popular demand to know wherein the guilt of the nation consists, that Iahvah is not really cognisant of their acts of apostasy.

"For Mine eyes are upon all their ways,
They are not hidden away from before My face;
Nor is their guilt kept secret from before Mine eyes."

The verse is thus an indirect reply to the questions of verse 10; questions which in some mouths might indicate that unconsciousness of guilt, which is the token of sin finished and perfected; in others, the presence of that unbelief which doubts whether God can, or at least whether He does regard human conduct. But "He that planted the ear, can He not hear? He that formed the eye, can He not see?" (Ps. xciv. 9). It is really an utterly irrational thought, that sight, and hearing, and the higher faculties of reflexion and consciousness, had their origin in a blind and deaf, a senseless and unconscious source such as inorganic matter, whether we consider it in the atom or in the enormous mass of an embryo system of stars.

The measure of the penalty is now assigned.

"And I will repay first the double of their guilt and their trespass
For that they profaned My land with the carcases of their loathly offerings,
And their abominations filled Mine heritage."[69]

"I will repay *first*." The term "first," which has occasioned much perplexity to expositors, means "the first time" (Gen. xxxviii. 28; Dan. xi. 29), and refers, if I am not mistaken, to the first great blow, the captivity of Jehoiachin, of which I spoke just now; an occasion which is designated again (ver. 21), by the expression "this once" or rather "at this time." And when it is said "I will repay the double of their guilt and of their trespass," we are to understand that the Divine justice is not satisfied with half measures; the punishment of sin is proportioned to the offence, and the cup of self-entailed misery has to be drained to the dregs. Even penitence does not abolish the physical and temporal consequences of sin; in ourselves and in others whom we have influenced they continue—a terrible and ineffaceable record of the past. The ancient law required that the man who had wronged his neighbour by theft or fraud should restore double (Ex. xxii. 4, 7, 9); and thus this expression would appear to denote that the impending chastisement would be in strict accordance with the recognised rule of law and justice, and that Judah must repay to the Lord in suffering the legal equivalent for her offence. In a like strain, towards the end of the Exile, the great prophet of the captivity comforts Jerusalem with the announcement that "her hard service is accomplished, her punishment is held sufficient; for she hath received of Iahvah's hand twofold for all her trespasses" (Isa. xl. 2). The Divine severity is, in fact, truest mercy. Only thus does mankind learn to realize "the exceeding sinfulness of sin," only as Judah learned the heinousness of desecrating the Holy Land with "loathly offerings" to the vile Nature-gods, and with the symbols in wood and stone of the cruel and obscene deities of Canaan; viz. by the fearful issue of transgression, the lesson of a calamitous experience, confirming the forecasts of its inspired prophets.

> "Iahvah my strength and my stronghold and my refuge in
> the day of distress!
> Unto Thee the very heathen will come from the ends of the
> earth, and will say:
> 'Mere fraud did our fathers receive as their own,
> Mere breath, and beings among whom is no helper.
> Should man make him gods,When such things are not
> gods?'

> "Therefore, behold I am about to let them know—
> At this time will I let them know My hand and My might,
> And they shall know that My name is Iahvah!"

In the opening words Jeremiah passionately recoils from the very mention of the hateful idols, the loathly creations, the lifeless "carcases," which his people have put in the place of the Living God. An overmastering access of faith lifts him off the low ground where these dead things lie in their helplessness, and bears him in spirit to Iahvah, the really and eternally existing, Who is his "strength and stronghold and refuge in the day of distress." From this height he takes an eagle glance into the dim future, and discerns—O marvel of victorious faith!—that the very heathen, who have never so much as known the Name of Iahvah, must one day be brought to acknowledge the impotence of their hereditary gods, and the sole deity of the Mighty One of Jacob. He enjoys a glimpse of Isaiah's and Micah's glorious vision of the latter days, when "the mountain of the Lord's House shall be exalted as chief of mountains, and all nations shall flow unto it."

In the light of this revelation, the sin and folly of Israel in dishonouring the One only God, by associating Him with idols and their symbols, becomes glaringly visible. The very heathen (the term is emphatic by position), will at last grope their way out of the night of traditional ignorance, and will own the absurdity of manufactured gods. Israel, on the other hand, has for centuries sinned against knowledge and reason. They had "Moses and the prophets"; yet they hated warning and despised reproof. They resisted the

Divine teachings, because they loved to walk in their own ways, after the imaginings of their own evil hearts. And so they soon fell into that strange blindness, which suffered them to see no sin in giving companions to Iahvah, and neglecting His severer worship for the sensuous rites of Canaan.

A rude awakening awaits them. Once more will Iahvah interpose to save them from their infatuation. "This time" they shall be taught to know the nothingness of idols, not by the voice of prophetic pleadings, not by the fervid teachings of the Book of the Law, but by the sword of the enemy, by the rapine and ruin, in which the resistless might of Iahvah will be manifested against His rebellious people. Then, when the warnings which they have ridiculed find fearful accomplishment, then will they know that the name of the One God is Iahvah—He Who alone was and is and shall be for evermore. In the shock of overthrow, in the sorrows of captivity, they will realize the enormity of assimilating the Supreme Source of events, the Fountain of all being and power, to the miserable phantoms of a darkened and perverted imagination.

xvii. 1-18. Jeremiah, speaking for God, returns to the affirmation of Judah's guiltiness. He has answered the popular question (xvi. 10), so far as it implied that it was no mortal sin to associate the worship of alien gods with the worship of Iahvah. He now proceeds to answer it with an indignant contradiction, so far as it suggested that Judah was no longer guilty of the grossest forms of idolatry.

1 "The trespass of Judah," he affirms, "is written with pen
of iron, with point of adamant;
Graven upon the tablet of their heart,
And upon the horns of their altars:
Even as their sons remember their altars,
And their sacred poles by the evergreen trees,
Upon the high hills.

2 "O My mountain in the field!
Thy wealth and all thy treasures will I give for a spoil,
For the trespass of thine high-places in all thy borders.

And thou shalt drop thine hand[70] from thy demesne
which I gave thee;
And I will enslave thee to thine enemies,
In the land that thou knowest not;

"For a fire have ye kindled in Mine anger;
It shall burn for evermore."

It is clear from the first strophe that the outward forms of idolatry were no longer openly practised in the country. Where otherwise would be the point of affirming that the national sin was "written with pen of iron, and point of adamant"—that it was "graven upon the tablet of the people's heart?" Where would be the point of alluding to the children's *memory* of the altars and sacred poles, which were the visible adjuncts of idolatry? Plainly it is implied that the hideous rites, which sometimes involved the sacrifice of children, are a thing of the past; yet not of the distant past, for the young of the present generation remember them; those terrible scenes are burnt in upon their memories, as a haunting recollection which can no more be effaced, than the guilt contracted by their parents as agents in those abhorrent rites can be done away. The indelible characters of sin are graven deeply upon their hearts; no need for a prophet to remind them of facts to which their own consciences, their own inward sense of outraged affections, and of nature sacrificed to a dark and bloody superstition, bears irrefragable witness. Rivers of water cannot cleanse the stain of innocent blood from their polluted altars. The crimes of the past are unatoned for, and beyond reach of atonement; they cry to heaven for vengeance, and the vengeance will surely fall (xv. 4).

Hitzig rather prosaically remarks that Josiah had destroyed the altars. But the stains of which the poet-seer speaks are not palpable to sense; he contemplates unseen realities.

"Will all great Neptune's ocean wash this blood
Clean from my hand? No, this my hand will rather
The multitudinous seas incarnadine,
Making the green one red."

The second strophe declares the nature of the punishment. The tender, yearning, hopeless love of the cry with which Iahvah resigns His earthly seat to profanation and plunder and red-handed ruin, enhances the awful impression wrought by the slow, deliberate enunciation of the details of the sentence—the utter spoliation of temple and palaces; the accumulated hoards of generations—all that represented the wealth and culture and glory of the time—carried away for ever; the enforced surrender of home and country; the harsh servitude to strangers in a far-off land.

It is difficult to fix the date of this short lyrical outpouring, if it be assumed, with Hitzig, that it is an independent whole. He refers it to the year b.c. 602, after Jehoiakim had revolted from Babylon—"a proceeding which made a future captivity well-nigh certain, and made it plain that the sin of Judah remained still to be punished." Moreover, the preceding year (b.c. 603) was what was known to the Law as a Year of Release or Remission (*shenath shemittah*); and the phrase "thou shalt drop thine hand," *i.e.* "loose thine hold of" the land (xvii. 4), appears to allude to the peculiar usages of that year, in which the debtor was released from his obligations, and the corn-lands and vineyards were allowed to lie fallow. The Year of Release was also called the Year of Rest (*shenath shabbathon*, Lev. xxv. 5); and both in the present passage of Jeremiah, and in the book of Leviticus, the time to be spent by the Jews in exile is regarded as a period of rest for the desolate land, which would then "make good her sabbaths" (Lev. xxvi. 34, 35, 43). The Chronicler indeed seems to refer to this very phrase of Jeremiah; at all events, nothing else is to be found in the extant works of the prophet with which his language corresponds (2 Chron. xxxvi. 21).

If the rendering of the second verse, which we find in both our English versions, and which I have adopted above, be correct, there arises an obvious objection to the date assigned by Hitzig; and the same objection lies against the view of Naegelsbach, who translates:

"As their children remember their altars,
And their images of Baal *by* (*i.e.* at the sight of) the green
trees, by the high hills."

For in what sense could this have been written "not long before the fourth year of Jehoiakim," which is the date suggested by this commentator for the whole group of chapters, xiv.-xvii. 18? The entire reign of Josiah had intervened between the atrocities of Manasseh and this period; and it is not easy to suppose that any sacrifice of children had occurred in the three months' reign of Jehoahaz, or in the early years of Jehoiakim. Had it been so, Jeremiah, who denounces the latter king severely enough, would certainly have placed the horrible fact in the forefront of his invective; and instead of specifying Manasseh as the king whose offences Iahvah would not pardon, would have thus branded Jehoiakim, his own contemporary. This difficulty appears to be avoided by Hitzig, who explains the passage thus: "When they (the Jews) think of their children, they remember, and cannot but remember, the altars to whose horns the blood of their immolated children cleaves. In the same way, by a green tree on the hills, *i.e.*, when they come upon any such, their Asherim are brought to mind, which were trees of that sort." And since it is perhaps possible to translate the Hebrew as this suggests, "When they remember their sons, their altars, and their sacred poles, by (*i.e.* by means of) the evergreen trees (collective term) upon the high hills," and this translation agrees well with the statement that the sin of Judah is "graven upon the tablet of their heart," his view deserves further consideration. The same objection, however, presses again, though with somewhat diminished force. For if the date of the section be 602, the eighth year of Jehoiakim, more than forty years must have elapsed between the time of Manasseh's bloody rites and the utterance of this oracle. Would many who were parents then, and surrendered their children for sacrifice, be still living at the supposed date? And if not, where is the appropriateness of the words "When they remember their sons, their altars, and their Asherim?"

There seems no way out of the difficulty, but either to date the piece much earlier, assigning it, *e.g.*, to the time of the prophet's earnest preaching in connexion with the reforming movement of Josiah, when the living generation would certainly remember the human sacrifices under Manasseh; or else to construe the passage in a very different sense, as follows. The first verse declares that the sin of *Judah* is graven upon the tablet of *their heart*, and upon the horns of *their* altars. The pronouns evidently shew that it is the guilt of *the nation*, not of a particular generation, that is asserted. The subsequent words agree with this view. The expression, "*Their* sons" is to be understood in the same way as the expressions "*their* heart," "*their* altars." It is equivalent to the "sons of Judah" (*benê Jehudah*), and means simply the people of Judah, as now existing, the present generation. Now it does not appear that image-worship and the cultus of the high-places revived after their abolition by Josiah. Accordingly, the symbols of impure worship mentioned in this passage are not high-places and images but altars and Asherim, *i.e.*, the wooden poles which were the emblems of the reproductive principle of Nature. What the passage therefore intends to say would seem to be this: "The guilt of the nation remains, so long as its children are mindful of their altars and Asherim erected beside[71] the evergreen trees on the high hills"; *i.e.*, so long as they remain attached to the modified idolatry of the day.

The general force of the words remains the same, whether they accuse the existing generation of serving sun-pillars (*maççeboth*) and sacred poles (*asherim*), or merely of hankering after the old forbidden rites. For so long as the popular heart was wedded to the former superstitions, it could not be said that any external abolition of idolatry was a sufficient proof of national repentance. The longing to indulge in sin is sin; and sinful it is not to hate sin. The guilt of the nation remained, therefore, and would remain, until blotted out by the tears of a genuine repentance towards Iahvah.

But understood thus, the passage suits the time of Jehoiachin, as well as any other period.

"Why," asks Naegelsbach, "should not Moloch have been the terror of the Israelitish children, when there was such real and sad ground for it, as in wanting in other bugbears which terrify the children of the present day?"

To this we may reply, (1) Moloch is not mentioned at all, but simply altars and *asherim*; (2) would the word "remember" be appropriate in this case?

The beautiful strophes which follow (5-13) are not obviously connected with the preceding text. They wear a look of self-completeness, which suggests that here and in many other places Jeremiah has left us, not whole discourses, written down substantially in the form in which they were delivered, but rather his more finished fragments; pieces which being more rhythmical in form, and more striking in thought, had imprinted themselves more deeply upon his memory.

> "Thus hath Iahvah said:
> Cursed is the man that trusteth in human kind,
> And maketh flesh his arm,
> And whose heart swerveth from Iahvah!
> And he shall become like a leafless tree in the desert,
> And shalt not see when good cometh;
> And shall dwell in parched places in the steppe,
> A salt land and uninhabited.

> "Blessed is the man that trusteth in Iahvah,
> And whose trust Iahvah becometh!
> And he shall become like a tree planted by water,
> That spreadeth its roots by a stream,
> And is not afraid when heat cometh,
> And its leaf is evergreen;
> And in the year of drought it feareth not,
> Nor leaveth off from making fruit."

The form of the thought expressed in these two octostichs, the curse and the blessing, may have been suggested by the curses and blessings of that Book of the Law of which Jeremiah had been so faithful an interpreter (Deut. xxvii. 15-xxviii. 20); while both the thought and the form of the second stanza are imitated by the anonymous poet of the first psalm. The mention of "the year of drought" in the penultimate line may be taken, perhaps, as a link of connexion between this brief section and the whole of what precedes it so far as chap. xiv., which is headed "Concerning the droughts." If, however, the group of chapters thus marked out really constitute a single discourse, as Naegelsbach assumes, one can only say that the style is episodical rather than continuous; that the prophet has often recorded detached thoughts, worked up to a certain degree of literary form, but hanging together as loosely as pearls on a string. Indeed, unless we suppose that he had kept full notes of his discourses and soliloquies, or that, like certain professional lecturers of our own day, he had been in the habit of indefinitely repeating to different audiences the same carefully elaborated compositions, it is difficult to understand how he would be able without the aid of a special miracle, to write down in the fourth year of Jehoiakim the numerous utterances of the previous three and twenty years. Neither of these suppositions appears probable. But if the prophet wrote from memory, so long after the original delivery of many of his utterances, the looseness of internal connexion, which marks so much of his book, is readily understood.

The internal evidence of the fragment before us, so far as any such is traceable, appears to point to the same period as what precedes, the time immediately subsequent to the death of Jehoiakim. The curse pronounced upon trusting in man may be an allusion to that king's confidence in the Egyptian alliance, which probably induced him to revolt from Nebuchadrezzar, and so precipitate the final catastrophe of his country. He owed his throne to the Pharaoh's appointment (2 Kings xxiii. 34), and may perhaps have regarded this as an additional reason for defection from Babylon. But the chastisement of Egypt preceded that of Judah; and when the day came for the latter, the king of Egypt durst no longer go to the help of his too trustful allies (2 Kings xxiv. 7). Jehoiakim had died, but his son and successor was carried captive to Babylon. In the brief interval between those two events, the prophet may have penned these two stanzas, contrasting the issues of confidence in man and confidence in God. On the other hand, they may also be referred to some time not long before the fourth year of Jehoiakim, when that king, egged on by Egypt, was meditating rebellion against his suzerain; an act of which the fatal consequences might easily be foreseen by any thoughtful observer, who was not blinded by fanatical passion and prejudice, and which might itself be regarded as an index of the kindling of Divine wrath against the country.

"Deep is the heart above all things else;
And sore-diseased it is: who can know it?
I, Iahvah, search the heart, I try the reins,
And that, to give to a man according to his own ways,
According to the fruit of his own doings.

"A partridge that gathereth young which are not hers,
Is he that maketh wealth not by right.
In the middle of his days it will leave him,
And in his end he shall prove a fool.

"A throne of glory, a high seat from of old,
Is the place of our sanctuary.
Hope of Israel, Iahvah!
All that leave Thee shall be ashamed;

Mine apostates shall be written in earth;
For they left the Well of Living Waters, even Iahvah.

"Heal Thou me, Iahvah, and I shall be healed,
Save Thou me, and I shall be saved,
For Thou art my praise.

"Lo, *they* say unto me,
Where is the Word of Iahvah? Prithee, let it come!
Yet I, I hasted not from being a shepherd after Thee,
And woeful day I desired not—*Thou* knowest;
The issue of my lips, before Thy face it fell.

"Become not a terror to me!
Thou art my refuge in the day of evil.
Let my pursuers be ashamed, and let not me be ashamed!
Let *them* be dismayed, and let not me be dismayed;
Let Thou come upon them a day of evil,
And doubly with breaking break Thou them!"

In the first of these stanzas, the word "heart" is the connecting link with the previous reflexions. The curse and the blessing had there been pronounced not upon any outward and visible distinctions, but upon a certain inward bent and spirit. He is called accursed, whose confidence is placed in changeable, perishable man, and "whose *heart* swerveth from Iahvah." And he is blessed, who pins his faith to nothing visible; who looks for help and stay not to the seen, which is temporal, but to the Unseen, which is eternal.

The thought now occurs that this matter of inward trust, being a matter of the heart, and not merely of the outward bearing, is a hidden matter, a secret which baffles all ordinary judgment. Who shall take upon him to say whether this or that man, this or that prince confided or not confided in Iahvah? The human heart is a sea, whose depths are beyond human search; or it is a shifty Proteus, transforming itself from moment to moment under the pressure of changing circumstances, at the magic touch of impulse, under the spell of new perceptions and new phases of its world. And besides, its very life is tainted with a subtle disease, whose hereditary influence is ever interfering with the will and affections, ever tampering with the conscience and the judgment, and making difficult a clear perception, much more a wise decision. Nay, where so many motives press, so many plausible suggestions of good, so many palliations of evil, present themselves upon the eve of action; when the colours of good and evil mingle and gleam together in such rich profusion before the dazzled sight, that the mind is bewildered by the confused medley of appearances, and wholly at a loss to discern and disentangle them one from another; is it wonderful, if in such a case the heart should take refuge in the comfortable illusion of self-deceit, and seek, with too great success, to persuade itself into contentment with something which it calls not positive evil but merely a less sublime good?

It is not for man, who cannot see the heart, to pronounce upon the degree of his fellow's guilt. All sins, all crimes, are in this respect relative to the intensity of passion, the force of circumstances, the nature of surroundings, the comparative stress of temptation. Murder and adultery are absolute crimes in the eye of human law, and subject as such to fixed penalties; but the Unseen Judge takes cognizance of a thousand considerations, which though they abolish not the exceeding sinfulness of these hideous results of a depraved nature, yet modify to a vast extent the degree of guilt evinced in particular cases by the same outward acts. In the sight of God, a life socially correct may be stained with a deeper dye than that of profligacy or bloodshed; and nothing so glaringly shows the folly of inquiring what is the unpardonable sin, as the reflexion that any sin whatever may become such in an individual case.

Before God, human justice is often the liveliest injustice. And how many flagrant wrongs, how many monstrous acts of cruelty and oppression, how many wicked frauds and perjuries, how many of those vile deeds of seduction and corruption, which are, in truth, the murder of immortal souls; how many of those fearful sins, which make a sorrow-laden hell beneath the smiling surface of this pleasure-wooing world, are left unheeded, unavenged by any earthly tribunal! But all these things are noted in the eternal record of Him who searches the heart, and penetrates man's inmost being, not from a motive of mere curiosity, but with fixed intent to award a righteous recompense for all choice and all conduct.

The calamities which marked the last years of Jehoiakim, and his ignominious end, were a signal instance of Divine retribution. Here that king's lawless avarice is branded as not only wicked but foolish. He is compared to the partridge, which gathers and hatches the eggs of other birds, only to be deserted at once by her stolen brood.[72] "In the middle of his days, it shall leave him" (or "it may leave him," for in Hebrew one form has to do duty for both shades of meaning). The uncertainty of possession, the certainty of absolute surrender within a few short years, this is the point which demonstrates the unreason of making riches the chief end of one's earthly activity. "Truly man walketh in a vain shadow, and disquieteth himself in vain: he heapeth up riches, and cannot tell who shall gather them." It is the point which is put with such terrible force in the parable of the Rich Fool. "Soul, thou hast much goods laid up for thyself for many years; take thine ease, eat, drink, and be merry." "And the Lord said unto him, Thou fool! this night shall thy soul be required of thee."

The covetousness, oppression, and bloodthirstiness of Jehoiakim are condemned in a striking prophecy (xxii. 13-19), which we shall have to consider hereafter. A vivid light is thrown upon the words, "In the middle of his days it shall leave him," by the fact recorded in Kings (2 Kings xxiii. 36), that he died in the thirty-sixth year of his age; when, that is, he had fulfilled but half of the threescore years and ten allotted to the ordinary life of man. We are reminded of that other psalm which declares that "bloody and deceitful men shall not live out half their days" (lv. 23).

Apart indeed from all consideration of the future, and apart from all reference to that loyalty to the Unseen Ruler which is man's inevitable duty, a life devoted to Mammon is essentially irrational. The man is most truly a "fool"—that is, one who fails to understand his own nature, one who has not attained to even a tolerable working hypothesis as to the needs of life, and the way to win a due share of happiness;—who has not discovered that

> "riches have their proper stint
> In the contented mind, not mint;"

and that

> "those who have the itch
> Of craving more, are never rich;"

and who has missed all apprehension of the grand secret that

> "Wealth cannot make a *life*, but love."

From the vanity of earthly thrones, whether of Egypt or of Judah, thrones whose glory is transitory, and whose power to help and succour is so ill-assured, the prophet lifts his eyes to the one throne whose glory is everlasting, and whose power and permanence are an eternal refuge.

> "Thou Throne of Glory, High Seat from of old,
> Place of our Sanctuary, Hope of Israel, Iahvah!
> All who leave Thee blush for shame;
> Mine apostates are written in earth;
> For they have forsaken the Well of Living Water, even
> Iahvah!"

It is his concluding reflexion upon the unblest, unhonoured end of the apostate Jehoiakim. If Isaiah could speak of Shebna as a "throne of glory,"[73] *i.e.*, the honoured support and mainstay of his family, there seems no reason why Iahvah might not be so addressed, as the supporting power and sovereign of the world.

The terms "Throne of Glory" ... "Place of our Sanctuary" seem to be used much as we use the expressions, "the Crown," "the Court," "the Throne," when we mean the actual ruler with whom these things are associated. And when the prophet declares "Mine[74] apostates are written in earth," he asserts that oblivion is the portion of those of his people, high or low, who forsake Iahvah for another god. Their names are not written in the Book of Life (Ex. xxxii. 32; Ps. lxix. 28), but in the sand whence they are soon effaced. The prophets do not attempt to expose

"The sweet strange mystery
Of what beyond these things may lie."

They do not in express terms promise eternal life to the individual believer.

But how often do their words imply that comfortable doctrine! They who forsake Iahvah must perish, for there is neither permanence nor stay apart from Iahvah, whose very Name denotes *He who Is*, the sole Principle of Being and Fountain of Life. If they—nations and persons—who revolt from Him must die, the implication, the truth necessary to complete this affirmation, is that they who trust in Him, and make Him their arm, will live; for union with Him is eternal life.

In this Fountain of Living Water Jeremiah now seeks healing for himself. The malady that afflicts him is the apparent failure of his oracles. He suffers as a prophet whose word seems idle to the multitude. He is hurt with their scorn, and wounded to the heart with their scoffing. On all sides men press the mocking question, "Where is the word of Iahvah? Prithee, let it come to pass!" His threats of national overthrow had not been speedily realized; and men made a mock of the delays of Divine mercy. Conscious of his own integrity, and keenly sensitive to the ridicule of his triumphant adversaries, and scarcely able to endure longer his intolerable position, he pours out a prayer for healing and help. *Heal me*, he cries, *and I shall be healed, Save me and I shall be saved*—really and truly saved, as the form of the Hebrew term implies; *for Thou art my praise*, my boast and my glory, as the Book of the Law affirms (Deut. x. 21). I have not trusted in man, but in God; and if this my sole glory be taken away, if events prove me a false prophet, as my friends allege, applying the very test of the sacred Law (Deut. xviii. 21 *sq.*), then shall I be of all men most forsaken and forlorn. The bitterness of his woe is intensified by the consciousness that he has not thrust himself without call into the prophetic office, like the false prophets whose aim was to traffic in sacred things (xiv. 14, 15); for then the consciousness of guilt might have made the punishment more tolerable, and the facts would have justified the jeers of his persecutors. But the case was far otherwise. He had been most unwilling to assume the function of prophet; and it was only in obedience to the stress of repeated calls that he had yielded. "But as for me," he protests, "I hasted not from being a shepherd to follow Thee." It would seem, if this be the correct, as it certainly is the simplest rendering of his words, that, at the time when he first became aware of his true vocation, the young prophet was engaged in tending the flocks that grazed in the priestly pasture-grounds of Anathoth. In that case, we are reminded of David, who was summoned from the sheepfold to camp and court, and of Amos the prophet-herdsman of Tekoa. But the Hebrew term translated "from being a shepherd" is probably a disguise of some other original expression; and it would involve no very violent change to read "I made no haste to follow after Thee fully" or "entirely"[75] (Deut. i. 36); a reading which is partially supported by the oldest version. Or it may be even better, as involving a mere change in the punctuation,[76] to amend the text thus: "But as for me, I made no haste, in following thee," more literally, "in accompanying thee" (Judg. xiv. 20). This, however, is a point of textual criticism, which leaves the general sense the same in any case.

When the prophet adds: "and the ill day I desired not," some think that he means the day when he surrendered to the Divine calling, and accepted his mission. But it seems to suit the context better, if we understand by the "ill day" the day of wrath whose coming was the burden of his preaching; the day referred to in the taunts of his enemies, when they asked "Where is the word of Iahvah?" adding with biting sarcasm: "Prithee, let it come to pass." They sneered at Jeremiah as one who seized every occasion to predict evil, as one who longed to witness the ruin of his country. The utter injustice of the charge, in view of the frequent cries of anguish which interrupt his melancholy forecasts, is no proof that it was not made. In all ages, God's representatives have been called upon to endure false accusations. Hence the prophet appeals from man's unrighteous judgment to God the Searcher of hearts. "*Thou* knowest; the utterance of my lips (Deut. xxiii. 24) before Thy face it fell": as if to say, No word of mine, spoken in Thy name, was a figment of my own fancy, uttered for my own purposes, without regard of Thee. I have always spoken as in Thy presence, or rather, in Thy presence. Thou, who hearest all, didst hear each utterance of mine; and therefore knowest that all I said was truthful and honest and in perfect accord with my commission.

If only we who, like Jeremiah, are called upon to speak for God, could always remember that every word we say is uttered in that Presence, what a sense of responsibility would lie upon us; with what labour and prayers should we not make our preparation! Too often alas! it is to be feared that our perception of the presence of man banishes all sense of any higher presence; and the anticipation of a fallible and frivolous criticism makes us forget for the time the judgment of God. And yet "by our words we shall be justified, and by our words we shall be condemned."

In continuing his prayer, Jeremiah adds the remarkable petition, "Become not Thou to me a cause of dismay!" He prays to be delivered from that overwhelming perplexity, which threatens to swallow him up, unless God should verify by events that which His own Spirit has prompted him to utter. He prays that Iahvah, his only "refuge in the day of evil," will not bemock him with vain expectations; will not falsify His own guidance; will not suffer His messenger to be "ashamed," disappointed and put to the blush by the failure of his predictions. And then once again, in the spirit of his time, he implores vengeance upon his unbelieving and cruel persecutors: "Let them be ashamed," disappointed in their expectation of immunity, "let *them* be dismayed," crushed in spirit and utterly overcome by the fulfilment of his dark presages of evil. "Let Thou come upon them a day of evil, And doubly with breaking break Thou them!" This indeed asks no more than that what has been spoken before in the way of prophecy—"I will repay the double of their guilt and their trespass" (xvi. 18)—may be forthwith accomplished. And the provocation was, beyond all question, immense. The hatred that burned in the taunt "Where is the word of Iahvah? Prithee, let it come to pass!" was doubtless of like kind with that which at a later stage of Jewish history expressed itself in the words "He trusted in God, let Him deliver Him!" "If He be the Son of God, let Him now come down from the cross, and we will believe on Him!"

And how much fierce hostility that one term "my pursuers" may cover, it is easy to infer from the narratives of the prophet's evil experience in chaps. xx., xxvi. and xxxviii. But allowing for all this, we can at best only affirm that the prophet's imprecations on his foes are natural and human; we cannot pretend that they are evangelical and Christ-like.[77] Besides, the latter would be a gratuitous anachronism, which no intelligent interpreter of Scripture is called upon to perpetrate. It is neither necessary to the proper vindication of the prophet's writings as truly inspired of God, nor helpful to a right conception of the method of revelation.

X
THE SABBATH—A WARNING

Jeremiah xvii. 19-27.

"Thus said Iahvah unto me: Go and stand in the gate of Benjamin, whereby the kings of Judah come in, and whereby they go out; and in all the gates of Jerusalem. And say unto them, Hear ye the word of Iahvah, O kings of Judah, and all Judah, and all inhabitants of Jerusalem, who come in by these gates!

"Thus said Iahvah: Beware, on your lives, and bear ye not a burden on the Day of Rest, nor bring it in by the gates of Jerusalem! Nor shall ye bring a burden forth out of your houses on the Day of Rest, nor shall ye do any work; but ye shall hallow the Day of Rest, as I commanded your fathers. (Albeit, they hearkened not, nor inclined their ear, but stiffened their neck against hearkening, and against receiving instruction.)

"And it shall come to pass, if ye will indeed hearken unto Me, saith Iahvah, not to bring a burden in by the gates of this city on the Day of Rest, but to hallow the Day of Rest, not to do therein any work; then there shall come in by the gates of this city kings [and princes] sitting upon the throne of David, riding on the chariots and on the horses, they and their princes, O men of Judah and inhabitants of Jerusalem! and this city shall be inhabited for ever. And people shall come in from the cities of Judah and from the places round Jerusalem, and from the land of Benjamin, and from the lowlands, and from the hill-country, and from the south, bringing in burnt-offering and thank-offering, and oblation and incense; and bringing a thanksgiving into the house of Iahvah.

"And if ye hearken not unto Me to hallow the Day of Rest, and not to bear a burden and come in by the gates of Jerusalem on the Day of Rest: I will kindle a fire in her gates, and it shall devour the palaces of Jerusalem, and shall not be quenched."

The matter and manner of this brief oracle mark it off from those which precede it as an independent utterance, and a whole complete in itself. Its position may be accounted for by its probable date, which may be fixed a little after the previous chapters, in the three months' reign of the ill-starred Jehoiachin; and by the writer's or his editor's desire to break the monotony of commination by an occasional gleam of hope and promise. At the same time, the introductory formula with which it opens is so similar to that of the two following oracles (chaps. xviii., xix.), as to suggest the idea of a connexion in time between the members of the group. Further, there is an obvious connexion of thought between chaps. xviii., xix. In the former, the house of Israel is represented as clay in the hand of the Divine Potter; in the latter, Judah is a potter's vessel destined to be broken in pieces. And if we assume the priority of the piece before us, a logical progress is observable, from the alternative here presented for the people's choice, to their decision for the worse part (xviii. 12 *sqq.*), and then to the corresponding decision on the part of Iahvah (xix.). Or, as Hitzig puts it otherwise, in the piece before us the scales are still in equipoise; in chap. xviii. one goes down; Iahvah intends mischief (ver. 11), and the people are invited to appease His anger. But the warning is fruitless; and therefore the prophet announces their destruction, depicting it in the darkest colours (chap. xix.). The immediate consequence to Jeremiah himself is related in chap. xx. 1-6; and it is highly probable that the section, chap. xxi. 11-xxii. 9, is the continuation of the oracle addressed to Pashchur: so that we have before us a whole group of prophecies belonging to the same eventful period of the prophet's activity (xvii. 20 agrees closely with xxii. 2, and xvii. 25 with xxii. 4).

The circumstances of the present oracle are these. Jeremiah is inwardly bidden to station himself first in "the gate of the sons of the people"—a gate of Jerusalem which we cannot further determine, as it is not mentioned elsewhere under this designation, but which appears to have been a special resort of the masses of the population, because it was the one by which the kings were wont to enter and leave the city, and where they doubtless were accustomed to hear petitions and to administer justice; and afterwards, he is to take his stand in all the gates in turn, so as not to miss the chance of delivering his message to any of his countrymen. He is there to address the "kings of Judah" (ver. 20); an expression which may denote the young king Jehoiachin and his mother (xiii. 18), or the king and the princes of the blood, the "House of David" of chap. xxi. 12. The promise "kings shall come in by the gates of this city ... and this city shall be inhabited for ever," and the threat "I will kindle a fire in her gates, and it shall devour the palaces of Jerusalem," may be taken to imply a time when the public danger was generally recognised. The first part of the promise may be intended to meet an apprehension, such as might naturally be felt after the death of Jehoiakim, that the incensed Chaldeans would come and take away the Jewish place and nation. In raising the boy Jehoiachin to the throne of his fathers, men may have sorrowfully foreboded that, as the event proved, he would never keep his crown till manhood, nor beget a race of future kings.

The matter of the charge to rulers and people is the due observance of the fourth commandment: "ye shall hallow the Day of Rest, as I commanded your fathers" (see Ex. xx. 8, "Remember the Day of Rest, to hallow it"— which is probably the original form of the precept. Jeremiah, however, probably had in mind the form of the precept as it appears in Deuteronomy: "Observe the Day of Rest to hallow it, as Iahvah thy God commanded thee:" Deut. v. 12). The Hebrew term for "hallow" means *to separate* a thing from common things, and devote it to God.

To hallow the Day of Rest, therefore, is to make a marked distinction between it and ordinary days, and to connect it in some way with religion. What is here commanded is to abstain from "bearing burdens," and doing any kind of work (*melakah*, Gen. ii. 2, 3; Ex. xx. 9, 10, xxxi. 14, 15; Gen. xxxix. 11, "appointed task," "duty," "business"). The bearing of burdens into the gates and out of the houses clearly describes the ordinary commerce between town and country. The country folk are forbidden to bring their farm produce to the market in the city gates, and the townspeople to convey thither from their houses and shops the manufactured goods which they were accustomed to barter for these. Nehemiah's memoirs furnish a good illustration of the general sense of the passage (Neh. xiii. 15), relating how he suppressed this Sabbath traffic between town and country. Dr. Kuenen has observed that "Jeremiah is the first of the prophets who stands up for a stricter sanctification of the seventh day, treating it, however, merely as a day of rest.... What was traditional appears to have been only abstinence from field-work, and perhaps also from professional pursuits." In like manner, he had before stated that "tendencies to such an exaggeration of the Sabbath rest as would make it absolute, are found from the Chaldean period. Isaiah (i. 13) regards the Sabbath purely as a sacrificial day." The last statement here is hardly a fair inference. In the passage referred to Isaiah is inveighing against the futile worship of his contemporaries; and he only mentions the Sabbath in this connexion. And that "tradition" required more than "abstinence from field-work" is evident from words of the prophet Amos, written at least a century and a half before the present oracle, and implying that very abstinence from trading which Jeremiah prescribes. Amos makes the grasping dealers of his time cry impatiently, "When will the new moon be gone, that we may sell corn? and the sabbath, that we may set out wheat for sale?" (Amos viii. 5); a clear proof that buying and selling were suspended on the sabbath festival in the eighth century b.c.

It is hardly likely that, when law or custom compelled covetous dealers to cease operations on the Sabbath, and buying and selling, the principal business of the time, was suspended, the artisans of town or country would be allowed by public opinion to ply their everyday tasks. Accordingly, when Jeremiah adds to his prohibition of Sabbath trading, a veto upon any kind of "work"—a term which includes this trafficking, but also covers the labour of handicraftsmen (cf. 1 Kings v. 30; 2 Kings xii. 12; Ex. xxxv. 35)—he is not really increasing the stringency of the traditional rule about Sabbath observance.

Further, it is difficult to understand how Dr. Kuenen could gather from this passage that Jeremiah treats the Sabbath "merely as a day of rest." This negative character of mere cessation from work, of enforced idleness, is far from being the sole feature of the Sabbath, either in Jeremiah's view of it, or as other more ancient authorities represent it. The testimony of the passage before us proves, if proof were needed, that the Sabbath was a day of worship. This is implied both by the phrase "ye shall hallow the Day of Rest," that is, consecrate it to Iahvah; and by the promise that if the precept be observed faithfully, abundant offerings shall flow into the temple from all parts of the country, that is, as the context seems to require, for the due celebration of the Sabbath festival. There is an intentional contrast between the bringing of innumerable victims, and "bearing burdens" of flour and oil and incense on the Sabbath, for the joyful service of the temple, including the festal meal of the worshippers, and that other carriage of goods for merely secular objects. And as the wealth of the Jerusalem priesthood chiefly depended upon the abundance of the sacrifices, it may be supposed that Jeremiah thus gives them a hint that it is really their interest to encourage the observance of the law of the Sabbath. For if men were busy with their buying and selling, their making and mending, upon the seventh as on other days, they would have no more time or inclination for religious duties, than the Sunday traders of our large towns have under the vastly changed conditions of the present day. Moreover, the teaching of our prophet in this matter takes for granted that of his predecessors, with whose writings he was thoroughly acquainted. If in this passage he does not expressly designate the Sabbath as a religious festival, it is because it seemed needless to state a thing so obvious, so generally recognised in theory, however loosely observed in practice. The elder prophets Hosea, Amos, Isaiah, associate Sabbath and new moon together as days of festal rejoicing, when men appeared before Iahvah, that is, repaired to the sanctuary for worship and sacrifice (Hos. ii. 11; Isa. i. 11-14), and when all ordinary business was consequently suspended (Amos viii. 5).

It is clear, then, from this important passage of Jeremiah that in his time and by himself the Sabbath was still regarded under the double aspect of a religious feast and a day of cessation from labour, the latter being, as in the ancient world generally, a natural consequence of the former characteristic. Whether the abolition of the local sanctuaries in the eighteenth year of

Josiah resulted in any practical modification of the conception of the Sabbath, so that, in the words of Professor Robertson Smith, "it became for most Israelites an institution of humanity divorced from ritual," is rendered doubtful by the following considerations. The period between the reform of Josiah and the fall of Jerusalem was very brief, including not more than about thirty-five years (621-586, according to Wellhausen). But that a reaction followed the disastrous end of the royal Reformer, is both likely under the circumstances, and implied by the express assertions of the author of Kings, who declares of the succeeding monarchs that they "did evil in the sight of the Lord according to all that their fathers had done." As Wellhausen writes: "the battle of Megiddo had shown that in spite of the covenant with Jehovah the possibilities of non-success in war remained the same as before": so at least it would appear to the unspiritual mind of a populace, still hankering after the old forms of local worship, with their careless connivance at riot and disorder. It is not probable that a rapacious and bloody tyrant, like Jehoiakim, would evince more tenderness for the ritual laws than for the moral precepts of Deuteronomy. It is likely, then, that the worship at the local high places revived during this and the following reigns, just as it had revived after its temporary abolition by Hezekiah (2 Kings xviii. 22). Moreover, it is with Judah, not ruined and depopulated Israel, that we have to deal; and even in Judah the people must by this time have been greatly reduced by war and its attendant evils, so that Jerusalem itself and its immediate neighbourhood probably comprised the main part of the population to which Jeremiah addressed his discourses during this period. The bulk of the little nation would, in fact, naturally concentrate upon Jerusalem, in the troublous times that followed the death of Josiah. If so, it is superfluous to assume that "most men could only visit the central altar at rare intervals" during these last decades of the national existence. [79] The change of view belongs rather to the sixth than the seventh century, to Babylonia rather than to Judea.

The Sabbath observance prescribed by the old Law, and recommended by Jeremiah, was indeed a very different thing from the pedantic and burdensome obligation which it afterwards became in the hands of scribes and Pharisees. These, with their long catalogue of prohibited works, and their grotesque methods of evading the rigour of their own rules, had succeeded in making what was originally a joyous festival and day of rest for the weary, into an intolerable interlude of joyless restraint; when our Lord reminded them that the Sabbath was made for man, and not man for the Sabbath (St. Mark ii. 27). Treating the strict observance of the day as an end in itself, they forgot or ignored the fact that the oldest forms of the sacred Law agreed in justifying the institution by religious and humanitarian considerations (Ex. xx. 8, 10; Deut. v. 12). The difference in the grounds assigned by the different legislations—Deuteronomy alleging neither the Divine Rest of Exodus xx., nor the sign of Exodus xxxi. 13, but the enlightened and enduring motive "that thy bondman and thine handmaid may rest as well as thou," coupled with the feeling injunction, "Remember that thou wast a bondman in the land of Egypt" (Deut. v. 14, 15)—need not here be discussed; for in any case, the different motives thus suggested were enough to make it clear to those who had eyes to see, that the Sabbath was not anciently conceived as an arbitrary institution established purely for its own sake, and without reference to ulterior considerations of public benefit. The Book of the Covenant affirmed the principle of Sabbath rest in these unmistakable terms: "Six days thou mayst do thy works, and on the seventh day thou shalt leave off, that thine ox and thine ass may rest, and the son of thine handmaid"—the home-born slave—"and the alien may be refreshed" (Ex. xxiii. 12), lit. recover breath, have respite. The humane care of the lawgiver for the dumb toilers and slaves requires no comment; and we have already noticed the same spirit of humanity in the later precept of the Book of the Law (Deut. v. 14, 15). These older rules, it will be observed, are perfectly general in their scope, and forbid not particular actions (Ex. xvi. 23, xxxv. 3; Num. xv. 32), but the continuance of ordinary labour; prescribing a merciful intermission alike for the cattle employed in husbandry and as beasts of burden, and for all classes of dependents.

The origin of the Sabbath festival is lost in obscurity. When the unknown writer of Gen. i. so beautifully connects it with the creation of the world, he betrays not only the belief of his contemporaries in its immemorial antiquity, but also a true perception of the utility of the institution, its perfect adaptation to the wants of humanity. He expresses his sense of the fact in the most emphatic way possible, by affirming the Divine origin of an institution whose value to man is divinely great; and by carrying back that origin to the very beginning, he implies that the Sabbath was made for mankind and not merely for Israel. To whom indeed could an ancient Jewish writer refer as the original source of this unique blessing of a Day of Rest and drawing near to God, if not to Iahvah, the fountain of all things good?

That Moses, the founder of the nation, gave Israel the Sabbath, is as likely as anything can be. Whether, in doing so, he simply sanctioned an ancient and salutary custom (investing it perhaps with new and better associations), dating from the tribal existence of the fathers in Chaldea, or ordered the matter so in purposeful contrast to the Egyptian week of ten days, cannot at present be determined. The Sabbath of Israel, both that of the prophets and that of the scribes, was an institution which distinguished the nation from all others in the period open to historical scrutiny; and with this knowledge we may rest content. That which made Israel what it was, and what it became to the world; the total of the good which this people realized, and left as a priceless heritage to mankind for ever, was the outcome, not of what it had in common with heathen antiquity, but of what was peculiar to itself in ideas and institutions. We cannot be too strongly on our guard against assuming external, superficial, and often accidental resemblances, to be an index of inward and essential likeness and unity. Whatever approximations may be established by modern archæology between Israel and kindred peoples, it will still be true that those points of contact do not explain, though to the apprehension of individuals they may obscure what is truly characteristic of Israel, and what alone gives that nation its imperishable significance in the history of the world. After all deductions made upon such grounds, nothing can abolish the force of the fact that Moses and the prophets do not belong to Moab, Ammon, or Edom; that the Old Testament, though written in the language of Canaan, is not a monument of Canaanite but of Israelite faith; that the Christ did not spring out of Babylon or Egypt, and that Christianity is not explicable as the last development of Accadian magic or Egyptian animal worship.

To those who believe that the prophets enjoyed a higher and less fallible guidance than human fancy, reflexion, experience; who recognise in the general aim and effect of their teaching, as contrasted with that of other teachers, the best proof that their minds were subject to an influence and a spirit transcending the common limits of humanity; the prominence given by Jeremiah to the law of the Sabbath will be sufficient evidence of the importance of that law to the welfare of his contemporaries, if not of all subsequent generations. If we have rightly assigned the piece to the reign of Jehoiachin, we may suppose that among the contrary currents which agitated the national life at that crisis, there were indications of repentance and remorse at the misdoings of the late reign. The present utterance of the prophet might then be regarded as a test of the degree and worth of the revulsion of popular feeling towards the God of the Fathers. The nation was trembling for its existence; and Jeremiah met its fears, by pointing out the path of safety. Here was one special precept hitherto but little observed. Would they keep it now and henceforth, in token of a genuine obedience? Repentance in general terms is never difficult. The rub is *conduct*. Recognition of the Divine Law is easy, so long as life is not submitted to its control. The prophet thus proposes, in a single familiar instance, a plain test of sincerity, which is perhaps not less applicable in our own day than it was then.

The wording of the final threat suggests a thought of solemn consequence for ourselves. "I will kindle a fire in her gates, and it shall devour the castles of Jerusalem—and shall not be quenched!" The gates were the scene of Judah's sinful breach of the Sabbath law, and in them her punishment is to begin. So in the after life of the lost those parts of the physical and mental organism which have been the principal seats of sin, the means and instruments of man's misdoing, will also be the seat of keenest suffering, the source and abode of the most poignant misery. "The fire that never shall be quenched"—Jesus has spoken of that awful mystery, as well as Jeremiah. It is the ever-kindling, never-dying fire of hopeless and insatiable desire; it is the withering flame of hatred of self, when the castaway sees with open eyes what that self has become; it is the burning pain of a sleepless memory of the unalterable past; it is the piercing sense of a life flung recklessly to ruin; it is the scorching shame, the scathing self-contempt, the quenchless, raging thirst for deliverance from ourselves; it is the fearful consciousness of self-destruction, branded upon the soul for ever and ever!

XI
THE DIVINE POTTER

Jeremiah xviii.

Jeremiah goes down into the Lower Town, or the valley between the upper and lower city; and there his attention is arrested by a potter sitting at work before his wheel. As the prophet watches, a vessel is spoiled in the making under the craftsman's hand; so the process begins afresh, and out of the same lump of clay another vessel is moulded, according to the potter's fancy.

Reflecting upon what he had seen, Jeremiah recognised a Divine Word alike in the impulse which led him thither, and in the familiar actions of the potter. Perhaps as he sat meditating at home, or praying in the court of the temple, the thought had crossed his mind that Iahvah was the Potter, and mankind the clay in His hands; a thought which recurs so often in the eloquent pages of the second Isaiah, who was doubtless indebted to the present oracle for the suggestion of it. Musing upon this thought, Jeremiah wandered half-unconsciously down to the workshop of the potter; and there, under the influence of the Divine Spirit, his thought developed itself into a lesson for his people and for us.

Cannot I do unto you like this potter, O house of Israel? saith Iahvah; Behold, as the clay in the potter's hand, so are ye in My hand, O house of Israel. Iahvah has an absolute control over His people and over all peoples, to shape their condition and to alter their destiny; a control as absolute as that of the potter over the clay between his hands, which he moulds and remoulds at will. Men are wholly malleable in the hands of their Maker; incapable, by the nature of things, of any real resistance to His purpose. If the first intention of the potter fail in the execution, he does not fail to realize his plan on a second trial. And if man's nature and circumstances appear for a time to thwart the Maker's design; if the unyielding pride and intractable temper of a nation mar its beauty and worth in the eyes of its Creator, and render it unfit for its destined uses and functions; He can take away the form He has given, and reduce His work to shapelessness, and remodel the ruined mass into accordance with His sovereign design. Iahvah, the supreme Author of all existence, can do this. It is evident that the Creator can do as He will with His creature. But all His dealings with man are conditioned by moral considerations. He meddles with no nation capriciously, and irrespective of its attitude towards His laws. *At one moment I threaten a nation and a kingdom that I will uproot and pull down and destroy. And that nation which I threatened returneth from its evil, and I repent of the evil that I purposed to do it. And at another moment, I promise a nation and a kingdom that I will build and plant. And it doeth the Evil in Mine eyes, in not hearkening unto My voice; and I repent of the good that I said I would do it* (vv. 7-10).

This is a bold affirmation, impressive in its naked simplicity and directness of statement, of a truth which in all ages has taken possession of minds at all capable of a comprehensive survey of national experience; the truth that there is a power revealing itself in the changes and chances of human history, shaping its course, and giving it a certain definite direction, not without regard to the eternal principles of morality. When in some unexpected calamity which strikes down an individual sinner, men recognise a "judgment" or an instance of "the visitation of God," they infringe the rule of Christian charity, which forbids us to judge our brethren. Yet such judgment, liable as it is to be too readily suggested by private ill-will, envy and other evil passions, which warp the even justice that should guide our decisions, and blind the mind to its own lack of impartiality, is in general the perversion of a true instinct which persists in spite of all scientific sophistries and philosophic fallacies. For it is an irrepressible instinct rather than a reasoned opinion which makes us all believe, however inconsistently and vaguely, that God rules; that Providence asserts itself in the stream of circumstance, in the current of human affairs. The native strength of this instinctive belief is shewn by its survival in minds that have long since cast off allegiance to religious creeds. It only needs a sudden sense of personal danger, the sharp shock of a serious accident, the foreboding of bitter loss, the unexpected but utter overthrow of some well-laid scheme that seemed assured of success, to stir the faith that is latent in the depths of the most callous and worldly heart, and to force the acknowledgment of a righteous Judge enthroned above.

Compared with the mysterious Power which evinces itself continuously in the apparent chaos of conflicting events, man's free will is like the eddy whirling round upon the bosom of a majestic river as it floats irresistibly onward to its goal, bearing the tiny vortex along with it. Man's power of self-determination no more interferes with the counsels of Providence than the diurnal revolution of the earth on its axis interferes with its annual revolution round the sun. The greater comprises the less; and God includes the world.

The Creator has implanted in the creature a power of choice between good and evil, which is a pale reflexion of His own tremendous Being. But how can we even imagine the dependent, the limited, the finite, acting independently of the will of the Absolute and Infinite? The fish may swim against the ocean current; but can it swim at all out of the ocean? Its entire activity depends upon the medium in which it lives and moves and has its being.

But Jeremiah exposes the secret of Providence to the eyes of his fellow-countrymen for a particular purpose. His aim is to eradicate certain prevalent misconceptions, so as to enable them to rightly apprehend the meaning of God's present dealings with themselves. The popular belief was that Zion was an inviolable sanctuary; that whatever disasters might have befallen the nation in the past, or might be imminent in the future, Iahvah could not, for His own sake, permit the extinction of Judah as a nation. For then His worship, the worship of the temple, the sacrifices of the one altar, would be abolished; and His honour and His Name would be forgotten among men. These were the thoughts which comforted them in the trying time when a thousand rumours of the coming of the Chaldeans to punish their revolt were flying about the land; and from day to day men lived in trembling expectation of impending siege and slaughter. These were the beliefs which the popular prophets, themselves probably in most cases fanatical believers in their own doctrine, vehemently maintained in opposition to Jeremiah. Above all, there was the covenant between Iahvah and His people, admitted as a fact both by Jeremiah and his opponents. Was it conceivable that the God of the Fathers, who had chosen them and their posterity to be His people for ever, would turn from His purpose, and reject His chosen utterly?

Jeremiah meets these popular illusions by applying his analogy of the potter. The potter fashions a mass of clay into a vessel; and Iahvah had fashioned Israel into a nation. But as though the mass of inert matter had proven unwieldy or stubborn to the touches of his plastic hands; as the wheel revolved, a misshapen product resulted, which the artist broke up again, and moulded afresh on his wheel, till it emerged a fair copy of his ideal. And so, in the revolutions of time, Israel had failed of realizing the design of his Maker, and had become a vessel of wrath fitted to destruction. But as the rebellious lump was fashioned again by the deft hand of the master, so might this refractory people be broken and built up anew by the Divine master hand.

In the light of this analogy, the prophet interprets the existing complications of the political world. The serious dangers impending over the nation are a sure symptom that the Divine Potter is at work, "moulding" an evil fate for Judah and Jerusalem. "And now prithee say unto the men of Judah and the inhabitants of Jerusalem:

> "Thus hath Iahvah said,
> Behold I am moulding evil against you,
> And devising a device against you!"

But Iahvah's menaces are not the mere vent of a tyrant's caprice or causeless anger: they are a deliberate effort to break the hard heart, to reduce it to contrition, to prepare it for a new creation in a more glorious likeness. Therefore the threat closes with an entreaty:

> "Return ye, I pray you, each from his evil way,
> And make good your ways and your doings!"

If the prophetic warning fulfil its purpose, and the nation repent, then as in the case of Nineveh, which repented at the preaching of Jonah, the sentence of destruction is revoked, and the doomed nation is granted a new lease of life. The same truth holds good reversely. God's promises are as conditional as His threats. If a nation lapse from original righteousness, the sure consequence is the withdrawal of Divine favour, and all of blessing and permanence that it confers. It is evident that the prophet directly contradicts the popular persuasion, which was also the current teaching of his professional opponents, that Iahvah's promises to Israel are absolute, that is, irrespective of moral considerations. Jeremiah is revealing, in terms suited to the intelligence of his time, the true law of the Divine dealings with Israel and with man. And what he has here written, it is important to bear in mind, when we are studying other passages of his writings and those of his predecessors, which foreshow judgments and mercies to individual peoples. However absolute the language of prediction, the qualification here supplied must usually be understood; so that it is not too much to say that this remarkable utterance is one of the keys to the comprehension of Hebrew prophecy.

But now, allowing for antique phraseology, and for the immense difference between ancient and modern modes of thought and expression; allowing also for the new light shed upon the problems of life and history by the teaching of Him who has supplemented all that was incomplete in the doctrine of the prophets and the revelation granted to the men of the elder dispensation; must we pronounce this oracle of Jeremiah's substantially true or the contrary? Is the view thus formulated an obsolete opinion, excusable in days when scientific thinking was unknown; useful indeed for the furtherance of the immediate aims of its authors, but now to be rejected wholly as a profound mistake, which modern enlightenment has at once exposed and rendered superfluous to an intelligent faith in the God of the prophets?

Here and everywhere else, Jeremiah's language is in form highly anthropomorphic. If it was to arrest the attention of the multitude, it could not well have been otherwise. He seems to say that God changes His intentions, according as a nation changes its behaviour. Something must be allowed for style, in a writer whose very prose is more than half poetry, and whose utterances are so often lyrical in form as well as matter. The Israelite thinkers, however, were also well aware that the Eternal is superior to change; as is clear from that striking word of Samuel: "The Glory of Israel lieth not nor repenteth; for He is not man, that He should repent" (1 Sam. xv. 29). And prophetic passages like that in Kings, which so nobly declares that the heaven and the heaven of heavens cannot contain God (cf. Jer. xxiii. 24), or that of the second Isaiah which affirms that the Divine ways and purposes are as much higher than those of His people, as the heavens are higher than the earth (Isa. lv. 9), prove that the vivid anthropomorphic expressions of the popular teaching of the prophets ought in mere justice to be limited by these wider conceptions of the Divine Nature and attributes. These passages are quite enough to clear the prophets of the accusation of entertaining such gross and crude ideas of Deity as those which Xenophanes ridiculed, and which find their embodiment in most mythologies.

There is indeed a sense in which all thinking, not only thought about God, but about the natural world, must be anthropomorphic. Man is unquestionably "the measure of all things," and he measures by a human standard. He interprets the world without in terms of his own consciousness; he imposes the forms and moulds of his own mind upon the universal mass of things. Time, space, matter, motion, number, weight, organ, function,— what are all these but inward conceptions by which the mind reduces a chaos of conflicting impressions to order and harmony? What the external world may be, apart from our ideas of it, no philosopher pretends to be able to say; and an equal difficulty embarrasses those who would define what the Deity is, apart from His relations to man. But then it is only those relations that really concern us; everything else is idle speculation, little becoming to creatures so frail and ephemeral as we.

From this point of view, we may fairly ask, what difference it makes whether the prophet affirm that Iahvah repents of retributive designs, when a nation repents of its sins, or that a nation's repentance will be followed by the restoration of temporal prosperity. It is a mere matter of statement; and the former way of putting the truth was the more intelligible way to his contemporaries, and has, besides, the advantage of implying the further truth that the fortunes of nations do not depend upon a blind and inexorable fate, but upon the Will and Law of a holy God. It affirms a Lawmaker as well as a Law, a Providence as well as an uniform sequence of events.

The prophet asserts, then, that nations reap what they have sown; that their history is, in general, a record of God's judgments upon their ways and doings. This is, of course, a matter of faith, as are all beliefs about the Unseen; but it is a faith which has its root in an apparently ineradicable instinct of humanity. Δράσαντι παθεῖν, "The doer must suffer," is not a conviction of Hebrew religion only; it belongs to the universal religious consciousness. Some critics are fond of pronouncing the "policy" of the prophets a mistaken one. They commend the high tone of their moral teachings, but consider their forecasts of the future and interpretations of passing events, as erroneous deductions from their general views of the Divine nature. We are not well acquainted with the times and circumstances under which the prophets wrote and spoke. This is true even in the case of Jeremiah; the history of the time exists only in the barest outline. But the writings of an Isaiah or an Amos make it difficult to suppose that their authors would not have occupied a leading position in any age and nation; their thought is the highest product of the Hebrew mind; and the policy of Isaiah at least, during the Assyrian crisis, was gloriously justified by the event.

We need not, however, stop here in attempting to vindicate the attitude and aims of the prophets. Without claiming infallibility for every individual utterance of theirs—without displaying the bad taste and entire lack of literary tact which would be implied by insisting upon the minute accuracy and close correspondence to fact, of all that the prophets foreboded, all that they suggested as possible or probable, and by turning all their poetical figures and similes into bald assertions of literal fact; we may, I think, steadfastly affirm that the great principles of revealed religion, which it was their mission to enunciate and impress by all the resources of a fervid oratory and a high-wrought poetical imagination, are absolutely and eternally true. Man does reap as he sows; all history records it. The present welfare and future permanence of a nation do depend, and have always depended, upon the strength of its adhesion to religious and moral convictions. What was it that enabled Israel to gain a footing in Canaan, and to reduce, one after another, nations and communities far more advanced in the arts of civilization than they? What but the physical and moral force generated by the hardy and simple life of the desert, and disciplined by wise obedience to the laws of their Invisible King? What but a burning faith in the Lord of Hosts, Iahvah Sabaoth, the true Leader of the armies of Israel? Had they only remained uncontaminated by the luxuries and vices of the conquered races; had they not yielded to the soft seduction of sensuous forms of worship;

had they continued faithful to the God who had brought them out of Egypt, and lived, on the whole, by the teaching of the true prophets; who can say that they might not have successfully withstood the brunt of Assyrian or Chaldean invasion?

The disruption of the kingdom, the internecine conflicts, the dynastic revolutions, the entanglements with foreign powers which mark the progressive decline of the empire of David and Solomon, would hardly have found place in a nation that steadily lived by the rule of the prophets, clinging to Iahvah and Iahvah only, and "doing justice and loving mercy" in all the relations of life. The gradual differentiation of the idea of Iahvah into a multitude of Baals at the local sanctuaries must have powerfully tended to disintegrate the national unity. Solomon's temple and the recognition of the one God of all the tribes of Israel as supreme, which that religious centre implied, was, on the other hand, a real bond of union for the nation. We cannot forget that, at the outset of the whole history, Moses created or resuscitated the sense of national unity in the hearts of the Egyptian serfs, by proclaiming to them Iahvah, the God of their fathers. It is a one-sided representation which treats the policy of the prophets as purely negative; as confined to the prohibition of leagues with the foreigner, and the condemnation of walls and battlements, chariots and horses, and all the elements of social strength and display. The prophets condemn these things, regarded as substitutes for trust in the One God, and faithful obedience to His laws. They condemn the man who puts his confidence in man, and makes flesh his arm, and forgets the only true source of strength and protection. To those who allege that the policy of the prophets was a failure, we may reply that it never had a full and fair trial.

> And they will say, Hopeless! for we will follow after our own devices, and will each practise the stubbornness of his own evil heart. Therefore thus hath Iahvah said:
>
> 1. "Ask ye now among the heathen,
> Who hath heard the like?
> The virgin (daughter) of Israel
> Hath done a very horrible thing.
>
> 2. "Doth the snow of Lebanon cease
> From overflowing the field?
> Do the running waters dry up,
> The icy streams?[80]
>
> 3. "For My people have forgotten me,
> To vain things they burn incense;
> And they have made them stumble in their ways, the

ancient paths,
To walk in bypaths, a way not cast up:

4. "To make their land a desolation,
Perpetual hissings;
Every one that passeth her by shall be amazed,
And shall shake his head.

5. "Like an east wind will I scatter them
In the face of the foe;
The back and not the face will I shew them,
In the day of their overthrow."

God foresees that His gracious warning will be rejected as heretofore; the prophet's hearers will cry "It is hopeless!" thy appeal is in vain, thine enterprise desperate; "for after our own devices" or thoughts "will we walk," not after thine, though thou urge them as Iahvah's; "and we will each practise the stubbornness of his own evil heart"—this last in a tone of irony, as if to say, Very well; we accept thy description of us; our ways are stubborn, and our hearts evil: we will abide by our character, and stand true to your unflattering portrait. Otherwise, the words may be regarded as giving the substance of the popular reply, in terms which at the same time convey the Divine condemnation of it; but the former view seems preferable.

God foresees the obstinacy of the people, and yet the prophet does not cease his preaching. A cynical assent to his invective only provokes him to more strenuous endeavours to convince them that they are in the wrong; that their behaviour is against reason and nature. Once more (ii. 10 *sqq.*) he strives to shame them into remorse by contrasting their conduct with that of other nations. These were faithful to their own gods; among *them* such a crime as national apostasy was unheard of and unknown. It was reserved for Israel to give the first example of this abnormal offence; a fact as strange and fearful in the moral world, as some unnatural revolution in the physical sphere. That Israel should forget his duty to Iahvah was as great and inexplicable a portent, as if the perennial snows of the Lebanon should cease to supply the rivers of the land; or as if the ice-cold streams of its glens and gorges should suddenly cease to flow. And certainly, when we look at the matter with the eye of calm reason, the prophet cannot be said to have here exaggerated the mystery of sin. For, however strong the temptation that lures man from the path of duty, however occasion may suggest, and passion urge, and desire yearn, these influences cannot of themselves silence conscience, and obliterate experience, and overpower judgment, and defeat reason. As surely as it is possible to know anything, man knows that his vital interests coincide with duty; and that it is not only weak but absolutely irrational to sacrifice duty to the importunities of appetite.

When man forsakes the true God, it is to "burn incense to vain gods" or things of nought. He who worships what is less than God, worships nothing. No being below God can yield any true satisfaction to that human nature which was made for God. The man who fixes his hope upon things that perish in the using, the man who seeks happiness in things material, the man whose affections have sole regard to the joys of sense, and whose devotion is given wholly to worldly objects, is the man who will at the last cry out, in hopeless disappointment and bitterness of spirit, Vanity of vanities! all is vanity! "For what shall it profit a man, if he shall gain the whole world, and lose his own soul? Or what shall a man give in exchange for his soul?" The soul's salvation consists in devotion to its Lord and Maker; its eternal loss and ruin, in alienation from Him who is its true and only life. The false gods are nought as regards help and profit; they are powerless to bless, but they are potent to hurt and betray. They "make men stumble out of their ways, out of the ancient paths, to walk in bypaths, in a way not cast up." So it was of old; so it is now. When the heart is estranged from God, and devoted to some meaner pursuit than the advancement of His glory, it soon deserts the straight road of virtue, the highway of honour, and falls into the crooked and uneven paths of fraud and hypocrisy, of oppression and vice. The end appears to sanctify the means, or at least to make them tolerable; and, once the ancient path of the Law is forsaken, men will follow the most tortuous, and often thorny and painful courses, to the goal of their choice. The path which leads away from God, leads both individuals and nations to final ruin. Degraded ideas of the Deity, false ideas of happiness, a criminal indifference to the welfare of others, a base devotion to private and wholly selfish ends, must in the long run sap the vigour of a nation, and render it incapable of any effectual resistance to its enemies. Moral declension is a sure symptom of approaching political dissolution; so sure, that if a nation chooses and persists in evil, in the face of all dissuasion, it may be assumed to be bent on suicide. Like Israel, it may be said to do thus, "in order to make its land an astonishment, perpetual hissings." Men will be surprised at the greatness of its fall, and at the same time will acknowledge by voice and gesture that its doom is absolutely just.

So far as his immediate hearers were concerned, the effect of the prophet's words was exactly what had been anticipated (ver. 18; cf. ver. 12). Jeremiah's preaching was a ministry of hardening, in a far more complete sense than Isaiah's had been. On the present occasion, the popular obduracy and unbelief evinced itself in a conspiracy to destroy the prophet by false accusation. They would doubtless find it not difficult to construe his words as blasphemy against Iahvah, and treason against the state. And they said: *Come and let us devise devices*—lay a plot—*against Jeremiah*. Dispassionate wisdom, mere worldly prudence, would have said, Let us weigh well the probability or even possibility of the truth of his message. Moral earnestness, a sincere love of God and goodness, would have recognised in the prophet's fearful earnest a proof of good faith, a claim to consideration. Unbiassed common sense would have asked, What has Jeremiah to gain by persistence in unpopular teaching? What will be his reward, supposing his words come true? Is it to be supposed that a man whose woeful tidings are uttered in a voice broken with sobs, and interrupted by bursts of wild lamentation, will look with glad eyes upon destruction when it comes, if it come after all? But habitual sin blinds as well as pollutes the soul. And when admonition is unacceptable, it breeds hatred. The heart that is not touched by appeal becomes harder than it was before. The ice of indifference becomes the adamant of malignant opposition. The populace of Jerusalem, like that of more modern capitals, was enervated by ease and luxury, altogether given over to the pursuit of wealth and pleasure as the end of life. They hated the man who rebuked in the gate, and abhorred him that spoke uprightly (Amos v. 10). They could not abide one whose life and labours were a continual protest against their own. And now he had done his best to rob them of their pleasant confidence, to destroy the delusion of their fool's paradise. He had burst into the heathenish sanctuary where they offered a worship congenial to their hearts, and done his best to wreck their idols, and dash their altars to the ground. He had affirmed that the accredited oracles were all a lie, that the guides whom they blindly followed were leading them to ruin. So the passive dislike of good blazes out into murderous fury against the good man who dares to be good alone in the face of a sinful multitude. That they are made thoroughly uneasy by his message of judgment, that they are more than half convinced that he is right, is plain from the frantic passion with which they repeat and deny his words. *Law shall not perish from the priest, nor counsel from the wise, nor the word from the prophet*: these things cannot, *shall not* be. When people have pinned their faith to a false system—a system which accords with their worldly prejudices, and flatters their ungodly pride, and winks at or even sanctions their vices; when they have anchored their entire confidence upon certain men and certain teachings which are in perfect harmony with their own aims in life and their own selfish predilections, they are not only disturbed and distressed but often enraged by a demonstration that they are lulled in a false security. And anger of this kind is apt to be so irrational, that they may think to escape from the threatened evil by silencing its prophet. *Come and let us smite him with the tongue, and let us not hearken to any of his words!* They will first get rid of him, and then forget his words of warning. Their policy is no better than that of the bird which buries its head in the sand, when its pursuers have run it down; an infatuated Out of sight, out of mind. And Jeremiah's recompense for his disinterested zeal is another conspiracy against his life.

Once more he lays his cause before the one impartial Judge; the one Being who is exalted above all passion, and therefore sees the truth as it is.

> "Hearken Thou, O Iahvah, unto me,
> And hear Thou the voice of mine adversaries.
> Should evil be recompensed for good?
> For they have digged a pit for my life.
> Remember my standing before Thee to speak good about them,
> To turn back Thy wrath from them."

Hearken Thou, since *they* refuse to hearken; hear both sides, and pronounce for the right. Behold the glaring contrast between my innocence of all hurtful intent, and their clamorous injustice, between my truth and their falsehood, my prayers for their salvation and their outcry for my blood.

As we read this prayer of Jeremiah's, we are reminded of the very similar language of the thirty-fifth and hundred and ninth psalms, of which he was himself perhaps the author (see especially Ps. xxxv. 1, 4, 5, 7, 11, 12; cix. 2, 5). We have already partially considered the moral aspect of such petitions. It is necessary to bear in mind that the prophet is speaking of persons who have persistently rejected warning, and ridiculed reproof; and now, in return for his intercessions on their behalf, are attempting his life, not in a sudden outbreak of uncontrollable fury, but with craft and deliberate malice, after seeking, apparently, like their spiritual successors in a later age, to entrap him into admissions that might be construed as treason or blasphemy (Ps. xxxv. 19-21).

> "Therefore give their sons to the famine,
> And pour them into the hands of the sword;
> And let their wives be bereaved and widows,
> And let their husbands be slain of Death;
> Let their young men be stricken down of the sword in the battle!
>
> "Let a cry be heard from their houses,
> When Thou bringest a troop upon them suddenly!
> For they digged a pit to catch me,
> And snares they hid for my feet.
>
> "But of Thyself, Iahvah, Thou knowest all their plan against me for death;

Pardon Thou not their iniquity,
And blot not out their trespass from before Thee;
But let them be made to stumble before Thee,
In the time of Thine anger deal Thou with them!"

The passage is lyrical in form and expression, and something must be allowed for the fact in estimating its precise significance. Jeremiah had entreated God and man that all these things might not come to pass. Now, when the attitude of the people towards his message and himself at last leaves no doubt that their obduracy is invincible, in his despair and distraction he cries, Be it so, then! They are bent on destruction; let them have their will! Let the doom overtake them, that I have laboured in vain to avert! With a weary sigh, and a profound sense of the ripeness of his country for ruin, he gives up the struggle to save it. The passage thus becomes a rhetorical or poetical expression of the prophet's despairing recognition of the inevitable.

How vivid are the touches with which he brings out upon his canvas the horrors of war! In language lurid with all the colours of destruction, he sets before us the city taken by storm, he makes us hear the cry of the victims, as house after house is visited by pillage and slaughter. But stripped of its poetical form, all this is no more than a concentrated repetition of the sentence which he has over and over again pronounced against Jerusalem in the name of Iahvah. The imprecatory manner of it may be considered to be simply a solemn signification of the speaker's own assent and approval. He recalls the sentence, and he affirms its perfect consonance with his own sense of justice. Moreover all these terrible things actually happened in the sequel. The prophet's imprecations received the Divine seal of accomplishment. This fact alone seems to me to distinguish his prayer from a merely human cry for vengeance. So far as his feelings as a man and a patriot were concerned, we cannot doubt that he would have averted the catastrophe, had that been possible, by the sacrifice of his own life. That indeed was the object of his entire ministry. We may call the passage an emotional prediction; and it was probably the predictive character of it which led the prophet to put it on record.

While we admit that no Christian may ordinarily pray for the annihilation of any but spiritual enemies, we must remember that no Christian can possibly occupy the same peculiar position as a prophet of the Old Covenant; and we may fairly ask whether any who may incline to judge harshly of Jeremiah on the ground of passages like this, have fully realized the appalling circumstances which wrung these prayers from his cruelly tortured heart? We find it hard to forgive small personal slights, often less real than imaginary; how should we comport ourselves to persons whose shameless ingratitude rewarded evil for good to the extent of seeking our lives? Few would be content, as Jeremiah was, with putting the cause in the hand of God, and abstaining from all attempts at personal vindication of wrongs. It surely betrays a failure of imaginative power to realize the terrible difficulties which beset the path of one who, in a far truer sense than Elijah, was left alone to uphold the cause of true religion in Israel, and not less, a very inadequate knowledge of our own spiritual weakness, when we are bold to censure or even to apologise for the utterances of Jeremiah.

The whole question assumes a different aspect, when it is noticed that the brief "Thus said Iahvah!" of the next chapter (xix.) virtually introduces the Divine reply to the prophet's prayer. He is now bidden to foreshow the utter destruction of the Jewish polity by a symbolic act which is even more unambiguous than the language of the prayer. He is to take a common earthenware bottle (*baqbûq*, as if "pour-pour"; from *baqaq*, "to pour out"), and, accompanied by some of the leading personages of the capital, heads of families and priests, to go out of the city to the valley of ben Hinnom, and there, after a solemn rehearsal of the crimes perpetrated on that very spot in the name of religion, and after predicting the consequent retribution which will shortly overtake the nation, he is to dash the vessel in pieces before his companions' eyes, in token of the utter and irreparable ruin which awaits their city and people.

Having enacted his part in this striking scene, Jeremiah returns to the court of the temple, and there repeats the same terrible message in briefer terms before all the people; adding expressly that it is the reward of their stubborn obstinacy and deafness to the Divine voice.

The prophet's imprecations of evil thus appear to have been ratified at the time of their conception by the Divine voice, which spoke in the stillness of his after reflexion.

XII
THE BROKEN VESSEL—A
SYMBOL OF JUDGMENT

Jeremiah xix.

The result of his former address, founded upon the procedure of the potter, had only been to bring out into clearer distinctness the appalling extent of the national corruption. It was evident that Judah was incorrigible, and the Potter's vessel must be broken in pieces by its Maker.

Thus said Iahvah: Go and buy a bottle (baqbûq, as if "a pour-pour"; the meaning is alluded to in the first word of ver. 7: *ubaqqothi*, "and I will pour out") *of a moulder of pottery* (so the accents; but perhaps the Vulgate is right: "lagunculam figuli testeam," "a potter's earthen vessel," A.V.; lit. *a potter's bottle*, viz., *earthenware*), and (take: LXX. rightly adds) *some of the elders of the people and of the elders of the priests, and go out into the valley of ben Hinnom at the entry of the Pottery Gate* (a postern, where broken earthenware and rubbish were shot forth into the valley: the term is connected with that for "pottery," ver. 1, which is the same as that in Job ii. 8), *and cry there the words that I shall speak unto thee,*—Jeremiah does not pause here, to relate how he followed the Divine impulse, but goes on at once to communicate the tenor of the Divine "words"; a circumstance which points to the fact that this narrative was only written some time after the symbolical action which it records;—*and say thou, Hear ye Iahvah's word, O kings of Judah and inhabitants of Jerusalem! Thus said Iahvah Sabaoth, the God of Israel: Lo, I am about to bring an evil upon this place, such that, whoever heareth it, his ears shall tingle!* If we suppose, as seems likely, that this series of oracles (xviii.-xx.) belongs to the reign of Jehoiachin, the expression "kings of Judah" may denote that king and the queen-mother. Another view is that the kings of Judah in general are addressed "as an indefinite class of persons," here and elsewhere (xvii. 20, xxii. 4), because the prophet did not write the main portion of his book until after the siege of Jerusalem (Ewald). The announcement of this verse is quoted by the compiler of Kings in relation to the crimes of king Manasseh (2 Kings xxi. 12).

Because that they forsook Me, and made this place strange—alienated it from Iahvah by consecrating it to "strange gods"; or as the Targum and Syriac, "polluted" it—*and burnt incense therein to other gods, whom neither they nor their fathers knew* (xvi. 13); *and the kings of Judah did fill this place with blood of innocents* (so the LXX. "Nor the kings of Judah" gives a poor sense; they are included in the preceding phrase), *and built the bamoth Baal* (High-places of Baal; a proper name, Josh. xiii. 17), *to burn their sons in the fire,* [*as burnt-offerings to the Baal:* LXX. omits, and it is wanting, vii. 31, xxxii. 35. It may be a gloss, but is probably genuine, as there are slight variations in each passage], *which I commanded not,* [*nor spake:* LXX. omits], *neither came it into My mind: therefore, behold days are coming, saith Iahvah, when this place will no more be called the Tophet and valley of ben Hinnom but the Valley of Slaughter!* [*and in Tophet shall they bury, so that there be*—remain—*no room to bury!* This clause, preserved at the end of ver. 11, but omitted there by the LXX., probably belongs here: see vii. 42]. *And I will pour out* (ver. 1; Isa. xix. 3) *the counsel of Judah and Jerusalem in this place*—that is, I will *empty* the land of all wisdom and resourcefulness, as one empties a bottle of its water, so that the heads of the state shall be powerless to devise any effectual scheme of defence in the face of calamity (cf. xiii. 13)—*and I will cause them to fall by the sword "before their enemies"* (Deut. xxviii. 25), *and by the hand of them that seek their life; and I will make "their carcases food unto the birds of the air and the beasts of the earth"* (Deut. xxviii. 26; chap. vii. 33, xvi. 4). *And I will set this city "for an astonishment"* (Deut. xxviii. 37) *and a hissing* (xviii. 16); *every one that passeth by her shall be astonished and hiss at all her "strokes"* (xlix. 17, l. 13) *or "plagues"* (Deut. xxviii. 59). *And I will cause them to "eat the flesh of their sons and the flesh of their daughters," and each the flesh of his fellow shall they eat*—"*in the stress and the straitness wherewith their enemies" and they that seek their life "shall straiten them."* It will be seen from the references that the Deuteronomic colouring of these closing threats (vv. 7-9) is very strong, the last verse being practically a quotation (Deut. xxviii. 53). The effect of the whole oracle would thus be to suggest that the terrible sanctions of the sacred Law would not remain inoperative; but that the shameless violation of the solemn covenant under Josiah, by which the nation undertook to observe the code of Deuteronomy, would soon be visited with the retributive calamities so vividly foreshadowed in that book.

And break thou the bottle, to the eyes of the men that go with thee, and say unto them: Thus said Iahvah Sabaoth; So will I break this people and this city, as one breaketh the potter's vessel so that it cannot be mended again! Thus will I do to this place, saith Iahvah, and to the inhabitants thereof and make (infin. constr. as in xvii. 10, continuing the mood and person of the preceding verb; which is properly a function of the infin. absol., as in ver. 13) *this city like a Tophet*—

make it one huge altar of human sacrifice, a burning-place for thousands of human victims. *And the houses of Jerusalem, and the houses of the kings of Judah*—the palace of David and Solomon, in which king after king had reigned, and "done the evil in Iahvah's eyes,"—*shall become like the place of the Tophet, the defiled ones! even all the houses upon the roofs of which they burnt incense unto all the host of heaven, and poured outpourings* (libations of wine and honey) *unto other gods.* (So the Heb. punctuation, which seems to give a very good sense. The principal houses, those of the kings and grandees, are called "the defiled," because their roofs especially have been polluted with idolatrous rites. The last clause of the verse explains the epithet, which might have been referred to "the kings of Judah," had it preceded "like the place of the Tophet." The houses were not to become "defiled"; they were already so, past all cleansing; they were to be destroyed with fire, and in their destruction to become the Tophet or sacrificial pyre of their inhabitants. We need not, therefore, read *Tophteh*, after Isa. xxx. 33, as I at first thought of doing, to find afterwards that Ewald had already suggested it. The term rendered "even all," is lit. "unto all," that is, "including all"; cf. Ezek. xliv. 9).[81]

The command *and break thou the bottle ... and say unto them ...* compared with that of ver. 2, *and cry there the words that I shall speak unto thee!* seems to indicate the proper point of view from which the whole piece is to be regarded. Jeremiah is recalling and describing a particular episode in his past ministry; and he includes the whole of it, with the attendant circumstances and all that he said; first to the elders in the vale of ben Hinnom, and then to the people assembled in the temple, under the comprehensive *Thus said Iahvah!* with which he begins his narrative. In other words, he affirms that he was throughout the entire occurrence guided by the impulses of the Spirit of God. It is very possible that the longer first address (vv. 2-9) really gives the substance of what he said to the people in the temple on his return from the valley, which is merely summarized in verse 15.

And Jeremiah came in—into the temple—*from the Tophet, whither Iahvah had sent him to prophesy, and took his stand in the court of Iahvah's House, and said unto all the people: Thus said Iahvah Sabaoth Israels God; Lo, I am about to bring upon* (ver. 3) *this city and upon all her cities [and upon her villages*: LXX. adds] *all the evil that I have spoken concerning her; because they stiffened their neck* (vii. 26), *not to hear My words!* In this apparent epitome of His discourse to the people in the temple, the prophet seems to sum up all his past labours, in view of an impending crisis. "All the evil" spoken hitherto concerning Jerusalem is upon the point of being accomplished (cf. xxv. 3).

In reviewing the entire oracle, we may note as in former instances, the care with which all the circumstances of the symbolical action are chosen, in order to enhance the effect of it upon the minds of the witnesses. The Oriental mind delights in everything that partakes of the nature of an enigma; it loves to be called upon to unravel the meaning of dark sentences, and to disentangle the wisdom wrapped up in riddling words and significant actions. It would have found eloquence in Tarquin's unspoken answer to his son's messenger. "Rex velut deliberabundus in hortum ædium transit, sequente nuncio filii: ibi inambulans tacitus summa papaverum capita dicitur baculo decussisse" (Liv. i. 54). No doubt Jeremiah's companions would watch his every step, and would not miss the fact that he carried his earthenware vessel out of the city by the "Sherd Gate." Here was a vessel yet whole, treated as though it were already a shattered heap of fragments! They would be prepared for the oracle in the valley.

It is worth while, by the way, to notice who those companions were. They were certain of "the elders of the people" and of the "the elders of the priests." Jeremiah, it seems, was no wild revolutionary dreamer and schemer, whose hand and voice were against all established authority in Church and State. This was not the character of the Hebrew prophets in general, though some writers have conceived thus of them. There is no evidence that Jeremiah ever sought to divest himself of the duties and privileges of his hereditary priesthood; or that he looked upon the monarchy and the priestly guilds and the entire social organisation of Israel, as other than institutions divinely originated and divinely preserved through all the ages of the national history. He did not believe that man created these institutions though experience taught him that man might abuse and pervert them from their lawful uses. His aim was always to reform, to restore, to lead the people back to "the old paths" of primitive simplicity and rectitude; not to abolish hereditary institutions, and substitute for the order which had become an integral part of the national life, some brand-new constitution which had never been tried, and would be no more likely to fit the body corporate than the armour of Saul fitted the free limbs of the young shepherd who was to slay Goliath.

The prophets never called for the abolition of those laws and customs, civil and ecclesiastical, which were the very framework of the state, and the pillars of the social edifice. They did not cry, "Down with kings and priests!" but to both kings and priests they cried, "Hear ye Iahvah's word!" And all experience proves that they were right. Paper constitutions have never yet redeemed a nation from its vices, nor delivered a community from the impotence and the decay which are the inevitable fruits of moral corruption. Arbitrary legislative changes will not alter the inward condition of a people; covetousness and hypocrisy, pride and selfishness, intemperance and uncleanness and cruelty, may be as rampant in a commonwealth as in a kingdom.

The contents of the oracle are much what we have had many times already. The chief difference lies in a calm definiteness of assurance, a tone of distinct certitude, as though the end were so near at hand, as to leave no room for doubt or hesitation. And this difference is fittingly and impressively suggested by the particular symbol chosen—the shattering of an earthenware vessel, beyond the possibility of repair. The direct mention of the king of Babylon and the Babylonian captivity, in the sequel (chap. xx.), points to the presence of a Babylonian invasion, probably that which ended with the exile of Jeconiah and the chief citizens of Jerusalem.

The fatal sin, from which the oracle starts and to which it returns, is forsaking Iahvah, and making the city of His choice "strange" to Him, that is, hateful and unclean, by contact with foreign and bloody superstitions, which were even falsely declared by their promoters to be pleasing to Iahvah, the Avenger of innocent blood! (chap. vii. 31). The punishment corresponds to the offence. The sacrifices of blood will be requited with blood, shed in torrents on the very spot which had been so foully polluted; they who had not scrupled to slay their children for the sacrifice, were to slay them again for food under the stress of siege and famine; the city and its houses, defiled with the foreign worships, will become one vast Molech-fire (xxxii. 35), in which all will perish together.

It may strike a modern reader that there is something repulsive and cold-blooded in this detailed enumeration of appalling horrors. But not only is it the case that Jeremiah is quoting from the Book of the Law, at a time when, to an unprejudiced eye, there was every likelihood that the course of events would verify his dark forebodings; in the dreadful experience of those times such incidents as those mentioned (ver. 9) were familiar occurrences in the obstinate defence and protracted sufferings of beleaguered cities. The prophet, therefore, simply affirms that obstinate persistence in following their own counsels and rejecting the higher guidance will bring upon the nation its irretrievable ruin. We know that in the last siege he did his utmost to prevent the occurrence of these unnatural horrors by urging surrender; but then, as always, the people "stiffened their neck, not to hear Iahvah's words."

Jeremiah knew his countrymen well. No phrase could have better described the resolute obstinacy of the national character. How were the headstrong self-will, the inveterate sensuality, the blind tenacity of fanatical and non-moral conceptions which characterized this people, to be purified and made serviceable in the interests of true religion, except by means of the fiery ordeal which all the prophets foresaw and foretold? As we have seen, polytheism exercised upon the popular mind a spell which we can hardly comprehend from our modern point of view; a polytheism foul and murderous, which violated the tenderest affections of our nature by demanding of the father the sacrifice of his child, and violated the very instinct of natural purity by the shameless indulgence of its worship. It was a consecration of lust and cruelty,—that worship of Molech, those rites of the Baals and Asheras. Meagre and monotonous as the sacred records may on these heads appear to be, their witness is supplemented by other sources, by the monuments of Babylon and Phenicia.

It is hard to see how the religious instinct of men in this peculiar stage of belief and practice was to be enlightened and purified in any other way than the actual course of Providence. What arguments can be imagined that would have appealed to minds which found a fatal fascination, nay, we must suppose an intense satisfaction, in rites so hideous that one durst not even describe them; minds to which the lofty monotheism of Amos, the splendid eloquence of an Isaiah, the plaintive lyrical strain of a Jeremiah, appealed in vain? Appeals to the order of the world, to the wonders of organic life, were lost upon minds which made gods of the most obvious subjects of that order, the sun, moon, and stars; which even personified and adored the physical principle whereby the succession of life after life is perpetuated.

Nothing short of the perception *that the word of the prophets had come to pass*, the recognition, therefore, that the prophetic idea of God was the true idea, could have succeeded in keeping the remnant of Judah safe from the contagion of surrounding heathenism in the land of their exile, and in radically transforming once for all the religious tendencies of the Jewish race.

In Jeremiah's view, the heinousness of Judah's idolatry is heightened by the consideration that the gods of their choice are gods "whom neither they nor their fathers knew" (ver. 4). The kings Ahaz, Manasseh, Amon, had introduced novel rites, and departed from "the old paths" more decidedly than any of their predecessors. In this connexion, we may remember that, while modern Romish controversialists do not scruple to accuse the Church of this country of having unlawfully innovated at the Reformation, the Anglican appeal has always been to Scripture and primitive antiquity. Such, too, was the appeal of the prophets (Hos. vi. 1, 7, xi. 1; Jer. ii. 2, vi. 16, xi. 3). It is the glory of our Church, a glory of which neither the lies of Jesuits nor the envy of the sectaries can rob her, that she returned to "the old paths," boldly overleaping the dark ages of medieval ignorance, imposture, and corruption, and planting her foot firmly upon the rock of apostolic practice and the consent of the undivided Church.

Disunion among Christians is a sore evil, but union in the maintenance and propaganda of falsehood is a worse; and the guilt of disunion lies at the door of that system which abused its authority to crush out legitimate freedom of thought, to retard the advancement of learning, and to establish those monstrous innovations in doctrine and worship, which subtle dialecticians may prove to their own satisfaction to be innocent and non-idolatrous in essence and intention, though all the world can see that in practice they are grossly idolatrous. God preserve England from that toleration of serious error, which is so easy to sceptical indifference! God preserve her from lending an ear to the siren voices that would seduce her to yield her hard-won independence, her noble freedom, her manly rational piety, to the unhistorical and unscriptural claims of the Papacy!

If we reverence those Scriptures of the Old Testament to which our Lord and His Apostles made their constant appeal, we shall keep steadily before our minds the fact that, in the estimation of a prophet like Jeremiah, the sin of sins, the sin that involved the ruin of Israel and Judah, was the sin of associating other objects of worship with the One Only God. The temptation is peculiarly strong to some natures. The continual relapse of ancient Israel is not so great a wonder to those of us who have any knowledge of mankind, and who can observe what is passing around them at the present day. It is the severe demand of God's holy law, which makes men cast about for some plausible compromise—it is that demand which also makes them yearn after some intermediary power, whose compassion will be less subject to considerations of justice, whom prayers and entreaties and presents may overcome, and induce to wink at unrepented sin. In an age of unsettlement, the more daring spirits will be prone to silence their inconvenient scruples by rushing into atheism, while the more timid may take refuge in Popery. "For to disown a Moral Governour, or to admit that any observances of superstition can release men from the duty of obeying Him, equally serves the purpose of those, who resolve to be as wicked as they dare, or as little virtuous as they can" (Bp. Hurd).

Then, too, there is the glory of the saints and angels of God. How can frail man refuse to bow before the vision of their power and splendour, as they stand, the royal children of the King of kings, around the heavenly throne, deathless, radiant with love and joy and purity, exalted far above all human weakness and human sorrows? If the holy angels are "ministering spirits," why not the entire community of the Blessed? And what is to hinder us from casting ourselves at the feet of saint or angel, one's own appointed guardian, or chosen helper? Let good George Herbert answer for us all.

"Oh glorious spirits, who after all your bands
See the smooth face of God, without a frown,
Or strict commands;

Where every one is king, and hath his crown,
If not upon his head, yet in his hands:

"Not out of envy or maliciousness
Do I forbear to crave your special aid.
I would address
My vows to thee most gladly, blessed Maid,
And Mother of my God, in my distress:

"But now, (alas!) I dare not; for our King,
Whom we do all jointly adore and praise,
Bids no such thing:
And where His pleasure no injunction lays,
('Tis your own case) ye never move a wing.

"All worship is prerogative, and a flower
Of His rich crown, from whom lies no appeal
At the last hour:
Therefore we dare not from His garland steal,
To make a posy for inferior power."

In this sense also, as in many others, the warning of St. John applies:

LITTLE CHILDREN, KEEP YOURSELVES FROM IDOLS!

XIII
JEREMIAH UNDER PERSECUTION

Jeremiah xx.

The prophet has now to endure something more than a scornful rejection of his message. *And Pashchur ben Immer the priest (he was chief officer in the house of Iahvah) heard Jeremiah prophesying these words. And Pashchur smote Jeremiah the prophet and put him in the stocks, which were in the upper gate of Benjamin in the house of Iahvah.* Like the priest of Bethel, who abruptly put an end to the preaching of Amos in the royal sanctuary, Pashchur suddenly interferes, apparently before Jeremiah has finished his address to the people; and enraged at the tenour of his words, he causes him—"Jeremiah *the prophet*," as it is significantly added, to indicate the sacrilege of the act—to be beaten in the cruel Eastern manner on the soles of the feet, inflicting probably the full number of forty blows permitted by the Law (Deut.), and then leaving him, in his agony of mind and body, fast bound in "the stocks." For the remainder of that day and all night long the prophet sat there in the gate, at first exposed to the taunts and jeers of his adversaries and the rabble of their followers, and as the weary hours slowly crept on, becoming painfully cramped in his limbs by the barbarous machine which held his hands and feet near together, and bent his body double. This cruel punishment seems to have been the customary mode of dealing with such as were accounted false prophets by the authorities. It was the treatment which Hanani endured in return for his warning to king Asa (2 Chron. xvi. 10), some three centuries earlier than Jeremiah's time; and a few years later in our prophet's history, an attempt was made to enforce it again in his case (Jer. xxix. 26). Thus, like the holy apostles of our Lord, was Jeremiah "counted worthy to suffer shame" for the Name in which he spoke (Acts v. 40, 41); and like Paul and Silas at Philippi, after enduring "many stripes" his feet were "made fast in the stocks" (Acts xvi. 23, 24). The message of Jeremiah was a message of judgment, that of the apostles was a message of forgiveness; and both met with the same response from a world whose heart was estranged from God. The heart that loves its own way, is only at ease when it can forget God. Any reminder of His Presence, of His perpetual activity in mercy and judgment, is unwelcome, and makes its authors odious. From the outset, transgressors of the Divine law have sought to hide *among the trees of the garden*—in the engrossing pursuits and pleasures of life—from the Presence of God.

Pashchur's object was not to destroy Jeremiah, but to break his spirit, and discredit him with the multitude, and so silence him for ever. But in this expectation he was as signally disappointed as his successor was in the case of St. Peter (Acts v. 24, 29). Now as then, God's messenger could not be turned from his conviction that *we ought to obey God rather than men*. And as he sat alone in his intolerable anguish, brooding over his shameful wrongs, and despairing of redress, a Divine Word came in the stillness of night to this victim of human tyranny. For it *came to pass on the morrow that Pashchur brought Jeremiah forth out of the stocks; and Jeremiah said unto him, Not Pashchur* [82]—as if "Glad and free"—*but Magor-missabib*—"Fear on every side"—*hath Iahvah called thy name!* Sharpened with misery, the seer's eye pierces through the shows of life, and discerns the grim contrast of truth and appearance. Before him stands this great man, clothed with all the dignity of high office, and able to destroy him with a word; but Iahvah's prophet does not quail before abused authority. He sees the sword suspended by a hair over the head of this haughty and supercilious official; and he realizes the solemn irony of circumstance, which has connected a name suggestive of gladness and freedom with a man destined to become the thrall of perpetual terrors. *For thus hath Iahvah said: Lo, I am about to make thee a Fear to thyself and to all thy lovers; and they will fall by the sword of their foes, while thine eyes look on!* This "glad and free" persecutor, wantoning in the abuse of power, blindly fearless of the future, is not doomed to be slain out of hand; a heavier fate is in store for him, a fate prefigured and foreshadowed by his present sins. His proud confidence is to give place to a haunting sense of danger and insecurity; he is to see his followers perish one after another, and evermore to be expecting the same end for himself: while the freedom which he has enjoyed and abused so long, is to be exchanged for a lifelong captivity in a foreign land. *And all Judah will I give into the hand of the king of Babylon, and he will transport them to Babylon, and smite them with the sword. And I will give all the store of this city*—the hoarded wealth of all sorts, which constitutes its strength and reserve force—*and all the gain thereof*—the produce of labour—*and all the value thereof*—things rare and precious of every kind, works of the carver's and the goldsmith's and the potter's and the weaver's art;—*and all the treasures of the kings of Judah will I give into the hand of their foes, that they may spoil them and take them and bring them to Babylon.*

And for thyself, Pashchur, and all that dwell in thine house, ye shall depart among the captives; and to Babylon thou shall come, and there thou shalt die, and there be buried, thyself and all thy lovers, to whom thou hast prophesied with untruth, or rather *by the Lie,* i.e., *by the Baal* (ii. 8, xxiii. 13, cf. xii. 16).

The play on the name of Pashchur is like that on Perath (ch. xiii.), and the change to Magor-missabib is like the change of Tophet into "Valley of Slaughter" (ch. xix.). Like Amos (vii. 16), Jeremiah repeats his obnoxious prophecy, with a special application to his cruel persecutor, and with the added detail that all the wealth of Jerusalem will be carried as spoil to Babylon; a detail in which there may lie an oblique reference to the covetous worldliness and the interested opposition of such men as Pashchur. Riches and ease and popularity were the things for which he and those like him had bargained away their integrity, prophesying with conscious falsehood to the deluded people. His "lovers" are his partisans, who eagerly welcomed his presages of peace and prosperity, and doubtless actively opposed Jeremiah with ridicule and threats. The last detail is remarkable, for we do not otherwise know that Pashchur affected to prophesy. If it be not meant simply that Pashchur accepted and lent the weight of his official sanction to the false prophets, and especially those who uttered their divinations in the name of "the Baal," that is to say, either Molech, or the popular and delusive conception of the God of Israel, we see in this man one who combined a steady professional opposition to Jeremiah with power to enforce his hostility by legalized acts of violence. The conduct of Hananiah on a later occasion (xxviii. 10), clearly proves that, where the power was present, the will for such acts was not wanting in Jeremiah's professional adversaries.

It is generally taken for granted that the name of "Pashchur" has been substituted for that of "Malchijah" in the list of the priestly families which returned with Zerubbabel from the Babylonian captivity (Ezra ii. 38; Neh. vii. 41; cf. 1 Chron. xxiv. 9); but it seems quite possible that "the sons of Pashchur" were a subdivision of the family of Immer, which had increased largely during the Exile. In that case, the list affords evidence of the fulfilment of Jeremiah's prediction to Pashchur. The prophet elsewhere mentions another Pashchur, who was also a priest, of the course or guild of Malchijah (xxi. 1, xxxviii. 1), which was the designation of the fifth class of the priests, as "Immer" was that of the sixteenth (1 Chron. xxiv. 9, 14). The prince Gedaliah, who was hostile to Jeremiah, was apparently a son of the present Pashchur (Jer. xxxviii. 1).

It is not easy to determine the relation of the lyrical section which immediately follows the doom of Pashchur, to the preceding account (vv. 7-8). If the seventh verse be in its original place, it would seem that the prophet's word had failed of accomplishment, with the result of intensifying the unbelief and the ridicule which his teachings encountered. There is also something very strange in the sequence of the thirteenth and fourteenth verses, where, as the text now stands, the prophet passes at once, in the most abrupt fashion imaginable, from a fervid ascription of praise, a heartfelt cry of thanksgiving for deliverance either actual or contemplated as such, to utterances of unrelieved despair. I do not think that this is in the manner of Jeremiah; nor do I see how the violent contrast of the two sections (7-13 and 14-18) can fairly be accounted for, except by supposing either that we have here two unconnected fragments, placed in juxtaposition with each other because they belong to the same general period of the prophet's ministry; or that the two passages have by some accident of transcription been transposed, which is by no means an uncommon occurrence in the MSS. of the Biblical writers. Assuming this latter as the more probable alternative, we see in the entire passage a powerful representation of the mental conflict into which Jeremiah was thrown by Pashchur's high-handed violence and the seeming triumph of his enemies. Smarting with the sense of utter injustice, humiliated in his inmost soul by shameful indignities, crushed to the earth with the bitter consciousness of defeat and failure, the prophet like Job opens his mouth and curses his day.

1. "Cursed be the day wherein I was born!
The day that my mother bare me,
Let it not be blest!

2. Cursed be the man who told the glad tidings to my
father,
'There is born to thee a male child;
'Who made him rejoice greatly.

3. And let that man become like the cities that Iahweh
overthrew, without relenting,
And let him hear a cry in the morning,
And an alarm at the hour of noon!

4. For that he slew me not in the womb,
That my mother might have become my grave,
And her womb have been laden evermore!

5. O why from the womb came I forth
To see labour and sorrow,
And my days fordone with shame?"

These five triplets afford a glimpse of the lively grief, the passionate despair, which agitated the prophet's heart as the first effect of the shame and the torture to which he had been so wickedly and wantonly subjected. The elegy, of which they constitute the proem, or opening strophe, is not introduced by any formula ascribing it to Divine inspiration; it is simply written down as a faithful record of Jeremiah's own feelings and reflexions and self-communings, at this painful crisis in his career. The poet of the book of Job has apparently taken the hint supplied by these opening verses, and has elaborated the idea of cursing the day of birth through seven highly wrought and imaginative stanzas. The higher finish and somewhat artificial expansion of that passage leave little doubt that it was modelled upon the one before us. But the point to remember here is that both are lyrical effusions, expressed in language conditioned by Oriental rather than European standards of taste and usage. As the prophets were not inspired to express their thoughts and feelings in a modern English dress, it is superfluous to inquire whether Jeremiah was morally justified in using these poetic formulas of imprecation. To insist on applying the doctrine of verbal inspiration to such a passage is to evince an utter want of literary tact and insight, as well as adhesion to an exploded and pernicious relic of sectarian theology. The prophet's curses are simply a highly effective form of poetical rhetoric, and are in perfect harmony with the immemorial modes of Oriental expression; and the underlying thought, so equivocally expressed, according to our ways of looking at things, is simply that his life has been a failure, and therefore it would have been better not to have been born. Who that is at all earnest for God's truth, nay, for far lower objects of human interest and pursuit, has not in moments of despondency and discouragement been overwhelmed for a time by the like feeling? Can we blame Jeremiah for allowing us to see in this faithful transcript of his inner life how intensely human, how entirely natural the spiritual experience of the prophets really was? Besides, the revelation does not end with this initial outburst of instinctive astonishment, indignation and despair. The proem is succeeded by a psalm in seven stanzas of regular poetical form—six quatrains rounded off with a final couplet—in which the prophet's thought rises above the level of nature, and finds in an overruling Providence both the source and the justification of the enigma of his life.

1. "Thou enticedst me, Iahvah, and I was enticed,
Thou urgedst[83] me, and didst prevail!
I am become a derision all the day long.
Every one mocketh at me.

2. "For as oft as I speak, I cry alarm,
Violence and havoc do I proclaim;
For Iahvah's word is become to me a reproach,
And a scoff all the day long.

3. "And if I say, I will not mind it,
Nor speak any more in His Name;
Then it becometh in my heart like a burning fire prisoned

in my bones.
And I weary of holding it in[84] and am not able.

4. "For I have heard the defaming of many, the terror on
every side;[85]
All the men of my friendship are watching for my fall;
'Perchance he will be enticed, and we shall prevail over him,
And take our revenge of him.'

5. "Yet Iahvah is with me as a dread warrior,
Therefore my pursuers shall stumble and not prevail;
They shall be greatly ashamed, for that they have not prospered,
With eternal dishonour that shall not be forgotten.

6. "And Iahvah Sabaoth trieth the righteous,
Seeth the reins and the heart;
I shall see Thy revenge of them,
For unto Thee have I committed my quarrel.

7. Sing ye to Iahvah, acclaim ye Iahvah!
For He hath snatched the poor man's life out of the hand of
evildoers."

The cause was of God. *Thou didst lure me, Iahvah, and I let myself be lured; Thou urgedst me and wert victorious.* He had not rashly and presumptuously taken upon himself this office of prophet; he had been called, and had resisted the call, until his scruples and his pleadings were overcome, as was only natural, by a Will more powerful than his own (chap. i. 6). In speaking of the inward persuasions which determined the course of his life, he uses the very terms which are used by the author of Kings in connexion with the spirit that misled the prophets of Arab before the fatal expedition to Ramoth Gilead. *And he said, Thou shalt entice, and also be victorious* (1 Kings xxii. 22). Iahvah, therefore, has treated him as an enemy rather than a friend, for He has lured him to his own destruction. Half in irony, half in bitter complaint, the prophet declares that Iahvah has succeeded only too well in His malign purpose: *I am become a derision all the day long; Every one mocketh at me.*

In the second stanza, the thought appears to be continued thus: *Thou overcamest me; for as often as I speak,* I am a prophet of evil, *I cry alarm* (`ez'aq; cf. zĕ`aqah, vers. 16); I proclaim the imminence of invasion, the *violence and havoc* of a ruthless conqueror. *Thou overcamest me* also, in Thy purpose of making me a laughing-stock to my adversaries; *for Iahvah's word is become to me a reproach, and a scoff all the day long* (the relation between the two halves of the stanza is that of coordination; each gives the reason of the corresponding couplet in the first stanza). His continual threats of a judgment that was still delayed, brought upon him the merciless ridicule of his opponents.

Or the prophet may mean to complain that the monotony of his message, his ever-recurring denunciation of prevalent injustice, is made a reproach against him. *For as often as I speak I make an outcry* of indignation at foul wrongdoing (Gen. iv. 10, xviii. 21, xix. 13); *wrong and robbery do I proclaim* (Hab. i. 2, 3)—the oppression of the poor by the covetous and luxurious ruling classes. A third view is that Jeremiah complains of the frequent attacks upon himself: *For as often as I speak I have to exclaim; Of assault and violence do I cry*; but the first suggestion appears to suit best, as giving a reason for the ridicule which the prophet finds so intolerable (cf. xvii. 15).

The third stanza carries this plea for justice a step further. Not only was the prophet's overwhelming trouble due to his having yielded to the persuasions and promises of Iahvah; not only has he been rewarded with scorn and the scourge and the stocks for his compliance with a Divine call. He has been in a manner forced and driven into his intolerable position by the coercive power of Iahvah, which left him no choice but to utter the word that burnt like a fire within him. Sometimes his fears of perfidy and betrayal suggested the thought of succumbing to the insuperable obstacles which seemed to block his path; of giving up once for all a thankless and fruitless and dangerous enterprise: but then the inward flame burnt so fiercely, that he could find no relief for his anguish but by giving it vent in words (cf. Ps. xxxix. 1-3).

The verse finely illustrates that vivid sense of a Divine constraint which distinguishes the true prophet from pretenders to the office. Jeremiah does not protest the purity of his motives; indirectly and unconsciously he expresses it with a simplicity and a strength which leave no room for suspicion. He has himself no doubt at all that what he speaks is "Iahvah's word." The inward impulse is overpowering; he has striven in vain against its urgency; like Jacob at Peniel, he has wrestled with One stronger than himself. He is no vulgar fanatic or enthusiast, in whom rooted prejudices and irrational frenzies overbalance the judgment, making him incapable of estimating the hazards and the chances of his enterprise; he is as well aware of the perils that beset his path as the coolest and craftiest of his worldly adversaries. Thanks to his natural quickness of perception, his developed faculty of reflexion, he is fully alive to the probable consequences of perpetually thwarting the popular will, of taking up a position of permanent resistance to the policy and the aims and the interests of the ruling classes. But while he has his mortal hopes and fears, his human capacity for anxiety and pain; while his heart bleeds at the sight of suffering, and aches for the woes that thickly crowd the field of his prophetic vision; his speech and his behaviour are dominated, upon the whole, by an altogether higher consciousness. His emotions may have their moments of mastery; at times they may overpower his fortitude, and lay him prostrate in an agony of lamentation and mourning and woe; at times they may even interpose clouds and darkness between the prophet and his vision of the Eternal; but these effects of mortality do not last: they shake but cannot loosen his grasp of spiritual realities; they cannot free him from the constraining influence of the Word of Iahvah. That word possesses, leads him captive, "triumphs over him," over all the natural resistance of flesh and blood; for he is "not as the many"—the false prophets—"who corrupt the Word of God; but as of sincerity, but as of God, in the sight of God, he speaks" (2 Cor. ii. 14, 17).

And still, unless a man be thus impelled by the Spirit; unless he have counted the cost and is prepared to risk all for God; unless he be ready to face unpopularity and social contempt and persecution; unless he knows what it is to suffer for and with Jesus Christ; I doubt if he has any moral right to speak in that most holy Name. For if the all-mastering motive be absent, if the love of Christ constrain him not, how can his desires and his doings be such as the Unseen Judge will either approve or bless?

The fourth stanza explains why the prophet laboured, though vainly, to keep silence. It was because of the malicious reports of his utterances, which were carefully circulated by his watchful antagonists. They beset him on every side; like Pashchur, they were to him a "magor-missabib," an environing terror (cf. vi. 25), as they listened to his harangues, and eagerly invited each other to inform against him as a traitor (The words "Inform ye, and let us inform against him!" or "Denounce ye, and let us denounce him!" may be an ancient gloss upon the term *dibbah*, "ill report," "calumny;" Gen. xxxvii. 2; Num. xiii. 32; Job xvii. 5. For the construction, cf. Job xxxi. 37. They spoil the symmetry of the line. That *dibbah* really means "defaming," or "slander," appears not only from the passages in which it occurs, but also from the Arabic *dabûb*; "one who creeps about with slander," from *dabba*, "to move gently or slowly about." The Heb. *ragal, riggel,* "to go about slandering," and *rakîl,* "slander," are analogous).

And not only open enemies thus conspired for the prophet's destruction. Even professed friends (for the phrase, cf. xxxviii. 22; Ps. xli. 10) were treacherously watchful to catch him tripping (cf. ix. 2, xii. 6). Those on whom he had a natural claim for sympathy and protection, bore a secret and determined grudge against him. His unpopularity was complete, and his position full of peril. We have in the thirty-first and several of the following psalms outpourings of feeling under circumstances very similar to those of Jeremiah on the present occasion, even if they were not actually written by him at the same crisis in his career, as certain striking coincidences of expression seem to suggest (ver. 10; cf. Ps. xxxi. 13, xxxv. 15, xxxviii. 17, xli. 9; ver. 13 with Ps. xxxv. 9, 10).

The prophet closes his psalm-like monologue with an act of faith. He remembers that he has a Champion who is mightier than a thousand enemies. Iahvah is with him, not with them (cf. 2 Kings vi. 16); their plots, therefore, are foredoomed to failure, and themselves to the vengeance of a righteous God (xi. 20). The last words are an exultant anticipation of deliverance.

We thus see that the whole piece, like a previous one (xv. 10-21), begins with cursing and ends with an assurance of blessing.

FOOTNOTES:

[1] The same root is used in the Targ. on i. 15 for *setting* or fixing thrones, cf. Dan. vii. 9: (וִימָר)

[2] Clem. Alex., *Strom.*, I., § 120.

[3] At least seven times.

[4] Hitzig.

[5] i. 6.

[6] i. 2, xxv. 3.

[7] רַעַנ *puer*; (1) Ex. ii. 6, of a three months' babe; (2) of a young man up to about the twentieth year, Gen. xxxiv. 19, of Shechem ben Hamor; 1 Kings iii. 7, of Solomon, as here.

[8] Hitzig, *Vorbemerkungen*.

[9] The Cimmerians are the Gomer of Scripture, the Gimirrâ'a of the cuneiform inscriptions.

[10] Ewald, *Die Psalmen*, 165.

[11] Zeph. ii. 4 *sqq.*, רקעת וזרקע ... היהת הבוזע הזע

[12] הרותה רפס, 2 Kings xxii. 8; תירבה רפס, 2 Kings xxiii. 2.

[13] Comparing the Hebrew verb with the Arabic مَ • ں *timuit, fastidivit*. LXX., κἀγὼ ἠμέλησα αὐτῶν, Cf. Jer. iii. 14. Gesenius rendered *fastidivit, rejecit*.

[14] So rightly the Syriac, for Jehoiakim.

[15] *i.e.* To scent food afar off, like beasts of prey. There was no occasion to alter A.V.

[16] Even in the history of the transmission of ancient writings.

[17] Isa. xliv. 24, וְעָבִם דְּרָצוּי, xlix. 5, וּל דבעֵל ֶ וְטבבמ יְרָצִי.

[18] For the words of this promise, cf. ver. 19 *infr.*, xv. 20, xlii. 11.

[19] תְנָמְלָצ, so far as the punctuation suggests that the term is a compound, meaning "shadow of death," is one of the fictions of the Masorets, like סִינֹוִיַאָגל and מִיַאָכלה and הְקלה in the Psalms.

[20] Perhaps, too, the immediate object of the prophet was attained, which was, as Ewald thinks, to dissuade the people from alliance with Psammitichus, the vigorous monarch who was then reviving the power and ambition of Egypt. Jeremiah dreaded the effects of Egyptian influence upon the religion and morals of Judah. Ewald notes the significant absence of all reference to the enemy from the north, who appears in all the later pieces.

[21] *She* saw: Pesh. This may be right. And the Traitress, her sister Judah, *saw it: yea, saw that even because the Turncoat Israel had committed adultery, I put her away.... And yet the Traitress Judah, her sister, was not afraid, etc.*

[22] 1 Kings ii. 4, מִבְבְל־לְכב‎ = תְּמָאֵב‎

[23] As if "Turn back, back-turning Israel!" *i.e.* Thou that turnedst thy back upon Iahvah, and, therefore, upon His pleasant land.

[24] Cf. also the Arabic ﺀ *pravus*, ﺀ *pravitas*, with the Hebrew term.

[25] The modern singer has well caught the echo of this ancient strain.

> "Wilt thou cover thine hair with gold, and with silver thy feet?
> Hast thou taken the purple to fold thee, and made thy
> mouth sweet?
> Behold, when thy face is made bare, he that loved thee shall hate:
> Thy face shall be no more fair at the fall of thy fate.
> "*Atalanta in Calydon.*

[26] The second *'awen*, however, probably means "trouble," "calamity," as in Hab. iii. 7. The Sept. renders πόνος, and this agrees with the mention of Dan in viii. 16. As Ewald puts it, "from the north of Palestine the misery that is coming from the further north is already being proclaimed to all the nations in the south (vi. 18)."

[27] With a different point: "When I had fed them to the full" (cf. Hos. xiii. 6).

[28] This term—*mashchîthîm*—is certainly not the plur. of the *mashchîth*, "pitfall" or "trap," of v. 26. The meaning is the same as in Isa. i. 4. The original force of the root *shachath* is seen in the Assyrian *shachâtu*, "to fall down."

[29] The form—*cārōf*—is like *bāchōn*, "assayer," in ver. 27.

[30] The omissions of the Septuagint are not always intelligent. The repetition of the "all" here intensifies the idea of the *totality* of the ruin of the northern kingdom. The two clauses balance each other: *all your brethren—all the seed of Ephraim*. The objection that Edom was

also a "brother" of Israel (Deut. xxiii. 8; Amos i. 11) shews a want of rhetorical sense.

In vii. 4 the Septuagint tastelessly omits the third "The Temple of Iahvah!" upon which the rhetorical effect largely depends: cf. chap. xxii. 29; Isa. vi. 3.

[31] Note on vii. 25.—The word answering to "daily" in the Heb. simply means "day," and ought to be omitted, as an accidental repetition either from the previous line, or of the last two letters of the preceding word "prophets." Cf. ver. 13, where a similar phrase, "rising early and speaking," occurs in a similar context, but without "daily."

[32] *Wa'etten lahem* can only mean "and I gave (in prophetic idiom 'and I will give') unto them," and this, of course, requires an object. "I will give them to those who shall pass over them" is the rendering proposed by several scholars. But *lahem* does not mean "to those," and the thought does not harmonize with what precedes, and this use of רבע is doubtful, and the verb "to give" absolutely requires an object. The Vulgate rendering is really more in accordance with Hebrew syntax, as the masc. suffix of the verb might be used in less accurate writing. Targum: "because I gave them My law from Sinai, and they transgressed against it;" Peshito: "and I gave unto them, and they transgressed them." So also the Syro-Hexaplar of Milan (participle: "were transgressing") between asterisks.

[33] It seems to take the ילע each time as ילע־ןוהיליע and to read םלעיגיס איתי for יתיגילבמ: thus getting "Scoffers! I will bring upon them sorrow; upon them my heart is faint."

[34] The irregular *Hiphil* form of the verb—cf. 1 Sam. xiv. 22; Job xix. 4—may be justified by Job xxviii. 8; we are not, therefore, bound to render the Masoretic text: *and they make their tongue bend their lying bow.* Probably, however, *Qal* is right, the *Hiphil* being due to a misunderstanding, like that of the Targum, "And they taught their tongue words of lying."

[35] Ewald prefers the reading of the LXX., which divides the words differently. If we suppose their version correct, they must have read: "They have trained their tongue to speak falsehood, to distort. They are weary of returning. Oppression in oppression, deceit in deceit! They refuse to know Me, saith Iahvah." But I do not think this an improvement on the present Masoretic text.

[36] If Jeremiah wrote Ps. lv., as Hitzig supposes, he may be alluding to the treachery of a particular friend; cf. Ps. lv. 13, 14.

[37] *Shahadhta lisânaka `alaina.* In this case, we should follow the Heb. margin or Q'rê.

[38] *Speak thou, Thus saith Iahweh*, is undoubtedly a spurious addition, and does not appear in the LXX. Jeremiah never says *Koh ne'um Iahvah*, and never uses the imperative *dabber!*

[39] LXX. "for *they* are afraid before them," מהינפל המה ותחי יכ.

[40] This is the most natural interpretation of the passage according to the Hebrew punctuation. Another is given below.

[41] It is against usage to divide the clause as Naegelsbach does, "Vain instruction! It is wood!" or to render with Ewald "Simply vain doctrine is the wood!" which would require the article (*ha'eç*).

[42] But perhaps it is rather the prophet's love for his people, which fervently prays that the oath of blessing may be observed, and Judah maintained in the goodly land.

[43] Hitzig supposed that the "vows" and "hallowed flesh" were thank-offerings for the departure of the Scythians. "It is plain that the people are really present in the temple; they bring, presumably after the retreat of the Scythians, the offerings vowed at that time." But, considering the context, the reference appears to be more general. I have partly followed the LXX. in emending an obviously corrupt verse; the only one in the chap. which presents any textual difficulty. Read: שדק רשבו םירבדגה התמזמה התושע ידידיל המ : יז לעת זא יכתער יכעלעם ורבעי. The article with a noun with suffix, and the peculiar form of the 2 pers. pron. f., are found elsewhere in Jer. But I incline to correct further thus: "What avail to My beloved is her dealing (or sacrificing: השע 2 Kings xvii. 32) in My house?" וגו שדק רשבו םיברה תוחבזמה. "Can the many altars (ver. 13) and hallowed flesh cause thine evil to pass away from thee (or pass thee by)?" This seems very apposite to what precedes. The Hebrew, as it stands, cannot possibly mean what we read both in the A. V. and R. V., nor indeed anything else.

[44] Reading וחלב, with Hitzig, instead of ומחלב, which is meaningless. Deut. xxxiv. 7; Ezek. xxi. 3. Perhaps it would be better to keep *all* the letters, and point ומחלב, understanding עץ as collective, "the trees."

[45] Not a vocative: xx. 12, xvii. 10.

[46] That "the swelling" or "the pride of Jordan" should rather be read "the wilds" or "jungles of Jordan," is clear from xlix. 19; Zech. xi. 3; quoted by Hitzig. וזאג means "growth," "overgrowth," among other things;

and the Heb. phrase coincides with the Ἰάρδην δρυμὸς of Josephus (*Bell. Jud.*, vii. 6, 5).

[47] The form of the Heb. verbs implies the *certainty* of the event. Hitzig supposes that ver. 6 simply explains the expression "land of peace" in ver. 5. At Anathoth the prophet was at home; if he "ran away" (reading חרוב "fleest" for חטוב "art confident") there, what would he do, when he had gone forth as a "sheep among wolves" (St. Luke x. 3)? But I think it is much better to regard ver. 6 as explaining the *whole* of ver. 5 in the manner suggested above.

[48] Or perhaps rather the holy land itself, as Hitzig suggested: Hos. ix. 15.

[49] Lit. "Is my domain vultures, hyenas, to me?" The dative expresses the interest of the speaker in the fact (dat. ethic.). The Heb. term עובץ only occurs here. It is the Arabic *dhabu`*, "hyena" (so Sept.). St. Jerome renders *avis discolor*. So the Targum: "a strewn" "sprinkled," or "spotted fowl."

[50] The references to "birds of prey," "beasts of the field," and "spoilers" (ver. 12), are interpreted by the phrase "mine evil neighbours" (ver. 14); and this constitutes a link between vv. 7-14 and 14-17.

[51] Such seems to be the best punctuation of the sentence. It involves the transfer of Athnach to הלכא.

[52] So the LXX. This agrees better with the context than "So be ye ashamed of *your* fruits."

[53] As Hitzig has observed, only a people, or a king, or a national god, could be spoken of as a "neighbour" to the God of Israel.

[54] Also xlviii. 12; Lam. iv. 2; Isa. xxx. 14.

[55] LXX. ἀπὸ κεφαλῆς ὑμῶν.. Read מְכַיתֹשׁאָרֶם = מְכִישׁאָרֶם; and cf. Assyrian *rešu*, plur. *rešêtu* (= תושאר).

[56] For סכיניע we might read, with LXX., Vat., דיניע (לשורי)מ. The Arabic has Israel. But Vulg. and Targ. agree with the Q'rê, and take the verbs as plur.: "Lift ye up your eyes and see who are coming from the north." The sing. fem. is to be preferred as the more difficult reading, and on account of ver. 21, where it recurs. Jerusalem is addressed (ver. 27), and "*your* eyes," plur. masc. pron., may be justified as indicating the *collective* sense of the fem. sing. The population of the capital is meant. Cf. Mic. i. 11; Jer. xxi. 13, 14. In ver. 23, the masc. plur. appears again, the figure for a moment being dropped.

[57] Hitzig: (1) xiv. 1-9, 19-22: "Lament and Prayer on occasion of a Drought." (2) xiv. 10-18. "Oracle against the false Prophets and the misguided

People" (Hitzig mistakes the import of the phrase עוֹנֵל וּבְהֹא זֶכ, "*Thus*
have they loved to wander,*" ver. 10; supposing that the "thus" refers
to xiii. 27, and that xiv. 1-9 is misplaced). (3) xv. 1-9. "The incorrigible
People will be punished mercilessly." Hitzig thinks C. B. Michaelis
wrong in asserting close connexion with the end of the preceding
chapter, because the intercession, vv. 2-9, does not agree with the
prohibition, xiv. 11; and because xiv. 19-22, merely prays for cessation
of the Drought; while the rejection of "the hypothetical intercession,"
xv. 1, delivers the people over to all the horrors which follow in the
train of war. xv. 1-9 may originally have followed xiv. 18. But this is
far from cogent reasoning. There is nothing surprising in the renewal
of the prophet's intercession, except on a theory of strictly verbal
inspiration; and xv. 1 *sqq.* in refusing deliverance from the Drought,
or rather in answer to the prayer imploring it, announces further and
worse evils to follow. (4) "Complaint of the Seer against Iahvah, and
Soothing of his Dejection," xv. 10-21. Hitzig thinks internal evidence
here points to the fourth year of Jehoiakim; and that xvii. 1-4 originally
preceded this section, especially as ch. xvi. connects closely with xv. 9.
(5) xvi. 1-20. "Prediction of an imminent general Judgment by Plague
and Captivity." Written immediately after xv. 1-9, and falls with that
in the short reign of Jehoiachin. (6) xvii. 1-4. "Judah's unforgotten
Guilt will be punished by Captivity." Wanting in LXX. (as early as
Jerome), but contains original of xv. 13, 14, and must therefore be
genuine. Belongs 602 b.c., year of Jehoiakim's revolt. (7) xvii. 5-18.
"The Vindication of Trust in God on Despisers and Believers. Prayer
for its Vindication." Date immediately after death of Jehoiakim. (8)
19-27. "Warning to keep the Sabbath." Time of Jehoiachin.

[58] The Heb. verb חָתַח "is broken" may probably have this meaning.
"Dismayed" is not nearly so suitable, though it is the usual meaning
of the term. Cf. Isa. vii. 8.

[59] Cf. viii. 9. "And no wisdom is in them."

[60] So Dathe, Naegelsbach.

[61] Lit. "all these things," *i.e.*, this visible world. There is no Heb. special
term for the "universe" or "world." "The all" or "heaven and earth,"
or the phrase in the text, are used in this sense.

[62] The reference to an eclipse of the sun in the words

"Her sun went down, while it yet was day;
He blushed and paled."

appears fairly certain. Such an event is said to have occurred in that part of the world, Sept. 30, b.c. 610.

[63] 13. Read בָּמֹתֶיךָ "Thine high places" for בְּמֹחִיר אֹל "without price"; and transpose תַאטחב (xvii. 3).

[64] 14. Read וְהַעֲבַדְתִּיךָ "and I will make thee serve" (xvii. 4) for יתרבעהו "and I will make to pass through...."

The third member is a quotation from Deut. xxxii. 22. In the fourth, read לְלֹ-עֹלָם "for ever" (xvii. 4) instead of עֲלֵיכֶם "upon you."

[65] The tone of all this indicates that the prophet was no novice in his office. It does not suit the time of Josiah; but agrees very well with the time of confusion and popular dismay which followed his death. That event must have brought great discredit upon Jeremiah and upon all who had been instrumental in the religious changes of his reign.

[66] Practices forbidden, Lev. xxi. 5; Deut. xiv. 1. Jeremiah mentions them as ordinary signs of mourning, and doubtless they were general in his time. An ancient usage, having its root in natural feeling, is not easily extirpated.

[67] Naegelsbach.

[68] The figure recalls the Persian custom of sweeping off the whole population of an island, by forming a line and marching over it, a process of extermination called by the Greek writers σαγηνεύειν, "fishing with a seine or drag-net" (Herod. iii. 149, iv. 9, vi. 31).

[69] For the construction, cf. Gen. i. 22; Jer. li. 11. Or "With their abominations they filled, etc.," a double accusative.

[70] *i.e.*, Loose thine hold of ... let go ... release. Read רְדִי for רְבוּ. The uses of שׁמט "to throw down," "let fall," resemble those of the Greek ἵημι and its compounds. I corrected the passage thus, to find afterwards that I had been anticipated by J. D. Michaelis, Graf, and others.

[71] There is something strange about the phrase "by (upon, `al) the evergreen tree." Twenty-five Heb. MSS., the Targ., and the Syriac, read "every" (kol) for "upon" (`al). We still feel the want of a preposition, and may confidently restore "under" (tahath), from the nine other passages in which "evergreen tree" (`ec ra`anan) occurs in connexion with idolatrous worship. In all these instances the expression is "under every evergreen tree" (tahath kol `ec ra`anan); from the Book of the Law (Deut. xii. 2), whence Jeremiah probably drew the phrase, to 2 Chron. xxviii. 4. Jeremiah has already used the phrase thrice (ii. 20, iii. 6, 13), in exactly the same form. The other passages are Ezek. vi.

13; Isa. lvii. 5; 2 Kings xvi. 4, xvii. 10. The corruption of *kol* into `al is found elsewhere. Probably *taḥath* had dropt out of the text, before the change took place here.

[72] A popular opinion of the time.

[73] Isa. xxii. 23.

[74] The Heb. term is probably written with omission of the final *mem*, a common abbreviation; and the right reading may be מירוסו "and apostates."

[75] אלם for הערמ.

[76] הָעֵרְמ for הָעֹרְמ.

[77] I have left this paragraph as I wrote it, although I feel great doubts upon the subject. What I have remarked elsewhere on similar passages, should be considered along with the present suggestions. We have especially to remember, (i) the peculiar status of the speaker as a true prophet; and (ii) the terrible invectives of Christ Himself on certain occasions (St. Matt. xxiii. 33-35; St. Luke x. 15; St. John viii. 44).

[78] The context is against supposing, with Graf, that the prophet's call "hear ye!" extends also to princes yet unborn (cf. xiii. 13; xxv. 18 is different). If, however, it be thought that Jeremiah addressed not the sovereigns personally, but only the people passing in and out of the gates; then the expression becomes intelligible as a generalised plural, like the parallels in 2 Chron. xxviii. 3 ("his children"), *ibid.* 16 ("the kings of Assyria" = Tiglath-pileser II.). The prophet might naturally avoid the singular as too personal, in affirming an obligation which lay upon the Judean kings in general.

[79] *Encycl. Britann., s.v.* Sabbath, p. 125.

[80] Instead of ידש רוצמ "from the rock of the field," I have ventured to read ידש וְצוּמ (Lam. iii. 54; Deut. xi. 4; 2 Kings vi. 6). For ושתני "plucked up" "uprooted," which is inappropriate in connexion with water, Schnurrer's ושתני "dried up" (Isa. xix. 5; Jer. li. 30), is probably right. In the second couplet, I read סיבז for סירז, which is meaningless, and transpose סירק with סילזון.

[81] LXX. ἀπὸ τῶν ἀκαθαρσιῶν αὐτῶν makes it possible that they read סיאמטמ which would represent סִיָאֲמֲמ "defiled."

[82] The name is probably a quadriliteral from פשח, ፠ Ethiopic ተፈሥሐ "to be glad," Assyrian ፠ ፠ -፠ *pashâchu* "to be at ease," "to rest," (which comes nearest to the Hebrew root). The Arabic verb means "The place was roomy, wide, ample"; whence ፠ "free from distress or narrowness

of mind." Thus Pashchur = "case," "tranquillity," and is formed like Achbor, *kaphtor*, "a capital," (LXX. Pashchor). But the name might remind a Hebrew of the root שׁוּפ "to leap," "prance," Jer. l. 11, and חֹר "free" (plur. only), as if it were a compound of *pāsh* and *chōr*. "Glad and free:" cf. the LXX. vocalisation Πασχώρ. I think this popular etymology pash chor is probably what Jeremiah thought of.

[83] Ex. xii. 33; Isa. viii. 11; Ezek. iii. 14; Jer. xv. 17.

[84] vi. 11 (or, of enduring, Mal. iii. 2).

[85] 'Denounce ye, and we will denounce him!'